RHETORIC AND POLITICS

Hispanic Issues

Volume 14.	*Rhetoric and Politics: Baltasar Gracián and the New World Order* Edited by Nicholas Spadaccini and Jenaro Talens
Volume 13.	*Bodies and Biases: Sexualities in Hispanic Cultures and Literatures* Edited by David William Foster and Roberto Reis
Volume 12.	*The Picaresque: Tradition and Displacement* Edited by Giancarlo Maiorino
Volume 11.	*Critical Practices in Post-Franco Spain* Edited by Silvia L. López, Jenaro Talens, and Darío Villanueva
Volume 10.	*Latin American Identity and Constructions of Difference* Edited by Amaryll Chanady
Volume 9.	*Amerindian Images and the Legacy of Columbus* Edited by René Jara and Nicholas Spadaccini
Volume 8.	*The Politics of Editing* Edited by Nicholas Spadaccini and Jenaro Talens
Volume 7.	*Culture and Control in Counter-Reformation Spain* Edited by Anne J. Cruz and Mary Elizabeth Perry
Volume 6.	*Cervantes's Exemplary Novels and the Adventure of Writing* Edited by Michael Nerlich and Nicholas Spadaccini
Volume 5.	*Ortega y Gasset and the Question of Modernity* Edited by Patrick H. Dust
Volume 4.	*1492–1992: Re/Discovering Colonial Writing* Edited by René Jara and Nicholas Spadaccini
Volume 3.	*The Crisis of Institutionalized Literature in Spain* Edited by Wlad Godzich and Nicholas Spadaccini
Volume 2.	*Autobiography in Early Modern Spain* Edited by Nicholas Spadaccini and Jenaro Talens
Volume 1.	*The Institutionalization of Literature in Spain* Edited by Wlad Godzich and Nicholas Spadaccini

HISPANIC ISSUES
VOLUME 14

RHETORIC AND POLITICS

BALTASAR GRACIÁN AND THE NEW WORLD ORDER

NICHOLAS SPADACCINI AND JENARO TALENS
◆
EDITORS

MIN
NE
SO
TA

UNIVERSITY OF MINNESOTA PRESS
MINNEAPOLIS LONDON

The editors of this volume gratefully acknowledge assistance from the Program for Cultural Cooperation between Spain's Ministry of Culture and United States' Universities and from the College of Liberal Arts and the Department of Spanish and Portuguese at the University of Minnesota.

Published by the University of Minnesota Press
111 Third Avenue South, Suite 290, Minneapolis, MN 55401-2520
Printed in the United States of America on acid-free paper

Library of Congress Cataloging-in-Publication Data

Rhetoric and politics : Baltasar Gracián and the new world order / Nicholas Spadaccini and Jenaro Talens, editors.
p. cm. — (Hispanic issues ; v. 14)
Includes index.
ISBN 0-8166-2910-2 (alk. paper). — ISBN 0-8166-2911-0 (pbk. : alk. paper)
1. Gracián y Morales, Baltasar, 1601–1658 — Criticism and interpretation. 2. Politics in literature. 3. Power (Social sciences) in literature. 4. Literature and society — Spain. I. Spadaccini, Nicholas. II. Taléns, Jenaro, 1946– . III. Series: Hispanic issues ; 14.
PQ6398.G4R5 1997
868'.309 — dc21 96-39456

Hispanic Issues

Contents

Introduction

The Practice of Worldly Wisdom: Rereading Gracián from the New World Order

Nicholas Spadaccini and Jenaro Talens

Of what use is knowledge if it is not practical?
[¿De qué sirve el saber si no es práctico?]
—*El discreto* 232

In recent years a good deal of cultural and literary theory has responded to the question asking how relations of power are part of a dynamic process that exceeds its negative attributes when it is seen only within the seemingly oppressive domain of the "state." Some of Michel Foucault's thoughts on this issue have become common currency, especially the assertion that power "doesn't only weigh on us as a force that says no, but . . . it traverses and produces things, it induces pleasure, forms knowledge, produces discourse. It needs to be considered as a productive network which runs through the whole social body, much more than as a negative instance whose function is repression" ("Truth and Power" 60–61). Similarly, others have argued for a "dialectic of control" in social systems (Giddens 145), contending that "all power relations . . . manifest autonomy and dependence 'in both directions'" (149). The reversible order of this scheme seems to be advanced as an expressed critique of Max Weber's conception of bureaucracy, which holds that, within bureaucracies, formal authority relations are accepted consensually at all levels of the organization, so that controlling bodies and their subjects work together.

Following general lines of thought that argue for the reciprocities of power relations, and keeping in mind José Antonio Maravall's well-known interpretation of the Baroque as a "conservative," "guided," "urban," and "mass-oriented" culture, we will do well to examine texts from the Spanish 1600s for the purpose of showing that while a homogeneous subject may indeed be posited through a variety of cultural and artistic products oriented toward "mass" consumption (especially certain types of theatrical performances, sermons, festivals, chapbooks, and so on), the possibility of alternative positions cannot be excluded. Such alternatives are implied in the subject's awareness that power relations involve reciprocity. In fact it could be argued that it is precisely this awareness that the culture of crisis—the Baroque—tries to suppress.

Gracián's *El héroe* (1637) is emblematic along these lines insofar as it advances the notion that the productive power that individuals and groups bring to every transaction is a kind of capital or "caudal" (*primor* 2, "Cifrar la voluntad"), and to the extent that such capital becomes someone else's object of desire, there is a need to anticipate the actions of one's potential antagonists through an understanding of their mental processes. This relationship of power may be viewed as productive insofar as the individual is involved in an exchange that allows for the possibility of gaining practical knowledge and, with it, additional "caudal." In Gracián's *Hero,* then, the accumulation of "caudal" in the form of practical knowledge is connected to a defense of the self. For this individual there emerges a break between knowledge viewed as an instrument or as a product of power relations and knowledge seen as an absolute explanation of oneself, grounded outside of concrete social relations (Sánchez and Spadaccini).

The individual's awareness of the relative reciprocity of power is dramatized in many texts of the Baroque period and, perhaps, especially in the writings of Cervantes, where the issue of communication between the individual subject and the various institutions of power resides at the very core of the debate on representation and modernity (Nerlich and Spadaccini; Spadaccini and Talens). In Cervantes the world of the mind or the imagination seems to be the possible core of an alternative self that can escape the total control of institutional power and, at the same time, produce a reality in which the individual sees herself as free from social constraints and memory. Along these lines one might think of characters such as Pedro de Urdemalas, Don Quixote, Berganza, Rinconete, Tomás Rodaja, Marcela, and others who struggle to achieve an identity beyond what was received through bloodline and social conventions.

The Renaissance conception of *virtù*, in which an individual is a producer of his own genealogy, reemerges with some insistence in Baroque texts (where the concept is also transformed). That production now depends upon the use of practical knowledge framed by prudence; by the ability to exercise a discursive constraint and, if need be, to effect the silencing of one's voice. This prudent use of knowledge will allow one to navigate through perilous waters of deception in which individuals are isolated and subjected to predators. This very idea is captured in Gracián's aphorism 181 of his *Art of Worldly Wisdom* (*Oráculo manual y arte de prudencia*), which advises ambiguity in words and deeds: "Don't lie, but don't tell the whole truth" (*"sin mentir no decir todas las verdades"* [Ed. Santa Marina 198]). One of the reasons for suppressing truth in this fashion is the unpredictability of its reception and its potential for creating misunderstandings and even personal harm:

> Nothing requires more skill than the truth, which is a letting of blood from the heart. It takes skill both to speak it and to withhold it. A single lie can destroy your reputation for honesty. The man deceived seems faulty, and the deceiver seems false, which is worse. Not all truths can be spoken: some should be silenced for your own sake, others for the sake of someone else.[1]

In the unstable world of the absolutist court, speaking the truth can often lead to bloody consequences ("sangrarse del corazón"). Thus, only those who practice a strategy and technique of prudence, of hiding their true selves, can successfully control their own destinies (See aphorism 21: "The art of success" ["arte para ser dichoso," Ed. Santa Marina 149]). This self-control is opposed to spontaneity or to the giving of oneself to passion. Gracián proposes an economy of language and behavior and a controlled self defined through a highly pragmatic (and programmatic) action that leaves nothing to chance.

The politics of self-control ostensibly predicated for courtiers in the cited writings of Gracián point to a world of uncertainties and dangers, demanding caution and silence: a constant cat-and-mouse game that compels the individual to anticipate possible dangers. In such a world one must think before one acts and, above all, one must plan and provide for deliberate action (see Gracián's aphorism 151: "Think ahead" ["Pensar anticipado," *Oráculo* 188–189]). In the aphorism "Think ahead," Gracián equates thinking and foresight with true living and survival. Thinking involves the visualization of oneself in the process of social interaction. Such a visualization or "rehearsal" entails the creation of an exterior self, a strategy for defending one's core. Such is the essence of what is stated in aphorism 130: "Do, but also seem" ("hacer y hacer parecer"), where Gracián says, "A fine exterior is the best recommendation of inner perfection" ("la buena exterioridad es la mejor recomendación de la perfección interior" [182]).

While the world of the Spanish absolutist court in Gracián's time demanded a strategy for self-preservation, it could be argued that the present-day court of public opinion–shaped discourses oriented by mass media demands a similar strategy—this despite the fact that the power of centralized states has shifted toward a multinational, diffused, and more complex world power.[2]

A few years ago, when Gracián's *The Art of Worldly Wisdom* appeared on one of the best-seller lists of the *New York Times*, we speculated on the possible reasons for its success. Even if for two active Hispanists, as we are, this success could be read as a symptom of the healthy state of Spanish Golden Age literature and culture, it seemed a little odd to find the Spanish Jesuit's name among other "mass-cultured" authors. Out of such a situation there arose a number of questions, including the following obvious ones: What does a seventeenth-century Jesuit thinker mean to a postmodern reader here and now, at the end of the millennium? Do his writings have any value, outside of their pure historical and/or archaeological interest?

Curiously, Gracián was also in the background of many political strategies in the socialist France of the late seventies. Even one of the noted French Hispanists, politically set in the left, Benito Pelegrín, published in Paris in 1978 his French version of Gracián's *Oráculo manual*, with the very revealing title of *Manuel de poche d'hier pour hommes politiques d'aujourd'hui* (Yesterday's textbook for contemporary politicians).

As we shall see, this newly reborn interest in Gracián's texts, an interest that has shifted from the classroom's closet to the public political arena, is not gratuitous. In effect, Gracián's aphorisms in particular and, in general, all his works seek to establish patterns of behavior that help people cope with the rules of an established social order that they do not want to transform but that, in any case, they seek to take advantage of. In this context the importance of rhetoric as a necessary discipline to manage public life is indisputable. Thus the question of the timeliness and significance of Gracián for our time is easily answerable: in some way, most of his proposals merge with what make discourses work in a reality where the real world as referent has been substituted by its simulacrum; politics and advertising are, at some point, synonymous, whereas "left and right" can be defined as obsolete terms.

In his recent book *Destra e sinistra* (Right and left), Norberto Bobbio has insisted on the necessity of maintaining the distinction between "right" and "left" in politics, since these two antithetic terms imply two different models of managing and dealing with everyday life in the real world, based upon the different and contradictory concept of equality inherent to each of them. Published just a few weeks before the general elections that brought the television mogul Silvio Berlusconi to the head of the Italian government, the reflections of the old Italian philosopher remind us how the so-called end of ideologies is, in itself, ideological:

> [And] then "left" and "right" do not merely indicate ideologies. To reduce them to a pure expression of ideological thought would be an oversimplification: for they indicate counterpoised programs regarding many problems whose solution normally belongs to the political sphere; [they signal] contrasts not only of ideas but also of interests and appraisals regarding the direction to be given to society, contrasts that exist in every society, and that do not seem likely to disappear.[3]

In his book *The Celluloid Mistress*, Rodney Ackland, speaking about his work with Alfred Hitchcock, says the following: " 'Surely,' I said to Hitch, 'we'll have to explain somehow why she's dumb, or the audience won't stand for it.' 'They stand for anything,' said Hitch, 'as long as you don't give them time to think,'" a statement remarkably similar to Cervantes's reflection on Lope de Vega's new mass-oriented theater in the early 1600s.

Hitchcock's extremely intelligent commentary, coming from a man who knew better than others how to manipulate the social imaginary of audiences, could be an appropriate way of defining the manner in which political discourse works in the New World Order, when speed is more important than communication and when discursive strategies on how to deal with things change as fast as possible, only to maintain things the way they are.

It is important to underline here that the crisis of Marxism, the fall of the Berlin Wall, and the disappearance of the Soviet Union are usually seen as demonstrations of the lack of usefulness of Critical Theory, to which they were related. The problem is how to think in a world where thinking seems to be out of tune. To what extent is there a place for political reflection in this supposed new paradise born from the ashes of what Fukuyama called the End of History? If we consider that the signals indicating that end have been the invasion of Panama, the Gulf War, civil war in the former Yugoslavia, genocide in Rwanda, and so on, it seems that one cannot underestimate rhetoric's power to make anything believable.

The appearance of new technologies (cable TV, private television, telex, fax, modem, and, in general, everything related to the computer world) is more than a simple technological step forward: first, it seems to imply a radical change in the redistribution of powers that are taking place in the modern world, even if such redistribution is more apparent than real. On the one hand the massive and almost simultaneous access to information, which produces an effect of "informative democratization," would seem to make the control of information by some groups of power nearly impossible. From this point of view, the increased supply, as well as rapid access to what is not considered an interpretation but a fact, would make more difficult, as an effect, a selective occultation. Such is the thesis maintained by many sociologists, political analysts, and communication scholars, for whom, literally, the generalized access to the media, with the increased number of information sources—more publishing houses, more journals, more radio and TV stations—would tend to prevent the manipulation exerted by these same sources when they are too few in number or too concentrated. The latter hypothesis does not take into account factors that we would like to highlight, namely that (1) the nominal increase in sources of information does not necessarily mean a dilution of power in the hands of a few corporations; in fact, within the economic structure of publishing houses and large media holdings, numerous enterprises flourish under different names but without real independence from the centralized entity that controls and designs the global functioning from the top of the pyramid; (2) such a democratic illusion does not grant any specific ideological function to the media, but to the people or groups that operate through them. Yet, we know that the media, as such, are not aseptic. Their function is not merely to stock, transmit, and make possible the circulation of contents that they do not control. On the contrary, the media *produce* the meaning of these contents, *establish* the rules of the communication interchange, and create typologies of readers and/or spectators, that is to say, predetermined social individuals. In the end what is at stake is to know how manipulation is exercised, where it emanates from, and to the service of what interests. Only then could we decide what position to take in relation to the media within the discursive and social framework in which they are both producers and participants.

These changes have modified both the technological media as such and the perception of the world by those traditionally passive users who, for the first time, see the possibility of participating actively in the process. While this could be considered positive, one should first clarify what it means to be an "active participant" in a context that gives such an extraordinary power of fascination, mystery, and omnipotence to the technological media, a power that is inherent to a universe that presents itself as scientific, but is experienced almost as a religion. Indeed, the infallibility that in our days is often attributed to machines does not differ much from the infallibility that the written word used to have in the Middle Ages, as a testimony beyond any discussion. Thus faith is fashionable once again. In fact, between the Islamic fundamentalists who kill in the name of God and this fundamentalism of technology that kills in the name of computer efficacy there is little difference, even if in the latter case we speak not of barbarism but of rationality. For that reason we cannot conceive of rhetoric as an abstract or theoretical matter, pertaining to the territory of academic discourse, but as a practice concerning the political and ideological universe of everyday life.

This point will be clear if we take the example of the Gulf War, when news of the first bombardments over Iraq were relayed to TV audiences under the format of an entertainment program. Thus, speaking to a reporter in front of a camera, a pilot indicated that the bombing mission from which he had just returned had been like "the movies." Another flier, clearly excited about the efficiency of the raid, said that he was going to have breakfast and take a shower prior to his next mission, which he seemed to be anticipating with enthusiasm. A third one compared the aerial attack to a football game in which the other team had suffered a severe defeat due to the superior quality of its opponent. At another moment, a reporter for the English-language Canadian TV interviewed a young marine who had been given a video camera by his father prior to the invasion of Panama in which he had participated as a member of the "salvation forces." In the faraway sands of the Persian Gulf the proud and improvised soldier-reporter sought to repeat his earlier exhilarating experience.

Such a degree of frivolity was strikingly surprising. Yet, the real problem was that almost no one seemed to perceive these facts as frivolous or obscene, and such is the point of the matter. The apparatuses for perception—which, like any other, are learned and assumed—had transformed a technical effect (the "live transmission") into a meaning effect (the "transmission of the truth"). Technology became the guarantor rather than the simple transmitter of what was being communicated.

These interviews, offered as if they were the last premiere at Hollywood Boulevard's Chinese Theater, alternated with press conferences and opinions by experts on everything, without the slightest desire to simulate a documentary effect. Spokesmen for the Defense Department, assuming their roles as protagonists in this movie, imparted lessons in applied technology. According to their accounts, their weapons had functioned perfectly, showing the high technological standards and reliability of the nation's weapons industry—even if those weapons had only been tested in mock wars, and even if systems such the Patriot were more patriotic than effective. On the networks it was ventured that no other country in the world was capable of doing things with such efficacy, speed, and intelligence ("smart bombs"). The seriousness of the problem was not that these speakers said so with utmost coolness, but that the television media gave its logistical support to these exhibitions, assuming the role of truth sanctioner with its very presence. Along with these spokesmen there were live interviews with international political analysts, economists, military strategists, and, even more unusual, with technology specialists who explained the functioning of guided missiles and fighters with special radars, as if they were talking about washing machines. In such a context, as Rey Chow (1991) wrote,

> the mediatization of both information and life has reached a point where "realities" are interchangeable. For to kill someone is as electronic as writing with a computer. Some of the American adolescents who used to stay home to manipulate video games on the screens of their TV sets found themselves flying over Iraq during the Gulf War. The simulacra they were used to appeared in their instrument panels, requiring from them the same moves or the pressing of buttons. Many kilometers above land where people were dying, the clean and cohesive video game became a persuasive substitution of war. (16–17)

The dirty and bloody part of the bombings *was not* a part of the play. In fact reality was replaced by "virtual reality" for the soldier-spectator.

The correspondence between "word" and "thing," which was proper to the stage of orality and which had been replaced by the notion of representation of "things" by "words" after the invention of printing, now gave way to the creation of simulacra. Such a production takes place from a language whose power does not come from the exteriority as a structure. As Mark Poster has stated, because of this autoreferentiality, the laws that supposedly regulate the truthfulness or the falsehood of a discourse do not depend upon their relationship with the world, but upon the internal coherence of the message.[4] Representativity still lasts in such a language but only as a "meaning" effect. This has been called the crisis of representation and has effects upon the social subjects receiving messages, because for them the objects tend to materialize not in language, but in the very flow of signifiers.

An anecdote whose implications one of us has developed elsewhere can serve as an example:[5] in October 1990 Saddam Hussein held a ninety-minute interview with CNN for U.S. public consumption. Even if no one was taking Saddam for a kind of Mother Teresa, many wanted to know what arguments he would use to justify a military action—the annexation of Kuwait by force—that a few months later would trigger the Gulf War. We watched stoically his long speech, and, the following morning, in seeking to discuss it in the classroom with American students in order to analyze the reasoning elaborated by the speaker as a practical mechanism for persuasion, we discovered that no one had watched the interview beyond the first few minutes—not because they were against its contents, but because of the length of the shots and the poor editing. For an audience used to the speed and concentration of the hegemonic model of discourse—that is, the video clip—the temptation to zap a discourse held in Arabic, with English translation in voice-over, was irresistible.

If we analyze what lies behind this behavior, some important conclusions come to the foreground. First of all, the process of communication only works out in a dialogic mode and under certain sociocultural conditions. To convince someone of something implies being able to establish a contact, that is to say, to make being heard functionally possible. In order to do so, one has to manage the codes of reception that have been institutionalized among the receivers.

Gracián's analysis of the power of discursive strategies facing the control of the social imaginary is not far from this idea. Moreover, the political set of ambiguities and the lack of clear goals that defines our era are not very different from those that were at stake in Spain in the first decades of the 1600s, the time in which Gracián's writings have to be contextualized. In both worlds a declining empire seeks to survive using not only armies but also the power of culture as a medium for control. In both of them, the goal of official thinkers is not to produce knowledge for the purpose of changing the material conditions of everyday life, but first and foremost, to analyze mechanisms in order to make people fit into them.

Let us recall that during the sixteenth and seventeenth centuries—which literary and cultural historians often refer to as the Spanish Golden Age or as the periods of the Renaissance and Baroque, respectively—the incipient modern state sought to systematize the sphere of cultural production as it moved to reorganize the space of social-political relations.[6] As we anticipated earlier, following the quote attributed to Hitchcock, Cervantes's critique of the Lopean *comedia* goes to the very heart of the institutional circuitry of theater production during the early phase of the Baroque period, when the monarcho-seigneurial segments of Spanish society muster all means at their disposal in seeking to preserve their privileges. Under these conditions the new theater, with its array of mechanical conventions, aims to construct a subject who identifies with the final resolution of dramatic conflicts. This subject is constructed through a desire for order elicited from the stage by means of his or her identification with the values and actions of the king and his loyal representatives. Even in those rare exceptions in which the king himself is a source of conflict, the dramatic resolution sustains the established system of authority.

Unlike the viewer or reader of Cervantes, who is posited as a critical "interlocutor" who sees obliquely and thus is not invested with a desire to identify with the illusions of the stage, the spectator of the Lopean *comedia* is placed at the central locus of a visually organized space that extends outward from the very body or embodiment of social and political power: the king (see Castillo and Spadaccini). Thus, the new theater may be said to perform certain representative functions that are essential to the continued legitimation of established authority; at the same time one can say that there are also other types of deployments from the center of power that structure desire through symbolic identification.[7] That is, royal authority is made omnipresent through an ever-growing bureaucracy and the proliferation of laws and institutions representing the will of the king.

Baroque urban life is full of cultural and religious representations that allow the various segments of society to partake of the splendor and spectacle associated with the central institutions of the Spanish state: the monarchy and the church. Thus, for example, sacramental plays performed on the feast of Corpus Christi to celebrate visually the miracle of transubstantiation or Baroque sermons staged from the pulpits to enhance ecclesiastical celebrations engulf the listener and viewer in a sea of emotion and make imminently present the teachings of the church (Barnes 57).[8] The dramatically articulated sermons were carefully crafted to make the greatest possible impact upon an audience that realized the limits of its own position within a power network that was a direct expression of the will of God. This is commensurate with the various modes of internalization of political power that in civil society are seen in the working out of the king-subject relation.[9] It is also important to emphasize that in the very midst of the culture of crisis of the Baroque (Maravall) there emerge radically different constructions of subjectivity, as can be seen, for example, in the work of Velázquez, whose paintings—like Cervantes's writing—constantly remind us of their status as artifice. A Velázquez painting calls attention to its compositional elements and thus manages to emphasize the distinction between the canvas and the world outside of it (see Castillo and Spadaccini).[10]

Velázquez's subjects are also represented in complex relation with their status in society as signified through outward signs such as clothing and gestures. Clothing signifies one's status and place in the social hierarchy, but neither clothing nor other outward signs tell all about the individual who is portrayed in the painting. The Velázquian subject emerges in the very gap created between social and inner life, between public representation and intimate emotions and thoughts (Maravall, *Velázquez y el espíritu de la modernidad*). For regardless of the social position of Velázquez's models—from kings, queens, and infantas to military protagonists, servants, street urchins, and dwarfs—all of them emerge as subjects through a process that might be defined as emotional and psychological. In the end "Velázquez's gaze represents the view of the state's citizens rather than that of the king, as Foucault (*The Order of Things*) would have it" (see Castillo and Spadaccini).[11] For in Velázquez's painting the king is displaced from the center and no longer exerts the mediating role in the production of meaningful life experience (the world and the self), as he does in the case of the Baroque *comedia.*

The gap perceived by Velázquez between public and inner self is often taken as a sign of disorder and chaos by privileged groups of his time. Hence the well-known image of a "world-upside-down" so dear to Quevedo and to those other authors who identify closely with a system of privileges and, therefore, exclusion. For them the "world" must be rearranged, its contradictions foreclosed, and displaced individuals reanchored. For a traditionalist such as Quevedo, that reanchoring hinges on the centrality of bloodline as a determinant for one's position in the social fabric, while for others the maintenance of the system of privileges depends upon the ability of the monarcho-seigneurial segments of society to incorporate those new dynamic groups whose status had been advanced through monetary wealth.

In stark contrast to Quevedo, the Jesuit moralist Baltasar Gracián offers a novel prescription to remedy the "crisis" at hand. For Gracián "a distinction is to be made between what he calls 'sujeto' (the human animal) as a category belonging to natural history and what he refers to as 'persona' (subject in the public sense), a category belonging to moral philosophy" (see Castillo and Spadaccini). To become a "persona" one must master the art of ostentation, that is, techniques for public representation. The supreme form of practical wisdom is to understand the demands exerted by public "opinion" and to manipulate appearances in order to meet expectations. It is important to recall here that when Gracián speaks of public opinion he is referring to that of the contemporary absolutist court, where bloodline is no longer the determining factor in the apportionment of one's privileges and influence. In effect, the changing structure of the absolutist court at this time was characterized by the emergence of a power elite that included nonnoble elements such as professional bureaucrats, statesmen, artists, and various moneyed groups (Maravall, *Poder, honor y élites*). It was this new elite that could afford to be public ("persona"). Thus, in accordance with this historical development, Gracián equates "being" with being public, what "is" with what is "seen," and thus the gap between public and inner self is closed.

To understand Gracián and the importance placed on rhetoric, we might recall—as Benito Pelegrín has brilliantly pointed out—that the Jesuit order, to which he belonged, was rooted on a contradiction that arose from the very personality of Ignatius of Loyola, its founder. A soldier and later on an ascetic, Loyola never separated action from contemplation. As a society constituted by Christ's soldiers, the Jesuits were mobilized to fight against the Reformation in order to impose Roman Catholicism the world over. The very structure of the Jesuit order is a military one, with a general on the top who expects obedience without discussion. As an army, it has to deal with masses and individuals. For the masses, there were missionaries and preachers; for the individual, there were educators and confessors. All of them had to address the conquered with the subtlest weapon they could find: the word. Thus, rhetoric is the glue that binds together the entire enterprise.

Obviously, as we said before, one cannot pretend to be understood without getting as close as possible to the cultural universe of the people one wants to convince. The Jesuits would learn Amerindian languages if necessary to better bring Amerindian peoples to their own sphere. In an Amerindian popular tapestry, seen during the summer of 1993 in Peter Gabriel's "Womad" rock concert in Bath (England), one of us could read the following inscription: "When the Jesuits came, we owned the land and they had the Bible; they offered us the Word of God; now we have the Bible and they own the land."

In the beginning, the goal to be achieved by the Counter-Reformists was related to morality and religion, but since to convince the other about something implies significant self-control, theatricality becomes part of the process of education. Dealing with human behavior works within a strategic, political conception of human interchanges. Those who have the power to master theatricality can impose their own ideas on others.

Machiavelli had founded a political science independent from morality and religion. In his writings, politics emerges as the art and theory of taking hold of, and maintaining, power (Pelegrín). Machiavelli's pragmatic and realistic ideas could not be denied in their own terms, even while they created moral problems among Christian political theorists. Since the latter did not want to abandon morality to judge the success or the lack of success of a social praxis, they tried to accommodate to the new winds of change by opposing to Machiavelli's Prince a "Christian" one who would change the "raison d'état" into a "bonne raison d'état." Thus, while lying was forbidden for the Christian Prince, a gradation could always be established between a lie and the truth. Nothing but the truth, but not the "entire" truth (let us recall Gracián's aphorism quoted above: "Don't lie, but don't tell the whole truth" ["sin mentir no decir todas las verdades"]). In short, there is no moral problem if something is told with enough ambiguity to allow other people to understand what has not been said. Moral responsibility thus shifts toward the receiver, who simply misunderstood.

The shift from discursive power as a medium to power as such happens because it becomes increasingly necessary to make the process efficient, that is to say, successful. Thus, only those who know can take hold of power. Gracián's writings seek to develop a methodology to prepare the elites for power. One can now understand why Gracián comes again to the foreground of the political arena in a time in which, as Paul Bové has stated, "even the most advanced industrial economies are subject to the operation of the law of value, [and] need not 'organic' intellectuals to provide leadership but specific intellectuals to provide expertise and to decode and control the discourses and technologies dominant in such a society" (40–41). Postmodern politicians are more actors than anything else, and those in politics who do not perform convincingly have no future. In a certain way Gracián wrote for people like these, and even if the goal of his writings—reactionary as they were—was not to deconstruct the mechanisms of manipulation but to enable them to work out, he describes with precision how to use rhetoric as a weapon, when to use it, and for what purposes. Going back to Gracián's thinking at the end of this millennium is thus a useful task for anyone who still believes in the political status of writing.

The present volume deals with most of the topics developed above. We have divided it into four sections, in line with the several approaches addressed by each of them. Part I, comprising the first two chapters, is "The Politics of Modernity." In an extensive essay focusing on *El criticón,* Alban Forcione views Gracián "as one of the last and the most conflicted of the Christian humanist writers of the Renaissance," and sees in the "apparently conventional scenes and amid their deceptively simple reformulations of traditional doctrines... some of the most revealing complexities in Gracián's drama of disengagement from the past."

His essay is divided into four sections. In sections one and two Forcione focuses on the metaphorical reconstitution of the traditional rational cosmos as the Baroque court, "in an image of plenitude integrated not through reason or love but through power and charismatic self-display"; he also examines the function and appeal of Baroque hexameral poems, which "are said to be connected with contemporary political realities as they display a universalist image of integration, pacification, coherence, and unity." Forcione goes on to argue that the "hexameral exaltation of man as a rational being made in God's image should be understood as a *progressive* response to nominalist theological currents and the pessimism of ascetic Christianity, an appeal that can be observed, not only in the enormous seventeenth-century appetite for miracle literature, but also in the writings of such influential contemporaries of Gracián as Calderón, Pascal, and Miguel de Molinos, as well as in numerous cultural and social manifestations of *desengaño.*"

In section three, "Gracián's Cosmic Disconnection," Forcione sees the most innovative aspect of *El criticón* with respect to traditional hexameral texts in "the transformation of the contemplating subject, the 'reader' of the Book of the World, who... has metamorphosed into an individual, an isolated being endowed with the freedom to shape the stars and the 'essential cosmic substance as he momentarily sees fit.' " Thus, "in the little drama beneath the stars that opens *El criticón,* Gracián would appear to be but a step away from the acosmic enthusiasm of the modern thinker who was so fascinated with the insights of his moral philosophy, Friedrich Nietzsche." Gracián would later provide a glimpse of the demonic realities of seventeenth-century politics that he was to "imaginatively develop in the spectacle of enslaving representation that Andrenio and Critilo witness in their subsequent encounter with the monstrous, 'invisible' politician in Spain."

In section four, titled "Closing the Book of the World," Forcione sees the *Criticón*'s fissured Book of the World as bearing "witness to a new condition of man as a distanced being, separated from the traditional cosmos, which had offered a reassuring model for his identity as a coequal with creator and created order in their shared rationality, and separated from the absolute state, to which he has yielded all independence."

Finally, Forcione argues that Gracián's most important response to the "decisive changes in the relationship of the individual to the cosmos was not in aesthetics, in epistemology, or in literary innovations of the type we associate with Cervantes and Góngora, two great visionaries of man in a world of his own making. It was rather in his worldly philosophy, in his understanding of a major alteration in this period in man's consciousness of himself as a social being."

In chapter 2, "On Power, Image, and Gracián's Prototype," Isabel Livosky argues for a timely reexamination of Gracián's prototype for the prudent politician, especially now, on the eve of the twenty-first century. Such a prototype is said to be based on the appropriation of political power through brutal methods under the guise of a higher purpose. What in Gracián is accomplished through the manipulation of words, the contemporary medium of television is said to manipulate through a poetics of power in images. Livosky goes on to point out that, "if in the early works of Gracián we were to perceive his nostalgia for the heroic possibilities and realizations of the 'modernity' embodied in Ferdinand's [i.e., Ferdinand the Catholic's] legitimation of the nation-state, perhaps in the atomization of the nation-state and the selective individualism reflected in his later work we can perceive the ethos of our own 'postmodernity.'" In her understanding of Gracián's work as related to our times, Livosky cites Roberto Rossellini, one of the first filmmakers to discover the social discursive power of television. Focusing on his film *La prise du pouvoir par Louis XIV* (produced in 1965 for French television), Livosky introduces the French absolutist king as a kind of human configuration of Gracián's ideas.

Part II of our volume comprises chapters 3 through 6 and appears under the heading "Subjectivities." In chapter 3, "Saving Appearances: Language and Commodification in Baltasar

Gracián," Malcolm Read reviews a wide spectrum of approaches to Gracián, "from those that recuperate the Jesuit for Spain and Morality, to those that legitimize only his secularism." Following materialist analyses, from Benjamin to Rossi-Landi and Eagleton, Read deals with the notion of language as commodity in relation to Gracián's use of economic metaphors and focuses on the linguistic ramifications of other, related problems, such as the conflict between the Jansenists and the Jesuits to arrive at an understanding of Gracián's work.

In chapter 4, "Surviving in the Field of Vision: The Building of a Subject in Gracián's *El Criticón,*" Luis Avilés sees Gracián as a means to analyze cultural responses to seventeenth-century Spain, as a way to describe through technologies of control, power, and domination—of which sight is the key manifestation of surveillance—the interplay between the writing of fiction and the writing of society. In *El criticón,* the deployment of the visual as a technology (in Foucaldian terms, "Technologies of the Self") to control space and gain access to the core vision is seen as pointing to what Martin Jay has called the scopic regime of the Baroque vision. Another observation—with Lacanian underpinnings—is that the narrative seeks an immediate elimination of childhood through a devaluation of motherhood and an identification with the father. Such an identification is then related to the construction of social subjects that "conform to the needs of the state."

The focus of Avilés's analysis is on "sight" and "confrontation," with the body viewed as a conflictive locus. The response to "crisis" is manifested in the feeding of the body with "new codes and filters of reality," through a "provisional screen." Thus, Andrenio's entrance into community and language occurs through the body of an other—Critilo. Here Avilés sees similarities between *El criticón* and Lacan's "mirror stage." Such a connection is also made in chapter 5, "Gracián and the Emergence of the Modern Subject," in which William Egginton analyzes Gracián's thought as a coherent moral system and goes on to compare it, within a Lacanian discursive framework, with the ethics of Kant. Egginton locates Gracián at "the crossroads between the universal anthropocentrism of the Renaissance and the transcendental subject of modernity." In many ways—according to Egginton—"the subject that Gracián describes, and implies, in *Oráculo manual* is already a modern subject. The essential defining quality of the modern subject is the fact that it is split . . . that the subject can only come to know himself through a reflective process, and that there is, perhaps, some inherent gap between the real self and its capacity to be known." Following Slavoj Žižek's idea that an event is conceived as traumatic only afterward, "with the advent of a symbolic space within which it cannot be fully integrated," Egginton concludes that in Gracián we have "a witness of the modern subject's traumatic birth, before that birth was conceived as traumatic and thereby repressed by the Enlightenment."

In chapter 6, "Gracián and the Ciphers of the World," Jorge Checa suggests that in *El criticón* Gracián presents "a circular idea of History, based on the principle of recurrence and repetition," just as several of Gracián's contemporaries recognize that "political action must also be grounded in the effective handling of contingencies." In *El criticón* the idea of decline is said to be introduced through the rhythmic irregularities of the Wheel of Time. Checa goes on to point out that in the "Episode of the World Deciphered," Gracián suggests that the task of the moralist is not the discovery, within an ethical reality, of "a syntax . . . made up of a limited number of elements," for the *mundo civil* requires a continuous rewriting, "which can transform the world's blurred appearances into the ciphered signs of a dynamic, provisional, and open-ended language."

Part III of this volume comprises chapters 7 through 10 and is titled "Representations." In chapter 7, "Gracián and the Art of Public Representation," David Castillo examines Gracián's understanding of the "public being" against the background of the evolution of art and public representation in early modernity. His basic line of argumentation is that, seen in relation to the fundamental changes that are taking place in the Spanish absolutist court, Gracián's moralistic discourse seems to be commensurate with the interests of the new power elites. "In fact," Castillo writes, "Gracián explicitly condemns a long list of manifestations of cultural production for favoring vulgar objects." This is why, ultimately, Gracián "explicitly blames the printing press, which has made possible the proliferation of books written for a wider and more heterogeneous market."

In chapter 8, "Symbolic Wealth and Theatricality in Gracián," Francisco Sánchez analyzes the notion of "caudal" as symbolic wealth, as a strategy for social exchange. Sánchez also makes an interesting connection between the aphoristic style of the *Oráculo manual* and *El político* and the intertextuality of imagery, reading, sight, and thinking, which "by the seventeenth century [had] become an inquiry into the status of vision in the acquisition of knowledge." Finally, Gracián's "prudencia" and "agudeza" are deemed to be "conceptual" in the sense that they establish relations between signs. Along these lines, Gracián's significance goes well beyond Baroque Spain to become part of the cultural debates of our own times.

In chapter 9, "Gracián and the Scopic Regimes of Modernity," Oscar Pereira, relying on Martin Jay's observation regarding the convergence between postmodernity and a rejection of "ocularcentrism," proposes to explain the function of "sight" in Gracián's thinking and to establish a relation between sight, hearing, and writing. Detecting a double tendency in the Spanish Baroque to either defend or reject sight, Pereira's study focuses on the sense of sight as a metaphor for understanding, on the observer's point of view, and on the metaphor of light with respect to reason.

Pereira questions both the dichotomy established by Lessing between arbitrary sign (word) and nonarbitrary sign (image) and the linguistic reductionism that, according to him, drives semiotics. For in Gracián the identification between looking and deciphering converts the image into a sign, while concept and image may be said to be inseparable. In the end it is the sense of sight that provides the materials for the constitution of mind and subjectivity. Finally, in the texts of Gracián, Pereira discovers elements of the three scopic regimes outlined by Jay: (1) "Cartesian perspectivalism," which structures *El criticón*, albeit as a projection not of a scientific method but of an abstract moral scheme; (2) the "Baconian art of describing," with which Gracián's *Discreto* and *Oráculo manual* share the incarnate eye but not the results of that looking—a blurred, dark, and changing world traversed by conflictive relations; and (3) the "Baroque vision," which rejects clarity and transparency and considers both language and image as enigmas. Among those three regimes, postmodern discourse is said to privilege Baroque vision.

In chapter 10, "Gracián and the Authority of Taste," Anthony Cascardi suggests that Gracián's work may be read as a sign "of the continuing need to assert the possibility of making discriminations of taste in the absence of a hierarchical social basis for such judgments." Taking as a point of departure Gadamer's reliance on Gracián "to recover the sensuous moment of taste," Cascardi argues that Gracián's notion of taste must be historicized in relation to the formation of social class, while Gracián's ideas of taste and of the education (*cultura*) of taste is seen as emerging "in the context of the crisis of values created by the weakening of the hereditary aristocracy in Spain, one of the consequences of which was a corresponding crisis in the authority of judgments of all kinds."

Part IV, "The Politics of Everyday Life," comprises chapters 11 and 12. In chapter 11, "*The Art of Worldly Wisdom* as an Ethics of Conversation," Carlos Hernández-Sacristán, relying on the work of Erving Goffman, examines Gracián in terms of a sociology of everyday life. Most aspects of Gracián's knowledge and ethics are said to be "decided within the confines of the social encounters that we know as conversations." Thus, Gracián's knowledge is referred to as being "conversable," as is "the reality of the subject involved in the social encounter.... The subject of knowledge discovers himself as a reality that must be constructed in his dialogical relationship with the other."

Hernández-Sacristán goes on to argue that while Goffman is "concerned with the study of repair mechanisms that come into play when the social image has deteriorated, or strategies that permit us to avoid the dangers that the social image is subject to in social situations," Gracián's "fundamental concern is those strategies that would improve the social image." Finally, for this critic, both Gracián and Goffman would hold that "the conceptualization of power is closely related to that of the practice of justice," while "morality and justice... both are founded on the believability of the self or person, understood as a subject involved in the construction of social reality."

In chapter 12, "Gracián in the Death Cell," Michael Nerlich discusses the lack of traces that Werner Krauss's book on Gracián has left on German research, perhaps as a result of Krauss's being identified as a Communist by well-known literati. The merits of Krauss's book, written while the author was awaiting execution in a Nazi death cell, are said to be implicit in his dialogue with the Spanish Jesuit thinker. Such a dialogue, according to Nerlich, is undertaken in order to question him about "his motivations and intentions and also perhaps to put Gracián face to face with his responsibility toward his contemporaries and toward posterity. Above all, however, Krauss enters the dialogue in order to inform us, his contemporaries, of what we can learn from Gracián and where we must contradict him."

We might end our introduction to this volume with a final observation: centuries ago, in the times when Greece was the center of the world, the sophist Gorgias said that he who has the word, has the sword. Rereading Gracián's writings nowadays might help to demonstrate that the so-called New World Order is nothing but old (Blanco Aguinaga, *Variaciones*), a simple footnote in the long journey into a night where a concentrated few go on controlling the lives and deaths of others, without even changing the alibi. As in Gorgias's times, everything is done in the sacred name of democracy.

Notes

1. "No hay cosa que requiera más tiento que la verdad, que es un sangrarse del corazón. Tanto es menester para saberla decir como para saberla callar. Piérdese con sola una mentira todo el crédito de la entereza. Es tenido el engañado por falto y el engañador por falso, que es peor. No todas las verdades se pueden decir: unas porque me importan a mí, otras porque al otro" (16–17).

2. See Poster, *The Second Media Age*. Echeverría also deals with this new configuration of personal and social relations in the electronic world in *Telépolis* and *Cosmopolitas domésticos*.

3. "[E] poi 'sinistra' e 'destra' non indicano soltanto ideologie. Ridurle a pura espressione di pensiero ideologico sarebbe un'indebita semplificazione: indicano contraposti programmi rispetto a molti problemi la cui soluzione appartiene abitualmente all'azione politica, contrasti non solo d'idee ma anche d'interessi e di valutazioni sulla direzione da dare alla società, contrasti che esistono in ogni società, e che non si vede come possano scomparire" (5).

4. Poster, *The Mode of Information: Poststructuralism and Social Context*.

5. Talens, "Writing against Simulacrum."

6. See Godzich and Spadaccini, Introduction. See also Luis Marin, *Portrait of the King*.

7. For a discussion of various mechanisms of identification with official, mass-oriented culture in Baroque Spain, see Godzich and Spadaccini, "Popular Culture and Spanish Literary History," in Godzich (72–95).

8. Francisco Caus's description of a colleague's sermon delivered on October 12, 1691, provides an illuminating example of the intimate connection between theater and pulpit: "Even though it [preaching] is so contrary to the theater, he behaved in this exercise as actors do. Actors, to attract audiences, and make a profit, commonly use scenic effects in the theater called *tramoyas,* that because of their novelty draw perhaps bigger crowds than Sermons do, and, in this way they increase their earnings" (cited by Barnes 57).

9. For a historical genesis of the subject and its contradictory nature in relation to absolutism, see Balibar 33–57. For the dynamics of the relationship between king and subjects in England as mediated by theater, pulpit, and political theory, see Dietz 91–119, and Orgel. See also Marin, *Portrait of the King.*

10. For an overview of Velázquez's work within the parameters of Baroque painting, see Brown.

11. The gaze of the king may be seen more properly in El Greco and other mannerist painters, whose synthesis of the spiritual and material domains parallel the manner in which the absolute monarchy theorizes its own legitimacy.

Works Cited

Ackland, Rodney, and Elspeth Grant. *The Celluloid Mistress; or, the Custard Pie of Dr. Caligari.* London: Wingate, 1954.

Balibar, Etienne. "Citizen Subject." In *Who Comes after the Subject?* Ed. Eduardo Cavada, Peter Connor, and Jean-Luc Nancy. New York: Routledge, 1991. 33–57.

Barnes, Gwendolyn. "Religious Oratory in a Culture of Control." In *Culture and Control in Counter-Reformation Spain.* Ed. Anne Cruz and Mary Elizabeth Perry. Hispanic Issues 7. Minneapolis: University of Minnesota Press, 1992.

Blanco Aguinaga, Carlos. *Variaciones sobre el Viejo orden mundial.* Eutopías/Documentos de trabajo 30. Valencia: Episteme, 1993.

Bobbio, Norberto. *Destra e sinistra: Ragioni e significati di una distinzione politica.* Roma: Donizelli Editore, 1994.

Bové, Paul A. "The Literary Critic in the Postmodern World." In *In the Wake of Theory.* Hanover and London: Wesleyan University Press, 1992. 25–47.

Brown, Jonathan. *Images and Ideas in Seventeenth-Century Painting.* Princeton, N.J.: Princeton University Press, 1978.

Castillo, David, and Nicholas Spadaccini. *La construcción de identidades en la primera modernidad española.* Eutopías/Documentos de trabajo 78. Valencia: Episteme, 1995.

Chow, Rey. "Media, Matter, Migrants." Valencia, Universidad Internacional Menéndez Pelayo, Valencia (mimeo), 1991. Published in Spanish as *Media, materia, migraciones.* Trans. Manuel Talens. Eutopías/Documentos de trabajo 39. Valencia: Episteme, 1994. Rpt. in Rey Chow, *Writing Diaspora: Tactics of Intervention in Contemporary Cultural Studies.* Bloomington: Indiana University Press, 1993.

Dietz, Mary G. "Hobbes's Subject as Citizen," In *Thomas Hobbes and Political Theory.* Ed. Mary G. Dietz. Lawrence: University of Kansas Press, 1990.

Echeverría, Javier. *Cosmopolitas domésticos.* Barcelona: Anagrama, 1995.

———. *Telépolis.* Barcelona: Destino, 1994.

Foucault, Michel. *Discipline and Punish.* Trans. Alan Sheridan. New York: Pantheon Books, 1977.

———. *The Order of Things.* New York: Vintage Books, 1973.

———. "Truth and Power." *Foucault Reader.* Ed. Paul Rabinow. New York: Pantheon Books, 1984. 51–75.

Fukuyama, Francis. *The End of History and the Last Man.* New York: Free Press, 1992.

Giddens, Anthony. *Studies in Social and Political Theory.* New York: Basic Books, 1977.

Godzich, Wlad. *The Culture of Literacy.* Cambridge: Harvard University Press, 1994.

Godzich, Wlad, and Nicholas Spadaccini, eds. *Literature among Discourses.* Minneapolis: University of Minnesota Press, 1986.

Gracián, Baltasar. *The Art of Worldly Wisdom: A Pocket Oracle.* Trans. Christopher Maurer. New York: Doubleday, 1992.

———. *El héroe. El discreto. Oráculo manual y arte de prudencia.* Ed. Luis Santa Marina. Barcelona: Planeta, 1984.

———. *Manuel de poche d'hier pour hommes politiques d'aujourd'hui.* Traduction, introduction, notes et classement des aphorismes par Benito Pelegrín. Paris: Edition-libres Hallier (Albin Michel), 1978.

Maravall, José Antonio. *La cultura del barroco.* Barcelona: Ariel, 1975. Trans. Terry Cochran as *Culture of the Baroque.* Minneapolis: University of Minnesota Press, 1986.

———. *Poder, honor y élites.* Madrid: Siglo XXI editores, 1977.

———. *Velázquez y el espíritu de la modernidad.* Madrid: Guadarrama, 1960.

Marin, Louis. *Portrait of the King.* Minneapolis: University of Minnesota Press, 1988.

Nerlich, Michael, and Nicholas Spadaccini, eds. *Cervantes's Exemplary Novels and the Adventure of Writing.* Minneapolis, Minn.: Prisma Institute, 1990.

Orgel, Steven. *The Illusion of Power: Political Theatre in the English Renaissance.* Berkeley: University of California Press, 1975.

Pelegrín, Benito. *Éthique et esthétique du baroque: L'espace jésuistique de Baltasar Gracián.* Arles: Actes Sud, 1985.

———. *Le fil perdu du "Criticón" de Baltasar Gracián: Objectif Port-Royal.* Aix-en-Provence: Publications Université de Provence, 1984.

Poster, Mark. *The Mode of Information: Poststructuralism and Social Context,* Chicago: University of Chicago Press, 1990.

———. *The Second Media Age.* London: Polity Press, 1995.

Sánchez, Francisco J., and Nicholas Spadaccini. "Baroque Culture and Individual Consciousness." *IJHL* 1.1 (1992): 63–81.

Spadaccini, Nicholas, and Jenaro Talens. *Through the Shattering Glass: Cervantes and The Self-Made World.* Minneapolis: University of Minnesota Press, 1993.

Talens, Jenaro. "Writing against Simulacrum." *boundary 2* 22.1 (1995): 1–21.

Part I
The Politics of Modernity

Chapter 1
At the Threshold of Modernity: Gracián's *El Criticón*

Alban K. Forcione

The Royal Cosmos

> *"Todo es corte ya."*
> —Francisco de Quevedo

Like other notable literary works of the early modern period—Montaigne's *Essays,* Cervantes's *Don Quixote,* and Milton's *Paradise Lost*—Gracián's *Criticón* is interesting not only for its innovative, in some cases one might say revolutionary, features, but also for its articulate dialogue with the traditional modes of conceptualizing and ordering human experience that the orthodox theology, philosophy, political and literary theory, and, of course, literature itself were continuing to affirm. To recall the insights and formulations of Hans Blumenberg's suggestive study of the origins and legitimacy of modernity, one might say that the most interesting features of these works lie in the tensions arising from their incorporation of a drama of epochal change, their reaccentuations of a rich and complex intellectual heritage, and their creative reoccupations of traditional forms of expression.[1] Reading them, one has the sense that one is witnessing something new, not as a given, but rather as something dramatically coming into being as new through a critical and self-conscious engagement with the old. And despite the enormous differences in form, doctrine, and ideological stance that separate them, in each case one feels that what is radically new is their conception of man as a self-assertive being, an individual in a cosmos that is in the process of losing its fundamental power of determining the human identity and offering him universally valid models for his self-creation and self-fulfillment within this world. It can be argued that all of these works "play off" the traditional cosmos, and whether the content of their play is metaphysical, religious, political, aesthetic, or literary, an appreciation of their creative dynamics and the ways in which all are rooted in *crisis* requires an understanding of modes of thinking and an order of things that since the end of Scholasticism have ceased to be integral to Western consciousness. Of these various figures, Gracián is the one who is probably the most remote, as his dialogue with the past is addressed to a great extent to Scholastic theological and philosophical traditions and articulated in their discarded idiom, and his "innovative" alternatives evidently did not respond to the central needs of a changing European society at the threshold of the modern era.[2] In other words, Gracián formulates his dialogue in the discourse of academic philosophy, even when it is framed within the most fantastical fictional constructs, a procedure that we might compare with the methods of one of his few modern descendants, Jorge Luis Borges. Moreover, he despises all forms of vulgar communication, and he demands a particular type of reader—an "aristocrat of the intellect"—a type that would survive in the modern world only in the most rarefied and "irrelevant" spaces of the academic elite.

Like his English contemporary, John Milton, the Spanish Jesuit Baltasar Gracián can be viewed as one of the last and the most conflicted of the Christian humanist writers of the Renaissance. The Christian humanists were intensely interested in man's perfectibility as a spiritual and a social being, and, while they turned decisively away from the theoretical speculation that had centered the philosophy of their Scholastic predecessors, they were nevertheless concerned with grounding their program for individual, social, religious, educational, and political reform in a traditional metaphysical order that had originated in classical antiquity and had reached its fullest development in medieval Scholasticism. In the opening scenes of the *Criticón*, Gracián describes this metaphysical order, and, although he appears to dismiss its significance when his characters leave the island of their encounter, one should recognize its carefully integrated place within the total structure of the *Criticón*. It is the first in a sequence of "constructive episodes" depicting the formation of a human being—significantly designated as a *persona*—and constituting a spiritual biography or wisdom narrative that develops in antithetical counterpoint to the more familiar succession of satirical visions of disintegration dominating the imaginative atmosphere of this "critical" narrative. At first glance this sequence of "upper worlds," where the heroes momentarily find refuge from the swarms of monsters and escape from the imprisoning spaces through which they must pass in their quest for enlightenment (or *Bildung*), might strike the reader as banal in their evident conventionality—the description of man the microcosm in the palace of Artemia, the enumeration of a canon of books for a proper education at the library of Salastano, the recreation of the ubiquitous *Tabula Cebetis* of humanist culture in the pilgrims' ascent of the hill of Virtelia's mansion in southern France, the celebration of the historical exemplars of moral heroism in the Armory of Valor. One is tempted to dismiss such constructive interludes as the product of a doctrinaire, mechanical, and inauthentic voice in Gracián, who clearly appears to be at his most forceful and original when working in the mode of the grotesque. However, it is precisely in such apparently conventional scenes and amid their deceptively simple reformulations of traditional doctrines that some of the most revealing complexities in Gracián's drama of disengagement from the past can be discerned.

In his edition of the *Criticón*, Miguel Romera-Navarro (1938, 1:103ff.) has noted that Gracián incorporated in the first three chapters (designated "crisis") of the work a number of passages from *La introducción del símbolo de la fe*, Luis de Granada's immense summa of Christian doctrine, and specifically from its opening section devoted to natural theology, "in which is discussed the creation of the world in order to come by way of the creatures to the knowledge of the Creator and His divine perfections."[3] Granada's work stands as one of the most influential of the numerous versions of the hexameral project in the age, a project through which orthodoxy reaffirmed the traditional picture of the universe and the biblical explanations of its origins in the face of the new astronomical, geographical, and anthropological discoveries and the challenges that they inspired.[4] Gracián's three introductory chapters describe the "Adamic" scene of Andrenio's awakening to consciousness and his discovery, through his use of his natural reason, of his identity as a human being and the presence of a divine creator manifest in the coherent design of nature and the cosmos. A close examination of these chapters reveals that Granada's text is even more pervasive than Romera-Navarro suspected and, more significantly, that it is modified in several interesting ways. In the following remarks I would like to consider some of these modifications because they tell us a good deal about Gracián's ambivalent stance toward the traditions that he appears to be endorsing and the numerous spokesmen for them whom he invokes apparently in order to authorize his own reading of the Book of the World.

The opening paragraph of the *Criticón* is based on Granada's description of Saint Helena as a marvelous island, firmly fixed in the abyss, confining the sea, despite its powerful surges, in its proper space and offering respite and provision to weary seafarers at the exact midpoint between East and West. Like other marvels of the natural world, the island bears witness to the providential designs of a rational creator; points clearly, as an intelligible cipher in God's coded book of nature—an image of stasis, restraint, centering, and symmetry—to moral values such as constancy and integrity; and arouses wonder and adoration in the beholder.[5] Gracián elaborates the passage in a dazzling display of Baroque figures that set the time and place of his narrative, naming the period of Philip IV periphrastically as the "time when both worlds had adored the foot of the universal monarch," and metaphorically identifying his crown with the fiery circle traced by the sun in its orbit around the earth and the island of Saint Helena with a pearl or an emerald set in its crystalline center. The copious metaphoric transmutation and imaginative relocation of objects in this textual world of spectacular unboundedness and instability continues as the island, the "jewel at the center of the sun-crown," is itself metamorphosed into the "crown of the ocean" and the "empress of its islands." The repeated elevating movement in the figuration—Philip-crown-sun; island-gem-crown—is intensified in the epithets dispersed throughout the passage—"august," "brilliant," "universal," "greatest," "immense," "Catholic"—which are drawn from the conventional discourse of imperial mythology and royal panegyric and constitute the imaginative field of majesty and power. It is here that the shifting figures and images converge. The entire passage points to the monarch, who has imaginatively possessed the cosmos and displaced the divine Creator as the object of adoration. Almost as an afterthought Gracián parenthetically includes the conception that centers, so to speak, Granada's entire passage: the beneficial character of divine providence, "a free hospice maintained by the provident clemency of God in the middle of immense waters."[6]

The most striking moment of such "political" destabilization of the traditional vision of man and his place in the order of things that Gracián would appear to be affirming and celebrating at the opening of his narration occurs following Andrenio's emergence from the cave, a moment that is, of course, allegorically identified with birth in this "curso de la vida en un discurso." Here again it is fruitful to approach the moment through the texts that Gracián is rewriting. In an act of philosophical imagination of the type found in several literary, philosophical, and political works of the seventeenth century, Gracián recreates a hypothetical primal scene, in which the naked subject stands before an unmediated order of reality and discovers or reveals his own essential reality, the nature of the world in which he is placed, and his essential relation to that world. Gracián's way of conceiving the scene is traditional, and his use of sources offers an interesting confirmation of the centrality of his conception in Western theorizing about man as a being defined by the fundamental urge to theorize.

Andrenio's birth is a reenactment of a parable written by Aristotle in his lost dialogue, "The Philosopher," transmitted by Cicero in *De natura deorum* and literally incorporated, then imaginatively reformulated in several permutations, in Granada's *Símbolo de la fe*. After exhorting his reader to raise his eyes to behold the sun and the stars so perfectly placed and so orderly in their movements that "if their places and positions were to change, the whole world would burn," Granada writes:

> And a little below the same Tully adds these words: Beautifully did Aristotle say that if some men dwelled beneath the earth, in palaces adorned with various paintings and with all the fine things with which the houses of those who are held to be fortunate and rich are decked out, and if those men dwelling in those subterranean regions had never seen the things that are on the earth and had heard the rumor that there is a sovereign divinity in the world; and if after this, the gorges of the earth having opened up, they were to come forth from those rooms: when they would see the earth, the sea, and the sky, the great size of the clouds, the force of the winds, and when they would fix their eyes on the sun and know its grandeur, its beauty, and its power, and how, illuminating the sky with its light, it is the cause of day, and when, at the arrival of night, they would see the entire sky adorned and painted with so many and such beautiful luminaries, and note the variety of the moon, with its waxing and waning forms, and consider the variety in the births and positions of the stars, so ordered and so constant in their movements throughout eternity—there can be no doubt that if such men, having come forth from the darkness of their caves, suddenly were to see all of this, then they would know that the rumor that had been told them was true, that is, that there is in this world a sovereign divinity, on which everything depends. Aristotle said this.[7]

In his imaginative reconstruction of this scene, Gracián initially would seem to be reaffirming the Aristotelian-Ciceronian conceptions of man's distinguishing natural impulse to know and his existence within a coherently designed and "readable" universe. However, he makes two striking changes as he constructs the traditional foundationalist scenario, and they bring complications that do not trouble Granada's version. The first concerns the principal and most awe-inspiring element in the sidereal system—the sun. For Granada, the description of the marvels of the sun is set within a celebration of the unity of the created things of the world, all bound to one another in mutual service within a chain extending upward to the first cause or mover, God. In emphasizing the *interdependencia* in the links of the chain, Granada presents the traditional musical analogies of the cosmos: the orderly "dance of the creatures" and the universal concert of numerous voices, the "harmony of the world, composed of an infinite variety of things reduced to this above-mentioned unity, which is the service of man."[8] God is a "choirmaster," who "reduces things to this unity and consonance." Paradoxically, it would appear, the sun, precisely because of its distinctive splendor, has the special role of demonstrating that "no thing is by itself sufficient for everything."[9] Although it exercises powers of procreation, endows the stars with their light and hence their power of influence over earthly life, and, in its cyclical movements, enables seasonal change and the terrestrial production of food, this heavenly body nevertheless finds itself dependent on the first sphere—the *primer mobile*—for its movement. In contemplating the sun, men learn to avoid the error of idolatry and recognize that even the most excellent creatures need the service and use of the others. The arbitrary character of such reasoning might strike us as quaint, but it is most interesting in that it reveals the way in which Granada's metaphysical vision is one that centers on *connection* and *community* and recognizes as the greatest threat to community the act of idolatry, which is a denial of dependency in a "companion" in being and, in effect, a rupture of the chain to God. Granada's association of the sun and the dangers of idolatry is an old motif in Christian meditations on the creation, and it appears in one of his earliest sources, Ambrose's *Hexameron* (4.125ff.). The anxieties surrounding it are much more striking in the contemporary hexameral literature and register the degree to which the old world picture was under stress from such threats as the developing heliocentricity in scientific circles and the discovery of widespread "solar idolatry" in the newly discovered lands of the Western Hemisphere.[10]

In Gracián's recreation of the parable of the cave and his elaboration of the solar moment of the hexameral tradition, the emphases are decisively altered. Driven by a desire to "ver y saber," a desire that has become "insatiable," Andrenio struggles toward the light and suddenly beholds the traditional "great theater of earth and heaven." At this point Critilo acclaims Andrenio as the only human being since Adam, "el primer hombre," to enjoy the privilege of truly seeing the world as it lies before man, unmediated by the customary modes of perception that have blinded him to its reality, beauty, and essential novelty and have prevented his living in a condition of cognitive and aesthetic plenitude. Gracián repeatedly describes this condition as "fruición," a term that can perhaps be understood as an aesthetic reaccentuation of the fundamental Augustinian conception of fruition in love of God and moral fulfillment, a plenitude fully comprehensible only in terms of its antithesis, the condition of nothingness that marks alienation from God.[11] If philosophers cannot *see* directly or innocently, but are compelled through reflection to *advertir,* Andrenio is gifted with the pure vision that man has irrecuperably lost and for which he nostalgically yearns. But what, in fact, does this objective observer of pure being discover in his first acts of cosmic perception? Amid a flood of sensations that nearly overwhelms him, causing him to "fill up" and nearly "burst with wonder, joy, and cognition," his attention is violently seized and fixed by what turns out to be the supreme object in Gracián's vision of the creation, the sun:

> Already the happy messengers of that great monarch of light that you call the sun, augustly crowned by blazing light, encircled by the guard of his rays, beseeched my eyes to render him the worship of attention and admiration. He began to display himself on that great throne of crystalline foam, and with silent sovereign majesty proceeded to spread his domain over the entire hemisphere, filling all the other creatures with his illustrious presumption. At this point I remained swallowed up and totally alienated from myself, placed within him, a rival of the most attentive eagle.[12]

In Gracián's extended conceit, what is really described is far more and far less than we are led to expect from the philosophical scenarios—Ciceronian and hexameral—framing the scene. In the heavens above the soaring cliff from which Andrenio looks out on the sublime spectacle of the macrocosm, we behold a ceremonial display of royal power, a baroque procession in which birds are metaphorically transformed into heralds, fixing the attention of spectators; rays encircling the rising sun appear as a brilliant royal guard accompanying the solemn entry of the sovereign; and the sea, given in metonymic-metaphorical transmutation as "cristalinas espumas," becomes a vast throne from which the royal figure displays himself ("ostentarse") in the theater of his court. As the imaginative metamorphoses continue, the brilliant solar effulgence flooding the creation and animating the creatures is figured as the silent sovereign majesty, which penetrates the body politic, ubiquitously reveals its "luminous presence," and dominates its subjects through the power of its self-display. In a reversal of the more typical metaphorical interchange between cosmology and politics in the seventeenth century, the portrait of the sun has become in Gracián's opening scene the portrait of the king. Politics has displaced metaphysics.

As Andrenio proceeds to describe his reaction to what he discovers in the universe, we see that the relation of subject to objects is one of total submission in which the self is dispossessed of its very being.[13] In contrast to the hypothetical spectators of Aristotle, Cicero, and Granada, Gracián's subject, whether situated in cognitive or aesthetic contexts, is in any case engaged in a form of apprehension in which reason and understanding fail to come into play. If the philosophical and literary traditions informing the opening scenes of the *Criticón* have led us to expect an affirmation of man's essential link with reality and participation in God's creative rationality—a triangular relationship "mediated by the divinity" (Blumenberg, *Legitimacy of the Modern Age* 391) celebrated widely in the didactic writings of the Counter-Reformation, most strikingly in the hexameral poems, which would restabilize a cosmos disintegrating under the impact of various assaults on its traditional rationality—we discover instead that Gracián's primal man, in raising his eyes toward the revealed, consubstantial deity, immediately prostrates himself as a disconnected "political" subject. The frightening hexameral theme of sun worship has been inverted, and its discursive space, traditionally assigned to the definition and rejection of idolatry, has been reoccupied by the scenario and rituals of seventeenth-century absolutist politics. In effect, the sun has been reidolized as the king. If countless contemporary theorists and celebrants of monarchy mythologize the solar king by associating him with the cosmos, Gracián's text, in what might strike one as a potentially blasphemous moment, has elevated the cosmos by associating it with the king.[14] As in the opening paragraph, the state and the court have imaginatively thrust themselves into the spaces of the traditional cosmos, and the kind of adoration that the vision of the created order elicits appears to have less to do with the cosmic wonder of the ancient tradition and its varied Christian assimilations, from the young Augustine to Granada, than with the kind of voluntary self-enslavement to images of power that the seventeenth-century absolutist state cultivated in its subjects or, once again recalling Granada, the kind of psychic experience that traditional theology associated with idolatry and attempted to recognize and to guard against in the cautionary moments of the hexameral poems. Behind the heavenly spectacle that Gracián's "Adam" confronts, we observe a metaphysical verification of Quevedo's colloquial lament "todo es corte ya" and the absolutism binding monarch and courtier-subject in seventeenth-century Spain. Or, looked at from another perspective, Cicero's natural man has become the image of the Baroque courtier.[15]

Gracián's deviation from Granada's treatment of the sun continues to reveal itself in the passage, even as Critilo, in his philosophical commentary on his companion's reactions, attempts to reconcile them with the orthodox positions of a rational theology and to contain the dispersive effects of his metaphorical language. Alluding to the basic principle of all hexameral writings and natural theology—that God's Book of the World is in reality an imperfect language accommodated to the human being's limited capacities for understanding his ineffable mysteries—Critilo reminds Andrenio that the sun is in reality but a shadow, a metaphor, or a mirror symbolizing a reality that man cannot perceive directly. Nevertheless, he too finds himself compelled to explain the aptness of the metaphor by invoking the absolute monarch and the familiar doctrines concerning his divine identity. His argument can be taken as a complete reversal of Granada's celebration of interdependence and community in the created order. Drawing on an etymological elaboration of the solar metaphor familiar in contemporary discussions of royalty, Critilo points out that the sun's name denotes its inaccessibility, its splendid isolation among the retiring heavenly lights ("el solo campea"), and its absolute freedom from dependency ("he is in need of nobody below himself, and all recognize their dependence on him").[16] Before this "creature that most ostentatiously portrays the majestic grandeur of the Creator...the most brilliant mirror in which the divine magnificence is represented,"[17] Andrenio spends a day in rapt contemplation, entirely "forgetful of himself."

If Andrenio has to be reminded that the sun is in reality a metaphor for God in the cosmic text, the reminder calls attention to the fact that there is *no qualification of the king* as the metaphor of the metaphor and, of course, contributes to the effect that the metaphor, in this case, has overwhelmed reality and the cosmos. Once again we observe the effects that strike us with the opening page: the political model of the absolutist state has imaginatively displaced the macrocosm. The "esclarecida presencia" of the divine remains the ubiquity of the absolute monarch.

The Baroque Hexameral Project: Reassurance, Integration, Submission

> *Este don, este fuego esclarecido,*
> *Este ingenio adornado de luz pura,*
> *En la esfera del hombre está incluido*
> *Como el inmenso Artífice en su altura.*[18]
>
> —Alonso de Acevedo, *La creación del mundo*

At this point in Gracián's narrative, we can say that the traditional rational cosmos has metaphorically reconstituted itself as the Baroque court, in an image of plenitude integrated not through reason or love but rather through power and charismatic self-display. A more complex and subversive moment of cosmic reconstitution follows shortly thereafter in Andrenio's contemplation of the stars. To understand its dynamics and implications, it is necessary to look more closely at the hexameral traditions informing the opening scenes of the *Criticón* and to consider their distinctive historical function in the epochal crisis marking the origins of the modern age.

Like another major literary genre of the Counter-Reformation, the miracle narrative, the hexameral epic centers on the colossal power of God. But while the miracle points toward the fundamental incomprehensibility of that power and the enormous gulf separating man in his helplessness from a divine will that is hidden and often seemingly complicitous with the agencies that bring disorder and tribulation to the earthly life, the hexameral narrative emphasizes that God, for reasons that man will never fully fathom, given the undeniable otherness of the divine will, chose to bridge that gulf and to make himself comprehensible within the limited capacities for understanding with which he has endowed man, a creature to this extent created in the divine likeness. In this perspective the hexameron should in fact be viewed as the antithesis of the rigidly dualistic miracle and as an orthodox response to the dark theological implications and ascetic admonitions of the latter regarding the dubious value of a hopelessly disordered created world and a pathetically inefficacious human will. As Luis de Granada put it in introducing his transcription of a series of miracle narratives, miracles have causes in an order completely alien to the order of natural reason and take place in fact to humiliate reason and compel man to fall back submissively on his faith.[19] Representing two fundamental elements of Christian doctrine that had always existed in an uneasy alliance—the wonders of the Creation and the mystery of the Redemption, the escape from a created world that is eventually to be destroyed—these two genres marked the extreme points of a dialogue that, while always latent in Christianity,[20] was orchestrated with unprecedented intensity in the comprehensive religious sentiment of the Counter-Reformation and was registered by innumerable works of art of an age that, to recall one of Spitzer's insightful formulations, seemed torn between *Weltsucht* and *Weltflucht*, between delight in worldly beauty, epic activism, fame, power, and pomp, and terror rising from an inescapable recognition of their emptiness (1927; 1932).[21]

In the Creation God determined to manifest himself in the Book of the World, to encode his reality and purposes in the letters and ciphers of a language universally intelligible through reason, and to endow the being whose gift it was to enjoy the fruits of that creation, man, with the divine attribute of reason. God, man, and cosmos are linked in their shared rationality:

> Esta obra, cuya gran circunferencia,
> Arte, rica labor, materia y forma
> Nos muestran que hagamos reverencia
> Al que de nada su edificio forma;
> Deste universal templo la excelencia,

Que del Eterno padre nos informa,
Es un gran libro, que el poder profundo
De Dios callando enseña al mismo mundo
Sagrado texto, do naturaleza
Nos muestra que una celestial idea
Desta máquina excelsa la grandeza
Gobierna con sus leyes y rodea:
No está escrito del roble en la corteza,
Ni con los puntos de la lengua hebrea,
Ni con griegos acentos, ni figuras
De símbolos y imágines escuras.
Que el que bebe las aguas del Hidaspe,
El más gentil, el más bárbaro scita,
El que en las tierras del inculto Caspe,
Mas inculto que el proprio monte habita,
El inhumano antártico, que al jaspe
Con la dureza de su vida imita,
Los caracteres desta fiel doctrina
Sabrá leer sin estudio y disciplina.[22]

One of the most influential attempts to read this universal language in Europe of the Counter-Reformation was Luis de Granada's eclectic summa of Christian doctrine, *El símbolo de la fe,* a voluminous work that strove to record and harmonize the numerous voices of the past that responded to the message of the divine text with comprehension and jubilation.[23] While Granada acknowledges that the prototypical models for this kind of contemplation and exegesis are to be found in the hexameral works of Basil and Ambrose, he in fact turns to Cicero and Seneca as his most eloquent initial witnesses, and their lengthy statements of cosmic piety are a powerful demonstration of the fundamental premise that the book of nature is a rationally apprehensible revelation and hence was readable before the Christian era. In the resonating cadences of his Ciceronian style, Granada praises the "university of the creatures" as superior to those of Athens and Paris. Eloquently recasting a traditional conflation of the Augustinian conception of the world as book with Pythagorean-

Platonic notions concerning the reflected and musical nature of the created order, he writes that the "grand and marvelous book" of the visible world, which God offered to the "eyes of all the nations of the world, Greeks as well as barbarians, the learned as well as the ignorant," is written in the "separated and illuminated letters" of the creatures, that each of the latter is a mirror placed before our eyes to reveal the radiant beauty of the Creator, and that each is a voice in a magnificent chorus, which "through so many differences of tones" hymns forth harmoniously the grandeur of the Creator's glory.[24]

The hexameral poet finds that his book has already been written. His function is to record, to translate, and to interpret the signs of a coherently designed, carefully integrated text, in which a multitude of differences—the innumerable discrete objects of the various orders of being and their respective containing spaces: stars, animals, rivers, plants, stones, and so on—ultimately collapses in a higher unity, and a clearly discernible net of correspondences continuously draws the contemplative eye upward to the One which unites the Many within itself:

> Y el soberano Artífice, como era
> *Uno* solo el maestro, *uno* el dechado,
> *Uno* el órden, así de *una* manera
> Para nos dar de su interior traslado,
> Hizo *uno* solo, y sola *una* es la esfera
> De la cual está el mundo rodeado,
> Si bien su circular y inmensa traza
> En contorno más círculos abraza.[25]

In a sense the poet is the epitome of the microcosmic being, man. For man is fundamentally a contemplative, a "reading" being. His supreme gift is the mind, or the rational faculty, a reflective power uniting him with God and exercising itself in the theoretical (i.e., noninterventionist) endeavor of recognizing the higher order to which the created book that it contemplates points, and in a sense contemplating itself—that is, the divine reason, with which it is consubstantial—in the world it gazes on. As Granada puts it in his Platonizing formulations of the hexameral material, ultimately in the condition of blessedness, man's mind will gaze on all the created things in the mirrorlike mind of God, in which it participates: "Just as in heaven you will be the mirror wherein we may see the creatures, so in this exile, they are for us a mirror in order that we may know you."[26]

As a reassertion of the mainstream philosophical positions of medieval Christianity and as a literary form revealing its design and effects most sharply when juxtaposed to the miracle narrative, the Baroque hexameron presents few problems of understanding. The epics of the Creation become, however, much more complex and much more revealing in their distinctive accentuations of conventional elements when we consider their significance, as testimony and agency, at a decisive moment of transition in European history. Hexameral writing had always been deeply concerned with apologetics and reassurance, taking up and refuting challenges to orthodox conceptions concerning the order of things and its providential design. In its didactive assertiveness it appears at first glance to be thoroughly dominated by a tone of confidence, and yet it curiously never quite manages to eradicate traces of underlying anxieties. This is particularly the case of its Baroque manifestations, which found themselves poised precariously between powerful challenges issuing from opposite extremes of the contemporary ideological spectrum. Looking backward, we can understand the Baroque hexameral project as a spectacular literary-ideological effort to defend orthodoxy from ascetic, nominalist, and Protestant religious currents, which would divorce a lost unregenerate man and his disordered, unintelligible worldly environment from an omnipotent, capricious, and fearsome divinity and encourage a resurgent theological absolutism as a mode of ordering experience.[27] If Luther denied that man can understand "even the natural works of God's creation" and characteristically saw in the skies above him the "heavens that the fearful conscience pictures as collapsing upon it,"[28] the hexameral writers continued to chart the perfect circles of God's cosmic rationality, to record his celestial music, and to place his privileged creation man, as *contemplator coeli,* at the center of the universe. Looking forward, however, we can see in the epics of the cosmos a programmatic reactionary effort to arrest the forces of disenchantment that were to "emancipate" man from that very anthropocentricity with which the traditional order had dignified and "disabled" him. While the firmly centered world picture of the past was disintegrating under the impact of startling astronomical, geographical, and anthropological discoveries and the society of Christian Europe was racked by the divisive effects of ascendant statism, religious sectarianism, emerging capitalism, social realignment, and constant warfare, the hexameral epics displayed, in the most grandiose terms conceivable, a universalist image of integration, pacification, coherence, and unity.[29]

In their incorporation of a dramatic engagement with the forces of modernity, the Baroque hexameral narratives developed a characteristic feature of their Dark Age ancestors—the speculative moment in which varying scientific hypotheses come under scrutiny and the heterodox are dismissed. In these moments of "enlightenment" and reassurance, we can readily calculate the fashionable appeal of such "subversive" doctrines as the motion of the earth, the infinity of space, the plurality of worlds, the celestial substance of the earth, and the centrality of the sun. For example, Tasso's *Mondo creato* clearly reveals the increasing advocacy of a heliocentric view of the cosmos and the ways in which sixteenth-century events were charging the old solar anxieties that had occasionally surfaced in the early hexameral writings with a new kind of power. Certainly the most famous case of such speculative engagement with the challenge of disquieting scientific views is in the one surviving member of this forgotten literary family, Milton's *Paradise Lost*. Attempting to read the "wondrous works" of the Book of God, the newly created Adam is scolded for his idle curiosity by his mentor, the angel Raphael, who goes on to inform him of the two competing versions of the universe, the Ptolemaic and the Copernican, and refuses to choose between them. In a moment that implicitly calls into question the entire hexameral project, he dismisses the value of metaphysical and scientific knowledge in favor of a practical approach to daily life on earth, which finds its fulfillment in humility before God, moral responsibility, and rational love of the creator through love of another human being. In turning from the cosmos toward man, Milton's momentary critical engagement with the hexameral project does not represent an essential rupture of the type we find in Gracián's nearly contemporaneous detachment of the individual subjectivity, and specifically the creative imagination, from the cosmos (to be discussed later), but rather a positive alternative to passive contemplation and theory that is easily reconcilable with the anthropocentric, ethical, and communitarian reaccentuation of the hexameral material characteristic of Christian humanism.[30]

Perhaps the most revealing register of the anxieties of epochal crisis in Baroque hexameral writings is their pervasive stress on God as a power that bounds and binds in his foundational acts. It is precisely because he has set the created objects so unalterably in carefully delineated and delimited spaces that man's understanding can encompass them:

> All the creatures have their natures and powers *bounded* and *limited*, because you created all of them in *number, weight*, and *measure*, and you made for them their *boundaries*, and you assigned the *limits of their jurisdictions*. Fire is very active in giving warmth, and the sun, in giving light; but still all these creatures recognize their *ends*, and have *boundaries that they cannot pass*. For this reason our soul's vision can *move from one end to the other and comprehend them*, because all of them are *enclosed, each one within its jurisdiction*.[31]

For all the energy and movement that the hexameral poet displays in the various orders of being, the general orientation of his universe is toward a condition of rest, a condition imaging the "unmoved mover" in which the scholastics found "their philosophical equivalent of God."[32] It is a universe bound by a rigid system of laws, traversing it centripetally, "from above to below, from outside to inside along the radii of the sphere" (Blumenberg, *Legitimacy of the Modern Age* 576–78). Its creator is a legislator, but more fundamentally, he is, in accordance with the wisdom of Solomon, a force that disposes of property—*omnia en mensura et numero, et pondere disposuisti*—a force that places, measures, encloses, and enchains.[33] "Oh mirabil del mondo, in un congiunta / con varie tempre e con tenaci nodi / catena indissolubile e più salda / che duro ferro o lucido adamante, / per magistero del superno fabro!"[34] As the richly ornamented sixteenth- and seventeenth-century world maps poured forth in a spectacular effort to provide informing and entertaining images of a world expanding at a bewildering pace, the hexameral God rose to his commanding height as the master cartographer, holding a cosmos firmly in order, making boundaries clearly visible to its inhabitants, and reminding them of the beneficence of him who has provided them with such marvels.[35] The Creator's characteristic gestures are the act of containment, an act frequently described as pacification of warring elemental forces that he himself has called into existence within the void; the redirection of "errant" motion toward its proper ends; and the suppression of transgression, the violations of boundaries as the distinctive objects and orders of being resist falling into place. For Acevedo God's division of the firmament above the waters is like the creation of an "inexpugnable fortaleza, / La cual batir el enemigo traza, / Que fabricada en circular figura, / Sus plazas fortalece y asegura." As the waters of the great flood recede beneath Noah's ark, "a entrar vuelve el Oceano / En su cárcel estrecha de crystales."[36] The elements are put "en prisión dura." The apparently errant movements and boundary violations of the tides are precisely regulated by the "poderosa mano de Dios." Man, in the most dignified of his acts, the "rational penetration" of the "movements of the heavens," is described as "bearing a sweet yoke beneath the command of God." The divine obsession with proper location and containment is echoed by the poet as he fashions the regular verbal forms of his imitative or "secondary" creation. At the beginning of the sixth day Acevedo invokes God's assistance in "subjugating," "dominating," "immobilizing," and "humiliating" the animals as he, like the divine "imperious voice" as it consigns the creatures to their respective cosmic orders, struggles to confine them in the "octavas derramadas" of his "canto numeroso."[37] The aim of the omnipotent but rational God is order, harmony, stasis, continuity, and the elimination of chance, a universal state of being analogically represented by the familiar image of predictable and uninterrupted movement, the well-regulated clock.

Such metaphors and motifs clearly indicate that the function and appeal of the Baroque hexameral poems, despite their theological origins, philosophical themes, and universalist aims, were intimately connected with contemporary political realities. As José Antonio Maravall has pointed out, the period of the European Baroque witnessed the intensification of nationalist sentiment, the centralization of the absolutist monarchies, the theorization of state power and of a state reason that in certain situations has priority over traditional metaphysical reason, the development by governments of rational techniques of fixation and control of a rigidly stratified society that was constantly menaced by internal energies of dispersion, the policing of urban environments rapidly expanding as a result of deep demographic movement and economic change, the construction of citadels and jails in chaotic cities, and the violent suppression of marginal groups and deviants.[38] If such historical realities are discernible in the epic recreations of the Book of Genesis primarily in imaginatively transfigured forms, the political substratum of the hexameral genre can occasionally appear less obliquely, as, for example, in Acevedo's poem, when a celebration of the creation of the heavenly bodies, some conflictive scientific speculations on the origins of the Milky Way, and the description of Jupiter, the political planet, are interrupted by a condensed historical narrative of the rise of the Spanish Empire, emphasizing its providential destiny, as a New Roman Empire, to carry out God's purposes and climaxing in a eulogy of Philip III as the extirpator of the errant Moriscos and as the unifier of Spain. The hexameral moment in which God regularizes the circular movement of the spheres and assures their powers of bringing "quietud" to the "mortal linaje" is correlated with the establishment of the Spanish king as "column and defender of the faith." The poet's apostrophe displays a harmonious coalescence of metaphysical, historical, and political teleologies, and its association of the king and the divine Creator with the restoration of clarity of vision, unanimity, and pure communication through linguistic purification is free of even the slightest trace of the kind of tensions destabilizing Andrenio's encounter with the "royal" sun at the opening of the *Criticón*:

> Tú, magnánimo Rey, que deseoso
> De augmentar la católica fe, esgombras
> Con la luz de tu celo piadoso
> De la morisca y infiel secta las sombras,
> No permites que idioma tenebroso
> En los estados, donde rey te nombras,
> Eclipse las unánimes ciudades,
> Fundadas en católicas verdades.[39]

Throughout the history of hexameral writings, from Basil on, the created universe has appeared as a theater, a location for seeing and hierarchical placing, but within that metaphorical construction relatively little attention is focused on man as the presumptive protagonist of the stage spectacle. In reality the epic hero of hexameral writing is God, the creator of the splendid theater that man is shortly thereafter to ruin.[40] The creation of man does in fact occupy one of the few highlighted moments that counter the tendencies of the Baroque hexamerons toward an undifferentiated accumulation of the many, tendencies that at times threaten to overwhelm the inflexibly fixed structural divisions by day and order of being that would hold the copious material in place. On the other hand, man is cast within the limits of his original noble creation, and he finds the fullest realization of his being in his role as a member of the audience—one who sees, correctly interprets, and imitates. What enables him to do so is his possession of the divine attribute of reason. Herein lie his link and his likeness to God. Through its exercise he connects with the reality in which he finds himself from birth. This connection—reason inhering in man and *in reality*—is so fundamental to the metaphysical order reaffirmed throughout the hexameral writings that without it the entire macrocosmic system would collapse. The fearsome *deus absconditus* of nominalism would preside over a universe in which man would live at risk of alienation and subjugation to arbitrary divine intrusion and chance and in which he would no longer find an assuring cosmic warrant for the "natural" order in which he chooses to live. The hexameralists' determination to "save" reality as rational and as an order rationally accessible to man is evident in Granada's discussion of the Incarnation, which can be read as an answer to the Lutheran disassociation of the central Christian mystery of the Redemption from an allegedly "rational" revelation offered by the created world: "Not for this reason did the divinity cease to be in everything that was created, as the first cause on which all other causes depend, and without whose power and attendance all of them would stop, just as the wheels of a clock would stop, if one were to remove the weight that moves them.... God does not fail to be in all things, giving them their natural being; this is all the more evident when we note that our intellective soul (which is a spiritual substance), while being enclosed in its body, wanders and roams through the entire world."[41] Just as the sun, a "creature of God," illuminates and gives warmth to the entire world, the spirit of God soars above the wings of angels, encompasses the entire created order in its gaze, and conserves, directs, and governs it with his divine providence, which, in conformity with the all-penetrating divine reason of the Stoic tradition with which it is generally associated, is fundamentally rational.

While the hexameral works devote relatively little attention to the actions and achievements of man, they do celebrate the moment of his creation. It is no surprise that the element that they emphasize is man's microcosmic character, his identification with the cosmos, and the nexus binding him to God and to the ordering principles of reality through his possession of the faculty of reason, the mark of his divine semblance and image. Granada points out that, while the created objects of the world about man are *traces* or *footprints* of God, man's *ánima intelectiva* is the very *image* of God and that its divine character is most evident in its function of bridging the spiritual and the material orders of being. Like the pure intellectual substance of the angels, it enjoys powers of understanding "high things." At the same time its participation in the "condición y propiedades de Dios" is fuller than such purely spiritual beings in that, as a formal principle, it animates and sustains the material bodies in which it dwells, overcoming the "disproportion" existing between the purely spiritual and the purely material "para adjectivarse las unas con las otras" (263b):

> Porque así como Dios, siendo uno, abraza
> Todas las cosas con potencia eterna,
> Y en todo asiste, y con divina traza
> Las produce, da ser y las gobierna,
> Así en la obra que fabrica y traza
> Del hombre hoy el Señor, el alma interna
> Toda está, y en cualquier miembro se anida
> Y le mueve, gobierna y le da vida.[42]

If Granada and Acevedo recall Aristotelian-Scholastic conceptions in the definition of man's divine *imago,* they supplement them with the traditional Stoic celebration—which had already been Christianized in Ambrose's *Hexameron*, one of Granada's acknowledged sources—of the mind as a power that, like the divine rationality in which it participates, can freely move about the universe of space and time, visiting its distant lands, penetrating its most hidden areas, encountering deceased friends, and conversing with the divine creator.

Insofar as man's faculties, activities, and achievements are incorporated in the hexameral poems, they are conceived as analogies of those of God and presented in schematic form. Man is a power that "dominates and subjects" the lower orders of the creation, controlling the animals with his "invincible *diestra*" and "enchaining" the disruptive passions in himself, fashioning himself according to the model associated with the rationality of the universal order, the well-regulated clock (Granada 457). Man builds cities and creates language, laws, art, and culture, all modeled on and metaphysically validated by the surrounding theater of reality erected by the supreme Creator and manifesting his rationality. Above all else man, like his creator, is distinguished by the divine mind and by his fundamental impulse to commune with his divine essence through contemplation:

Y como con suprema providencia
El inmenso poder estableciese
Que la figura simil a su esencia
Sola entre las demás celestial fuese,
Enderezó en dos pies su real presencia
Para que el hombre contemplase y viese
El sitio, que inmortal asiento tiene,
De donde su divino origen viene.
Y a la celestial mente dió morada
En la parte mas ardua y excelente
Del cuerpo . . .
Este don, este fuego esclarecido,
Este ingenio adornado de luz pura,
En la esfera del hombre está incluido
Como el inmenso Artífice en su altura;
Y como Dios con natural vestido

La cumbre ornase desta criatura
Adornó juntamente al mismo instante
Con necesarios miembros su semblante.[43]

Alone upright among the creatures, man naturally looks upward from the earth toward the starry manifestations of his divine origin. Nothing frustrates his inquiring gaze. He "penetrates the swift course of the circling heavens and the journey of the sun." All that he sees he "possesses with his perspicacious mind" ("ingenio perspicaz" [279]). The Book of the Creation is written in his own language. Its messages are instantly available.

For all his splendor, there is a static, abstract character in the figure that comes into being at what is almost, but not quite, a genuine climactic moment in these monumental, detemporalized narratives of the Creation. He is firmly bound within preestablished spaces; his fullness of being is instantaneous; his "godlike" dignity is exhausted in his origins; he is the *picture* brought to life; his perceptions are limited to the essential, the already made, with which he is consubstantial; his affective state is an unchanging condition of jubilation and fruition. Insofar as he is a creature of will, his choice is simple: integration within the total order. In a sense his possibilities and limitations are analogous to those of the poet who can do little more than transcribe and applaud his creation. As the beautiful sea comes into existence and displays its "foaming and twisted arms" "before the eyes of the divine and unchanging mind," Tasso's narrator pauses to express his wonder in a scene comparable to Andrenio's emergence onto his high "balcony":

Ma da qual alto e in mar pendente scoglio
e da qual più sublime eccelsa rupe,
da qual sommo di monti alpestre giogo
che signoreggi d'ambe parti il mare,
vedró la sua beltà sì chiaro, e tanto,
quant'ella innanzi al suo fattor s'offerse?[44]

At the top of the frontispiece of Sylvester's widely read English version of Du Bartas's *La sepmaine,* above a world sphere in which all continents are neatly placed, stand the words of Genesis 1:31, which can be taken as an appropriate motto for the entire European hexameral project: "Vidit cuncta que fecerat et erant valde bona" (*Divine Weeks*, vol. 2, frontispiece). God, reader, and poet stand in satisfaction before an orderly cosmos and recognize that it is good.

Viewed in the perspective of his microcosmic role, man, although hailed as the "finished image inspired with life by the inimitable art of the true Prometheus" — "O complet Creature!" (*Divine Weeks* 1:282, 289)—is in an important sense himself a Prometheus confined. He remains fundamentally an *imitator* of a preexistent text and of the actions of a being shining through the script of that text.[45] The most influential of the hexameral poems, Du Bartas's *La sepmaine*, a work widely read in all the major European languages during the late sixteenth and the seventeenth centuries, offers a revealing picture of the splendors and the *limitations* in the conception of the cosmic being whose creation marks the culmination of the divine week:

> This curious Lust to *imitate* the best
> And fairest Works of the Almightiest,
> By rare effects beares record of thy Linage
> And high discent; and that his sacred Image
> Was in thy Soule ingrav'n . . .
> And thy mature and setled Sapience,
> Hath some aliance with his Providence:
> He works by Reason, thou by Rule: He's glorie
> Of th'Heav'nly Stages, thou of th'Earthly Storie;
> He's great High-Priest: thou his great Vicar heere:
> He's Soveraigne Prince, and thou his Vice-Roy deere.
> (*The Divine Weeks*, 1:289; italics added)

Hans Jonas's analysis of the "limitations" of cosmically conceived man is precise and pertinent:

> Man's cosmic piety *submits* his being to the requirements of what is better than himself and the source of all that is good. But at the same time man is not just a part like other parts making up the universe, but through the possession of a mind a part that enjoys *identity* with the *ruling principle* of the whole. Thus the other aspect of man's proper

> relation to the universe is that of *adequating* his own existence, confined as it is as a mere part, to the essence of the whole, of reproducing the latter in his own being through understanding and action. The understanding is one of reason by reason, cosmic reason by human reason, i.e., of like by like: in achieving this knowing relation, human reason assimilates itself to the kindred reason of the whole, thereby transcending the position of a mere part. (246–47; see also Blumenberg, *Legitimacy of the Modern Age* 215)

In discussing the historical function of the Baroque creation epics, I suggested that the early modern hexameral exaltation of man as a rational being made in God's image should be understood as a *progressive* response to nominalist theological currents and the pessimism of ascetic Christianity, the appeal of which can be observed not only in the enormous seventeenth-century appetite for miracle literature, but also in the writings of such influential contemporaries of Gracián as Calderón, Pascal, and Miguel de Molinos, as well as in numerous cultural and social manifestations of *desengaño*.[46] Before turning to Gracián's complex engagement with the hexameral project, I would emphasize the equally striking *conservative* character of the popular cosmogonic epics. The change in perspective can perhaps be most readily grasped if we compare the monumental hexameral image of God-man-poet in blissful repose above a completed created order with three countervailing images of modernity that would radically recast it: Góngora's restlessly wandering pilgrim-poet, who "reoccupies" the divine vantage point and gazes from his towering "green balcony" on a vast, "unmapped," and indeterminate landscape below, in which a river aimlessly meanders, continually changing form and undergoing imaginative reconfiguration in the poet's own "cosmic reconstruction";[47] Cervantes's writer, who, finding himself lost and homeless amid the archetypes of his official culture, humorously displaces the omnipotent nominalist God as he creates a new literary image of "unbounded" man, not demiurgically from preexistent models, but ex nihilo, from the resources of his own emancipated, singular fantasy;[48] and Bernardo de Vargas Machuca's explorer-conquistador, who stands above the terrestrial globe, holding, like the hexameral

God, a compass to the earth while he clasps his sword. Beneath this striking reassembly of hexameral images ornamenting the frontispiece of his *Milicia y descripción de las Indias* (1599), the motto celebrates man's control over an expanding cosmos through science, technology, and force: "A la espada y el compas / Mas y mas y mas y mas."[49] Man has replaced the transcendent divinity as cosmic cartographer and property holder.

When considered beside such expansive visions of the universe, the human imagination, and man's possibilities for movement and self-assertion,[50] the hexameralists' celebration of the "divine image" of man becomes most striking for its insistence on *limitation* in the proper determination and understanding of man's microcosmic character. In this perspective their efforts can in fact be seen in cultural history as a critical response to the revolutionary destabilizations of the firmly founded Scholastic conception of the relations of God, man, and cosmos that Ernst Cassirer and, more recently, Hans Blumenberg have traced from Nicholas of Cusa's reconception, in terms of mathematics and a reconciled version of the relation of the Incarnation to the Creation, of man's active, or projective, role in the determination of the cosmic order, to Galileo's declaration that the vast book of the universe is written in the accessible language of mathematics (Cassirer, *Individual and the Cosmos* chap. 2; Blumenberg, *Legitimacy of the Modern Age*, pt. 4, chap. 2; Blumenberg, *Genesis*, pt. 3, chap. 6). Of the various philosophical allies from this tradition that one might connect with the exhilarating vision of creative freedom observable in the literary worlds of Góngora and Cervantes, perhaps the most relevant is Giordano Bruno. Like the hexameral poems, his dialogues can be approached as a contestation to the challenge of the nominalists' and the *desengañados'* assaults on the rationality of a comprehensible world order. But rather than reconstructing and reasserting that order, Bruno in fact transvalues its destruction, just as Góngora can be said to transvalue the "unbinding" (*desatar*) of the universe of the creation epics and Cervantes can be said to "positivize" the dis-integration of the traditional paradigms of literature—genres, plots, character types, and symbolic schemas—that reflect that order. In all cases the process of *desengaño* is redirected away from its conventional Christian goals of eliciting the deep terror of the formless and emptying out the illusory substances and structures of the world and simultaneously re-cognized as a paradoxical source of world-affirming energy.

In his heretical writings Bruno celebrates an acentric, infinite cosmos, expressing and *exhausting* the creative power of a self-sufficient, "simple" deity, free from all compulsions toward self-glorification and self-reflection, a cosmos not at all bound by or subordinate to the "hidden" significances of an "original" reality that it merely reflects as image or text, for example, as a "book of nature." Bruno's universe is not a space for commentary, admonitions, and prohibitions. The fixed web of ciphers or correspondences of the type Andrenio sets out to read in the world unveiled at the threshold of his cave has here vanished. Its features contradict the hexameral vision in every way—the plurality of created worlds and times, the rejection of gradation and privileged, foundational spaces and times, the "overcoming of the ontological comparatives that had proliferated since Plato and of their legitimation of predestinations behind which thought could not penetrate" (Blumenberg, *Legitimacy of the Modern Age* 568–69), and the universality of motion, change, and metamorphosis in unbounded space. One might contrast the anxiety of Tasso, the hexameral poet, concerning the scandalous existence of hybrids and monstrosities (e.g., the mule) in God's providentially ordered universe and his attribution of their origin to defective, rebellious matter rather than to the divine will (*Il mondo creato* 6.1221ff., *Opere,* 4: 263ff.) with Bruno's exaltation of matter as divine and inexhaustible as it passes into its multiplicitous particular forms and his sympathy "with the pagan metamorphosis of the gods—even with the animal multiformity of the Egyptian pantheon" (Blumenberg, *Legitimacy of the Modern Age* 573, 589). Wiping away the highly integrated hexameral order and the Incarnation, in which its justification (and limitation) of the world as unique and of interest to God was frequently founded, Bruno's universe in effect represented "a *positivization* of the nominalist destruction of the traditional *ordo* of reality" and hence an important transitional moment at the epochal threshold through which man passed on his way, amid the terrors and temptations of formlessness, to the reconnected, serviceable cosmos that characterized the modern age, enabled its scientific methods and technological achievements, and allowed for a fundamental emancipation of man from his age-old cosmic bindings (Blumenberg, *Legitimacy of the Modern Age* 568–69, 575, 581, 584–85).

Gracián's Cosmic Disconnection: Andrenio as Cosmic Man and Hexameral Reader

> *"Un pien teatro di maraviglie."*
> —Emmanuele Tesauro
>
> *"Desde lejos es mayor la reverencia."*
> —Diego de Saavedra Fajardo/Tacitus[51]

A work that continually affirms its determination to "construct a human being," the *Criticón* begins by bringing the traditional cosmic figure of the hexameral project to life and dramatizing the spectacle of his proper recognition of and "adequation" to the universal order whose essence he shares. Initially we appear to be witnessing the unfolding of a thoroughly conventional metaphysical drama, as the awakened "Adam" proceeds to read the ciphers of the world book correctly and to express the epistemological wonder and cosmic veneration appropriate to his discoveries. In reality, Gracián's Andrenio can be seen as an activation of the abstract entity of the hexameral poets or as an imaginative expansion of the fleeting images of the natural man in Cicero's and Granada's philosophical parables. He concentrates the mood of wonder that attends the fulfillment of man's licit curiosity as reader of the divine script of the world and as applauding spectator within the vast theater around him. His repeated reactions to what he sees and understands are "rapture," "astonishment," "suspense," "entertainment," "fruition," and "applause." He shares with his author the task of providing edifying commentary on that script and disclosing its mysterious but reassuring senses. Moreover, in his interrogations of his philosophical mentor he creates a familiar Scholastic philosophical format that enables the proper elucidation of that commentary for an imaged reader. In all of these roles, Andrenio's presence is perfectly consistent with the doctrinal and generic traditions framing his appearance.

Insofar as his initial responses to the created theater of the universe are conventional, Andrenio would appear to be carrying out the admonition that climaxes Gracián's prologue to the scene. His introductory fable contains a critical response to the challenge to the traditional stable relationship of Creator, man, and the cosmos raised by the celebrative treatises on man's dignity that we associate with the Italian Renaissance. In effect, the prologue can be read as a parody of the most famous work in this tradition, Pico della Mirandola's *Oration on the Dignity of Man,* a parody that radicalizes and strikes at Pico's most subversive metaphysical message—that man is created with no place, that he is "heterogeneous to the primary order of things," and that his supreme responsiblity lies not in imitating or imaging a divine likeness but rather in his creation of an identity as "sculptor of himself."[52] Man's desire to go beyond "any center" and to encompass the entire universe is exposed in Gracián's version as "*exorbitante* ambición," and the traditional glory of man in the service rendered him by the creatures is unmasked as culture's gilding of man's vanity, avarice, and monstrosity. The fable concludes by emphatically restabilizing man's place *within* the cosmos by the affirmation of the mind as a power that enables him to traverse the cosmos as *reader* or exegete, one who sees in all the places it visits traces and connections pointing ultimately to the Supreme Creator. Man is decisively, if paradoxically, reinserted and "immobilized" in the center as "king of the created order."[53]

As he begins the account of his experiences following his "birth" and emergence from the cave, Andrenio and his mentor would appear to be following the admonition of the fable and reenacting its reassuring restoration of man to his traditional center. However, as he reconstructs the hexameral tradition, occasionally appealing to the pronouncements of that "gran filósofo" Luis de Granada in his interpretations of the ciphers of the wonderful "teatro del universo" and its "uniformes variedades," we discover occasional modifications or displacements in the articulated body of conventional elements that bring unsettling effects to what traditionally is a foundationalist scenario of absolute stability. Earlier we noted the intrusion into Gracián's primal scene of conceptions and metaphorical figurations familiar in the contemporary discourse of sovereign power and their drastic alteration of its metaphysically conceived context—their striking displacement of traditional cosmic veneration by monarchical political idolatry and their implicit disruption of the harmonious triangular connection in shared rationality of the creator, man, and reality marking the inherited world order. A more complex and subversive moment in Andrenio's initial encounter with the world occurs in Gracián's rearticulation of the sidereal motifs of the tradition of natural theology.

In its brevity, concentration, and enigmatic reverberations, the moment is characteristic of Gracián's laconic style at its most challenging. It is conceptually dense and highly determined, providing a glimpse of the author's aesthetic and political insights as they converge on his metaphysical vision. In order to appreciate its implications, we must bear in mind that in the central stream of classical philosophy the starry sky was "the purest embodiment of reason in the cosmic hierarchy, the paradigm of intelligibility and therefore of the divine aspect of the sensible realm" (Jonas 255). One of the most influential expressions of this optimistic metaphysical vision was precisely the work that, mediated by Luis de Granada's celebration of the creation, provides the imaginative conception of Gracián's opening scenes, Cicero's *De natura deorum*. Paraphrasing the Latin text, Granada asks:

> Who will hold for a man of reason someone who, though seeing the motions of the heavens and the order of the stars, so firm and constant, and though seeing the connection and concert that all these things have with one another, claims that all of this was made without prudence or reason, and believes that things made with such counsel that no council or individual understanding can manage to comprehend them were in fact made by chance? . . . And seeing the impetus with which the heavens move, with such wonderful swiftness and how they follow their courses, which are so certain and so well ordered for the health and conservation of the created order, would we not then begin to see that all of this is made according to reason, and not only reason, but excellent and divine reason?[54]

Supplementing his argument with citations from the Psalms, Granada concludes that the stellar order is perhaps the most eloquent page in the book of nature, that accommodated language that "se oye en todas las tierras" (is heard in all lands) and assures human beings that they can live confidently in an "orden invariable" (192b) designed by a "sapientísimo y potentísimo hacedor," a "soberano presidente," and protected through his providential ordinances.

In his first night beneath the stars Gracián's natural man finds himself gazing on a celestial spectacle that is far different from Granada's image of rational order. Placed in a "labyrinth of stars, some twinkling, others shining," Andrenio attempts to comprehend a "total picture or system." "I proceeded to survey them all, taking note of their great variety in size, locations, movements, and colors, as some came forth and others concealed themselves."[55] Although his "Platonic" mentor is quick to naturalize such apparently disorderly phenomena within his intelligible cosmic text by advising Andrenio that such changes and movements point clearly to an idea (*ideando*), that of the course of human life from birth to death, Andrenio continues to voice his ingenuous impressions concerning the "imperfections" of the heavenly order. If his reaction to the sun is given a peculiar accentuation by the discourse of the political order of absolutism, his meditation on the stars is marked by a shift into the discourses of poetics and rhetoric. Noting the bewildering complexities and striking asymmetries in the divine artificer's ornamentation of his cosmos, he wonders why the latter, in the disposition of his marvelous materials ("florón y estrella"), had not decorated the "artesonada bóveda" (paneled vault) of the world with "order and concert so that they would entwine attractive lacings and form exquisite pieces of needlework."[56] If the artificer would have distributed the parts with "arte" and "correspondencia," as in an "artistically crafted embroidery" ("artificioso recamado"), a "spectacular garden" ("vistoso jardín"), and a "precious pendant of gems" ("precioso joyel"), he would not only have created an agreeable spectacle ("they would shine forth even more and would be a spectacle very pleasant to behold, a most brilliant piece of art"),[57] but he would also have stifled the "foolish scruple" that such irregularities arouse in the viewer—the suspicion that the entire resplendent panorama has been made by chance rather than by the rational direction of Divine Providence. Andrenio's comments would appear to be introducing a traditional challenge contained and rebutted in Christian natural theology and its exemplifications in hexameral narratives—the Epicurean conception of randomness at the heart of the creation, a conception that, of course, strikes at the fundamental premise of a rationally and providentially designed universe. As Gracián's English contemporary Robert Burton put it, "How comes or wherefore is this *temeraria siderum dispositio,* this rash placing of stars, or as Epicurus will, *fortuita,* or accidental? Why are some big, some little, why are they so confusedly, unequally situated in the heavens, and set so much out of order?"[58]

In its metaphorical formulations, which clearly evoke classical aesthetic values and the medieval poetics of correspondences underlying the contemporary hexameral epics and their cosmologies, Gracián's passage, in fact, appears to be addressed to Luis de Granada's exposition and definitive resolution of the philosophical confrontation. For Granada the world is conceived as a beautiful painting, displaying a plenitude of stars, trees, birds, flowers, and colors. Were it created by chance, according to the "madness of the Epicurean atheists" ("locura de los ateistas epicúreos"), it would not only lack the clear composition that locates its multitudinous objects in a well-ordered system of places, but it would in fact resemble a "blot of ink that managed to fall on a board" ("un borron de tinta, que acertó á caer sobre una tabla" [192a]). Granada insists that the "celestial vault" is *compasada*: the movements of the stars are regular, order is invariable, and predictability is the condition of the world upon which man looks. The spectacle elicits admiration, understanding, assurance, and veneration, but there is no place for the excitement aroused by the experience of mutability, novelty, and "defamiliarizing" metamorphoses and asymmetries. There is no interest in the complexities of the observer's confrontation of the flux about him or the way in which recollections and fantasies might mediate the unchanging present of that confrontation. Severely limited in his responses and activity, Granada's essential subject can simply see what is already and always known.

In Gracián's text Critilo's response to Andrenio's apparent desire for the reassuring simplicities of the familiar refutation of Lucretius brings instabilities to this metaphysical drama that go well beyond those of the speculative moments of the traditional hexameral examinations of conflicting scientific and philosophical explanations of the order of things. While acknowledging that in their visual configurations the stars do not reveal a symmetrical pattern, a "classical" image of "arte y correspondencia," he nevertheless insists that their apparently disorderly spatial and temporal interrelationships conceal an absolutely rational system of movements and correspondences by which they moderate their respective influences for constructive and stabilizing effects on the world order. Critilo's argument is entirely conventional, and, if he stopped here, the interchange could be viewed as a seventeenth-century example of hexameral speculative reassurance, bearing a superficial trace of the Baroque taste for the asymmetrical.[59] However, Critilo goes further in exploring the aesthetic implications of Andrenio's interrogation, and in so doing, he suddenly springs beyond the traditional limits framing the speculative encounter:

> The other artful disposition that you speak of would be affected and *uniform*; leave it to the *playthings of art and human childishness*. This way every night the *sky is made new for us, and it is never boring to look at; each individual proportions the stars as he wishes.*[60]

Within the traditions inspiring the opening of the *Criticón* and informing its philosophical fictions, we appear to be facing something entirely new and something that calls into question the very metaphysical foundations that these traditions were so concerned with establishing and protecting.[61] The most astonishing innovation is the transformation of the contemplating subject, the "reader" of the Book of the World, who, from Cicero's natural man to Milton's Adam, was placed before a "completed" text, metaphysically founded, its higher meanings preordained, and given the obligation of translating, imitating, and incorporating these meanings and celebrating their truth. And the guarantee of that subject's correct, and limited, reading was figured most directly in the stars—the images of reason that symbolized the mediating bridge of rationality connecting man, the Creator, and the created world. In Gracián we find that this microcosmic subject, ever identical with himself, with his cosmic environment, and with his essentially rational fellow members of the species man, has momentarily metamorphosed into an individual, an isolated being endowed with the freedom to shape the stars and the "essential" cosmic substance as he momentarily sees fit. In the changing constructions of individual "readings," the monumentally constructed cosmos loses all determinacy, its shifting figures manifesting no longer the unchanging principles of a uniform rationality, but rather the arbitrary, and perhaps capricious, efforts of the human imagination to create "the new" in the face of the boredom that is the inescapable consequence of human beings' subjection to temporality.[62] At this most subversive moment of Gracián's articulation of the Book of the World, man's cosmic connection springs apart, the created world loses its essential and indelible character, a new subject stands as reader and creator before a potentially chaotic reality, the imagination (*ingenio*) makes a powerful ontological claim in the face of reason's traditional enthronement and present collapse, and the products of the imagination, as well as "the new" in general, are released from their traditional stigma through association with falsehood, the irrational, the "sophistic," the "unauthorized," and the fruits of illicit curiosity. In the little drama beneath the stars that opens the *Criticón,* Gracián would appear to be but a step away from the acosmic enthusiasm of the modern thinker who was so fascinated with the insights of his moral philosophy, Friedrich Nietzsche:

> Trümmer von Sternen
> Aus diesen Trümmern baute ich eine Welt.[63]

As a restless, "threshold" moment, in which the new dramatically emerges within a restatement of the old and calls into question its foundations, Andrenio's and Critilo's exchange and its implications concerning man's freedom to construct his own artistic cosmos can be compared with Don Quixote's challenge to the Canon of Toledo's reaffirmation of art's traditional responsibility to mirror reality, to appeal to the rationality common in all men, and to replicate in its verisimilar, symmetrical, and unified imitations the *dissimilium concordia* of a rational universe (Cervantes, vol. 1, chaps. 47–50). For Don Quixote the writer constructs a world in which "the sun shines with a *new* radiance" and art "conquers nature," an imagined "other" order of reality that "is bound to cause *pleasure* and arouse *wonder* in any reader of the story, whoever he may be" ("ha de causar *gusto* y *maravilla* a cualquiera que la [historia] leyere" [Cervantes 2:500–501]). As I have argued elsewhere, one finds concentrated in the canon's discussion of the romance of chivalry most of the central principles of the neoclassical theoretical project. The effort to standardize and control literary activity through the dissemination of rules based on a rationalistically and rhetorically reinterpreted Aristotelian poetics is a notable feature of the culture of the Counter-Reformation. In its biases toward authority, tradition, edification, and unity, and in its emphasis on the fundamental obligation of the poet to imitate a rational universe, it is perfectly consistent with the hexameral poetic project, which originated precisely in the decades of its maximum influence in Italy. Most relevant to Gracián's subversive textual moment are Cervantes's echoes and reaccentuations of the influential poetics of Tasso, specifically the latter's discussion of the poem as a "picciolo mondo." For Tasso, who ultimately turned to the hexameral "world text" as the most appropriate and undeniably true subject of imitation, the "nonmimetic" art of the uncontrolled "fantasia sensitiva," characteristic of the *romanzi*, is associated with the sophist and the magician, who do not deal with "cose sussistenti" and who produce idols and chimeras, things that "are nothing." Such monsters represent the diabolical antithesis of the substantial artistic products, the "imitazione icastica," of the "fantasia intellettuale" and the truthful poet, whose model is Orpheus (*Discorsi* 523–31; 587–90). In his rejoinder to the Canon of Toledo's condemnation of the monstrosities of the books of chivalry, Don Quixote presents an appealing image of Tasso's frightening "art of the sophist." His narrative of the journey of a knight-errant to a marvelous lower world replaces the traditional cosmic panorama with a far more beautiful one ("There it seems to him that the sky is more transparent, and that the sun shines with a newer radiance" ["Allí le parece que el cielo es más transparente, y que el sol luce con claridad más nueva"; Cervantes 2:500]) and climaxes in the depiction of a grotesque fountain that reveals the triumph of art over nature in its creator's elaboration of his own *dissimilium concordia* ("orden desordenada"). The entire vision implies a conception of art in which the creative imagination, freed from all responsibility to duplicate the cosmos, creates from within itself and its "lower," interior order a "higher," autonomous order of reality over which the artist stands as god and which requires no legitimation through a substantial connection with an "objective," rationally apprehensible order in reality or nature.[64]

Insofar as Gracián maintains in the background of Critilo's clarification of the celestial spectacle a God who acknowledges the monotony and "childishness" of a "classical" world picture, encourages man's expression of his individual subjectivity, and permits his freedom to intervene in cosmic construction, it is tempting to conclude that he has suddenly shifted theological positions, displacing the providential, self-displaying deity of natural theology with a God far more remote from human purposes, although, unlike the fearsome or unconcerned God of the nominalists, one who is quite well disposed toward man's subjective reconstitutions of the created order. At this point the hexameral *Theatrum Mundi* appears to have collapsed and been replaced by the "pien teatro di maraviglie" that four years later (1655) Emmanuele Tesauro would celebrate in the most fantastic poetic creations of his contemporaries. The very title of Tesauro's massive revision of Aristotle's *Poetics,* the *Cannocchiale Aristotelico,* implies that a revolution in cosmic perception has brought with it a major revision in man's understanding of literature. For Tesauro God's created order can be viewed as a multitude of marvelous metaphors, but their relevance for mankind lies not in any essential, intelligible truths that they allegedly signify but in the dynamics of their production and their inspiration to man as a creator ex nihilo of his own realities rather than as an imitator or an exegete of a preexistent reality.[65] However, the shocking final argument in Critilo's rejoinder to Andrenio's ingenuous complaint about the apparent spectacle of chaos in the multitude of stars may in fact suggest the omnipotent, nonrational, and hidden god of nominalism, who shows himself only through miracle and enigma and confounds his adorers' efforts to reach him through human modes of understanding. If we have witnessed an unexpected contextual leap from the metaphysical into the aesthetic, here the abrupt change of perspective is even more startling, as the aesthetic converges with the political. Critilo continues his explanation of the apparent stellar disorder:

> In this natural variety and *oppressive confusion,* the stars appear to be so much greater in number that the *common people consider them to be innumerable,* and as a result *the supreme governance remains as if hidden within an enigma, one that is very clear and comprehensible to the experts.*[66]

At various points in Andrenio's reading of the Book of the World, we note a conception of the creative deity as a force that exercises colossal powers of domination, suppression, and containment. A characteristic example is his sublime description of the sea as he surveys the world from a cliff soaring above the angry breakers battering the shore. He finds himself nearly overwhelmed by rapture as he witnesses the "horrifying monster" of the sea being "imprisoned," "subdued," "restrained," "incarcerated," and "enclosed," by the "prevención" of a divinity that appears to stand triumphantly embattled between universal order and its violent overthrow. The degree of repressive violence and threatening chaos at the border areas of the assembled cosmos is particularly striking when compared with the harmonious effects marking the spatial junctures of the *discordia concors* of the created cosmos in Gracián's principal intertext, the *Símbolo de la fe.* In Granada's work, the sea lovingly "enters into an embrace with the land," with its numerous shores and beaches, so that "from two things so different there is made a nature common to both."[67] Truer to the Pythagorean-Platonic traditions standing behind all of these texts, his deity has more of the musician and the lover than of the absolute monarch. Nevertheless, even in such extreme elaborations of the violence latent in the paradoxical *discordia concors* of the universe, Gracián, in most of such passages, remains fundamentally consistent with the orthodox premises of the hexameral tradition regarding the creation. One could say that his deity represents a particularly striking development of the traditional image of the creator in his role of measuring, placing, and harnessing the oppositional energies released in his fundamental building blocks, the warring elements of the Empedoclean philosophical tradition. However, in Critilo's depiction of the deity as the supreme "asistencia" and the beings created in his likeness and image as manipulated subjects, overwhelmed by the confusing spectacles and unfathomable "enigmas" of a totalitarian order of monarch and accomplices, who rule the ignorant through fear and secrecy, we find not only a shocking inversion of the self-revealing God of natural theology, but once again, a conspicuous displacement of the cosmic order by the most disquieting scenarios of contemporary absolutist politics. In his *Empresas políticas,* Diego de Saavedra Fajardo describes the undulating movements of the serpent, which leaves no traces and gives no hint of his "intención" or direction. He concludes that "the counsels and designs of princes should be concealed in a similar way," and, in words that can be taken as a complete reversal of the discourse of Granada's natural theology, he justifies such secrecy by the model of God, "the great Governor of the created order, whose moves can be understood by nobody." Going beyond the political cynicism evoked by Gracián's text, he notes that nature's concealment of man's heart within his breast is its warrant for the normality of individual isolation and suggests that the king should keep even his closest associates in ignorance so that "the people might drink from them their deception, so that it might spread and flow everywhere."[68] Although in one of his more idealistic moments Saavedra Fajardo can speak of the king as a being who should display himself fully and directly to his subjects to inspire love and community feeling and, like the self-revealing God, maintain his palace doors open to all, more characteristically he holds to the Tacitan principle that "lo que no se ve se venera más" (what is unseen is venerated more), despises the populace's capacities for judgment, suggests that it is not fitting for it to know whether the "chain of its servitude is of iron or of gold," and argues that, since it tends toward the conditions of "furia" and "confusión," "a great skill of the prince is to guide it with its own reins and to proceed at the pace of its ignorance." Saavedra Fajardo's ruminations on the concealing surface enclosure of the beehive, a striking example of the age's characteristic reoccupation of archaic modes of expression with the insights of a decisively modern mentality, are perhaps even more relevant to Gracián's momentary vision of the universal ruler's enigmatic "multiplication" of the stars. The bees show us that government is most effective when it conceals designs, veils the dressing room wherein its theatrically displayed ordinances are costumed, cultivates fear of the unknown in its audience, and projects grandiose phantasms that, if glimpsed in their substantial dimensions, would inspire laughter. The justification for such procedures lies in the example of the Old Testament God, who, while communicating to Moses on Mount Sinai, maintained distance and incomprehensibility behind the fires and clouds surrounding its summit.[69]

If Gracián's sharp rupture with his natural theological context has transformed the traditional hexameral author and spectator-reader of the Book of the World momentarily into the individuated Baroque artist, creatively indulging his "ingenio" in the novelties of an imaginatively recreated, "hollow" cosmos, he has, almost immediately thereafter, presented an image of that very spectator-reader as a transported, imaginatively dominated subject, whose irrational responses to illusions can be viewed as the glory both of the absolutist state and the Baroque artist.[70] In the place of the universal hexameral audience—an envisaged society of authentic communication and essential connectedness, transcending all distinctions of culture, class, and language[71]—we observe a group divided, ignorant, and confused, subject to the manipulations of a capricious power whose source it neither sees nor understands. In this momentary disruption in the heavens, which is as fleeting and as portentous as the intrusion of a comet flashing across the perfect circles of a rational cosmos, we already have a brief glimpse of the demonic realities of seventeenth-century politics that Gracián will imaginatively develop in the spectacle of enslaving representation that Andrenio and Critilo witness in their subsequent encounter with the monstrous, "invisible" politician in Spain (1:vii). The cosmic "theater of marvels" is simultaneously a theater of power, engineered by a hidden god.

Closing the Book of the World: The Distancing of Man

Laberintos, retruécanos, emblemas,
Helada y laboriosa nadería,

. . . .

No hubo música en su alma; sólo un vano
Herbatio de metáforas y argucias
Y la veneración de las astucias
Y el desdén de lo humano y sobrehumano.

> *No lo movió la antigua voz de Homero*
> *Ni esa, de plata y luna, de Virgilio;*
> *No vió al fatal Edipo en el exilio*
> *Ni a Cristo que se muere en un madero.*[72]
> —Jorge Luis Borges, "Baltasar Gracián"

If we consider the implications of Gracián's scene of cosmic severance, we are led to a seemingly paradoxical conclusion. On the one hand man asserts his *distance,* his detachment from the world around him and his interior freedom to create as an individual. In this distance we see an analogy of the artist's release from his binding to a mimetic theory of poetry that would limit him to imitating or reading a coherent, divinely ordained cosmos.[73] The artist is free to explore the imagination and to value his own works as offspring of his *ingenio* quite apart from any reflective or utilitarian function they might have.

On the other hand we see the apparently contradictory imaginative transformation of the cosmos into the absolutist monarchic court and the relationship of man to that court as one of total submission and surrender of self. We see quite literally, projected into the heavens, the primary imaginative setting of Western metaphysics, the mythification of state and king that Strong has described as absolutism's transmutation of "the physical reality of the ruler into a metaphysical idea." On the one hand the individual submits to the state and adores it; on the other hand the individual preserves his inner autonomy, his distance from any completed metaphysical order, his right to construct imaginatively any such order, and perhaps his sense of the arbitrary, constructed character of the very political order to which he freely and totally submits. Seen in this perspective, the absolutist state might appear as the most spectacular of Baroque metaphors.[74]

In either case we can say that the *Criticón's* fissured Book of the World bears witness to a new condition of man as a *distanced* being, separated from the traditional cosmos, which had offered a reassuring model for his identity as a coequal with creator and created order in their shared rationality, and separated from the absolute state, to which he has yielded all independence. In his study of Tesauro's Baroque rewriting of Aristotle's *Poetics,* Eugenio Donato notes that the most important change that took place between the Renaissance and the Baroque periods was the "breakdown of the rationality of the cosmos," a "devaluation of reality," and the formation of "a new concept of the I." In his inescapably subjective creations the poet is in one sense the master of the universe that he is free to create as if he were a god. At the same time he is entirely dependent on his readers' subjectively founded approval, since there is no conceptual truth inherent in the "autonomous" products of his imagination. Gracián's most important response to such decisive changes in the relationship of the individual to the cosmos was not in aesthetics, in epistemology, or in literary innovations of the type we associate with Cervantes or Góngora, two great visionaries of man in a world of his own making.[75] It was rather in his worldly philosophy, in his understanding of a major alteration in this period in man's consciousness of himself as a social being, the "comprehensive transformation of human beings" that Norbert Elias has described as "distancing" and associated with the social conditions of the absolutist courts and the kind of rationality that they fostered: "The courts were not the only figurations in which people forming them developed greater self-control, and with it an increased detachment from nature, from each other and from themselves. But they were among the first, and for a time they were undoubtedly the most powerful and influential of these figurations."[76]

Gracián was, of course, most famous in Europe for presenting the strategies for success in the court, emphasizing, in his treatises on heroism and discretion and in his collection of aphorisms, the *Oráculo manual*, the importance of theatrical self-presentation, the control of the audience of others through a carefully calculated projection of appearances, reflective self-distancing from affects and spontaneous inclinations, and extreme caution regarding unmasked communication with others. That Gracián was aware of the implications of isolation, distrust, duplicitous impersonation, and a ruthless power drive in his reaccentuation of the traditional Stoic philosophical anthropology becomes clear in his satirical visions of the court in the *Criticón*.[77] The most striking refashions Ariosto's famous labyrinth of obsessive desire and delusion, the castle of Atlante, as a *social* image, a claustrophobic palace with neither doors nor windows, where invisible inhabitants reveal their presence only in the glow of rapacious hands that can be perceived at a banqueting table, where disembodied voices can be heard and an impenetrable darkness enshrouds all human relationships, separating even husband, wife, and child.[78]

Such metaphysical and social distancing finds its parallel in Gracián's most interesting vision of the seventeenth-century political order. From the protagonists' entry into the smoky city of the hidden monarch to the theatrical *descubrimiento* of the empty banquet plates of his public festival—"on uncrowning the meat pie [*empanada*], he found only the echo [i.e., *nada*], and of the leg of the roast [*pernil*], he found the *nihil* . . . the fruits, of Sodom, without fruits [i.e., fruitfulness]" ("al descoronar la empanada hallaba sólo el eco, y del pernil el *nihil* . . . las frutas, de Sodoma, sin fruto")—to the entrapment of Andrenio in a compulsive daily ritual of going to an empty palace "to idolatrize in the fantastic grandeur of a king devoid of reality" ("en la fantástica grandeza de un rey sin nada de realidad"), the entire episode is imaginatively dominated by motifs of nothingness. It reaches its climax in a "community-forming" rite on the public square, where a "mecánico teatro," with "many pieces of stage machinery and illusion-producing devices" ("muchas tramoyas y apariencias"), has been constructed "in the middle of that great theater of the world" ("en medio de aquel gran teatro de todo el mundo"). The dramatic production is a spectacle of loneliness, deception, cruelty, and scapegoating that enthralls the audience, whose members are completely unaware that the theatrical representation is being duplicated simultaneously in their own victimization by pickpockets: "so that in the end the observed and the observers all turned out to be equal: naked in the street and likewise on the face of the earth."[79] At a further remove in the complex metatheatrical construction of this "ceremonia inviolable," as if in the royal box of a theater, the "escondido monarca" (hidden monarch) views from beneath the protective shield of a "lattice" the festival that he has arranged—"toda tropelía" (everything illusionism)—in order to "deceive the people, not allowing them the chance to think about more serious things."[80] Aside from its direct attack on Machiavelli, who, on the day preceding the production of the play, appears on the central square as a grotesque charlatan and stupefies the "innumerable vulgaridad abobada" with his spellbinding eloquence, this episode is most interesting in disclosing Gracián's insights into the disconnection of the foundation of the political order from an evident natural order, the inadequacy of traditional organicist metaphors as explanations of its cohesion, the hiddenness of its origin and source of control, and its reliance on illusion and a "technology of power" for legitimation and self-perpetuation. Such insights are characteristic of the most advanced political thinking of the century (see Zarka), but they are insights that Gracián evidently associates with emptiness, futility, chaos, and monstrosity. When the incessant labors of Andrenio as courtier are finally rewarded with an opportunity to gaze on the king, he discovers that he "is most distant from him when most near." In the magical mirror provided by the benevolent artificer, Artemia, the source of power holding the modern state together is unveiled as a figure of absolute disproportion ("no corresponde parte a parte") and obliquity ("no puede ir derecho"). It is an "agregado de monstruosidades," a mass of coiling lines and twisted forms, which grotesquely intermingles the animal and the human orders of being and continually eludes the observer's fixing glance in its restless movements and metamorphoses. In Gracián's satirical epiphany the "monstruo coronado" and his labyrinthian city of masked subjects ("there was not a man or a woman who did not come forth with his or her [mask], and all of them were other than themselves")[81] should certainly be seen as an inversion of the traditional rational, "illuminated," and cosmically founded political order, which was commonly reasserted in Gracián's age and even reconciled with the pragmatic doctrines of such modernist political thinkers as Saavedra Fajardo. However, what is most striking here is Gracián's recoil from his own modernist insights into the realities and consequences of political power. Where the traditionalists situated the animating heart or head of the corporate body, and the modernists, the stabilizing machinery of rationally institutionalized power, Gracián finds nothing but nothingness. His pessimism becomes even more evident as the image of the "monstruo coronado" is easily lifted to a more general level of allegorization and becomes, at the scene's conclusion, an embodiment of the powers and pervasiveness of *engaño* in the world (*Criticón* 1:108–14, 123–30). The reward of political lucidity could hardly be more devastating. As a metaphorical vehicle perfectly adequated to illusion, politics becomes finally a privileged figure in Gracián's distinctive rhetoric of nothingness.

Such phantasmagoric visions suggest that for Gracián cosmic disconnection was a condition that, while releasing man's imaginative faculties from their classical fetters and endowing him with unprecedented powers for mastering himself and his social environment, forced him to the painful confrontation of the hollowness hidden behind the dazzling surfaces of his creations. Man himself can in fact be no more than persona, an entity invested with being only by the gaze of others who observe his performance. Near the end of their pilgrimage, the heroes are rewarded with perhaps Gracián's most revealing image of man as he achieves full self-realization in the glow of his theatrical existence. Above the streets of Rome a tightrope walker "dances and leaps" with the "lightness of a bird" and the "temerity of a madman," enthralling a large mob of spectators below, "who were watching him, their amazement matching his intrepidity, they trembling on seeing him, he dancing so that they might see him."[82] Caught in the success and exhilaration of his performance, man fails to realize that he walks "not with sane, but with very insane confidence" on a "silk thread; less, on a hair; that is even a lot; on the thread of a spider; that is still something; on the thread of life, which is even less."[83] The lesson in fragility and *desengaño* is abrupt and severe. One might recall Tesauro's acknowledgment that the splendid "autonomous" metaphors of the liberated poet are in reality "like the apples of the Black Sea; when seen they are lovely and rosey, but if you bite into them, they leave your mouth full of ashes and smoke."[84]

The ashes and smoke that pervade the imaginative atmosphere of the *Criticón* thicken noticeably in its final book, and it is no surprise that, when Gracián returns to the cosmic panorama at his conclusion, he makes no effort whatsoever to find reassurance by reopening the traditional Book of the World. Here we find that the cave in which Andrenio discovered his identity as a human being through the exercise of the universal, inherent light of reason has been transformed into the devouring Cave of Nothingness, which yawns beneath a swarm of nobodies who chatter incessantly in a pathetic effort to become something, an entity founded solely in the inconsequential response of recognition that they can provoke in others. After viewing the spectacle of "el nadilla y el nonadilla" (little nothings and mere nothings) who want to "parecer algo, y mucho" (appear to be something, and a lot), the protagonists descend to the cave and watch as three-quarters of the inhabitants of the world eagerly hurl themselves into its oblivion and display in their grotesque postures of self-cancellation "how much is nothing and how nothing would like to be everything" ("cuán mucha es la nada y que la nada querría serlo todo" [3:191, 208, 222]).

At the climax of the *Criticón* the protagonists arrive at Rome, the center of the world and the goal of their quest for enlightenment and felicity. They ascend a hill and turn their gaze to the heavens. If, from their heights above the sea, Andrenio and Critilo could comfortably contemplate the splendors of the created universe and decipher the significances that the deity manifests in it, here their vision requires the assistance of a marvelous "Archimedean" glass, which enables them to gaze "much farther into reality than Galileo's telescope." On raising it to the heavens they discover a spectacle of celestial spinning wheels, which, unlike the musical spheres of the deluded Pythagoras, turn silently and treacherously as they draw out the slender threads of innumerable balls of yarn, "extracting their substance and consuming their life until leaving them totally spent and unraveled, so that all that managed to remain of each was a piece of rag of a poor shroud, for this is where everything comes to a stop."[85] Gracián's final image of the flexibility of the persona that man can heroically construct to replace his monumental microcosmic ancestor and soar beyond his providential fetters could hardly be more insubstantial. In his greatest efforts he is merely "leaping, springing, and bobbing" ("brincando, saltando, rodando"), unaware that he is disintegrating constantly, helplessly prey to the arbitrary movements of the machinery of time and death, the emblems of the ultimate meaning of a universe that has fallen silent.

Notes

1. Blumenberg, *Legitimacy.* See also Nicolson's study of the impact of the "new science" on the literature of this period, a period when "man, like the world and universe, gradually ceased to be part of an animate universe . . . when men were living between an old world and a new" (129).

2. It is perhaps revealing that the most significant recognition that Gracián's writings received in philosophical circles during the following three hundred years came from two "outsiders" to and critics of the mainstream western metaphysical traditions that reasserted themselves in the seventeenth-century triumph of Cartesianism—Schopenhauer and Nietzsche. Two recent efforts to recuperate Gracián as a philosophical "outsider" and an important precursor of postmodern philosophy (e.g., Heidegger and Derrida) are the studies of Hidalgo-Serna and Pelegrín.

3. "... en la cual se trata de la creación del mundo para venir por las criaturas al conoscimiento del Criador, y de sus divinas perfecciones" (181). All translations are my own unless otherwise indicated. I am grateful to Edmund L. King for his assistance in the translation of several of Gracián's most difficult texts.

4. For the enormous popularity of the hexameral epics in the period, see Thibaut de Maisières. The most influential, Du Bartas's *La sepmaine, ou Création du monde,* appeared in some 230 editions, in all the major European languages, as well as in Latin, during the seventy years following its publication in 1578.

5. Granada 202b. For the importance of epistemological wonder in the *Criticón's* opening scenes and their evocation of philosophical traditions descending from Aristotle's *Metaphysics* and Plato's *Thaetetus,* see Armisen.

6. "Venta franca, mantenida de la divina próvida clemencia en medio de inmensos golfos" (Gracián, *El criticón* (1971) 1:9–10). Subsequent volume and page references to the *Criticón* are to this edition.

7. "Si mudasen sus lugares y puestos, ardería todo el mundo. Y un poco más abajo añade el mismo Tulio estas palabras: Hermosamente dijo Aristóteles que si habitasen algunos hombres debajo de la tierra, en algunos palacios adornados con diversas pinturas, y con todas las cosas con que están ataviadas las casas de los que son tenidos por bienaventurados y ricos, los cuales hombres morando en aquellos soterraños nunca hubiesen visto las cosas que están sobre la tierra, y hubiesen oído por fama que hay una divinidad en el mundo soberana; y despues desto, abiertas las gargantas de la tierra, saliesen de aquellos aposentos: cuando viesen la tierra, la mar, y el cielo, la grandeza de las nubes, la fuerza de los vientos, y pusiesen los ojos en el sol, y conosciesen la grandeza, y hermosura, y eficacia dél, y cómo él esclaresciendo con su luz el cielo, es causa del día, y llegada la noche viesen todo el cielo adornado y pintado con tantas y tan hermosas lumbreras, y notasen la variedad de la luna, con sus crescientes y menguantes, y considerasen la variedad de los nascimientos, y puestos de las estrellas tan ordenados y tan constantes en sus movimientos en toda la eternidad; sin duda cuando los tales hombres salidos de la escuridad de sus cuevas, súbitamente viesen todo esto, luego conoscerían haber sido verdadera la fama de lo que les fué dicho, que era haber en este mundo una soberana divinidad, de que todo pendía. Esto dijo Aristoteles" (189b).

8. "... armonía del mundo, compuesta de infinita variedad de cosas reducidas a este unidad susodicha que es el servicio del hombre" (191a). For the traditional musical conceptions of the universe and their Pythagorean-Platonic origins, see Spitzer, *Classical and Christian Ideas,* and Heninger, Chap. 4. For the *scala mundi,* the classical study is Lovejoy.

9. "... maestro de capilla ... reduce las cosas a esta unidad y consonancia ... ninguna cosa por sí sola basta para todo" (191b).

10. See Tasso's *Il mondo creato* 3.862ff., a long passage in which the poet laments that solar worship is common in the New World and reminds the reader that the earth is older and far more honorable than the sun and that the latter's apparent powers of fecundation have nothing to do with the original ornamentation of the globe with plant and animal life. See also 4.159ff., where he deplores the false guides who lead his contemporaries into error concerning the power of the sun (*Opere* 4:98, 125–126). For the hexameral literature as a confirmation of a geocentric universe in the face of the new astronomical discoveries associated with the Copernican revolution (e.g., heliocentricity, the infinity of the immeasureable space of the universe, a plurality of worlds) and their harmonization with the ancient Pythagorean-Platonic "metaphysics of light," which was so prominent in Renaissance philosophy, see Lara Garrido: "En Kepler, la heliolatría platonizante se perfila hasta hacer del sol el Dios visible al que en el *Mysterium cosmographicum* (1596) asigna el papel de motor y llama 'Corazón del Mundo, Rey y Príncipe de las estrellas.'" Lara Garrido maintains that the most systematic effort to wipe out heliocentricity was Bodin's *Universae naturae theatrum* (1592) (see 245). For Copernicus's and Kepler's "sun worship," see Nicolson 151–155. It is perhaps worth pointing out that Philip II's efforts to obliterate all traces of the Indians' cosmologies and religious practices appearing in the anthropological accounts of the pre-Columbian cultures written in the New World reached their climax precisely in the years in which the great hexameral project of early modern literature was inaugurated in Du Bartas's internationally admired *La sepmaine* (1578) (see Baudot, esp. Chap. 9).

11. Gracián's modernist reconception of the condition of nothingness is discussed later in this chapter. Its obsessive presence in his writings and the unprecedented imaginative effects in its evocations can be similarly clarified in part as secularizing reaccentuations of powerful religious conceptions.

12. "Ya en esto los alegres mensajeros de ese gran monarca de la luz que tú llamas sol, coronado augustamente de resplandores, ceñido de la guarda de sus rayos, solicitaban mis ojos a rendirle veneraciones de atención y de admiración. Comenzó a ostentarse por ese gran trono de cristalinas espumas, y con una soberana callada majestad se fue señoreando de todo el hemisferio, llenando todas las demás criaturas de su esclarecida presunción. Aquí yo quedé absorto y totalmente enajenado de mí mismo, puesto en él, émulo del águila más atenta" (1:22–23).

13. For the way in which the traditional subject's cosmic "submission" is in fact the key to his self-acquisition, see Jonas (Chap. 10).

14. See, for example, Strong's description of a royal entry of Henry IV in Avignon. The ceremony "includes an arch dedicated to Henry as Apollo Economico, the god who *'gouverne tout l'Universe par ses rayons et occultes influences,'* and in which the king appeared bearing up the celestial sphere" (*Art and Power* 71). Strong points out that, in celebrating an imperialist vision of spiritual unity, artists and humanists of the Renaissance courts exploited all the techniques of spectacular theater to identify rulers with cosmic powers and harmonies. As for the image of the king, Strong notes that "royal portraiture transmuted the physical reality of a ruler into a metaphysical idea" (Henry, Prince of Wales 113). In Gracián's text we discover that in fact a metaphysical idea has been transformed into the physical reality of a ruler.

15. Andrenio's solar idolatry should be understood in terms of seventeenth-century rituals of gazing on the "solar" king: "¡Dichoso el que alcanza a ver / del sol del Rey sólo un rayo! ... Como sin el sol el hombre no es hombre, es estatua, es piedra, / así aquel que nunca vio / la cara al Rey" (Blessed is the man who manages to see but a single ray of the sun of the King! ... Just as a man without the sun is a statue or a stone / So the man who never saw / The face of the King") (Lope de Vega 190). Lope's play is one of the most penetrating studies of this central ritual of absolutism in that it lays bare and problematizes the surrender of being and loss of connection of the individual within the organic body of the state, the very connection that the ubiquitous solar myth allegedly confirmed. For Saavedra Fajardo, the king, as sun, penetrates, unifies, and warms with love all spaces of the body politic; in its continual movements the sun emblematizes a king's attendance to the state's needs everywhere (810). For Edward Forsett, the subject gazes on the majesty shining in the body of the king like the sun in a glass and through its miraculous effects finds concord, civility, love, and the mutuality of an integrated rational society (32–34). Relevant to Andrenio's alienation from himself and self-prostration before the gigantic royal apparition striding toward him in the heavens is perhaps the most famous image of absolutism in the age, Hobbes's Leviathan, rising like the sun at the horizon of the Commonwealth, spreading its shadowy image across the landscape, and literally incorporating into its colossal figure the innumerable diminutive subjects whose eyes are riveted in awe on its fearsome face. For the phantasmal basis and the irrational, "eclipsing" dynamics of this "absolutist" mode of connection of individual and state-cosmos, see Pye (esp. 296ff.). La Rochefoucauld's maxim "le soleil ni la mort ne se peuvent regarder fixement"(47) provides a deeper insight into the dynamics of the "monarch-sun's" interaction with his subject in Gracián's scene than do the writings of such rational theorists of absolutism as Saavedra Fajardo and Forsett.

16. "A nadie ha menester de sí abajo, y todos le reconocen dependencias" (1: 23). See, for example, Sancho de Moncada's *Nueva, e importante Universidad en la Corte de España* (Madrid, 1619). He discusses the appropriateness of the sun as a *blasón* for Philip III, "unico, y sin segundo en el Orbe": "Un sol. Lo primero, porque V. Mag. tiene grandeza sin segunda en el Orbe, y el Sol se llama Sol, porque es solo. Lo segundo, porque ninguna cosa declara tanto el Oficio Real, como el Sol, pues Egypto le tuvo por geroglyfico del Rey" (ed. J. A. Maravall; see Maravall, *Estudios* 3:115–149, esp. 148). For the classical and Christian traditions lying behind the elaborate solar mythology and imagery in the court ceremonial of seventeenth-century absolutist monarchy, see Ernst Kantorowizc. Gracián's epiphany of the sun as a monarchic ritual of self-display, power, and adoration is all the more striking when compared with the corresponding solar moment of the hexameral epics. For Acevedo, who reveals no anxiety about solar idolatry or "scientific" heliocentricity, the sun is continually associated with harmony. While fecundating the earth, it moderates planetary influences and brings warring elements into concord. It is like the "third string of the musical instrument, which brings the discordant strings into pleasing harmony" (*Creación del mundo* 267). Tasso and Du Bartas similarly emphasize scientific properties of the sun, although both analogize its appearance with the joyful bridegroom striding forth from his

heavenly tent in Psalm 19:6, and the latter briefly likens it to a royal procession (Tasso, *Il mondo creato* 4.298ff.; Du Bartas 4.547ff.).

17. "... criatura que más ostentosamente retrata la majestuosa grandeza del Criador... el más luciente espejo en quien las divinas grandezas se representan" (1:23).

18. "This gift, this illustrious fire, / This intelligence adorned with pure light / Is included in the sphere of man / Like the immense Artificer in his sublimity."

19. Granada 358–359. For the miracle as a literary form, see Forcione, *Cervantes and the Humanist Vision*, Chap. 4.

20. See Blumenberg (*Genesis* 22ff., 333–334): "To put it in extreme form: Christ would not have had to die for man's benefit if the world had really been created for man's benefit."

21. On the two, potentially conflictive, tendencies of Baroque cultural production (e.g., worldliness, activism, and epic heroism vs. renunciation, quietism, and spiritual heroism), see Weisbach, Weise, and Skrine.

22. "This work, whose great circumference, art, rich labor, matter, and form show us that we should bow in reverence to Him who fashions his edifice from nothing; the excellence of this universal temple, which informs us of the Eternal Father, is a great book, which in silence teaches that very world the profound power of God. A sacred text, where nature shows us that a celestial idea governs and encompasses with its laws the grandeur of this sublime machine. It is not written on the bark of the oak, nor with the marks of the Hebrew language, nor with Greek accents, nor with dark figures of symbols and images. For he who drinks the waters of Hydaspes, the most heathen, the most barbarous Scythian, he who inhabits the lands of the untilled Caspian, wilder than the wilderness itself, the inhuman dweller of the Antarctic, who, in the hardness of his life, imitates jasper, all will know how to read the characters of this reliable doctrine without study and discipline" (Acevedo 247).

23. Granada's compendium incorporates the entirety of the Christian vision, passing from the hexameral material to the fundamental mystery of the Incarnation and Redemption. Yet its most influential and widely disseminated part was its initial book, dealing with the beauty, rationality, and providential design of the Creation. For its connections with hexameral traditions, as well as its tremendous popularity, attested by numerous editions and translations, see Balcells.

24. "... ojos de todas las naciones del mundo, así de griegos como bárbaros, así de sabios como de ignorantes... letras quebradas y iluminadas... por tantas diferencias de tonos" (186b).

25. "And as the master was *one alone, one the model, one the order,* so, in order to give us a copy of his mind within, the sovereign Artificer made in *one manner, one single copy;* and a *single one* is the sphere by which the world is encompassed, although its circular and immense design embraces more circles within its circumference" (Acevedo 247). See Tasso, *Il mondo creato* 2.93–98, and 3.1445–1451, where the poet expresses anxiety about the danger of not being able to complete an adequate depiction of the seemingly boundless created order but recognizes that the most minute objects point in the same direction, toward the revealed power and grandeur of the Creator. For hexameral theology and its narrative manifestations as "a kind of fixed enclosing structure or substance which compre-

hends all that is known or experienced, and thus defines the space of knowledge," see Kendrick 126. Kendrick presents some suggestive insights into the essentially static character of hexameral epic. The poet's task is "a methodical filling in of a serialized space, a space broken into discrete fragments which have been preordained by creation." The poem, in a sense, is in reality a commentary. For the powerful containing effects of the elaborate and systematic categorizing structures of hexameral narrative, see Pfandl's discussion of Granada's work (163–165) and Balcells 39.

26. "... así como en el cielo vos seréis espejo en que veamos las criaturas, así en este destierro ellas nos son espejo, para que conozcamos a vos" (186b).

27. For the threat of theological absolutism at the threshold of modernity, see Blumenberg (*Legitimacy*, esp. Part 2, Chaps. 3 and 4). He notes nominalism's dominating concern with the immediacy of the operation of the absolute power of divinity, its conception of the "secondary" character of created reality, and its "shift of interest and accent onto the miracle, the paradigmatic reduction of the bindingness of nature." In this sense a "system of breaches of system," it directs its speculative interest not at the "power that could give rise to the world but the power that can give rise to something other than this world" (189).

28. See Blumenberg (*Genesis* 320–321). Luther's rejection of natural reason and the attitudes and premises underlying natural theology and the hexameral project was uncompromising. The way to the hidden God can only be through the nonrational experience of the passions of suffering and humiliation, the way of the cross. Those who wish to find God in His "visibilia" and "posteriora," through rational interpretation of the created order, are in reality fools: "Non ille digne Theologus dicitur, qui invisibilia Dei per ea, quae facta sunt, intellecta conspicit.... Sed qui visibilia et posteriora Dei per passiones et crucem conspecta intelliget" (Luther 361–362). Since I am postulating a cultural need for the stabilizations, reassurances, and occultations provided by the resurgent natural theology of the period, it is worth recalling the success of Montaigne's translation of Raymond de Sebonde's fifteenth-century *Theologia naturalis sive liber creaturarum*, a translation that he undertook at the urgings of his father, who no doubt considered it a "very useful book and suited to the time... when the innovations of Luther were beginning to gain favor and to shake our old belief in many places" (Montaigne 319–320). At the same time, I would suggest that the infiltration of fideistic and anthropologically oriented destabilizing elements into Montaigne's formulation of Sebonde's reading of the "book of nature," with its metaphysical gradualism and elaborate relations of analogy, and the subsequent radical disarticulation of that text in the skeptical and nominalist criticisms of the "Apologie" are comparable, as signs of a general cultural crisis, to Gracián's ambivalent articulation and disarticulation of the same fundamental and rational world text at the beginning of the *Criticón*. For Montaigne and Sebonde, see Friedrich (*Montaigne* 91ff.). For the popularity of Sebonde's ideas in Spain and the favor his book found among the Jesuits, see De Bujanda. I am grateful to my colleague François Rigolot for bringing this study to my attention.

29. For the disenchantment of the world, see Blumenberg (*Legitimacy, Genesis*); also the fundamental studies of Cassirer (*Individual and the Cosmos*) and Haydn. For the socioeconomic context of the process, see Maravall (*Culture of the Baroque*).

A suggestive critical view of the process is available in Toulmin's recent retrospective study of modernity's "hidden agenda."

30. This is not to deny the strong theocentrism of Raphael's introductory excursus on cosmology and his traditional denunciation of *vana curiositas*: "Solicit not thy thoughts with matters hid, / Leave them to God above, him serve and fear" (Milton, *Paradise Lost* 8.167–168), words that certainly suggest a theological absolutism underlying all the practical implications of the injunctions to "be lowly wise" and to immobilize the "errant" imagination ("But apt the Mind or Fancy is to rove / Uncheckt, and of her roving is no end" [188–189]). As for the humanist traditions and their reconcilability with the Baroque hexameral project, it should be pointed out that, while Erasmus's Christianity is fundamentally acosmic and antimetaphysical, he nevertheless edited Ambrose's and Basil's hexamerons. The nature of his affirmative attitude toward the creation is revealed clearly in his most influential dialogues. For example, in the *Godly Feast,* at the gate of Eusebius's garden, an image of Christ stands over the inscription "I am the way" and points with one hand to heaven. But simultaneously his other hand invites passersby to dwell within a delightful garden, where plants, flowers, and objects of art regale them with pleasures, beauties, and higher significances that they symbolize. In the *Epicurean* Erasmus describes his attitude toward the created order in very precise terms. One gazes at the heavens through the desire to love rather than in response to the curious impulse to comprehend and to find fault in imperfections. In the created objects one discerns traces of the Creator's omnipotence, wisdom, and goodness. And in an imaginative reelaboration of the Ciceronian wisdom parable informing Andrenio's emergence from the cave, Erasmus contrasts two kinds of spectators who suddenly gaze on Psyche's palace—one a "detached" stranger, motivated by curiosity alone, the other, bonded personally with the object of knowledge through love of its architect, who happens to be his father. Pleasure in the created object is the reward of such knowledge. One should contrast this with Luther's words on the way of the cross and the limitations of the *visibilia* (see n. 28), as well as Augustine's admonition to race quickly through the world of temporal things in his clarification of the mystery of Christ as the way (*On Christian Doctrine* 1.34). The Erasmian reform movement remained deeply attached to man's "detour" through the created order, and in its philosophical context it is perhaps instructive to approach its distinctive "Epicurean" kind of Christianity as the complex negotiation of an intermediary position between the unacceptable extremes of Protestant transcendence, spiritualism, and theocentrism and Epicurean worldliness, materialism, and dissociation of eudemonism from theoretical absorption in inherent purposes. Despite his disdain for the metaphysical speculations and priorities of scholasticism, Erasmus's humanistic position remained fundamentally compatible with the mainstream Counter-Reformation reconciliation of divine omnipotence; the goodness, purposefulness, and beauty of the created universe; and the value of man's achievements in the free exercise of his creative powers. Although focusing on divine power and the creation, the hexameral project was founded precisely on this reconciliation. For the humanists' reaccentuation of the traditional elements of classical and scholastic world pictures, their anthropocentric teleology, their derivation of moral and political duties from a cosmic vision linked genetically with rhetoric, and their impact on

the theological positions adopted by the Council of Trent and celebrated in Baroque culture, see Blumenberg (*Genesis* 200–208). See also Bouwsma's concise study of Stoic and Augustinian currents in Renaissance thought.

31. "Todas las criaturas tienen *finitas* y *limitadas* sus naturalezas y virtudes, porque todas las criastes en *número, peso y medida,* y les hecistes sus *rayas,* y señalastes los *límites de su jurisdiccion.* Muy activo es el fuego en calentar, y el sol en alumbrar, y mucho se extiende su virtud; mas todavía reconoscen estas criaturas sus *fines,* y tienen *términos que no pueden pasar.* Por esta causa puede *la vista de nuestra ánima* llegar de *cabo á cabo,* y *comprehenderlas,* porque todas ellas están *encerradas cada una dentro de su jurisdiccion*" (Granada 185b–186a, my emphasis).

32. Blumenberg (*Legitimacy* 576). Tasso's poem concludes by looking forward to the Judgment Day, when this "mobile theater" will tumble down and be replaced by an order of quietude: "Allor quiete e pace / avran le menti rapide e rotanti, / c'han sì vari pensier, sì vario el moto" (Then and only then, / will there be final quietude for all / the swift-rotating minds that have today / so much variety of thought and speed). The created beings, running erratically in their "distorti giri," will find repose "nel fisso punto de la Divinità" in its eternal rest (*Il mondo creato* 7.145–152, 362–363, 400–424; *Opere* 4:291, 299, 300–301; trans. Tusiani, *The Creation of the World* 197.)

33. For Blumenberg a crucial aspect of modernity's alteration in the traditional consciousness of the relations of the divinity and this world is its overcoming of the notion that the cosmos-nature, as "property," belongs to God and not to man, his creature. For the nominalists' denial that man's "measurements" could possibly be commensurate with those of the omnipotent creator and the Cartesians' reinterpretation, under the influence of Stoic ethical thought, of "possessing" and "mastering" as knowing correctly, see *Legitimacy* 348–349, 541–542. The undermining of the hexameral position—where God is revealed and reliable as measurer and property holder—from these two opposite extremes was, for Blumenberg, essential in the origins of modernity with its empowerment of man. As I shall suggest, Gracián's fictional world, which is poised so bewilderingly between the traditional and the modern, discloses both points of assault: in the instabilities surrounding its articulation of the hexameral position and in its pessimism and evident anxieties concerning the fixation of proper place and boundaries by man in a world that he has totally ruined and that presumably is moving toward destruction.

34. "Oh, wonderful, indissoluble chain / of this great world, strong-fastened into one / in various ways and with tenacious bonds, / and made by the High Smith's great mastery / more hard and bright than steel or adamant!" (Tasso, *Il mondo creato* 3.718–722; *Opere* 4:93; trans. Tusiani 197).

35. In 1570 the "first systematic compendium of current geographical information," Abraham Ortelius's *Theatrum orbis terrarum,* was published at Antwerp. Constantly expanding through the incorporation of new maps, descriptions, and pictures of the earth's wonders, the atlas went through forty editions, in seven languages, in its historical life in the following half century—precisely the period in which the hexameral project arose and enjoyed its universal success (see Welu).

36. "... impregnable fortress, which the enemy plots to batter down, which, constructed in the figure of a circle, fortifies and secures its center.... The ocean once again enters its narrow jail of crystals" (Acevedo 251).

37. Acevedo 276. An instructive contrast can be found in Góngora, a poet whose masterpiece, *Soledades,* with its imaginative commingling of diverse orders of being; its delight in transgressing boundaries; its cultivation of the fragmentary, the incomplete, the open, and the multiform; and its reiterated motifs of unbinding—*desatar,* the very opposite procedure of the hexameral God and poet—can be approached fruitfully as a "de-creation" epic in its disengagement from inherited cosmic structures and their numerous poetic celebrations. In connection with the earlier mentioned cosmic motifs, for example, one might contrast the hexameralists' discussions of God's marvelous regularization of the tides within tightly drawn boundaries with Góngora's depiction, at the opening of the second *Soledad,* of endless metamorphosis, imaginative hybridization, and perpetual movement at a breach in the shore line where a mountain stream and the ocean tides wash together (2.1–29). Similar contrasts can be found in the centrifugal metaphorical transformations that mark Góngora's processional spectacle of the creatures (1.288–341); in his eroticization and unfixing of the marvelous instrument of science, cartography, and "hexameral binding through navigation," the compass (1.386–403); in his metaphorical displacement of the sun in its firmly bound, repetitious movements along the ecliptic by a frantic crow caught between two attacking birds of prey; and, most spectacularly, in his vision from above of the erotic dalliances of a meandering river, which is strikingly indifferent to its "hexameral functions" of representing the cycle of the waters and offering an allegory of life and death (1.182–218). In its implicit transposition of creative powers from God to man, Góngora's "de-creation" epic might have justified the contemporary attacks on *gongorismo* as heretical in a way that its critics could hardly have imagined. In any event, *Las soledades* stands as coequal beside the other principal literary witnesses of the birth of modernity in Spain, Cervantes's *Don Quixote* and Gracián's *Criticón.* An approach to the *Soledades* and their poetic "fullness" as an "emptying out" of the creation epics would be compatible with Krauss's suggestive remarks on Góngora's effort to create an elementary world prior to the darkening effects of moral judgment ("diesseits von Gut und Böse"). Words with highly charged moral connotations (e.g., "infame," "lascivo," "mentir") are articulated only to be "de-ethicalized" through figurative function and context.

38. See Maravall, *Culture of the Baroque,* particularly the discussion of *dirigismo* and techniques of integration (Chap. 2). In analyzing the economic roots of such political realities, Maravall emphasizes the reestablishment of a seigneurial system within a modern monarchy dependent on a landed aristocracy for financial support. It is worth noting, in this context, that at the beginning of his account of the third day of the creation, Acevedo supplements the traditional metaphors of God's created order, the book and the theater, with the fief: "Mas cuando de su mano omnipotente, / Como en feudo, el imperio y el gobierno / Del orbe quiso dar liberalmente / Al hombre el justo Rey y Padre Eterno" (257). For an interesting effort to locate the socioeconomic foundations of late hexameral poetry—viewed as "an attempt to reconstruct in cultural space the ideological underpinnings of feudalism proper"—a *reassertive* literary form whose tensions disclose a complex historical interaction of absolutism, a retrenched aristocratic power, and the ethos of a rising commercial class, see Kendrick 127–131. The argument is based on the historical conditions of England and to a great extent on the complexities in Milton's *Paradise Lost.*

39. "You, magnanimous King, who, desirous of increasing the Catholic faith, dispel with the light of your pious zeal the shadows of the infidel and Moorish sect, in the states where you are named king, do not permit a tenebrous idiom to plunge into darkness the unanimous cities, founded on Catholic truths" (Acevedo 265).

40. The "absence" of man (or the confinement of the Promethean figure) as epic protagonist in this narrative of the Creator and the created world is most striking in Tasso's self-conscious dismissal of the traditional subjects of Renaissance epic (and implicitly his own previous highly celebrated achievements) at the beginning of the third day. Arms and loves, chivalry and fame, the monuments of antiquity, celebrations of cities, their foundations and historical achievements—all of this will have no place in this work, which, more ambitiously than its predecessors, seeks to contemplate the marvelous art and labor of the "king of heaven." Acevedo follows Tasso's text at this point very closely. For Tasso's anxieties regarding the problematic connection with cosmic truth in sixteenth-century theories and practices of poetic imitation and the dangers of the independent, "disconnected" fantasy and its endorsement by the sophist, anxieties that can be traced from his expurgations of the *Liberata,* through his creation of the *Conquistata,* to his ultimate turn to the reassuring hexameral materials and all the limitations on artistic autonomy that they imposed, see Leo.

41. "No por eso dejaba [la divinidad] de estar en todo lo criado, como primera causa de que penden todas las otras causas, sin cuya virtud y asistencia todas ellas pararían, como lo harían todas las ruedas de un reloj si les quitásedes el peso que las mueve. . . . [Dios] no deja de estar en todas las cosas, dándoles ser natural; mayormente pues vemos que nuestra ánima intelectiva (que es substancia espiritual), estando encerrada en su cuerpo, discurre y anda por todo el mundo" (Granada 457b–458a).

42. "Because just as God, being one, embraces all things with eternal power, and attends on everything, and with a divine plan produces them, gives them being, and governs them, so in the work of man, which the Lord today fashions and designs, the internal soul is everything, and dwells in every member and moves it, governs it, and gives life to it" (Acevedo 281).

43. "And since, with supreme providence, the immense power would bring it about that the figure resembling its essence alone among the rest of the creatures would be celestial, it raised his regal presence on two feet, so that man might contemplate and see the place that holds his immortal seat, whence his divine origin proceeds. And for the celestial mind, it provided a dwelling in the most hard and excellent part of the body. . . . This gift, this illustrious fire, this intelligence adorned with pure light is included in the sphere of man like the immense Artificer in his sublimity. And just as God with natural dress adorned the highest point of this creature, so in the very same moment He embellished his image with necessary parts" (Acevedo 280).

44. "But from what high and downward-hanging cliff / or from what lofty, aery mountain top, / from what sublime, enchanting alpine peak / towering from both sides above the sea, / shall I now watch the beauty that was seen / by its supernal Maker on that day?" (*Il mondo creato* 3.813–818; *Opere* 4:96; trans. Tusiani; see Tasso, *Creation* 59).

45. For the metaphysical foundations of the doctrine of mimesis, its limitations, and its domination of the history of western thinking about art and aesthetics, see Blumenberg ("Nachahmung der Natur"). For its importance in the Renaissance and for Cervantes's liberation of fiction from its inhibiting control, see Forcione (*Cervantes, Aristotle, and the "Persiles"*).

46. For the outpouring of miracle literature, see Forcione (*Cervantes and the Humanist Vision*, Chap. 4); for the popularity of Molinos, whose cult of nothingness and self-annihilation can be viewed as the antithesis of the hexameral celebration of the plenitude of the Creation, see Forcione ("El desposeimiento del ser"). Cosmic unfathomability in the face of human reason's efforts to penetrate nature's signs and control events is of course a recurrent motif of Calderón's dramatic worlds. For the pervasiveness of *desengaño* and melancholy in Spanish society of the seventeenth century and their impact on behavior, dress, etiquette, and ceremony, see Pfandl 221–227, and Gumbrecht 443–452; see also Schulte. Social distrust parallels cosmic distrust, and it is possible that its cultivation as a virtue was not limited to the literary and paradoxical worlds of picaresque fiction. In 1593 Guillén de Castro delivered a "Discurso contra la confianza," commissioned by the Academy of Nocturnals in Valencia, detailing the calamities that confidence in others has brought to the world (see Maravall, *Culture of the Baroque* 161).

47. Góngora, *Soledades* 1.189–218. Góngora's defender and imitator, the Conde de Villamediana, celebrated the independent and transgressive creative power of his master. As Phaeton, Góngora displaces the sun, his father; defies Jupiter; and reilluminates the very cosmos he has grasped and consumed: "Cogit et ardenti perfundit lumine mundum." See Schmidt: "One would be hard pressed to fashion a more heroic image of the poet, grasping the reins of the father and overcoming the chastisement of the gods, in order to re-form and re-light the world through fire." For Villamediana's text, see Martínez Arancón 279–280.

48. Cervantes, *Don Quijote de la Mancha*, vol. 1, "Prólogo." One might also recall Cide Hamete Benengeli's mockery of the limitations on fictional spaces imposed by the rationalistic neo-Aristotelian theorists ("los estrechos límites de la narración"), his oblique assertion of imaginative freedom and the "habilidad, suficiencia y entendimiento para tratar del universo todo," and his request for praise for "lo que ha dejado de escribir" (what he has refrained from writing [II, Chap. 44]). Like the all-powerful nominalist God, Cide Hamete is perhaps most interesting for the *worlds he could have created.* For Cide Hamete as a celebrant of creative freedom, see Forcione, *Cervantes, Aristotle* 155–166. For the figure of the writer in the *Prólogo* to *Don Quijote*, see Forcione, "Exemplarity, Modernity" 333–352.

49. "To the sword and the compass / More and more and more and more" (Vargas Machuca frontispiece reproduced in Elliott, n.p. It is worth noting that Góngora's admirers defended his radical poetic and linguistic innovations against the denunciations of the "ancients" by invoking the example of Columbus in his curiosity, courage, and determination to "discover the new" (see Paravicino, cited by Krauss 73).

50. As I shall point out below, Andrenio's drama beneath the stars attests similarly to the value of human exertion in the face of "cosmic" limitation and submission, but in the ambivalences of its hexameral context and its "threshold"

character, it is more meaningful as an image of crisis than as an image of affirmation.

51. "A full theater of marvels"; "From afar reverence is greater."

52. See Blumenberg, *Legitimacy* 524–525. Perhaps nothing is more revealing of the peculiar restlessness and anxiety of place that mark Gracián's entire fictional world than his choice of Pico's oration as the basis of the first of the numerous "miniprologues" that proliferate in a multitude of genres, forms, and tones throughout the *Criticón*, his imaginative concentration of its argument into a conflict over place, and his determination to immobilize its freely moving, "superfluous" protagonist through the decisive delineation of his simultaneously limiting and empowering space. For the significance of Pico's statement as summarizing "with grand simplicity and in pregnant form the whole intent of the Renaissance," man's "turning towards the world" while "distinguishing" himself from it, see Cassirer, *Individual and the Cosmos* 86.

53. The "Supreme Artificer" and "sovereign owner" of the "universal theater" of Gracián's fable makes man's limitations very clear: "Como rey que es pretende señorearlo todo. Pero entiende ¡oh hombre!... que esto ha de ser con la mente, no con el vientre.... Todo lo has de ocupar con el conocimiento tuyo y reconocimiento mío; esto es, reconociendo en todas las maravillas criadas las perfecciones divinas y pasando de las criaturas al Criador." (As the king that he is, he seeks to take command of everything. But understand, oh, man!... that this is to be with your mind, not with your belly.... You are to take possession of all things by knowing them and so knowing me; that is, recognizing in all of the created marvels the divine perfections and passing from the creatures to the Creator.) As for the "dignity of man," Gracián includes at the convocation of the creatures a "lisonjero" (flatterer) who defends man's refusal to accept any "center" and his desire to possess the "entire universe" as springing from his "grandeza de ánimo" (*El criticón* 1:18–19).

54. "¿Quién tendrá por hombre de razón al que, viendo los movimientos del cielo, y la órden de las estrellas, tan firme y constante, y viendo la conexion y conveniencia que todas estas cosas tienen, diga que todo esto se hizo sin prudencia ni razón, y crea que se hicieron acaso las cosas que ningun consejo ni entendimiento puede llegar á comprehender con cuánto consejo hayan sido hechas?... Y viendo el ímpetu con que se mueven los cielos, con tan admirable ligereza, y que hacen sus cursos, tan ciertos y tan bien ordenados para la salud y conservacion de las cosas, ¿no echarémos de ver que todo esto se hace con razon, y no solo con razon, sino con excelente y divina razon?" (Granada 190a; for the echoes of Cicero, see *De natura deorum* 2.36–38).

55. "... laberinto de las estrellas, unas centelleantes, otras lucientes.... Ibalas registrando todas, notando su mucha variedad en la grandeza, puestos, movimientos y colores, saliendo unas y ocultándose otras" (*El criticón* 1:24).

56. "... orden y concierto, de modo que entretejieran vistosos lazos y formaran primorosas labores" (ibid.).

57. "Campearan otro tanto y fuera un espectáculo muy agradable a la vista, brillantísimo artificio" (ibid.).

58. Burton, *Anatomy of Melancholy* 2.2, Mem. 3; cited by Nicolson 189.

59. The most orthodox evocations of the Book of the World in Gracián's age could acknowledge its *labyrinthian* character. For example, Nieremberg described

the creation as a great poem or "Panegírico de Dios": "Es como un laberinto que por todas partes se lee y haze sentido y dicta a su Autor" (*Oculta filosofía de la sympatía y antipatía de las cosas* [Barcelona, 1647]; cited by Checa, *Gracián y la imaginación* 121).

60. "La otra disposición artificiosa que tú dices fuera afectada y *uniforme*; quédese para los *juguetes del arte y de la humana niñería*. De este modo se nos hace cada noche *nuevo el cielo y nunca enfada el mirarlo, cada uno proporciona las estrellas como quiere*" (1:25).

61. It is instructive to compare Saavedra Fajardo's formulation of the same argument. In discussing the "gran volumen, en cuyas hojas... escribió el Autor de lo criado con caracteres de luz, para gloria de su eterna sabiduría, las mudanzas y alteraciones de las cosas" (the great volume, on whose pages... the Author of the created world wrote with characters of light, for the glory of his eternal wisdom, the changes and alterations of things), he reaches Andrenio's point, admitting that "están sus luces desconcertadas, unas por su colocación fija y otras por su movimiento" (his lights are confused, some because of their fixed location, others because of their movement). Nevertheless he insists that such lack of concert is not to be interpreted as an indication of the operation of chance. In a perfect example of traditional hexameral speculative reassurance, he acknowledges the appeal of Critilo's final argument only to reject it: "no sirve su desorden a la hermosura" (their disorder is not for the sake of beauty), and insists that the order in such apparent asymmetry is to be found in the complexities of stellar influence) (see 821).

62. A dramatic representation of the subject's imaginative freedom to play with the traditional cosmic ciphers follows shortly when Andrenio discovers that time, repetition, and changing bodily conditions have had an exhausting effect on his perceptions and that the lapidary cosmos has begun to fade. With unintentional philosophical irony, he remetaphorizes the customary cipher "sun-king" as "sun-page," whose diminished light "serves" him and hence proves the sun's "creatureliness" as he tries to follow the dark path downward on the "mal segura escala" of the ruins of his cave world (*El criticón* 1:27).

63. "Dionysus Dithyramben," cited by Blumenberg, *Genesis* 73: "Wreckage of stars: / Out of this wreckage, I constructed a world." For Nietzsche's admiration of Gracián—"Europa hat nichts Feineres und Komplizierteres (in der Moralisterei!) hervorgebracht"—see Hidalgo-Serna 38. See also Bouillier.

64. See Forcione, *Cervantes, Aristotle* Chap. 3. A relevant discussion of differing "conceptions of reality" and the problematic status of the *new* in traditional poetics can be found in Blumenberg, "Wirklichkeitsbegriff."

65. "Tesauro transcends both the ornamental and the conceptual function of the metaphor, moving towards a new reality which is centered on the *I* and oriented by the *I*" (Donato 24). See also Friedrich (*Epochen* 630–631, 639). The fact that Tesauro's theories have been interpreted as continuing a traditional poetics of correspondence is another indication of the complexities that distinguish the cultural production of this "threshold" period in its preservation and reaccentuation of the traditional in the face of the radically new (see Mazzeo, and Donato's discussion of his thesis [25]).

66. "Que en esta variedad natural y *confusión grave* parecen tanto más que *el vulgo las juzga innumerables*, y con esto *queda como en enigma la suprema asistencia*: si bien *para los sabios muy clara y entendida*" (1:25).

67. "Se abraza con la tierra . . . de dos cosas tan diferentes viene a hacerse una comun naturaleza de ambas" (Granada 190a).

68. "Así ocultos han de ser los consejos y desinios de los príncipes . . . aquel gran Gobernador de lo criado, cuyos pasos no hay quien pueda entender . . . beba el pueblo dellos el engaño, con que se esparza y corra por todas partes" (409–410).

69. "Es gran destreza del príncipe gobernalle con su misma rienda, e ir al paso de su ignorancia" (see 369–374, 376, 431, 615–619).

70. The importance of visualization and theatricalization of dogma and power in the religious culture of the period has been well studied, but only relatively recently have critics looked closely at the importance of visibility and self-representation in the absolutist state's establishment and maintenance of authority. As Hobbes put it, the state must rely upon a manifest "visible power to keep the subjects in awe, and tye them by fear of punishment to the performance of their covenantes." Rather than eliciting a condition of cognitive detachment or activating an innate tendency to concord through the ceremonial display of a sovereign analogously linked to man's highest faculty, the (all-penetrating) soul, universal reason, or the rational divinity, the king's power and mystery must be made visible to exploit the subject's "natural tendency to 'relish nothing but what is eminent'" (see Pye 279, 292). The spectacle aims at the arousal of the subject's awe, which, despite claims concerning its elevating effects by the theorists of sovereignty, in effect "subverts his human power to comprehend" (293). Since his early work (*Teoría*), Maravall has continued to emphasize the rich emblem literature of the seventeenth century as an instrument of social and political control directed at a new kind of public in the expanding urban centers, an instrument that, through enigmatic and rhetorical procedures, as opposed to conceptual demonstration, exploits the power of imagery to "move," "overwhelm," and "persuade" its audience. See "La literatura de emblemas en el contexto de la sociedad barroca," in *Teatro* 149–188, esp. 176ff., and "Sociopolitical Objectives of the Use of Visual Media," in *Culture*, 251–263. See also Geertz, "Centers, Kings, and Charisma: Reflections on the Symbolics of Power" 121–146. Geertz notes that there has recently been a "small explosion of books" concerning this subject and offers a useful bibliography (see 123).

71. Granada writes that the "grande y maravilloso libro" of the visible world, which God offered to the "ojos de todas las naciones del mundo, así de griegos como de bárbaros, así de sabios como de ignorantes," is written in the "letras quebradas y iluminadas" of the creatures, and that each of the latter resembles a mirror placed before our eyes and revealing the radiant beauty of the Creator, and that each is like a voice in a grand harmonious chorus, which "por tantas diferencias de tonos nos predican la grandeza" of God (186b). As Acevedo (247) makes clear, his hexameral epic is little more than a commentary on the great Book of the World, which, in its universal language, unites the single audience of mankind in a single universe beneath a single God (see n. 22).

72. "Labyrinths, quibbles, emblems, / Such bleak laborious minutiae / . . . No music in his soul; but this inane / Herbarium of metaphors and punning / And a veneration of cunning / And contempt for the human and the superhuman. / Homer's ancient voice he never heard, / Or the voice—silver and moonlight—of Virgil; / Nor saw Oedipus the accursed in exile / Nor Christ who is dying on a piece of board" (translation by Feldman, with some modification; cited by Ramos Foster 70–71).

73. Gracián's few references to verisimilitude, probably the most theorized concept in sixteenth-century poetics and certainly the concept that was essential to their metaphysical validations of literary creation in the face of traditional assaults on the insubstantiality of artistic illusion, are very revealing. In a context of moral satire in the final book of the *Criticón,* the pilgrims learn from the "Decifrador" that the book of the earthly or social world, as opposed to the heavenly world, is "closed when most open," that one must learn to read "counterciphers" ("la contracifra de todo") with the mind rather than the eye, in order to survive, and that in a world of insubstantial appearances and concealed intentions, "no hay mejor enemigo de la verdad, que la verisimilitud" (3:100; see also 3:255). Whatever his intentions might have been, I am arguing that Gracián was closing the ultimately unreadable book of the heavens even as he was explicating the rather monotonous book of society that *human beings* have written in their garbled, generally grotesque "letras." For this "reconception" of the Book of the World as a "parody Platonism," rooted in a pessimistic conviction concerning this world's absolute unreliability and its separation from a transcendent order, see Blumenberg's analysis of Gracián's elaboration of the old philosophical metaphor of the cave exit (*Höhlenausgänge* 450–464; see also *Die Lesbarkeit* 108–120). For its modernity among the various seventeenth-century efforts to rewrite the traditional Book (e.g., Galileo, Descartes, Comenius), its "anti-Platonism," and its optimistic implications concerning man's capacities to achieve rational control over his own world, comprehended in situational as opposed to essentialist terms, see Maravall, "Un mito platónico en Gracián" (*Estudios* 3:377–383).

74. See Donato's observations on the broad scope of metaphor implied by Tesauro's theories: "The metaphor in the Baroque period becomes much more than simply a rhetorical figure; it becomes significant form." He cites Getto: "per questa civiltà si potrebbe addirittura parlare di un 'metaforismo' e di un 'metamorfismo' universale come di essenziali modi de avvertire e di esprimere la realtà" (in this civilization one could without hesitation speak of a "metaphorism," and of a universal "metamorphism," as of essential modes of perceiving and expressing reality) (28–29).

75. By saying this I do not mean to deny the importance of Gracián's place in the history of aesthetics. I would in fact suggest that some of the difficulties of his most baffling treatise, the *Agudeza y arte de ingenio*—its eccentric terminology, its proliferating pseudoclassifications, its illusory, frustrating gestures toward systematic completeness and consistency—can be accounted for if one recognizes that, in aesthetics, just as in metaphysics, epistemology, anthropology, politics, and morality, its author stands in the "in between." He claims that the *agudeza,* the highest offspring of the *ingenium,* represents a *modern* art, that it has its origins in the "fuente de su mente" and can be distinguished from traditional poetry, which flows from the "fuente de su monte" (*Agudeza* 2:254–257). In other words, he situates the distinctively modern art in a creative faculty of the human mind rather than in a "higher" objective truth to be divulged through "Parnassian" inspiration or in the truth of a universal created order of things to be imitated. The imaginative faculty is both perceptive and creative, discerning unusual or hidden relationships in objects and circumstances and, in an act that Gracián associates frequently with subjugation and heroism, constructing an autonomous, "illuminated" order of culture in the face of nature's chaos. Intellectual historians

have justifiably acclaimed Gracián's insights into the imagination, genius, and taste and found in his writings anticipations of Kantian, Romantic, modernist, and even postmodernist aesthetics. However, it is important to recognize the degree to which such insights were incapable of disengaging from traditional conceptions of art's subordination to truth, reason, and cognitive operations. Their limitations are in part due to the fact that they were thought through within the conceptual field of Scholasticism and formulated in its anachronistic vocabulary. For example, while the *ingenio,* through the conceit, produces beauty as well as truth and, in its superiority to judgment, is associated positively with madness, its "vivifying" power of conjoining seemingly incongruous objects is theorized in intellectualist terms recalling the powers of the Aristotelian-scholastic abstracting *intellectus agens*: the pleasing or marvelous analogy discloses a common truth inhering in each particular. In his creation of metaphor, the writer remains bound by an essential correspondence, a truth link, despite his subtlety in "minimalizing" it for unexpected imaginative effects. In this respect they might suggest a mechanical wit and a belated Scholasticism, as well as a reconceived *ingenium* (i.e., no longer practically assimilable to reason or *judicium,* as in the classical rhetorical tradition) and an anticipation of art's final conquest of autonomy. Here the residues of the past are just as telling as in the case of Gracián's attachment to the hexameral vision. Moreover, Gracián frequently insists on the didactic responsibilities of the poet, and maintains that erudition and imitation of the ancients are absolutely essential in his creative acts (see May, esp. 61). For a more favorable view of the *Agudeza,* see Hidalgo-Serna, who finds in Gracián's *ingenio* a faculty that is primarily cognitive and as such a coherently theorized mode of access to reality that offers an alternative to both Aristotelian-Scholastic and Cartesian rationality and can be best understood in the context of postmodernist critiques of rationality (e.g., Heidegger). On the seventeenth-century reconception of *ingenium* as revealed by Gracián's follower in France, Dominique Bouhours, see Cassirer, *Philosophy of the Enlightenment* 317–318. For Tesauro, *ingenium,* and the rhetorical tradition, see Friedrich, *Epochen* 631–632. Gracián's importance in the history of aesthetics has been noted by Gadamer, Borinski, and, most recently, Ferry. For my purposes, the limitations in Gracián's aesthetic theories are most interesting as they suggest his awareness of the darker consequences of the full emancipation of *homo aestheticus*—the "democratization" and relativization of artistic experience, the ambiguities surrounding taste as an adjudicating faculty and a subjectively determined value, the problem of assessing the spurious in an environment indiscriminately mingling cultural, political, and marketplace activity, and the very real possibility of a tyranny of mass or vulgar judgments. One infers this awareness, not, of course, from the treatises, which are notable for their confident tone and their elitist celebrations of the intelligence, discretion, artistry, and "technique" of those who possess, recognize, and presumably can impose standards of good taste, but rather from various satirical scenes in the *Criticón,* particularly those investing the image of the *vulgo* with a nightmarish power unprecedented in the history of literature. Among the most notable are the depiction of the "great man," a dwarf (*nonada*) metamorphosed into a giant by the power of public opinion and the artifices—mirrors, ink, smoke—of its squidlike manipulators (3:108–120), the spectacle of the acrobat in Rome, and the concluding epiphany of the three epic heroes on the Island of Immortality. In perhaps the most devastating of the numerous seventeenth-century assaults on the epic genre in its moment of historical crisis, Gracián displays the three great heroes, "el Cid español, el Roldán francés y el portugués Pereira," standing on a fragile island amid a sea of ink and recoiling in embarrassment—literally covering their faces in an act of self-erasure—as they witness, at the climactic moment of their *descubrimiento,* the foundation of their epic fame and immortality disintegrate into the notoriety that is the gift of a "tasteless" howling mob (3:316–319). Gracián continually associates the *vulgo* and *nada,* and, if the abyss of nothingness looms on the far side of his metaphysical advances, the mob rushes forward menacingly and prophetically as he opens the path toward a modern acosmic aesthetics. The correlation of the emptiness of the heavens and the hollowness of culture is impossible to overlook at the end point in the great narrative of eclipse.

76. See Elias 242–246. See also Blumenberg's remarks on the new area of professional expertise demanded by man's discovery of the complexities in his "sociability": "Was der neuzeitlichen Wissenschaftsidee die Rechtfertigung theoretischer Professionalität eingebracht hatte: die Begründung ihrer Schwierigkeit mit der mathematischen Verschlüsselung ihrer Sachverhalte und deren Auflösbarkeit allein durch Sachverstand, das findet in Graciáns 'Entzifferung' der Welt seine Anwendung auf eine Sphäre der Realität, die bis dahin überhaupt nicht im Verdacht exklusiver theoretischer Bedürfnisse gestanden hatte, nun aber den 'Weltmann' als einen eigens eingeweihten Professional der Moralistik zu erfordern scheint" (The same process that had brought to the modern period's idea of science the justification of theoretical professionalism—the foundation of its difficulty in the mathematical encoding of its facts that is then solvable only through expertise—is observable, in Gracián's "deciphering" of the world, in reference to a sphere of reality that previously had not stood under any suspicion whatsoever of exclusive theoretical needs but that now appears to demand the "man of the world" [den Weltmann] as an expressly initiated professional in moral philosophy) (*Die Lesbarkeit* 112).

77. Particularly relevent for my argument is Gracián's reinterpretation of Stoic independence (autarky) as tactical isolation, self-concealment, and self-control, as well as his striking redefinition of *synteresis,* traditionally the light of conscience and reason binding all men and the divinity (see Altenstaig 854–856) and associated with the Stoic cosmic fire of rationality uniting the created universe (see, for example, Vives 260–261). Gracián discusses "la prudentísima sindéresis" as a faculty or capacity for regulating the powers of the imagination to bring contentment to consciousness (see *Oráculo manual* 24, 155) and as a restraining capacity enabling one to avoid errors of taste, poor social performance, and excessively singular or extravagant behavior (see 168). As "la gran sindéresis" it is the fundamental *piece of armor* protecting (and hence separating) him in his embattled social condition (see 96). One might compare the transformation of the fundamental idea of the microcosm. If nature makes man a "compendio de todo lo natural por su eminencia," art makes him a "universo por ejercicio y cultura del gusto y del entendimiento." His "universality" consists not in his "cosmic rationality," but rather in his total knowledge of circumstances and tastes ("varón universal de ingenio en noticias y de genio en gustos"), and it enables him to be a "discreet Proteus," adapting his image to the specific needs of each observer,

"haciendo política transformación" and "ganando a todos" (see 77, 93). For Gracián's "Tacitan," or political reformulation of Stoic and Scholastic principles of moral philosophy, see Friedrich, "Gracián"; Schröder, Chap. 2; and Blüher, 371–447. For the importance in Schopenhauer of Gracián's redirection of *synteresis* as an instinct for self-preservation, see Borinski 36. A penetrating critique of the underlying cynicism of Gracián's moral philosophy can be found in Jankelévitch. It has been recently rebutted, from an allegedly Nietzschean perspective, by Pelegrín, 200 ff. Studies of Gracián as a moral philosopher have generally focused on such drastic revisions of classical doctrines, whether their assessments have been negative or positive. What is not so often recognized is the fact that Gracián frequently celebrates such ethical values of traditional Stoicism as magnanimity, fortitude, virtue, patience in adversity, constancy, consistency, and integrity of self, and occasionally allows their metaphysical foundation to assert itself. See, for example, his descriptions of the self-reliant sage and his model in the "Entidad Suma" (*Oráculo manual* 137), the "hombre de entereza," a "constante varón" who, like his cosmic analogue, never "pisa la raya de la razón" (29), and the "verdadera soberanía," which "consiste en la entereza de costumbres" (103; see also 116, 120, 128, 131, 159, 165, 167). Equally revealing in this context are such important episodes of the *Criticón* as the ascent to Virtue's Palace and the climactic wisdom symposium in Rome. Blüher's presentation of Gracián as the culminating spokesman in the rich Spanish tradition of Stoicism is certainly justified. What I would emphasize is that even in Gracián's "constructive" or straight incorporations of Stoic values, it is Stoicism's *defensive* accent on a stable subject who can resist all temptations to self-alienation rising from the delusionary worlds of society and politics that is prominent and not the element in Stoicism that was especially appealing to Renaissance humanists in their turn from speculative *sapientia* and *scientia* to civic wisdom—the strong emphasis on the conception of cosmic orderliness and wholeness as enjoining a deep concern for community ("haec communitas, quae maxime est apta naturae" [Cicero, *De officiis* 1.45]) and the responsibilities of citizenship, and a faith in language and rhetoric as an instrument grounded in trust. See Blumenberg, *Genesis* 200–208; for the community orientation in Roman Stoicism, see Groethuysen 54–69. The ambiguities in Gracián's Stoicism should be viewed as yet another manifestation of his complexity as a "threshold" figure. In ethics, as well as in metaphysics, epistemology, aesthetics, anthropology, and politics, he stands in the "in between." For the ambiguous character of his writings on politics and heroism in the development of early modern political thought, see Zarka. I am grateful to my colleague Thomas Pavel for drawing my attention to this study.

78. See Checa, "Gracián lector." One can easily read this episode as a grotesque realization of a particularly shocking precept in Gracián's "reason of state" for the individual, the *Oráculo manual.* In another metaphorical reformulation of the traditional language of metaphysics and the Book of the World, he counsels dissimulation by advising his reader to "turn the will into ciphers" ("cifrar la voluntad") and conceal his interiority in the impenetrable ink of the squid ("a linces del discurso, jibias de interioridad" [*Oráculo* 98]). In its appropriation of cosmic motifs, the aphorism can be compared with Gracián's formulation of the complementary principle of simulation: "Empeñarse con novedades de bizarría, amane-

ciendo muchas veces como el sol, variando teatros al lucimiento, para que, en el uno la privación y en el otro la novedad soliciten aquí el aplauso, si allí el deseo" (One should continually present novelties of splendor, like the sun, dawning many times, displaying brilliance in a variety of theaters, so that in one the deprivation and in another the novelty might solicit in the former desire, in the latter applause) (81).

79. "De suerte que, al cabo, el mirado y los que miraban todos quedaban iguales, pues desnudos en la calle y aun en tierra."

80. "... engañar el pueblo no dejándole lugar para discurrir en cosas mayores."

81. "No hubo hombre ni mujer que no saliese con la suya, y todas eran ajenas."

82. "... los que le miraban tan pasmados cuanto él intrépido, ellos temblando de verle, y él bailando porque le viesen."

83. "... no cuerda, sino muy loca confianza ... una hebra de seda; menos, sobre un cabello; aun es mucho, sobre un hilo de araña; aun es algo, sobre el de la vida, que aun es menos" (3:264–265).

84. "... come le mele nel Mar Negro, di veduta son belle, & colorite: ma se le mordi, ti lasciano le fauci piene di cenere, & di fumo" (cited by Donato 19). "Tesauro ... gives us a clue as to the new grounds on which the *I* of the Baroque poet can stand. Inasmuch as he takes upon himself to found the rationality of the real upon himself, he does indeed assume the function of God, and yet inasmuch as he himself is part of the same world to which he has denied any rationality, his whole creation is bound to crumble in ashes and smoke" (28). Such *desengaño* would appear to underlie the pathos in one of Gracián's most startling assertions of man's freedom to create. In a paradoxical reformulation of the central metaphor of western metaphysics, he claims that the autonomous products of the artist's imagination are valued because they shield the viewer from the unbearable light of the "naked truth": "There is no mouthful more bitter than a naked truth. The light that wounds directly torments the eagle's and the lynx's eyes; how much more will it torment those that are weakening. For this reason the sagacious physicians of the soul invented the art of gilding truths, of sugaring disillusionments" ("No hay bocado más amargo que una verdad desnuda. La luz que derechamente hiere atormenta los ojos de una águila, de un lince, cuanto más los que flaquean. Para esto inventaron los sagaces médicos del ánimo el arte de dorar las verdades, de azucarar los desengaños" [*Agudeza y arte de ingenio* 2:lv; see 2:192]). The specious splendor of the baroque conceit momentarily darkens the chilling light of a cosmos that is still frightening in its meaninglessness.

85. "... sacando la sustancia y consumiendo la vida hasta dejarlos de todo punto apurados y deshechos, de tal suerte que no venía a quedar en cada uno sino una pedazo de trapo de una pobre mortaja, que en esto viene a parar todo" (3:260).

Works Cited

Acevedo, Alonso de. *Creación del mundo*. Ed. Don Cayetano Rosell. Madrid: B.A.E., vol. 29, 1948.

Altenstaig, Joannes. *Lexicon Theologicum*. Facsim. of 1619 Cologne edition by J. Tytz. Hildesheim: Olms, 1974.

Ambrose of Milan, Saint. *Hexameron.* Trans. J. J. Savage. Vol. 42 of *The Fathers of the Church.* Ed. J. Deferrari. New York: Fathers of the Church, 1961.

Armisen, A. "Admiración y maravillas en *El criticón* (más unas notas cervantinas)." *Gracián y su época: Actas de la I reunión de filólogos aragoneses.* Zaragoza: Institución Fernando el Católico, 1986. 201–242.

Augustine, Saint. *On Christian Doctrine.* Tr. D. W. Robertson Jr. New York: Bobbs-Merrill, 1958.

Balcells, José María. Introduction to his edition of Luis de Granada's *Introducción del símbolo de la fe.* Madrid: Cátedra, 1989.

Basil, Saint. *Exegetic Homilies.* Trans. A. C. Way. Vol. 46 of *The Fathers of the Church.* Ed. J. Deferrari. Washington, D.C.: Catholic University Press, 1963.

Baudot, Georges. *Utopía e historia en México.* Trans. V. González Loscertales. Madrid: Espasa-Calpe, 1983.

Blüher, Karl Alfred. *Seneca in Spanien.* Munich: Francke, 1969.

Blumenberg, Hans. "'Nachahmung der Natur': Zur Vorgeschichte der Idee des schöpferischen Menschen." *Studium Generale* 10 (1957): 266–283.

———. "Wirklichkeitsbegriff und Möglichkeit des Romans." *Nachahmung und Illusion.* Ed. Hans-Robert Jauss. Munich: Eidos, 1964.

———. *Die Lesbarkeit der Welt.* Frankfurt am Main: Suhrkamp, 1981.

———. *The Legitimacy of the Modern Age.* Trans. R. M. Wallace. Cambridge, Mass.: MIT Press, 1983.

———. *The Genesis of the Copernican World.* Trans. R. M. Wallace. Cambridge, Mass.: MIT Press, 1987.

———. *Höhlenausgänge.* Frankfurt am Main: Suhrkamp, 1989.

Borges, Jorge Luis. *Obra poética: 1923–1976.* Buenos Aires: Emecé, 1977.

Borinski, Karl. *Baltasar Gracián und die Hoflitteratur in Deutschland.* Halle: Niemeyer, 1894.

Bouillier, Victor. "Baltasar Gracián et Nietzsche." *Revue de Littérature Comparée* 6 (1926): 381–401.

Bouwsma, William J. "The Two Faces of Humanism: Stoicism and Augustinianism in Renaissance Thought." *Itinerarium Italicum: The Profile of the Italian Renaissance in the Mirror of Its European Transformations.* Ed. H. A. Oberman, with T. A. Grady Jr. Leiden: Brill, 1975. 3–60.

Cassirer, Ernst. *Philosophy of the Enlightenment.* Trans. F. C. A. Koelln and J. P. Pettegrove. Boston: Beacon Press, 1962.

———. *The Individual and the Cosmos in Renaissance Philosophy.* Trans. M. Domandi. New York: Harper and Row, 1964.

Cervantes Saavedra, Miguel de. *El ingenioso hidalgo Don Quijote de la Mancha.* 2 vols. Ed. M. de Riquer. Barcelona: Juventud, 1958.

Checa, Jorge. *Gracián y la imaginación arquitectónica: Espacio y alegoría de la Edad Media al Barroco.* Potomac, Md.: Scripta Humanistica, 1986.

———. "Gracián lector de Ariosto: Huellas del *Orlando furioso* en el *Criticón.*" *Hispania* 71 (1988): 743–751.

Cicero. *De natura deorum.* Loeb Classical Library. Cambridge, Mass.: Harvard University Press, 1956.

———. *De officiis.* Loeb Classical Library. Cambridge, Mass.: Harvard University Press, 1990.

De Bujanda, J. M. "L'influence de Sebond en Espagne au XVIe siècle." *Renaissance and Reformation* 10 (1974): 78–84.

Donato, Eugenio. "Tesauro's Poetics: Through the Looking Glass." *Modern Language Notes* 77 (1963): 15–30.

Du Bartas, Guillaume Salluste. *La sepmaine.* Ed. Y. Bellenger. 2 vols. Paris: Nizet, 1981.

———. *The Divine Weeks and Works of Guillaume de Saluste Sieur Du Bartas.* 2 vols. Trans. J. Sylvester. Ed. S. Snyder. Oxford: Oxford University Press, 1979.

Elias, Norbert. *The Court Society.* Trans. E. Jephcott. New York: Pantheon, 1983.

Elliott, John H. *The Old World and the New.* Cambridge: Cambridge University Press, 1970.

Erasmus, Desiderius. *The Colloquies of Erasmus.* Trans. C. R. Thompson. Chicago: University of Chicago Press, 1965.

Ferry, Luc. *Homo Aestheticus: L'invention du goût à l'âge démocratique.* Paris: Bernard Grasset, 1990.

Forcione, Alban. *Cervantes, Aristotle, and the "Persiles."* Princeton: Princeton University Press, 1970.

———. *Cervantes and the Humanist Vision.* Princeton: Princeton University Press, 1982.

———. "El desposeimiento del ser en la literatura renacentista: Cervantes, Gracián, y los desafíos de *Nemo*." *Nueva Revista de Filología Hispánica* 34 (1985–86): 654–690.

———. "Exemplarity, Modernity, and the Discriminating Games of Reading." *Cervantes's "Exemplary Novels" and the Adventure of Writing.* Ed. M. Nerlich and N. Spadaccini. Minneapolis: University of Minnesota Press, 1989. 333–352.

Forsett, Edward. *A Comparative Discourse of the Bodies Natural and Politique.* London, 1606.

Friedrich, Hugo. *Epochen der Italienischen Lyrik.* Frankfurt am Main: Klostermann, 1964.

———. *Montaigne.* Bern: Francke, 1967.

———. "Gracián, *El Criticón*." *Romanische Literaturen.* 2 vols. Frankfurt am Main: Klostermann, 1972. 2: 162–180.

Gadamer, Hans-Georg. *Wahrheit und Methode.* Tübingen: Mohr, 1960.

Geertz, Clifford. "Centers, Kings, and Charisma: Reflections on the Symbolics of Power." *Local Knowledge: Further Essays in Interpretive Anthropology.* New York: Basic Books, 1983. 121–146.

Góngora y Argote, Luis de. *Soledades.* Ed. D. Alonso. Madrid: Alianza, 1982.

Gracián, Baltasar. *Agudeza y arte de ingenio.* Ed. E. Correa Calderón. 2 vols. Madrid: Castalia, 1969.

———. *El criticón.* 3 vols. Ed. M. Romera-Navarro. Philadelphia: University of Pennsylvania Press, 1938–40.

———. *El criticón.* 3 vols. Ed. E. Correa Calderón. Madrid: Espasa-Calpe, 1971.

———. *El discreto. Obras completas.* Ed. A. del Hoyo. Madrid: Aguilar, 1960.

———. *Oráculo manual y arte de prudencia.* Ed. M. Romera-Navarro. Madrid: Jura, 1954.

———. *Oráculo manual y arte de prudencia. Obras completas.* Ed. A. del Hoyo. Madrid: Aguilar, 1960.

Granada, Luis de. *Introducción del símbolo de la fe.* Ed. D. Buenaventura Carlos Aribau. Madrid: B.A.E., vol. 6, 1944.

Groethuysen, Bernhard. "Philosophische Anthropologie." *Mensch und Charakter.* Munich and Berlin: Oldenbourg, 1931.

Gumbrecht, Hans Ulrich. *"Eine" Geschichte der spanischen Literatur.* Frankfurt am Main: Suhrkamp, 1990.

Haydn, Hiram. *The Counter-Renaissance.* New York: Harcourt, Brace and World, 1950.

Heninger, S. K., Jr. *The Cosmographical Glass: Renaissance Diagrams of the Universe.* San Marino, Calif.: Huntington Library, 1977.

Hidalgo-Serna, Emilio. *Das ingeniöse Denken bei Baltasar Gracián.* Munich: Fink, 1985.

Hobbes, Thomas. *Leviathan.* Ed. C. B. Macpherson. Baltimore, Md.: Penguin, 1968.

Jankelévitch, Vladimir. "Apparence et Manière." *Homenaje a Gracián.* Ed. C. Aubrun et al. Zaragoza: Institución Fernando el Católico, 1958. 119–129.

Jonas, Hans. *The Gnostic Religion.* Boston: Beacon Press, 1963.

Kantorowizc, Ernst. "Oriens Augusti-Lever du Roi." *Dumbarton Oaks Papers* 17 (1963): 119–177.

Kendrick, Christopher. *Milton: A Study in Ideology and Form.* New York: Methuen, 1986.

Krauss, Werner. "Das neue Góngorabild." *Romanische Forschungen* 51 (1937): 71–82.

Lara Garrido, José. "La creación del mundo en la poesía barroca: De la tradición neoplatónica a la ortodoxia contrarreformista." *Estudios sobre literatura y arte dedicados al Profesor Emilio Orozco Díaz.* Granada: Universidad de Granada, 1979. 2: 241–262.

La Rochefoucauld, François de. *Maximes et réflexions diverses.* Ed. J. Truchet. Paris: Garnier-Flammarion, 1977.

Leo, Ulrich. *Torquato Tasso: Studien zur Vorgeschichte des Secentismo.* Bern: Francke, 1951.

Lovejoy, Arthur O. *The Great Chain of Being.* Cambridge, Mass.: Harvard University Press, 1948.

Luther, Martin. *Disputatio Heidelbergae habita* (1518). Vol. 1 of *Werke.* Weimar, 1883.

Maravall, José Antonio. *Teoría española del Estado en el siglo XVII.* Madrid: Instituto de estudios políticos, 1944.

———. "Las bases antropológicas del pensamiento de Gracián." *Revista de la Universidad de Madrid* 7 (1958): 403–445.

———. *Teatro y literatura en la sociedad barroca.* Madrid: Seminarios y Ediciones, 1972.

———. *Estudios de historia del pensamiento español.* 3 vols. Madrid: Cultura Hispánica, 1984.

———. *Culture of the Baroque: Analysis of a Historical Structure.* Trans. T. Cochran. Minneapolis: University of Minnesota Press, 1986.

Martínez Arancón, Ana. *La batalla en torno a Góngora.* Barcelona: Bosch, 1978.

May, T. E. "Gracián's Idea of the 'Concepto.'" *Wit of the Golden Age.* Kassel: Reichenberger, 1986. 53–79.

Mazzeo, Joseph. "Metaphysical Poetry and Poetic of Correspondence." *Journal of the History of Ideas* 14 (1953): 221–235.

Milton, John. *Paradise Lost*. Ed. M. Y. Hughes. New York: Odyssey Press, 1935.
Montaigne, Michel de. *The Complete Essays of Montaigne*. Trans. D. M. Frame. Stanford, Calif.: Stanford University Press, 1968.
Nicolson, Marjorie H. *The Breaking of the Circle: Studies in the Effect of the "New Science" on Seventeenth-Century Poetry*. New York: Columbia University Press, 1965.
Pelegrín, Benito. *Ethique et esthétique du Baroque: L'Espace jésuitique de Baltasar Gracián*. Arles: Actes Sud, 1985.
Pfandl, Ludwig. *Geschichte der Spanischen Nationalliteratur in ihrer Blütezeit*. Freiburg im Breisgau: Herder, 1929.
Pye, Christopher. "The Sovereign, the Theater, and the Kingdome of Darknesse: Hobbes and the Spectacle of Power." *Representing the English Renaissance*. Ed. S. Greenblatt. Berkeley: University of California Press, 1988. 279–291.
Ramos Foster, Virginia. *Baltasar Gracián*. Boston: Twayne, 1975.
Saavedra Fajardo, Diego de. *Empresas políticas: Idea de un príncipe político-cristiano*. Ed. Q. Aldea Vaquero. 2 vols. Madrid: Editora Nacional, 1976.
Schmidt, Rachel. "Challenging the Order of the Sun in Góngora's *Soledades*." *Imagining Culture: Essays in Early Modern History and Literature*. Ed. Jonathan Hart. New York: Garland, forthcoming.
Schröder, Gerhart. *Baltasar Graciáns "Criticón": Eine Untersuchung zur Beziehung zwischen Manierismus und Moralistik*. Munich: Fink, 1966.
Schulte, Hansgerd. *El Desengaño: Wort und Thema in der spanischen Literatur des Goldenen Zeitalters*. Munich: Fink, 1969.
Skrine, Peter N. *The Baroque*. London: Methuen, 1978.
Spitzer, Leo. "Zur Kunst Quevedos in seinem *Buscón*." *Archivum Romanicum* 11 (1927): 511–580.
———. *Die Literarisierung des Lebens in Lope's Dorotea*. Bonn: Röhrscheid, 1932.
———. *Classical and Christian Ideas of World Harmony: Prolegomena to an Interpretation of the Word "Stimmung."* Baltimore, Md.: Johns Hopkins University Press, 1963.
Strong, Roy. *Art and Power: Renaissance Festivals, 1450–1650*. Suffolk: Boyd, 1984.
———. *Henry, Prince of Wales, and England's Lost Renaissance*. New York: Thames and Hudson, 1986.
Tasso, Torquato. *Creation of the World*. Trans. J. Tusiani. Binghamton: State University of New York at Binghamton, Center for Medieval and Early Renaissance Studies, 1982.
———. *Discorsi del poema eroico*. *Prose*. Ed. E. Mazzali. Milan: Ricciardi, 1959.
———. *Il mondo creato*. Vol. 4 of *Opere*. Ed. B. Maier. Milan: Rizzoli, 1964.
Tesauro, Emmanuele. *Il cannocchiale aristotelico*. Facsim. of 1670 Turin edition. Ed. A. Buck. Berlin: Gehlen, 1968.
Thibaut de Maisières. Maury Dieudonné. *Les Poèmes inspirés du début de la Genèse a l'epoque de la Renaissance*. Louvain, 1931.
Toulmin, Stephen. *Cosmopolis: The Hidden Agenda of Modernity*. New York: Free Press, 1990.
Vega, Félix Lope de. *El villano en su rincón*. Ed. J. M. Marín. Madrid: Cátedra, 1987.
Vives, Juan Luis. *De institutione feminae christianae*. Vol. 4 of *Opera omnia*. Ed. G. Mayáns y Siscar. Valencia: Monfort, 1783.
Weisbach, Werner. *Der Barock als Kunst der Gegenreformation*. Berlin: Cassirer, 1921.

Weise, Georg. "Das Element des Heroischen in der spanischen religiösen Literatur der Zeit der Gegenreformation." *Gesammelte Aufsätze zur Kulturgeschichte Spaniens, Spanische Forschungen der Görresgesellschaft* 10 (1955): 161–304.

Welu, James A. "Strange New Worlds: Mapping the Heavens and Earth's Great Extent." *The Age of the Marvelous.* Ed. J. Kenseth. Hanover, N.H.: Hood Museum of Art, 1991. 103–112.

Zarka, Yves Charles. "Héros et antihéros: Baltasar Gracián et la naissance de la théorie moderne de l'individu." *Situations de la démocratie,* May 1993, 260–275.

Chapter 2
On Power, Image, and Gracián's Prototype

Isabel C. Livosky

Gracián's prescription for success in a world he characterizes as being in constant struggle is based on concealment, disguise, and opportunism. In the first "primor" of his first prescriptive treatise, *The Hero* (1637), the injunction to the candidate for greatness is "All should know you, nobody should encompass you; with this rule, a little will seem a lot" (8).[1] In *The Politician* (1640) he states, "Astuteness has its own way of founding [empires], always availing itself of chance," (41)[2] which is later corroborated in *The Oracle* (1647): "288. The direction of affairs, discourse, everything, must be appropriate to the occasion. Resolve while you can, for time and tide wait for no man. . . . The wise man, however, knows that the first rule of prudence demands that he should behave as the occasion demands" (269).[3] The carefully chosen vocabulary—*parecer, astucia, ocasión*—sets the tone for what Forcione calls "the prudent ethics of accommodation" ("la prudente ética de acomodo" [682]).

Gracián's construct of the prototype for the prudent politician and man-about-court in seventeenth-century Spain bears reexamination as we approach the end of a millennium with doubts about issues of dominance in a world struggling with cultural and political instabilities. The dilemma for Gracián and his contemporaries was to justify and reconcile the brutal methods necessary to acquire and maintain power with the moral teachings of the church. In the following pages I shall argue that they did so through an ingenious sophism that allowed unacceptable or questionable means to be used for the seizure and maintenance of political power under the guise of a higher purpose, and that this constitutes the foundation of Gracián's prototype. I shall then suggest that what in the seventeenth century is mostly enunciated through the manipulation of words finds visual expression in the most popular media of our own time, the television screen—I refer to Rosellini's *La prise de pouvoir par Louis XIV* (1965). We travel in time from the power of the word to the power of the image.

In *The Hero* Gracián's intention is "to forge with a small book a giant of a man" ("formar con un libro enano un varón gigante" [5]). As he addresses the duke of Nochera at the beginning of *The Politician: Don Ferdinand the Catholic,* Gracián purports to offer "not so much the body of [Ferdinand's] history, as the soul of his politics; not a narrative of his exploits, as a discourse of his achievements; judgment of many kings, but not a panegyric of only one" (39). The poetics of power articulated in *The Politician* rests on the construction of a quasi-mythical figure: Ferdinand emerges as the paradigm of an ideal king to be admired and emulated at a time when the Spanish monarchy he founded is in decline. Ferdinand is shown as the founder of a monarchy that eventually encompasses a diversity of lands and peoples brought together by force, cunning, and chance—his merit consists in imposing on them his kingly authority and the religion of the hegemonic metropolis, Castile. Although Providence is said to play a crucial role in the making and unmaking of empires for its secret and high purposes (48), it is Ferdinand's combined abilities ("capacidad"), single-minded purpose, and hard work that are signaled for his monumental achievements. Ferdinand's acquisition of territories and peoples (by force or cunning) with the ostensible purpose of propagating the faith rests on the personal qualities of the king: valor, prudence, sagacity in dealing with others, aptness in choosing the appropriate occasion. At a time when heterogeneous ethnic and linguistic divisions within the realm were a matter of great concern, Gracián could be inducing Philip IV to look back upon Ferdinand as a model in the exercise of royal authority and political acumen. His accommodation to circumstances and single-minded commitment to the imperial enterprise and to the church make of Ferdinand the perfect paradigm for Gracián's similar ideology.

In his lucid introduction to *El político,* Tierno Galván discusses the background against which Gracián's text is conceived: Machiavelli's *The Prince* (written in 1513, published in 1532), as well as his *Discourses* (probably finished by 1518, published in 1532), and the problem of the political theoreticians of the Counter-Reformation as they grapple with the concept of "reason of state," which, although never mentioned as such by Machiavelli, was implicit in *The Prince.* Tierno observes that "what is very clearly proposed in *The Prince* is the recognition that in terms of facts, the justification or legitimacy of politics lies in political success and not in moral principles." He subsumes that this leads to "a political order constructed according to the relationship power-submission," and thus "politics becomes a theory of power, of its acquisition and its preservation" (9).[4]

Tierno traces the predicament of the Catholic *tratadistas* as they search for a formula that would find "a theory that, according to the good reason of state, would make of moral politics an efficient instrument in practical terms" (11–12). As enunciated, among others, in Giovanni Botero's *Della ragion di Stato* (1589), Pedro de Rivadeneyra's *El príncipe cristiano* (1595), and Juan de Mariana's *De rege et regis institutione* (1599), the theory of the "good reason of state" ("buena razón de Estado") purports to reconcile political action and moral principles by proposing that "politics is a science, and as such it is subordinated to morality, but it should not be confused with morality" (12–13).[5] Tierno concludes by stating that Gracián's novelty consists in his introducing casuistic doctrine into politics, and thus the concept of "directed intention," much used by the Society of Jesus. As an example of casuistic reasoning, he cites Father Escobar of the Society: "If your enemy seeks to hurt you, you must not desire his death on account of a feeling of hate, but rather to avoid your being harmed" ("Si tu enemigo procura hacerte daño no debes desear su muerte por un sentimiento de odio, pero sí para evitar tu propio perjuicio" [13]).

It is this recourse to sophistry that makes it possible for Gracián to refer to Machiavelli's "reason of state" as "reason of stable" ("razones, no de Estado, sino de establo" [*Criticón* 1:vii]), although in fact he also condones the principle that the attainment of the end justifies the means. Tierno's comment is very telling: "Evidently, without moral casuistry applied to politics, Baroque politics is a barely understandable monstrosity" (14).[6] For Gracián, supposedly, this construction means that as long as the policies and actions enacted redound not merely in preserving the state, but rather the state as it adheres to the tenets of the church and the propagation of the faith, they are legitimate and praiseworthy. It bears remembering that in 1629 Pope Gregory XV had established the Congregation for the Propagation of the Faith, that Gracián was a member of a very active order committed to proselytism on behalf of the church, and that the propagation of the faith was one of the mainstays of the Spanish monarchy's imperial enterprise. Quevedo's *Política de Dios y gobierno de Cristo* (1625) and Saavedra Fajardo's *Política y razón de Estado* (1631) and *Empresas políticas, o Idea de un príncipe político-cristiano representada en cien empresas* (published in 1640) also belong to this period.

Gracián's contemptuous rejection of Machiavelli notwithstanding, it is interesting to note how they coincide in their treatment of the concept that the end justifies the means, as well as in their conception of what constitutes a good ruler.

In chapter 18 of *The Prince,* "How princes should keep their promises," Machiavelli is considering the opposition integrity-trickery in terms of the prince's actions to "maintain the state": "And it is essential to realize this: that a prince, and above all a prince who is new, cannot practice all those things for which men are considered good, being often forced, in order to keep his position, to act contrary to truth, contrary to charity, contrary to humanity, contrary to religion. Therefore he must have a mind ready to turn in any direction as Fortune's winds and the variability of affairs require, yet, . . . he holds to what is right when he can but knows how to do wrong when he must" (66).[7]

Gracián's formulation in *The Oracle* is less qualified, more direct, even more blunt:

> 66. *Take care that your affairs reach a successful conclusion.* Some people are more concerned with the accuracy of their aim than with the satisfaction of attaining their object; but the disgrace of failure invariably counts for more than the recognition of diligence. *A victor need give no explanations.* The majority do not look closely into circumstantial detail but only at a successful, or unsuccessful, outcome: thus *one's reputation never suffers if one's object is attained. A satisfactory issue puts everything to rights, although mistaken means belie it.* It is, therefore, an art in itself to transgress the rules of art, when there is no other way of winning the joy of success.[8] (97–99, my emphasis)

Conspicuously, Machiavelli and Gracián coincide in praising Ferdinand of Aragon as a paragon of a king. Gracián's opening sentence in *The Politician* sets the tone for his eulogy: "I offer a king against all those in the past, I propose a king against all those in the future: Don Ferdinand the Catholic King, that great master in the art of kingship, the greatest oracle of the reason of State" (38); he later remarks that "the true and masterly policy was that of Ferdinand, assured and firm, which did not end up in unrealistic ideas. . . . His greatest talent, and the sun of all his natural gifts, was a prodigious capability, the sure foundation of his royal greatness" (55). For Gracián, "capacidad" consists of quick intelligence and mature judgment, qualities that he judges characterize Ferdinand, "the king with the greatest capability that ever existed" ("el rey de mayor capacidad que ha habido" [58]). His recapitulation reveals Gracián's conception of what constitutes greatness in a monarch as much as it summarizes what Ferdinand did for the Spanish monarchy:

> He made it religious by purging it from all infidels and by exalting the sacred and vigilant tribunal of the Inquisition. He made it valiant, showing the courage of the Spaniards to foreign nations, so they were in awe of its power. Majestic, perfecting royal authority, so trampled and even contested before. Rich, not with tributes, but rather with its perennial fleets, rivers of gold, silver, pearls, and other riches that arrive each year from the Indies. He used to bring [to Spain] learned and renowned men in literature and divinity. Finally, fortunate in all kinds of perfection and culture. (68–69)

Writing nostalgically, well over a century after Ferdinand had laid the foundations for the empire now disintegrating, Gracián is acutely aware of the historical import of his own perspective: "He reigned at the onset of the empire, which helps greatly the praiseworthiness of a monarch; a king's greatness or smallness depends much on the state of the monarchy, for there is great difference between reigning as it is rising or declining" (46–47).[9]

When Machiavelli needs a paradigm to illustrate "XXI. How a prince conducts himself in order to gain a high reputation," his foremost example is the Catholic king, his contemporary:

> Nothing makes a prince so highly esteemed as do great undertakings and unusual actions. An example in our times is Ferdinand of Aragon, the present king of Spain. He can be called almost a new prince because through fame and glory he has transformed himself from a petty ruler to the foremost king among the Christians. If you consider his actions, you find them all very great and some of them extraordinary. In the early part of his reign he attacked Granada; this undertaking was the foundation of his power. First, he acted when he was otherwise unengaged and had no fear of being hindered; by invading Granada he kept employed the minds of the unruly barons of Castile, who when thinking about war did not think about rebellion. In the meantime he also gained a high reputation and sovereignty over his nobles without their realizing it. With money from the Church and from the people he maintained armies, and in that long war laid the foundation for his military organization, which since has done him honor. Besides this, for the sake of engaging in greater enterprises, he continually availed himself of religion, for he turned to a pious cruelty, hunting down and clearing out of his kingdom the Marranos; no memorable act could be more pitiable than this or more extraordinary. Under this same cloak of religion, he invaded Africa; he then undertook his expedition to Italy; recently he attacked France; and so always he performed and planned great actions, which kept the minds of his subjects always in suspense and wonder, watching for the outcome. These actions have in such a way grown one from another that between one and the next never has he given people any interval of leisure for working against him.[10] (*The Prince* 81)

In the light of Gracián's demonstrable acceptance of the axiom that the end justifies the means, it seems appropriate to examine his position when this concept converges with that of gaining ascendancy, or power, over others, and the use made of that power. His meticulous enumeration of strategies necessary to attain and maintain power, originally enunciated in *The Hero* (dedicated in the first edition of 1637 to Philip IV), remain present, consistent, and constant in *The Politician* and *The Oracle*—his eminently pragmatic political discourse on power persists throughout. Virtue, on the other hand, is praised summarily at the end of *The Hero* and of *The Oracle* without being defined and without a disquisition of what it consists of. It seems to be rather summarily mentioned after a long and systematic listing of pragmatic advice on how to conduct oneself in order to acquire superiority and power over others, as the headings from *The Oracle* seem to indicate. Interspersed with aphorisms about how to acquire wisdom, we find in *The Oracle* very mundane, and perhaps morally questionable, injunctions about how to learn the skills necessary to succeed in a hostile society. In the case of a prince, it entails how to acquire ascendancy and power over others and thus become a successful ruler. Typical examples are the following:

3. *Keep your affairs in suspense.*
5. *Make people depend upon you.*
7. *Avoid victories over your superior.*
31. *Recognize the fortunate so that you may choose their company and the unfortunate so that you may avoid them.*
66. *Take care that your affairs reach a successful conclusion.*
99. *Reality and appearance.*
120. *Live practically.*
130. *Act, and let it be seen that you are doing so.*
149. *Know how to put your troubles on someone else's shoulders.*
181. *Without lying, do not tell the whole truth.*
187. *Do everything pleasant yourself; everything unpleasant through intermediaries.*
212. *Always keep the ultimate tricks of your trade to yourself.*
220. *When you cannot clothe yourself in a lion's skin, don that of a fox.*
232. *Be a bit of a business man.*

234. *Never trust your reputation to another unless you have his honour in pawn.*
236. *Grant beforehand as a favour what you would later have to give as a reward.*
253. *Do not make your thoughts too clear.*
255. *Know how to do good a little at a time, and often.*
288. *Live as the occasion demands.*

The critical reading of Gracián in our own century consistently remarks on the eminently pragmatic character of his works. L. B. Walton, translator of *The Oracle,* declares that "the 'hero' of Gracián . . . is, first and foremost, an astute man of sound judgment, great-hearted, quick in action, courageous" (9), and elaborates: "What kind of work is the *Oráculo*? It is, as the author describes it, a 'handbook' and its object is severely practical. The literature of the period abounded in guides to heaven above; the *Oráculo* is strictly concerned with man's fortunes on the earth beneath." He then characterizes *The Oracle* as "an odd compound of shrewdness, cynicism, and moralizing" (15).

Romera-Navarro concurs:

> His *Oráculo manual* holds the doctrines and teachings of worldly morals. They are practical, utilitarian admonitions. Neither the idealistic evangelical nor the pious sentimental speaks, but rather the man experienced in the struggle of life. And his advice is sometimes addressed to the common man, sometimes to the great man, the prince, and even the king; also to the politician, the ruler, the man who fights actively in the midst of interests, intrigue, and rivalries. The author adapts the aphorisms to the state and condition of each of them. Thus, the aphorisms run all over the moral scale, from the hardest and most selfish addressed to the ruler to the most honest intended for the common man. As a whole, it endeavors to fashion not a model of a virtuous man, although this is not missing, but rather a prudent, astute and mundane successful individual.[11] (xiv)

For R. O. Jones,

> the book [*Oracle*] teaches prudent management of one's affairs so as to achieve success, which appears to be measured in exclusively social terms. Life is represented as

> a tacit struggle for influence and esteem. Gracián is much concerned with appearances, since these are important in that struggle.... Social *Realpolitik* informs many... aphorisms.... This book is not (of course) a treatise on morality: its subject is the prudent management of affairs, and in this opportunism must have a place. Gracián is concerned less with ends than with means.... This is a worldly book, but it concludes: *"En una palabra, santo, que es decirlo todo de una vez."* This may seem to modern readers an abrupt change of direction, but it did not in Gracián's day. The book's subject is worldly prudence; the divine is taken for granted. (199–200)

The subject to whom Gracián's advice and aphorisms are addressed must be taken into consideration as we examine his works. In general, the content, the language, and the style are purposefully rendered difficult—the intended reader is the cultivated man ("el hombre culto"). Two recent approaches to the Spanish Baroque that deal to a certain extent with individualism during that period are pertinent here. John Beverley points out "the paradoxical conjunction of the principle of submission to authority with the practical and theoretical ideal of the self-willed, independent individual" (225); Anthony J. Cascardi takes exception to certain tenets of José Antonio Maravall's approach to the Spanish Baroque and suggests the need to "articulate the problem of cultural control in terms of the crisis of subject formation in early modern Spain" (236–237). His analysis of the mechanisms of control lead him to conclude that "the... 'rational' model of psychology evident in Gracián both incorporates and subsumes the psychological models developed during the Counter-Reformation" (251).

As we inscribe Gracián in the complex mosaic of seventeenth-century Spanish culture, the emergence of the "probabilist" movement and its impact within the church, particularly among the Jesuits, adds another dimension to the discussion of the conflict between a hierarchical society and individualism. The keystone to probabilism is the conviction that in matters of the legality or illegality of an action, it is permissible to follow conscientiously a less probable opinion against one that is more probable. The corollary of this axiom, reliance on one's judgment, clearly challenges the principle of authority inherent in the hierarchical structure of the church, and gets dangerously close to heterodoxy. The polemic was hard-fought and long—from about 1577 until 1679, when Pope Innocent XI condemned a series of propositions that included the tenets of probabilism. Gracián could not have ignored the import of the theological dispute, and his failure to conform to the vow of obedience, for which he was repeatedly punished, bespeaks his taking an "individualist" position. But we must be cautious, for in his treatises, Gracián's individualism applies to the discriminating individual who aspires to become a *hero* or *discreto,* someone who belongs to an elite group, not the common man.

As we attempt to better contextualize the literature of the period, to in fact cross the imaginary line between literary and nonliterary texts, the work of Maravall and J. H. Elliott, among others, provides a historical analysis of the sixteenth and seventeenth centuries that allows us to gain an insight into the interplay between Gracián's texts, the time and place when and where they were produced, and us today.

Elliott proposes that the ideological underpinnings of the Spanish monarchy were a "sense of global mission, conceived both in religious and dynastic terms," from which ensued the justification "to preserve, defend, and extend the faith," the "identification of throne and altar," and the peculiar "combination of constitutional pluralism with unitary kingship" that brought under one crown a diversity of peoples that managed to preserve their individual institutional prerogatives (165–170).

Maravall's analysis of the social alterations that took place during this period of strenuous economic fluctuations facilitates the understanding of the conflictive nature of the interaction and the relations among the various groups that made up the social fabric of Spain at the time. For him, a change in values and in behavior provoke alterations in the processes of integration by those marginalized, which in turn bring about frustration, resentment, tensions, and, from the perspective of the dominant group, abhorrent conduct that manifests itself in revolutions (*Cultura del Barroco* 66–70). Maravall brings to the fore the texts mostly ignored by the official record. In the face of the historical evidence presented by Maravall, his reading of Gracián is extremely telling:

"in order to try to understand the Baroque aspects that on one hand offer support for the aristocratic conception of society and on the other hand present a definitive erosion of aristocratic social morals, we can conveniently use the Gracianesque versions of a debased aristocraticism in *The Oracle,* of an elitism without heroic meaning in *The Hero,* of a calculated and efficient synteresis, in as much as it is bourgeois, in *The Critic*" (76–77).[12] Maravall concludes that "the Spaniards of the seventeenth century, very differently from those of the Renaissance period, appear to us as shaken by a serious crisis in their process of integration (from 1600 on, it is a generally accepted opinion that the fall of the Spanish monarchy is cosmically unstoppable in terms of its being an integrated group; and the only thing to be done is to give it provisional support). This translates into a state of anxiety—which in many cases can be regarded as anguished—and thus of instability, with a consciousness of irremediable 'decadence' that the Spaniards themselves had" (95).[13]

The theme of power, how to acquire it, how to exercise it, and how to maintain it is of particular interest to the aristocracy in seventeenth-century Europe. It is a century of fierce European rivalry and strife, it is the century of the decline of imperial Spain and the building of empires by England, France, and Holland. From the perspective of the media culture of our own late twentieth century, it seems appropriate to consider here a visually eloquent dissection of the mechanisms of power as exercised by the master of absolutism, Louis XIV of France, in Roberto Rosellini's *La prise de pouvoir par Louis XIV.* The film was made in 1965 for French television. The title in English has been translated as *The Rise to Power of Louis XIV,* which does not convey the meaning of the French: "prise" suggests the capture, the seizing of something, and implies an active agent, in this case the king, who by design concentrates all the power in himself. Thus, *The Seizure of Power by Louis XIV* would not only be more accurate, but would also reflect the point of the film: the cunningly devised and systematically implemented manipulation by which the king relentlessly affirms his control over the court, and the implied subsequent use of similar strategies to consolidate his power over the other orders in the society.

A brief summary of some salient points made by Rosellini in the film would serve as a contemporary commentary on how seventeenth-century absolutist ideology is made to inform the codes of language, dress, deportment, and daily life, with the aim of acquiring and consolidating power, thus exposing the interplay between ideology, discourse, and power.

On his deathbed, Mazarin (1601–1661) acknowledges to the priest confessing him that he used his high office to accumulate riches; he then tells the king (Louis XIV, 1638–1715, reigned 1643–1715) that he wishes to leave him this fortune; the king refuses in the name of the Crown. This scene provides one of the first glimpses of the king's sagacity, for he explicitly refuses not on account of principle, but rather on account of the effect that his acceptance would have on public opinion. Immediately after Mazarin's death the king decides at the age of twenty-two to govern himself, muses that "power is in too many hands that are guided by conflicting interests," that "the nobles need money, and only the merchants have it," and relies on his minister Colbert (1619–1683) to carry out his policies. Louis XIV concludes that only absolutism will preserve the Crown, and devises the means by which he will attain his goal: he decrees that everyone must owe everything to the monarch; he reduces the importance of the nobility and controls it by keeping it occupied with elaborate dress, meals, and ceremonial functions; he removes the court from the center of power in Paris to Versailles; he rules the mind by the appearance of things, not by the essence. The vivid images of the king designing and then wearing an amazingly elaborate suit, or making a theatrical production of his meals, point clearly to his strategies. He does not, however, neglect to implement Colbert's economic policies, which will ultimately consolidate his power: we also see images of the king and his minister analyzing economic and social issues, of the king making acute evaluations of historical circumstances and of human nature—these are the underpinnings of the policies the king adopts and Colbert implements to gain control of the nobility as the first step in the attainment of absolute power. The last scene shows the king alone reading La Rochefoucauld and reflecting on the qualities necessary to prevail over others by instilling in them a sense of awe: "There is a loftiness that does not depend at all on fortune: it is a certain air of superiority that seems to destine us to great things; it is a value that we award imperceptibly to ourselves; it is through this quality that we usurp the deference of other men, and it is this quality that usually places us above them more than birth, honours, and merit themselves would."[14] The last line he reads, "Neither the sun nor death can be faced steadily" ("Le soleil ni la mort ne se peuvent regarder fixement" [*Maximes* 26, p. 15]) foreshadows the role he assigns for himself in his own scheme.

Gracián had written in *The Hero*: "14. *On natural self-command.* There shines on some an innate dignity, a secret force of mastery, that elicits obedience without external precepts, without the art of persuasion" (26).[15] It seems pertinent to note the coincidence of thought between Gracián's "innate dignity" ("señorío innato") and La Rochefoucauld's "certain air," in that both evoke a theatrical connotation of performance. J. H. Elliott points out the importance accorded to "the application of the arts of the theatre to political life, and especially to the projection of kingship" (163) by the monarchies of seventeenth-century Europe, and points to the usefulness of the ceremonial aspects of the court for the purpose of subjecting the Spanish aristocracy into obedience to the king, Philip IV. Yet, lest we oversimplify the issue, he incisively notes that although in our time we have a "sharpened awareness of the significance of symbolism and the creation of images" (164), more than the manipulation of images is needed to exercise power. With this in mind, Elliott thoroughly investigates the economic and political agenda of the Conde-Duque de Olivares, Philip IV's minister, just as Rosellini shows Louis XIV and Colbert discussing the implementation of the economic plan that will consolidate the power of the Crown.

The background against which Gracián is writing during the first half of the seventeenth century is a period during which the Conde-Duque de Olivares is striving unsuccessfully to unify, to give cohesion to a fragmented monarchy by forcing the diverse kingdoms under the Crown to come under the effective control of Castile. Gracián's dedication of *The Hero* to Philip IV in the manuscript of 1637, subsequently substituted by a dedication to Vincencio Juan de Lastanosa in the edition of 1639, read: "Dedicado ala S[acra] C[atólica] R[eal] M[ajestad] del Rey N[uestro] S[eñor]

D[on] Felippe el Quarto. Candidato dela Grandeça. Amante dela fama, pretendiente dela imortalidad" (Romera-Navarro 77).[16] By 1639 the disillusion of Gracián with the king's policies, particularly as they concerned Catalonia, is clear. And in hindsight, there is no question but that the Spanish empire and its triumphant vision of itself declined precipitously.

Gracián was fated to live during the period of decline and disintegration of the Spanish empire, in pointed contrast to the era of his admired Ferdinand of Aragon. The politician, the hero, the discreet, all creatures conceived and designed as prototypes for interaction in society, and constructed by a discourse of power based on disguise, strategies, and manipulation of one's own image, eventually lead to the introspection and the *desengaño* of *The Critic*—from interaction with the world to the man within. We have also traveled from rhetoric to image, from a poetics of power in words to a poetics of power in images, from Machiavelli through Gracián to Rosellini. Is there sufficient similitude between Gracián's *espacio vital* and ours, between his political discourse in a declining society and our own in a world we perceive as a fragmented, disconnected, pluralistic, ironic, subversive, and subverted construction? If in the early works of Gracián we were to perceive his nostalgia for the heroic possibilities and realizations of the "modernity" embodied in Ferdinand's legitimation of the nation-state, perhaps in the atomization of the nation-state and the selective individualism reflected in his later work we can perceive the ethos of our own "postmodernity."

Notes

1. "Todos te conozcan, ninguno te abarque; que con esta regla, lo moderado parecerá mucho." All translations are my own, except those from *The Oracle* and *The Prince*.

2. "Tiene la astucia su propio modo de fundar, que fue valerse siempre de la ocasión."

3. "288. *Vivir a la ocasión*. El gobernar, el discurrir, todo ha de ser al caso; querer cuando se puede, que la sazón y el tiempo a nadie aguardan.... Mas el sabio sabe que el norte de la prudencia existe en portarse a la ocasión" (227–228).

4. "En *El Príncipe* es muy claro que se postula el reconocimiento de que en el orden de los hechos la justificación o legitimidad de la política está en el éxito político y no en los principios morales"; "... un orden político construído según la relación poder-sumisión"; "La política se convierte en una teoría del poder, de su adquisición y de su mantenimiento."

5. "... una teoría que hiciera de la política con moral, según la buena razón de estado, un instrumento eficaz en la práctica"; "... que la política es una ciencia y que como tal ciencia está subordinada a la moral, pero que no se ha de confundir con la moral."

6. "Evidentemente, sin un casuismo moral aplicado a la política, la política barroca resulta una monstruosidad apenas comprensible."

7. "In che modo e'principi abbino a mantenere la fede." "Et hassi ad intendere questo, che uno principe, e massime uno principe nuovo, non può osservare tutte quelle cose per le quali li uomini sono tenuti buoni, sendo spesso necessitato, per mantenere lo stato, operare contro alla fede, contro alla carità, contro alla umanità, contro alla relligione. E però bisogna che elli abbi uno animo disposto a volgersi secondo ch'e'venti e le variazioni della fortuna li comandono, e, come sopra dissi, non partirsi dal bene, potendo, ma sapere intrare nel male, necessitato" (104–105).

8. "66. *Atención a que le salgan bien las cosas.* Algunos ponen más la mira en el rigor de la dirección que en la felicidad del conseguir intento, pero más prepondera siempre el descrédito de la infelicidad que el abono de la diligencia. *El que vence no necesita dar satisfacciones.* No perciben los más la puntualidad de las circunstancias, sino los buenos o los ruines sucesos; y así, *nunca se pierde reputación cuando se consigue el intento. Todo lo dora un buen fin, aunque lo desmientan los desaciertos de los medios.* Que es arte ir contra el arte cuando no se puede de otro modo conseguir la dicha del salir bien" (171, my emphasis).

9. "Opongo un rey a todos los pasados, propongo un rey a todos los venideros: don Fernando el Católico, aquel gran maestro del arte de reinar, el Oráculo mayor de la razón de Estado"; "La verdadera y magistral política fue la de Fernando, segura y firme, que no se resolvía en fantásticas quimeras.... Su mayor prenda, y el sol de las demás, fue una prodigiosa capacidad, fundamento seguro de una real grandeza"; "El la hizo religiosa con purgarla de unos y otros infieles y con ensalzar el tribunal sacro y vigilante de la Inquisición. El la hizo valerosa, dando a conocer el esfuerzo de los españoles a las naciones extranjeras, con súbito espanto de su potencia. Majestuosa, poniendo en su punto la autoridad real, tan atropellada antes, y aun tan competida. Rica, no con tributos, sino con sus flotas perennes, ríos de oro, plata, perlas y otras riquezas que entran cada año de la India. Sabía contraer a ella varones doctos e insignes en letras humanas y divinas. Finalmente, feliz en todo género de perfección y de cultura"; "Reinó en creciente de imperio, que ayuda mucho a la plausibilidad de un monarca; depende mucho de la grandeza o la pequeñez de un rey del estado de la monarquía, que va mucho de reinar en su creciente, al reinar en su menguante" (46–47).

10. "XXI. *Che si conviene a un principe perché sia stimato.* Nessuna cosa fa tanto stimare uno principe, quanto fanno le grande imprese e dare di sé rari esempli. Noi abbiamo ne'nostri tempi Ferrando di Aragonia, presente re di Spagna. Costui si può chiamare quasi principi nuovo, perchè d'uno re debole è diventato per fama e per gloria il primo re de'Cristiani: e, se considerrete le azione sua, le troverrete tutte grandissime e qualcuna estraordinaria. Lui nel principio del suo regno assaltò la Granata; e quella impresa fu el fondamento dello stato suo. Prima, e'la fece ocioso e sanso sospetto di essere impedito: tenne occupati in quella li animi di quelle baronbi di Castiglia, li quali, pensando a quella guerra, non pensavano ad innovare; e lui acquistava in quel mezzo reputazione et imperio sopra

di loro, che non se ne accorgevano. Posse nutrire con danari della Chiesa e de'populi eserciti, e fare uno fondamento con quella guerra lunga alla milizia sua, la quale lo ha di poi onorato. Oltre a questo, per possere intraprendere maggiori imprese, servendosi sempre della relligione, si volse ad una pietosa crudeltà, cacciando e spogliando el suo regno de'Marrani: né può esser questo esemplo piú miserabile né piú raro. Assaltò sotto questo medesimo mantello l'Affrica: fece l'impresa di Italia: ha ultimamente assaltato la Francia: e cosí sempre a fatte et ordite cose grandi, le queli sempre hanno tenuto sospesi et ammirati li animi de'sudditi et occupati nello evento di esse. E sono nate queste sue azioni in modo l'una dall'altra, che non ha dato mai, infra l'una e l'altra, spazio alli uomini di potere quietamente operarli contro" (125–126).

11. "Su *Oráculo manual* encierra las doctrinas y enseñanzas de la moral mundana. Son avisos prácticos, utilitarios. No habla el idealista evangélico, ni el piadoso sentimental, sino el hombre experimentado en el batallar del vivir. Y se dirigen sus consejos, a veces, al hombre común, y a veces, al gran señor, al príncipe y aun al rey, también al político, al gobernante, al hombre que lucha activamente en medio de intereses, intrigas y rivalidades. Acomoda el autor los aforismos al estado y condición de cada uno de ellos. Así, los aforismos recorren toda la escala moral, desde el más duro y egoísta al gobernante hasta el más honrado al hombre común. En conjunto, pretende formar, no un modelo de varón virtuoso, aunque tampoco falte éste, sino un sujeto prudente, sagaz y triunfador en la vida" (Introducción, xiv).

12. ". . . para tratar de entender esos aspectos barrocos que, por un lado, ofrecen un apuntalamiento de la concepción aristocrática de la sociedad, y, por otro, presentan una erosión definitiva de la moral social aristocrática, podemos muy bien servirnos de las versiones gracianescas de un aristocratismo aplebeyado en el *Oráculo manual,* de un elitismo sin sentido heroico en *El héroe,* de una sindéresis calculada y eficaz, en tanto que burguesa, en *El criticón.*"

13. "Los españoles del XVII, muy diferentemente de los de la época renacentista, se nos presentan como sacudidos por grave crisis en su proceso de integración (la opinión general, a partir de 1600, es la de que se reconoce cósmicamente imparable la caída de la monarquía hispánica, en tanto que régimen de convivencia del grupo, a la que no cabe más que apuntalar provisionalmente). Ello se traduce en un estado de inquietud—que en muchos casos cabe calificar como angustiada—, y por tanto de inestabilidad, con una conciencia de irremediable 'decadencia' que los mismos españoles tuvieron." For an analysis of what he calls "las tendencias adversas al régimen oficial," see Maravall's *La oposición política bajo los Austrias* (Barcelona: Ariel, 1972).

14. "Il y a une élévation qui ne dépend point de la fortune: c'est un certain air qui nous distingue, et qui semble nous destiner aux grandes choses; c'est un prix que nous donnons imperceptiblement à nous-mêmes; c'est par cette qualité que nous usurpons les déférences des autres hommes, et c'est elle d'ordinaire qui nous met plus au-dessus d'eux que la naissance, les dignités et le mérite même" (*Maximes* 399, p. 80).

15. "XIV. *Del natural imperio.* . . . Brilla en algunos un señorío innato, una secreta fuerza de imperio, que se hace obedecer sin exterioridad de preceptos, sin arte de persuasión."

16. For a detailed study of the MS of *El héroe,* see Miguel Romera-Navarro, *Estudio del autógrafo de "El Héroe" graciano.* Madrid: *Revista de filología española,* Anejo 35, 1946.

Works Cited

Beverley, John R. "On the Concept of the Spanish Literary Baroque." In *Culture and Control in Counter-Reformation Spain.* Ed. Anne J. Cruz and Mary Elizabeth Perry. Hispanic Issues 7. Minneapolis: University of Minnesota Press, 1992. 216–230.

Cascardi, Anthony J. "The Subject of Control." In *Culture and Control in Counter-Reformation Spain.* Ed. Anne J. Cruz and Mary Elizabeth Perry. Hispanic Issues 7. Minneapolis: University of Minnesota Press, 1992. 231–254.

Elliott, J. H. *Spain and Its World, 1500–1700.* New Haven and London: Yale University Press, 1989.

Forcione, Alban. "El desposeimiento del ser en la literatura renacentista: Cervantes, Gracián, y los desafíos de *Nemo.*" *Nueva Revista de Filología Hispánica* 34.2 (1985–86): 654–690.

Gracián, Baltasar. *Obras completas.* Ed. Arturo del Hoyo. Madrid: Aguilar, 1967.

———. *The Oracle: A Manual in the Art of Discretion.* Trans. L. B. Walton. London: Dent, 1953.

———. *Oráculo manual y Arte de prudencia.* Edición crítica y comentada por Miguel Romera-Navarro. Madrid: *Revista de Filología Española,* Anejo 42, 1954.

———. *El político.* Ed. E. Correa Calderón. Introducción de E. Tierno Galván. Madrid: Ediciones Anaya, 1961.

Jones, R. O. *A Literary History of Spain: The Golden Age: Prose and Poetry.* London: Ernest Benn, 1971.

La Rochefoucauld, François de. *Réflexions sentences et maximes morales.* Précedés d'une notice par M. Sainte-Beuve. Paris: Garnier Frères, n.d.

Machiavelli, Niccolò. *Il principe di Niccoló Machiavelli: Con commento storico, filologico, e stilistico, a cura di Giuseppe Lisio.* Firenze: Sansoni, 1924.

———. *The Prince.* In *The Chief Works and Others.* Vol. 1. Trans. Allan Gilbert. Durham: Duke University Press, 1989.

Maravall, José Antonio. *La cultura del Barroco.* Barcelona: Ariel, 1975.

———. *Culture of the Baroque: Analysis of a Historical Structure.* Trans. Terry Cochran. Minneapolis: University of Minnesota Press, 1986.

Romera-Navarro, Miguel. *Estudio del autógrafo de "El Héroe" graciano.* Madrid: *Revista de filología española,* Anejo 35, 1946.

Part II
Subjectivities

Chapter 3

Saving Appearances: Language and Commodification in Baltasar Gracián

Malcolm K. Read

If confirmation is required that reading and interpreting an author are activities that presuppose committed interests and social pressures, then it is surely provided by the spectrum of different critical "approaches" to Gracián, from those that recuperate the Jesuit for Spain and Morality, to those that legitimize only his secularism. We will understand more about such critical conflict when we have learned to relate it to the broader process by which society channels literature. Provisionally, we will suggest that a classically "liberal" education, at the tertiary level, aimed to cultivate a higher subjectivity, to inculcate degrees of (aesthetic) sensitivity considered to be beyond the capacity of the solid rump of mankind: "Gracián remains . . . a complete man, a man in the round, a true Spaniard who is, at the same time, an outstanding example of the *homo europaeus* whose very existence is threatened by the ant-heap 'civilization' of our own day" (Walton 34).

Walton is able to arrive at such a conclusion only after having negotiated some dangerous terrain, which includes the extent to which Gracián's commands to serve the state can be bent to totalitarian purposes; what the Jesuit and totalitarianism have in common, which is "repugnant to the scientific humanist" (30);

and the Jesuit's seemingly amoral counsels. Walton resolves these difficulties by confining moralism to the superstructure of Victorian England and claiming Gracián for the reality of capitalism's productive practice: "the majority of successful people undoubtedly followed [the counsels] in Gracián's day and continue to do so in our own, even though some of these would certainly 'profess and call themselves Christians' " (30).

Gracián's "cold objectivity," however much in tune with "the tastes of an age of 'realism' in politics, both foreign and domestic" (38), probably accounts for his relative neglect by classical liberalism. Hispanists struggled to accommodate the Jesuit within a tradition that discovered in literature, or so it believed, values that transcended exchange value, and served precisely to counter, within national culture, the kind of "disingenuous opportunism which characterizes so much of [Gracián's] advice" (38). Canonic status was granted to works that, given the peculiar abstractness of capitalist relations, were able to "provide and sustain a basis for symbolic exchange value" (Doyle 14). Macabre attitudes to rationality, time, money, and energy could be offset by the arts and seemingly authenticated by human values prior and external to exchange. Hence the importance attributed to "literary value" or, as Walton would have it, Gracián's "universality." Doyle explains: "This issue is important for the discipline not so much because it helps sustain an inherent value for literature itself, but because in so doing it provides an apparently self-sustaining transcendental (objective) ground for *all* use and exchange values" (14).

Spain's advantage over England, as far as this antiutilitarian conservative ethic was concerned, lay in its preservation of certain mystic, ritual values that had been obliterated in more advanced economies. It lent itself far more readily, as a result, to the simulation of an organic community. Here again, for all his universal appeal, Gracián's insincerity, cynicism, and monadic selfishness jarred with the liberal ethic. His willful inconsistencies have continued to plague more recent critics, enamored as they are of architectonic order and unity (see Smith 70, 71–72). Again Doyle indicates a broader, sociological relevance:

> As an even greater requirement is placed upon the discipline to resolve problems of quantifying exchange value, the discipline has itself entered a condition of

> accelerating crisis. While even today much critical discourse is driven by an imperative towards symbolic harmonization this has taken the form of increasingly desperate attempts to reduce disparate and dissonant fictions to some kind of simulacrum of harmonic unity. (Doyle 15)

Literature as Value

Our point of access to Gracián will be his association with his patron, Don Vincencio Juan de Lastanosa, a cultivated nobleman of Huesca, whose home contained a scientific museum, an art gallery, and a library and served as the venue for a brilliant literary salon. Like the earlier Neoplatonic circles, in the tradition of which it stands, Lastanosa's literary salon provided a haven from an outside world hostile to finer feeling, in which Gracián was able to enjoy the "parentesco de corazones y de genios" (kinship of hearts and minds) (Gracián 163).[1]

While Gracián's relationship with Lastanosa demonstrates a residual dependence upon a feudal system of patronage, his desire to evade his order's control over his literary activity registers the impact of emergent relations of literary production (see Rodríguez 40). Gracián no longer circulates manuscripts privately: he sells his works publicly. Furthermore, within the nascent capitalist mode of production, exchange takes place via the market, which finds Gracián in his private correspondence discussing the book trade, along with financial transactions connected with his publishing ventures (e.g., Gracián 1130, 1142).

Lastanosa's private museum symptomizes a reaction to the consequent sense of degradation by market forces. For what does the Baroque tendency to pile up objects ceaselessly signify other than their withdrawal from circulation (see Hoyo, in Gracián xxxii–xxxiii)? It was Walter Benjamin who first pointed to the Baroque fascination with amorphous fragments: the seventeenth century conceived of knowledge as the process of storing—hence the creation of its vast libraries—in which all sense of totality is lost (Benjamin 184). The obsessive nature of the collector's zeal, Benjamin suggests, is offset by the chaotic arrangement of his curios.

We owe the market connection, however, to Terry Eagleton, who first noticed that eloquent silence in *The Origin of German*

Tragic Drama that is the commodity (see Eagleton, *Walter Benjamin* 25 ff.). Just as the common substance of all commodities—their "value"—allows them to circulate freely, so also can one symbol be exchanged, semantically, for any other in allegory. The collector—Lastanosa is a perfect example—raises things onto the same level of abstraction, through a process that sees metaphors transformed endlessly into metonymy: "Snatched into this space [of sheer contiguity], the object is liberated from the drudgery of usefulness, stripped of its exchange-value and so rescued from the fate of the commodity. Yet though what remains is in one sense its use-value, the collected object is not in fact used; thus it emerges from the fetishism of the commodity only to dip back once again" (61).

There is a connection that deserves to be pursued between the collector and Gracián's archetypal pilgrim, and between both and Benjamin's *flâneur.* The Baroque melancholic, as Benjamin himself discerned (Benjamin 149) and Gracián evinces, had a predilection for long journeys; he drifts somewhat aimlessly from court to court, "logrando en ellas todo género de prodigios de la naturaleza y del arte en pinturas, estatuas, tapicerías, librerías, joyas, armas, jardines y museos" (acquiring in them every kind of prodigy of nature and of art—relating to paintings, statues, tapestries, books, jewels, arms, gardens, and museums) (Gracián 144–145). Like his bourgeois descendant in the nineteenth century, this decadent aristocrat "displays in living motion something of the commodity's self-contradictory form" (Eagleton, *Walter Benjamin* 25). Both pilgrim and *flâneur* move through a comparable entrepreneurial ambiance, are drawn to the crowds yet remain aloof from them through the same garish dress, which "signifies the protest of a fading aura in the face of commodity production" (26). The *flâneur*'s "shabby-genteel peregrinations" (29) are already prefigured in the only too secular perambulations of Gracián's *Discreto*: "Buscó y gozó de todo lo bueno y lo mejor del mundo" (He sought after and experienced the best that there is) (Gracián 144). They share the same object of desire, the commodity: "más gusta de los objectos el que los ve una vez que el que muchas" (the one who enjoys objects most is the one who sees them not many times but once) (144). Once purchased, this commodity quickly loses its glitter and will soon be discarded as so much trash: "el primer día es una cosa para el gusto de su dueño, todos los demás para el de los extraños" (the first day's enjoyment belongs to the owner, the other days' to others) (144). For subject and object, it is a story of endless renewal, after the manner of the phoenix.

Organicism versus Animism

Juan Carlos Rodríguez discerns in Golden Age culture a clash between two productive matrices, associated respectively with feudalism and capitalism (Rodríguez 115–116). He characterizes the first as *organicism,* a term taken from Gaston Bachelard but broadened considerably so as to encompass a tradition that postulates the notion of substance as determinant. Organicism contrasts with *animism,* likewise taken from Bachelard but extended by Rodríguez to describe an ideology that derives from various medieval strands but that blossoms in the first, mercantilist phase of bourgeois development (i.e., in the "Renaissance").

Under organicism, the divine and earthly spheres are separated by an abyss: perfection stands opposed to imperfection, decay to eternal life. But these two spheres are also mutually dependent. Thus, if the sublunar world could not exist without being "informed" by the celestial, conversely the only evidence for the supernatural are its signs in nature. Hence the need to "save appearances," a concept that derives from the Scholastic, Aristotelian tradition and that is sometimes confused with superficially similar requirements of scientific empiricism (see Rodríguez 61 ff.). "Beauty" is the effect of informing influence on the order of the creation.

What is true of the relationship between the celestial and terrestrial spheres also applies to the body/soul dichotomy. For organicism, the notions of body and soul are radically different, in the sense that the soul is never "expressed" in the body, that is, "unified" with it or made to shine through it. The soul is the body's informing principle, without which the body could not live. The solution to disorders in the body, whether individual or social, is bleeding and the elimination of waste matter. The need to save appearances thus helps explain the relentless anality of the organicist vision, and in turn the melancholy of the Baroque.

For in the event of God's even partial withdrawal, the body ceases to be proximately informed, and turns into ugly, stinking matter (see Read, *Visions* Chap. 3).

The organicist need to "save appearances" derives from the very infrastructure of organicism and, not surprisingly, is clearly in evidence as regards language (see Bursill-Hall 39–40). Modistic or speculative grammar is based on a tripartite division between external objects, mediatory concepts, and words. For Thomists, the mind per se is a blank sheet or tabula rasa, dependent for its ideas on stimuli from the outside world, operating via the senses. In its extreme form, this model presupposes a naive realism, according to which consciousness contains a mirror image of external phenomena. As the modistae were the first to insist, however, what is actually conveyed by language is the mind's recreation of the universe it perceives, achieved through the creative power of the mind, called the *intellectus agens*. It was possible to distinguish within language itself between an *internal* discourse (*verbum mentis*) and an *external* discourse (*verbum oris*). The latter was derived from the former by specific transformational processes, a relatively embryonic distinction between inside and outside that allows little space for a subject. "Soy quien soy" (I am who I am) was the rallying cry of a remarkably unfissured aristocrat, who, even in his villainy, lacks interstices of being (see Read, *Birth and Death* 16–17).

The medieval view of the world as a book accords closely with this "speculative" view of language. Thus, if one must struggle to decipher its signs, the Book of Nature remains an "espejo grande de Dios" (huge mirror of God) (Gracián 539) and in consequence amenable to interpretation: "deformes caracteres, pero informados de mucho espíritu" (deformed characters, but informed with much spirit), as Gracián comments of his own "inscriptions" (37). Even though we have only a few traces ("borrones") to guide us, Truth is not hidden in the depths of learned minds but "en los inmortales caracteres de los libros" (in the immortal characters of books) (739). It is, one might say, visible in principle.

Language, it follows, is integral to the whole dialectic of life as a dream or a theatrical performance. The spirit is revealed in the earthly sphere only through appearances, which are something to be admitted, at least until the passions are corrected and the eyes disenchanted. In striking contrast to the animist facility to produce nudes, organicism balks at the vacuum that is the bare body—the young girl is always veiled ("siempre atapada" [97]). Perforce it treats nudity as a sign, for example, of poverty or of licentiousness. Language is the most important body of signs, the indispensable dress of a Truth obliged to disguise itself in a world that despises the unadorned (472–473). Faced by the distinction between the redundant ("Asiatic") and concise ("laconic") styles, Gracián can hedge his bets, support the virtues of both according to occasion, by recommending the former to orators and the latter to moral philosophers. But in the last instance his preferences must lie with the historian's need to expand, comment upon, and decorate. Otherwise, we are left with only the bare facts and events: "La desnuda narración es como el canto llano; sobre él se echa después el agradable artificioso contrapunto. Es anómalo el humano gusto, que apetece en un mismo manjar mil diferencias de sainetes" (The bare narration is like a simple melody to which is subsequently added the pleasing artifice of the counterpoint. Human taste is unusual insofar as it craves a thousand different seasonings in one and the same dish) (500). In Gracián's hands, the "laconic" style becomes a source of difficulty, that is, a kind of dress.

(Bodily) appearances, then, are indispensable. As Rodríguez insists (205), strictly speaking, feudal organicism never posed the problem of the relation between inside and outside. It was, quite simply, an opposition incompatible with the "fullness" of the Chain of Being. Feudalism is characterized by social transparency, deriving from the homogenizing writing that the signs of God impose on things. In a manner of speaking, the superstructure collapses into the base, so that social appearances become substantial. Differences of estate between individuals (equal in spirit only) were accordingly marked by their clothes. When a sign proved incomprehensible, it was simply because it had not been *read* as it should, not because its interior was hidden by an opaque crust. The distinction between public and private only became really possible with the contradictory coexistence of two types of social relations. The pressure of animism forced organicism to accommodate the view that things have a hidden interior, which cannot be reached at first glance. The opposition becomes a commonplace in the pages of Gracián: "Las cosas comúnmente no pasan por lo que son, sino por lo que parecen. Son muchos más los necios que los entendidos, páganse aquéllos de la apariencia, y aunque atienden éstos a la substancia, prevalece el engaño y estímanse las cosas por de fuera" (Things are commonly not taken for what they are but for what they seem. Fools outnumber the wise: the former are guided by appearances, and although the latter take substance into account, deceit prevails and only the outside of things counts) (Gracián 109).

Even under the new conditions, however, the inside/outside distinction remains a problem of reading. Organicism's interior has nothing to do with the "inner spirit" of which the animist speaks. Its "substantial forms" involve acts of incarnation, which preclude the very idea of an interior that can be unhitched from its exterior, a spirit separable from its shell (see Rodríguez 206–207). Transubstantiation, as such, is unthinkable. So when Gracián contrasts appearances with reality, he is simply registering the partial eclipse of God's signs, in conditions of life that are no longer feudal: "son raros los que miran por dentro, y muchos los que se pagan de lo aparente" (rare are those who look within, and many are those who rest content with what they can see) (Gracián 178).

The Ideology of the *Ingenio*

The attack upon corporativism derives in the first instance from a latent medieval Augustinianism, along with other voluntaristic traditions that involved the relinquishing of things corporeal (see Rodríguez 66 ff.). In the process the rift between inner and outer reality widens: nominalists, for example, doubted whether the interaction between the senses and the active intellect could actually produce true knowledge of the universe (see Padley 233). The ground is thus prepared for the emergence of the Neoplatonic free soul or protosubject. Michelangelo—the example is Rodríguez's (Rodríguez 88)—sees in the marble an inner nucleus, to be extracted by the removal of all superfluous, contingent matter. The process is one of denuding, of bringing to light, typically (as far as literature is concerned) in the form of a sonnet. It involves not the suppression of matter, but its spiritualization. The soul is liberated after a long peregrination, enacted literally by Gracián's Critilo, along with other shipwrecked swains of the Baroque (94–95). Gracián, however, is writing at a point by which the animist attack upon substantialism has been effectively neutralized by a resurgence of organicism. While mercantile relations continued to develop throughout the sixteenth century, ideologically the bourgeoisie was obliged to compromise increasingly with feudalism. As Rodríguez explains: "En el XVII es ya imposible distinguir: el organicismo domina en todos los terrenos y, por ejemplo, no se puede decir con precisión si la construcción de un soneto es debida a la *adopción*, por parte del organicismo, de una temática animista, o si es debida a la *intervención* del animismo sobre ciertos temas organicistas y feudalizantes" (By the seventeenth century it is impossible to differentiate: organicism predominates in all fields and, for example, one cannot say precisely whether the construction of a sonnet is due to the adoption, on the part of organicism, of animist thematics, or whether it is due to intervention by animism in certain organicist, feudalizing themes) (354).

The "ingenio" (wit), a quintessentially animist concept (although prefigured in the Thomistic "intellectus agens"), still bears in Gracián much of the ideological load of the animist project. Under its benevolent rays, the world is redeemed from sin, particularly in Spain where, even in Roman times, writers refused to "subject themselves" to the "rigors" of discourse (Gracián 457–459). By its very nature, the "ingenio" is an insane *excess* ("grado de demencia" [512]) destined to conflict with law and order: "Socorra la razón a la autoridad. Un ingenio anómalo siempre fué mayor, porque se deja llevar del conatural ímpetu en el discurrir y de la valentía en el sutilizar; que el atarse a la prolijidad de un discurso, y a la dependencia de una traza, le embaraza y le limita" (Let reason lend assistance to authority. An unpredictable mind is always above such things, since it is governed by the natural impetus of thought and by the rigors of discriminating discourse. It feels constrained and thwarted when tied to the prolixity of discourse and to dependence upon any preestablished plan) (459).

Of course, Gracián's support of the "ingenio" was by no means unqualified. To begin with, as an ideologue of the absolutist state, he recognized the need to channel its (re)productive energy in the interests of the prevailing (feudal) relations of production: "Toda agudeza que participa de razonamiento y de discurso es más ingeniosa, porque es asunto de la más noble acción del ánimo" (The kind of wit that depends upon reasoning and discourse is more subtle, because it falls within the most noble action of the soul) (349). Moreover, absolutism was the result of pressure from the bourgeoisie, which itself had a vested interest in avoiding social anarchy. Clearly, the debate over the freedom of the "ingenio" was bound to be intense.

Gracián's preoccupation with tidiness ("aliño") and cleanliness ("artificioso aseo") is the hallmark of the bourgeoisie and contrasts notably with the organicist's slackness and overt anality. The disorder of the Baroque magicians' dens and alchemists' laboratories, not to mention the confusion of allegorical scenery (see Benjamin 188), stand opposed to the tight-fitting clothes of the bourgeoisie and its commitment, even on the level of syntax, to "hacer un cuerpo atado con alguna traza" (construct a body subject to some specific plan) (Gracián 460). In contrast, the virtues of narrative closure and textual unity, as the thinly disguised analogue of social harmony in general, could be made to serve different ideological purposes: "Todo compuesto ha de tener partes, unas principales y mayores, y éstas no han de ser muchas, otras, menores, que componen aquellas primeras. Todas requieren conexión y orden" (Every composite thing must have parts, some important and essential (and these cannot be many), other parts, less important, which constitute the former. All presuppose interconnection and order) (469). Closure is achieved not merely vertically, when disparate threads are drawn together under a common "head," but horizontally, on the level of discourse: "como sucede en los empeños, que cuanto más se van dificultando, se goza más de la acertada salida" (as in the case of pledges, the greater the complexity, the greater the chance of a happy outcome) (471).

Gracián's ultimately ambiguous attitude to the "ingenio" underlines the ideological complexity of the textual dynamics he is describing, which facilitate not merely the play of desire but its playing *out*. The initiated who are occupied in making sense of a piece of language are distracted from other things, including social subversion: "no se les ha de dar lugar a la censura, ocupándolos en el entender" (they are to be given no opportunity for censorship, by occupying them in the task of understanding) (217). Desire is drawn into the labyrinth of minutiae and kept circulating until it seeps quite harmlessly away. Art, on this basis, serves to defuse social tensions. It teaches us to relinquish our disruptive desires through a delicate interplay between the sublimely infinite and the prudently finite: "Habló del ingenio con él, quien le llamó finitamente infinito" (He who described it as finitely infinite spoke of wit with wit) (453). It is this interplay, I believe, that Benjamin had in mind when he spoke, regarding the Baroque, of "the playful miniaturization of reality and the introduction of a reflective infinity of thought into the finite space of a profane fate" (Benjamin 83). Such discussion must connect at some point, which we prefer to leave unspecified, after the manner of Benjamin himself,[2] with the successful attempt by the aristocracy to block the growth of an *autonomous* state, and thereby the logic of capitalist development in the Spain of the Transition.

Gracián's predilection for discursive complexity naturally colored his attitude toward the "plain" style ("liso, corriente, sin afectación, pero propio, casto y terso" [smooth, fluid, without affectation, but proper, pure and polished] [Gracián 504]) of the emergent bourgeoisie. He appreciates the importance of this style when the onus is upon the communicative *use* of language: "es sustancial, verdadero, y así el más apto para el fin del habla, que es darnos a entender" (it is substantial, truthful, and therefore most appropriate for the purpose of speech, which is to make ourselves understood) (504), and on such occasions he is only too eager to wax lyrical upon the wholesome nature of plain bread. But he was also only too aware that language performs a crucial role in the maintenance of social distinctions. Accordingly, he is careful to draw attention to stylistic nuances *within* the plain style that help sustain them (507).

Comparable ideological tensions and overdeterminations are in evidence in Gracián's discussion of conceits. To begin with, his theory of "agudeza" presupposes the centrality of the organicist metaphor of the world as a book, insofar as the drawing of equivalencies is unthinkable outside the notion of the Chain of Being. However, these same punctual exchanges that appear and disappear in a flash correspond, in their abstraction, with the operations of exchange value within a capitalist mode of production. Value or meaning is generated from the positions assumed within a system of relationships. Crucially, conceits conceal the labor that went into them, through the purely spontaneous coupling of objects (see Eagleton, *Walter Benjamin* 11). (Gracián himself, we recall, repeatedly insists that the essence of all artifice is its own dissimulation.) However, at the same time as it is robbed of its referential value, the conceit foregrounds the material qualities of language: "Mas el nervio del estilo consiste en la intensa profundidad del verbo" (But the nerve of style lies in the intense profundity of the word) (Gracián 499). The convulsion of language lends great plasticity to its elements; words recharged with meaning glow with the aura of commodities.

Finally, the body is also transformed into a locus for ideological conflict. A lingering animism causes Gracián to resist all corporeal influence. To the tyranny of the humors he opposes the power of the will: "Una gran capacidad no se rinde a la vulgar alternación de los humores" (A superior talent never succumbs to the common sway of the humors) (113); and to the attraction of nature, the discipline of art. Culture and civilization constitute an act of defiance in the face of the inertia of matter. And yet, by that strangest of ironies that is the return of the repressed, an art seemingly mortgaged to morality rediscovers the sensuous surfaces that are the body. The activity of the "ingenio" is, when all is said and done, an aesthetic: "No se contenta el ingenio con sola la verdad, como el juicio, sino que aspira a la hermosura" (Wit never rests content with truth alone, as does judgment, but rather aspires to beauty) (239). Its driving force is not reason but desire. And on this basis, which was paradoxically the negation of all essentialism, Gracián proceeded to outline a whole new way of life.

Market Strategies

The degree to which Gracián was able to isolate *jouissance,* or "la fuerza del deleite" (47), as an abstract category, corresponds with the material level of development of capitalist exchange in (parts of) contemporary Spain. The dynamics of the concept are those of commodification, the secret of which is the constant "soliciting" of desire through the stimulation of both literal and intellectual appetites (105). The quest for novelty, whereby to offset the familiarity that diminishes desire, results in a spiral of increasingly imaginative creations. One need only attend to the packaging, "echando un papel blanco y nuevo" (by throwing on some new, white paper) (974). As far as the commodity is concerned, the surface is the true essence of life. Readers are attracted only by the rhetorical form of language, whatever its actual content. To sell anything, essential qualities are largely irrelevant: as with food, it is the sauces that whet the buyer's appetite (136–137).

But if desire must be constantly fed—its converse is the disgust provoked by all repetition—it should never be to the point of satiety. The one golden rule of all commodification is that it should leave the individual unsatisfied (228); while being as ostentatious as possible, any purchase should allow room for innovation (167). It must, in other words, combine instant availability with a certain remoteness. The more it "costs" to plumb its depths, the higher the commodity's price: "Entendimiento con fondos logra eternidades. Lo que mucho vale, mucho cuesta" (An understanding with hidden depths is equivalent to eternities. What is worth a lot costs a lot) (167).

What may seem like the outer reaches of the universe is in fact the confined space of the capitalist mode of production. Fetishized and estranged appearances are, after all, a necessary feature of this system. The value of a commodity is the quantity of socially necessary labor required for its production, but it enters consciousness as a property of things. As Callinicos observes, capitalism "dissimulates itself in presenting itself" (Callinicos 50). "Reality," given a slight Althusserian twist, is no "hidden mystery" underlying appearances, but the structured relations of these appearances. Historically, these relations enter into crisis during the Transition: "Política contienda es qué importe más, la realidad o la apariencia" (It is a political question as to which is more important, reality or appearance) (Gracián 112), with the balance of power tilted suddenly in favor of appearance: "Donde pensaréis que hay substancia, todo es circunstancia, y lo que parece más sólido, es más hueco, y toda cosa hueca, vacía" (Where you think there is substance, all is circumstance, and what seems most solid is actually empty, and what seems empty is emptier still) (879).

The sublime, the infinite, the mysterious, the hidden are all categories indispensable to the smooth functioning of the market economy: "Gran leción es ésta del saberse hacer estimar, de saber vender una eminencia, afectando el encubrirla, para conservarla y aun aumentarla con el deseo" (A great lesson is that which teaches how to assert one's value, how to sell a singular object, by feigning to cover it, in order to preserve it, and so enhancing its desirability) (105). Thus the more freely available jewels are, the less they are worth, whatever their actual carat value. For exchange-value is the phenomenal form of "value," that is, the form in which value usually *appears* to us: "*Saber vender sus cosas*. No basta la intrínseca bondad dellas, que no todos muerden la sustancia ni miran por dentro" (*Know how to sell your wares*. Their intrinsic worth does not suffice, since not all men test for quality or look within) (191). Gold and silver, as the universal equivalence ("medida y contrapeso de todas las cosas" [measure and counterweight for all things] [375]) constitute the most abstract category of all. However, while intrinsically worthless, money is the appearance assumed by the productive forces of labor. Its richness is the converse of the worker's alienation. Money is power (81–82), and consequently to be respected, even worshipped.

The world of commodification can conceive of no other possible scheme of things. El Siri's suggestion that true happiness lies in an absence of desire is greeted with genuine incomprehension and horror by El Valvezi: "es un querer reducir la noble humana naturaleza a la nada. Pues desear nada, conseguir nada y gozar nada ¿qué otra cosa es que aniquilar el gusto, anonadar la vida y reducirlo todo a la nada?" (it is tantamount to reducing our noble human nature to naught; since to desire nothing, to aim for nothing, and to attain nothing—what is it but to annihilate taste, to negate life, and to reduce everything to nothingness?) (957). And if desire is life, its absence can only be the ultimate horror of death: "si nada hay que desear, todo es de temer: dicha desdicha. Donde acaba el deseo comienza el temor" (if there is nothing desired, all is feared: happiness, unhappiness. Where desire finishes, fear begins) (204).

The whole world is recast in the image of the fair. Commercial thinking penetrates into the very core of Gracián's being, colors his very turns of phrase: we are told, by way of quite general advice, "no hacer negocio del no negocio" (not to make a deal of something) (184), "tomar el pulso luego a los negocios" (to know how to sell oneself) (187), and so on. Face-to-face encounters of quite an ordinary kind are seen, in an increasingly alienated society, through the prism of business: "Es ardid del hombre negociante descuidar la voluntad para acometerla, que es vencida en siendo convencida" (It is a favorite trick of the salesman to disregard the will one moment, only to assail it the next, for once it is convinced, it is conquered) (208). It is all a question of buying and selling: a little sweetness here, a little steel there. Human virtues are remodeled according to commercial values, from which it is but a short step to the denigration of the intellectual in favor of the more practical man: "*Tener un punto de negociante.* No todo sea especulación, haya también acción. Los muy sabios son fáciles de engañar, porque, aunque saben lo extraordinario, ignoran lo ordinario del vivir" (*Have a touch of the businessman.* Let not all be speculation; there should also be action. The very wise are easy to deceive, because although they know about the extraordinary, they are ignorant of what is ordinary in life) (212). The root of the problem, as Gracián explains, is the division of labor, primarily between manual and mental work. Daringly, established hierarchies are reversed: "Procure, pues, el varón tener algo de negociante. . . . ¿De qué sirve el saber si no es pláctico? Y el saber vivir es hoy el verdadero saber" (A man should endeavor, then, to be something of a businessman. What is the use of knowledge if it serves no practical purpose? And to know how to live is these days true knowledge) (212).

Clearly, Gracián is a writer who awaits discovery by the New Right. Neoliberals are notoriously less easily shocked than their classical forebears. Appropriately read, Gracián might well be deployed to justify a little corporate fraud: "Floreció en el siglo de oro la llaneza; en éste de yerro, la malicia" (Plain speaking flourished in the golden age; in our age of iron, wickedness) (209). Justification would equally not be lacking for the dismantling of the welfare state. Great skill is required, Gracián warns, to help someone without personal risk: "*No perecer de desdicha ajena.* Conozca al que está en el lodo, y note que le reclamará para hacer consuelo del recíproco mal" (*Do not die of another's woe.* Take note of who is stuck in the mire, and be warned that he will try to alleviate his suffering by making it yours) (225). True, the Jesuit sometimes strives for balance: we should live (he recommends) neither entirely for ourselves, nor entirely for others. But the very existence of the "individual" and "society" as prevailing conceptual categories indicates the real drift of his thought: individualism is the order of the day.

Counting the Cost

"De lo que gustaba mucho Andrenio, y tanto que no pudo contener la risa, era de ver rodar los trajes y dar vueltas los usos, y más mirando hacia España, donde no hay cosa estable en esto del vestir" (What pleased Andrenio most—so much so that he could not contain his laughter—was seeing the relay in fashion and the shifts in custom, particularly in the case of Spain, where there is nothing stable in matters of dress) (969). Once desire has emerged as an entity, abstracted from particulars, it can be seen in all its irrationality; one fashion follows frenetically upon the next in one long mad pursuit. Andrenio finds the phenomenon amusing, but is aware of its more serious, even pathological implications. The movement of desire is a symptom of social decay; it charts a course away from Paradise. The dire consequences of the pervasiveness of exchange value are particularly apparent as regards the "ingenio," which, as one more commodity, is the mere function of obsessions that work through it. A subject that would possess the whole world lacks any self-possession, in other words, is incapable of self-knowledge. A utopian impulse survives in the almost unthinkable absence of desire: "Estoy tan lejos de decir que consiste la felicidad en tenerlo todo, que antes digo que en tener nada, desear nada y despreciarlo todo; y ésta es la única felicidad" (I am not saying by any means that happiness consists of having everything, rather of having nothing, desiring nothing and despising everything. This is true happiness) (951).

As Terry Eagleton reminds us, the preconditions of desire's affirmation, namely its isolation as an independent force, are also those of its denunciation (see Eagleton, *Ideology* 159–160). The perennial creativity of the "ingenio" is the "tyranny of pleasure" (Gracián 621) that drives the market; it is the "vile profiteering" (610) of the modern city, raised to aesthetic status. The "interest" generated by a work of art is strictly financial, "the king of all vices, served and obeyed by all" (702). The average grasping bourgeois is a philistine, who can talk of nothing else but money and how to make it. The "discreto," in the face of such widespread crassness, tries to live the age of gold within (95), only to discover that gold is gold, and that solitude is itself but a symptom of the social sterility he flees.

The miseries of life, portrayed by Gracián in existential, universal terms, are in reality historically localized, in a society unable to "assume" a mercantilist infrastructure. Ideologically, secularization proceeds, but subject to notable compromises. In the literature of the period—*El criticón* is a classic example—chronological movement is grasped spatially, "as in the days of the creation, when it was not history which was taking place" (Benjamin 91). The same loss of historical dynamic is apparent elsewhere. In language, for example, laws of change mimic the process of commodification, as one product of labor exchanges with another: "Hasta en el hablar hay su novedad cada día, pues el lenguaje de hoy ha docientos años parece algarabía.... Atendieron y oyeron en el primero decía *fillo,* en el segundo *fijo,* el tercero, *hijo,* y el cuarto ya decía *gixo,* a lo andaluz" (Even in speech novelty is the order of the day: today's language two hundred years ago seems gibberish.... They took notice and heard the first man saying *fillo;* the second, *fijo;* the third, *hijo;* and the fourth was even saying *gixo,* as in Andalusia") (971). A fifth cognate exists, but cannot be identified (and so is not heard); language does not (d)evolve teleologically, but in accordance with the frozen lunges of desire. Nostalgic for an earlier age, Andrenio wonders why language was not left in its pristine perfection, instead of being subjected to change. Why, after all, does language change? "No más de por mudar, sucediendo lo mismo en las palabras que en los sombreros" (Simply for the sake of change, in which respect words are no different from hats) (971).

For Gracián, language is the best barometer of social decay. Debased in itself, it is also the very medium of the general perversion: "negóciase en el aire con el aire" (air is traded through air) (221). The organicist counterpoises his own physiocratic conception of language to the mercantilist equation of constant linguistic capital with money. His experience of language was conditioned by barter, as opposed to commodification. Work was less remote to him than it was to those who simply lived off their income. Accordingly he was less tempted to equate language with true wealth: "Los desvanecidos se pagan del viento. Las palabras han de ser prendas de las obras, y así han de tener el valor" (Vain folk take pleasure in wind. Words should be the tokens of deeds, if they are to have any value) (196). Gracián doubtless found confirmation of his persuasions in the spiraling inflation currently ravaging the Spanish economy, the reach of which appeared to extend to verbal currency. The area of the lexicon that had suffered most damage was that which sustained organicist ideology. Some came to feel that to give one's word of honor was in effect to give nothing of value: "Hacen precio de la honra y pagan con el viento de unas buenas palabras" (People prize honor and pay with the wind of a few nice words) (202). This kind of semantic shift in language is often quite slow, to be measured in terms of centuries rather than decades, but in certain cultural situations—the Baroque is an obvious example—it can be much more rapid (see Williams 11–12).

Needless to say, Gracián attributes the decline of Spain not to the defeat of the new elements ("amigos de mudanzas peligrosas" [those enamored of dangerous changes] [972]) but, on the contrary, to their pervasive influence and success in promoting their own interests (Gracián 562, 727–728). As an argument, it was far from being implausible: "progress" had been achieved at some cost, as far as some sections of the population were concerned (see Maravall, Chap. 1). Social displacement, particularly from the land to urban centers, was occurring on a large scale, with catastrophic consequences, not least of all for the most elemental human relationships: "Ninguno se ahorraba con el otro, ni hermanos con hermanos, ni padres con hijos" (Nobody empathized with anyone else, neither brothers with sisters nor parents with children) (Gracián 704). Gracián's attention naturally focused on the cities, as the center of bourgeois activity: "Sabed que con el tiempo, que todo lo trastorna, fué creciendo esta ciudad, aumentándose en gente y confusión, que toda gran corte es Babilonia" (And so, with the passing of time, which transforms everything, this city arose, growing in population and confusion, to become the Babylon that every court is) (802). Here, the modern experience of living was taking place in a new structuration of space and time. The massed inhabitants were lonely crowds; for the first time, people had the experience of not knowing their neighbors: "No se conocían ya unos a otros, achaque de poblaciones grandes" (People no longer knew one another, one of the drawbacks of large towns) (802–803). Friendships were an oasis in the desert that was modern life, but in a society corroded by market relations, how was one to know a *true* friend? "Más vale ser engañado en el precio que en la mercadería" (It is preferable to be deceived over price than over the quality of the merchandise) (193).

Divisions are not simply inter- but intra-individual. With the inside now radically split from the outside, the organicist struggles to make sense of the world as a book: "los humanos corazones est[á]n tan sellados y inescrutables, asegúros que el mejor letor se pierde" (human hearts are so sealed and inscrutable that, I assure you, even the best reader is lost) (877). What chance has one of reading others when it is impossible to read oneself? In the world of capitalist monads, what is most hidden from us is what is closest. Ironically, as the individual's geographical horizons expanded, those of the self gradually shrank. The ego was the last bit of private property, an emptiness, hollowed out of being, that clamored to be filled: "Aquel decir *mío, mío* y todo es *mío* y siempre *mío,* y nada para vos" (That insistent *mine, mine* and all is *mine* and always will be *mine,* and nothing for you) (706).

It is difficult for us to fully appreciate the shock of Gracián's confrontation with the modern, and inevitably so: by definition, modernity has been integrated fully into our own structure of feeling. In contrast, what we do see as strange, bizarre, even slightly mad are those organicist values, such as "honor," that Gracián's own texts naturalize. However, the Devil's Advocate would not be alone in insisting that Gracián's values at least have the virtue of being *social.* As such, they serve to defamiliarize the individualism that is now taken so much for granted and is characterized by its own kind of insanity. By an act of imagination, we may come to see the solipsism of the modern windowless monad through Gracián's eyes: "No decían ya '¿Qué dirán?'; sino '¿qué diré yo dél que no diga él de mí, y mucho más?' Desta suerte, mancomunados todos, echaron fuera el *¿Qué dirán?*, y al punto se perdió la vergüenza, faltó la honra, retiróse el recato, huyó el pundonor; ya no se atendía a obligaciones, con que todo se asoló" (One no longer asked "What will people say?," but "what can I say about him that he will not say about me, and much more besides?" In this way everyone generally forgot about "What will people say?," and instantly all sense of shame disappeared, honor was no more, modesty retired, and self-respect took flight; obligations were no longer recognized, with the result that desolation reigned) (803).

In response to bourgeois pressure, organicism attacks animism at its key points, one of the most important of which is women. That Gracián participates in the strong misogynist tradition is obvious even from the most cursory glance at his work. In addition to numerous negative references to women, of a perfunctory nature, there are Oedipal myths that foreground the violence of emasculating maternal figures (707), not to mention conspiracy theories recounting the usurpation of power by women (565). Not surprisingly, they are accompanied by male fantasies about the possibility of bypassing woman in the procreational process (375). The absurdity of such beliefs—by any reckoning Gracián's was a staunchly patriarchal society—suggests that something more than gender is at issue.

Predictably, the postmodernist critic has made much of this aspect of Gracián's work, insisting that "man's self-realization is at the expense of woman's submission" (Smith 73). But his discussion remains abstract and idealist. "Public" and "private" are not the universal categories Smith takes them to be but, as we have seen, are associated historically with the rise of animism, "donde la 'mujer' comienza a representar (a condensar) el significado eje que la especial estructura familiar supondrá siempre en las relaciones burguesas" (in which "woman" begins to represent (to condense) the crucial meaning that the particular structure of the family will always have in bourgeois relations) (Rodríguez 368). From within its private sphere, animism developed a new kind of discourse, which, while aggressively lean and masculine, was also archetypally feminine in its ability to defy feudal law through a play of masks and personae. Art and the aesthetic embody the values that will fuel the bourgeois enterprise: the feminine will return through concepts "fertile" in origin and words "pregnant" with meaning, which divide and multiply endlessly.

The Time before First

The postmodern critic engages "the most radical critique of metaphysics" (Smith 93) to explore in Gracián the "ethnic and sexual 'deviance' which obstinately refuses to be integrated" (92). Predictably, in his deconstructive capacity, he is drawn to Gracián's discourse on origins in the opening pages of *El criticón*. As Smith is quick to point out, even before he acquires the power of speech, "Andrenio is determined by his relation to *écriture*.... Even the naked body is not innocent of inscription; and nor is the desert island untouched by culture" (68). With telling skill, Smith illustrates how Andrenio arrives at a sense of (social) identity in isolation, that is, even before he meets Critilo. Andrenio tells his story from fragments that point to what cannot be acknowledged, "a time before first" (69). The problem, as the deconstructionist suggests, is one of allocating an origin for Andrenio's discourse: "Gracián inadvertently reveals that there can be no zero knowledge and experience, that the pure presence or still center of subjectivity is always preceded and under-written by textuality (69).

Now this attempt to assimilate language to textual play is all very well, but it is necessary to remind deconstructionists, along with their petit bourgeois Romantic forebears, that the foundation of language lies in production. As Rossi Landi has argued, objects must be produced before they can be used in a nonproductive way (Rossi Landi 181). Language, in this respect, is no different from a motorcar. Nobody wishes to contest the validity of the ludic dimension—made much of by modern philosophers of the pleasure principle, such as Marcuse and Norman O. Brown—but if play is to be a serious possibility for most people, the question of liberation from need has to be debated, together with the kind of future (classless) society that is likely to bring it about. By the same token the "potential of play [in Gracián] would be properly addressed" (Smith 72) if we had rather more from the postmodernist in the way of sociopolitical analysis, as opposed to gestural references to "those historical and material factors that go to make up the place from which he wrote" (91).

It is above all in matters of language that Smith demonstrates the deconstructionist's horror of the materiality of productive labor. Gracián, it is true, encourages his idealism: "dos niños arrojados de industria en una isla se inventaron lenguaje para comunicarse y entenderse" (two children abandoned on purpose on an island invented language in order to be able to communicate with, and understand, each other) (Gracián 522). What is so scandalous about this fantasy is the fact that it ignores the generations of labor required for the production of any natural language. The "artifice" without which nature is, according to Gracián, "perverted" (522) is a code word for this labor. For labor is what transforms nature into artifact. The materials may be natural, the product is not. There can be no "zero knowledge," to use Smith's phrase, because language is underwritten not by "textuality" but by past work accumulated within language as within any artifact. Its "inexhaustible proliferation" is the condensed labor of earlier linguistic workers.

Language offers to every member of a speech community an immediately accessible legacy, a "constant capital," in the form of the labor crystallized in it (see Rossi Landi 146 ff.). Andrenio draws unthinkingly upon it when he reflects learnedly upon the nature of being and identity (Gracián 523–524) and when he eludes himself as to his own linguistic self-sufficiency: "¡Qué de veces, y *sin voces,* me lo pregunté a mí mismo, tan necio como curioso!" (How many times, and *without words as such,* did I ask myself this, as foolish as I was curious) (523, emphasis added). It is an act of ingratitude perilously easy to commit, insofar as the artifact presents itself as a seamless whole, as if it were a product of nature rather than of work. But when Andrenio, like certain modern linguists, starts to flaunt his innate *creativity* ("¡Qué de soliloquios hacía tan interiores[!]" [How many silent soliloquies I delivered!] [524]), it is time to point to the individual's dependence upon the other, and consequently upon the inalienably social basis of language. This other is initially an "imaginary" self ("duplicábame, aun no bien singular" [I duplicated myself, was singular no longer] [523]), subsequently an Oedipal imago, identification with which completes the process of socialization: "Tú, Critilo, me preguntas quién soy yo y yo deseo saberlo de ti. Tu eres el primer hombre que hasta hoy he visto y en ti me hallo retratado más al vivo que en los mudos cristales de una fuente" (You, Critilo, ask me who I am, and I wish to learn this from you. You are the first man that I have seen until today, and in you I find myself depicted in a manner more lifelike than in the silent mirror of the stream) (523). The natural man can only become civilized if he acquires the necessary tools, be these hammers, rescued from his wrecked boat, or words, bequeathed to him by a shipwrecked comrade.

If Andrenio is less natural than at first he seems, the "Man" who presides over the Creation is similarly less universal than Gracián would have us believe. Indeed, he is none other than the aggressive, grasping subject of mercantile capitalism: "no se contentaba con menos que con todo el Universo y aun le parecía poco" (he was content with nothing less than the whole Universe, and even this seemed to him insufficient) (525). Gracián's grandly totalizing gestures belie the historical specificity of this flawed subjectivity, whose freedom enchains its victim and drives it to self-destruction. The extension of Spain's empire depended upon individuals modeled upon this prototype: "Corta le parece la superficie de la tierra, y así penetra y mina sus entrañas en busca del oro y de la plata, para satisfacer en algo su codicia; ocupa y embaraza el aire con lo empinado de sus edificios, dando algún desahogo a su soberbia; surca los mares y sonda sus más profundos senos" (The surface of the earth seems limiting [to Man], and so he penetrates and mines its insides in search of gold and silver, in order to satisfy his greed to some extent; he occupies and obstructs space with his towering buildings, giving vent to his pride; he ploughs the seas and plumbs its most hidden depths) (525). Masquerading in this way as the very essence of Christian mythology are the degraded appetites of everyday bourgeois existence.

Having naturalized bourgeois ideology (and so to some extent neutralized his critique of it), Gracián lacks any *historical* alternative to the social perversion he describes. The only recourse is to disengage from society, through a process of regression. Critilo confirms our suspicion that Andrenio is civilized man reborn: "Privilegio único del primer hombre y tuyo llegar a ver con novedad y con advertencia la grandeza, la hermosura, el concierto, la firmeza y la variedad de esta gran máquina creada. Fáltanos la admiración comúnmente a nosotros, porque falta la novedad, y con ésta la advertencia" (It is yours and the first man's sole privilege to see with freshness and awareness the grandeur, beauty, design, stability, and variety of this great created machine. Others often lack the element of astonishment, because the novelty is lacking, and with it the awareness) (527). Art serves to liberate us from the deadening effect of reification, to teach us to appreciate the loving labor bestowed upon the world by its Creator. But this can only be a partial, temporary solution: contemplative suspension must be constantly renewed, for the simple reason that the act of contemplation itself defines the process of commodification. And so at the very moment when he or she seems most to evade the effects of reification, the subject is caught up further in its mechanisms.

The tensions in Gracián's text are better understood if we peel away its separate layers: on the purely mental level, God and his creation are a result of men's self-estrangement, whereby the latter attribute their essential powers to entities lying outside themselves; in materialist terms, it is capitalist relations of production that alienate the worker both from the product of his labor and from his labor itself. Myth and history combine to produce a text scarred by the dynamics of commodification: "Pero está ya muy vulgarizada [la perfección], que nos suspenden las cosas, no por grandes, sino por nuevas. No se repara ya en los superiores empleos por conocidos, y así andamos mendigando niñerías en la novedad, para acallar nuestra curiosa solicitud con la extravagancia. Gran hechizo es el de la novedad, que como todo lo tenemos tan visto, pagámonos de juguetes nuevos, así de la naturaleza como del arte" (But [perfection] is now commonplace; we are overawed not by the grandeur but by the novelty of things. We no longer notice superior feats through sheer familiarity, and so go around begging knickknacks in order to satisfy our curious craving for the extravagant. Powerful is the spell of novelty; as we know only too well, we are charmed by new playthings, whether of nature or of art) (531). Grim necessity, in the form of the hunger, brings to an end Andrenio's stroll through the marvels of the Creation, and reminds him (and us) of the drab division of labor that makes such leisurely activity possible only for the few: "abatiéndome de la más alta contemplación a tan materiales empleos" (falling from the highest contemplation to the most material of concerns) (531).

"Cartesian Linguistics"

Whereas the importance of the conflict between the Jesuits and the Jansenists to an understanding of the work of Gracián has been realized for some time (see Pelegrín 85 n. 1), its linguistic ramifications, so far as I am aware, remain unexplored. In what follows, I propose to illustrate how these ramifications relate to the discussion so far.

As is well known, in recent years linguists have debated the ideas on language emanating from the Jansenists' schools of Port Royal.[3] In order to legitimate his own Transformational Generative Grammar, Chomsky traced it back to Cartesian mentalism, particularly as embodied in Port Royal linguistic scholarship. He saw Cartesian linguistics as having an inner and an outer aspect, or, to use his technical terms, a "deep" and a "surface structure." The transformation of the former into the latter is accomplished by certain inborn principles of the mind, which presupposes a rationalist subject possessed of a sophisticated mental apparatus. Such a view is anathema to most present-day descriptive linguists, whose perspective has been far more empiricist and inductive.[4]

How does this confrontation relate to the question of subjectivity in the Baroque? According to Rodríguez, animism, rationalism and mechanism "tienen como eje determinante la noción clave de *sujeto,* sin la cual la lógica burguesa no puede existir" (are determined crucially by the key notion of the *subject,* without which bourgeois logic cannot exist) (Rodríguez 372 n. 76). Animism breaks with the feudal obsession with blood to produce a "free soul." Even in its most secular forms, it does not laicize globally, and with the reassertion of aristocratic control from the mid–sixteenth century it compromises further with organicism. The result is a nonorganic Aristotelianism, a kind of discourse that operates without the determining presence of the subject, which can be put to different ideological uses. These include the legitimation of both bourgeois and aristocratic positions. A bourgeois unconscious that cannot thematize its own logic is forced to retreat to this kind of academic Aristotelianism, which in France "va a servir sobre todo como punto de confluencia, de coexistencia, para racionalistas cartesianos y jesuitas escolastizantes" (will serve above all as the point of confluence, of coexistence, for rationalist Cartesians and scholasticizing Jesuits) (373 n. 76).

The rationalist position lies midway between animism and mechanistic doctrine. In Descartes's works, for example, the mechanical sections are fewer and less insistent than in Galileo's. The soul has assumed the form of Cartesian "reason," which, in turn, will become the transcendental subject of empiricism, the bourgeois subject proper. The latter has nothing previous to itself, no inner capacity to experience (see Rodríguez 374). In the seventeenth century there was an animist presence in the French Baroque, especially in the spiritualism of Pascal, in Jansenism, and also in the Spanish Baroque. But it is in England where it is most visible, in Donne and later Blake, passing through the Cambridge school ("reivindicada por Chomsky" [rediscovered by Chomsky] [382]).

On the basis of the above, Rodríguez proceeds to deal with the problem of whether it can be said that there is an "autonomous" bourgeois ideology in England. Despite the importance of their various contrasting contributions, Marxist historians (so Rodríguez believes) have in general been hamstrung by the assumption of an empiricist notion of the subject as the origin of historical change. They have failed or, rather, been unable to perceive that ideology is an objective unconscious, the "internal logic" deriving (in this case) from bourgeois social relations (380–381). Now while all this is not directly relevant to our concerns, it does throw interesting light upon the controversy over Port Royal linguistic scholarship. For while this controversy led to some advance, it too has failed to focus issues of subjectivity adequately, by raising them to a sufficient level of awareness. I will concentrate on the work of Padley, which contains an excellent résumé of the major positions and the general state of play.

Padley's narrative of a rationalist tradition that, developing from the Middle Ages, enters a decisive new stage around 1540, before feeding eventually into Port Royal, gradually falls into incoherence, for the simple reason that it can conceive of the category of the subject only from the position of its own empiricist ideology. The problem is compounded by the absence of anything that resembles historical analysis, in the sociological sense. Padley postulates a grammatical theory that "had to decide whether to continue with the inherited mixed formal-semasiological approach" or to "transfer its attention decisively from *verbum oris* to *verbum mentis*" (Padley 259), a "Society" that "no longer has the same need of an education based on classical norms," and "the growing spirit of scientific inquiry [that] demands a culture orientated towards discovery" (261).

Now while such rampant personification will be to the taste of some, it does not amount to an adequate theory of agents, and of how these operate within social structures. The year 1540 and the mid–seventeenth century *are* significant, but for reasons that totally transcend Padley's perspective. (They mark, respectively, the collapse of animism in Spain and the transition in France from animism to rationalism, with corresponding repercussions for the category of the subject.) Given the frailty of his own theoretical underpinning, Padley faces a proliferation of mysteries. For example, Sanctius is the "victim of a curious confusion," a scholar "who has muddled his argument" (109). Padley is destined to find equally curious the survival, despite bitter condemnation, of Scholastic doctrine in the seventeenth century (226–227), not to mention its commingling with Neoplatonic and even Stoic elements in Lord Herbert (235). And once this kind of confusion sets in, the empiricist's whole conceptual edifice begins to crumble: "Locke, just as much as Descartes, is a mentalist" (230); "even an out-and-out Sensualist such as Hobbes equally believes in the existence of mental concepts" (237); everyone accepts the existence of mental concepts that precede the words used to express them (239); and, in the last instance, both empiricism and rationalism share a distrust of words, as opposed to concepts (239). As Rodríguez comments (in his own context):

> Cualquier variante es posible y podrá sin muchas dificultades legitimarse, recurriendo a los hechos sociales, a la cita de textos o a la cronología. Habrá "pruebas" para todos los gustos y para todos los argumentos (¡"Verificaciones" —dice el *Empirismo*— para las "Hipótesis"!), porque, en realidad, no hay problemas que plantear, o mejor dicho, se discuten como problemas cosas que están ya perfectamente resueltas de antemano. (Rodríguez 384)

> [Any variant is possible and can be legitimated, without too much difficulty, through recourse to social facts, to the citation of texts or to chronology. "Proofs" will be found for all tastes and all approaches ("Verifications," as Empiricism says, for all "hypotheses"!), because in reality there are no problems to be posed, or, to be more precise, things are discussed as problems that are already, beforehand, perfectly settled.]

Padley is not entirely oblivious to the importance of issues of subjectivity. He concedes, for example, that the *Grammaire générale* has a Cartesian bias since its authors privilege the representation of concepts of the mind, at the expense of language's relation to external phenomena (Padley 224). The *Grammaire,* he adds later, "seems to lose sight altogether of the *vox* or formal component of the word" (241). As Padley himself explains, this indifference to the world of appearances clearly distinguishes Port Royal doctrine from the medieval conception of linguistic signs. However, in the last instance, he is unable to theorize this difference, since he is bound by empiricist presuppositions, which include the belief in a basic, unchanging psychology. As we have seen, this psychology is wont to assume various personified guises.

To conclude, it matters little (pace Padley) whether Cartesianism is or is not the *origin* of the specifically linguistic ideas in the Port Royal grammar. Nor should one be guided excessively by the "ultimate" sources of these ideas in Scholasticism, from which all seems to "flow." "Influences" can, after all, be accommodated to everyone's taste: "Cuando se trata de 'espíritus,' los caminos son brumosos y las fronteras imprecisas; cualquiera puede llevar a cualquier parte" (When it is a question of 'spirits,' all paths are blurred and all frontiers imprecise; any one can lead any where) (Rodríguez 384–385). Moreover, as Rodríguez insists, it is not "psychology" that is at issue but "la existencia de un nivel ideológico inconsciente" (the existence of an unconscious ideological level) (388). This suggests the need to reformulate the questions, within different conceptual horizons, which would take into account the objectivity of social relations of production, along with the (unconscious) ideological level that corresponds to these relations. Reposited in this manner, the Augustinian spiritualism of the Jansenists emerges as the religious statement not of bourgeois animism but of the impact of objective bourgeois relations on the feudal ambit. The linguistic ideas of Port Royal, we are implying, were bound to be contradictory.

The *Persona*

Port Royal stood opposed to Claude Vaugelas (1647) and the humanistic descriptive tradition that concerned itself with details of usage and general rhetorical matters. Such concerns were shunned by the Jansenists, who exhibited a bourgeois suspicion of rhetoric and verbal ornamentation as aristocratic manipulation and who opposed the demands of reason to discursive authoritarianism. In a furious polemic, Father Bouhours supported Vaugelas (see Rosset).[5]

Gracián's attitude to language was perfectly consonant with his order's religion of exteriority, not to mention its cultivation of refined casuistry (see Pelegrín 30–39). He concedes the communicative role of language as an afterthought to his preoccupation with its rhetorical power (Gracián 208). The authority of any statement from this standpoint derives largely from its obscurity. Such a view of language is diametrically opposed to that of the Jansenists. Baroque ornamentation obscures the logicality of speech, through a process in which words, syllables, and sound disengage from their "proper" meaning to assume different allegorical guises. Such textual *jouissance,* at least as Benjamin describes it, is fueled by the death drive: "For the baroque sound is and remains something purely sensuous; meaning has its home in written language. And the spoken word is only afflicted by meaning, so to speak, as if by an inescapable disease; it breaks off in the middle of the process of resounding, and the damming up of the feeling, which was ready to pour forth, provokes mourning" (Benjamin 209).

Who is the killjoy who puts an end to the festivities by enforcing the norms of logic? In Benjamin's view, it is none other than that master of meaning, the intriguer, so familiar to us from the pages of Gracián. This figure functions, within the context of the Transition, as a new subject, to be distinguished from both the feudal citizen and the "free soul" of animism. Gracián gives us a good thumbnail sketch: *"Hombre con fondos, tanto tiene de persona.*

Siempre ha de ser otro tanto más lo interior que lo exterior en todo" (*The greater a man's depths, the more of a person he is.* There should always be twice as much to the inside as to the outside in its entirety) (Gracián 164). This "*persona*" is a product of the burgeoning bureaucracy of the absolutist state. The corridors of power are his haunt, his expertise the techniques of survival in them. Those who perish are distinguished by their one-dimensional character structures: "Hay sujetos de solo fachata, como casas por acabar, faltó el caudal; tienen la entrada de palacio, y de choza la habitación" (There are subjects who are all facade, like houses unfinished through lack of funds; they have the entrance of a palace, and the living quarters of a shack) (164).

Gracián's Hero is but one version of the *persona,* defined by his capacity to penetrate the defenses of others, but to remain himself eternally elusive. The would-be Hero is advised to lure his victim by constantly feeding but never satisfying her curiosity: "Prometa más lo mucho, y la mejor acción deje siempre esperanzas de mayores" (Tactically, it is best to promise a lot, and always to leave people expecting more) (6–7). Like the commodity, he should promise instant availability, while remaining tantalizingly out of reach. In its characteristic dynamics, his persona betrays its etymological roots: it is an exchange value or abstract equivalence that *masks* the true self: "Las cosas no pasan por lo que son, sino por lo que parecen. Valer y saberlo mostrar es valer dos veces" (Things pass not for what they are, but for what they seem. To be of value and to know how to show it is to be worth twice as much) (186). *Seduction* is another word that describes this process, and is the clue to the Hero's actual identity: "el héroe no es más que una versión política de Don Juan" (the hero is no more than a political version of Don Juan) (Pelegrín 58). For Don Juan (as for Gracián), social interchange is the "desire of the Other," raised to the level of the sublime and dignified to spiritual discipline: "si no el ser infinitos, a parecerlo" (if not to be infinite, at least to seem so) (7). As such it is endlessly specular; through a process of synecdochic sublation, in which the half repeatedly promises more than the whole, we approach the vanishing point of desire: "Todos te conozcan, ninguno te abarque; que, con esta treta, lo moderado parecerá mucho, y lo mucho, infinito, y lo infinito, más" (Let all know you, but let no one encompass you, for in this way the moderate will seem a lot, the lot, infinite, and the infinite, still more) (8).

Desire, elevated to cosmic status, has certain practical uses, not the least important of which is the maintenance of bureaucratic secrecy: the aura that surrounds the Baroque persona not only dignifies his exclusiveness but, intensified by linguistic obscurity, facilitates the exclusion of the mass of the population from the affairs of state: "Los ingenios claros son plausibles, los confusos fueron venerados pero no entendidos; y tal vez conviene la escuridad para no ser vulgar" (Clear minds are plausible; confused ones are venerated but not understood; and perhaps obscurity is desirable in order not to be ordinary) (208). The persona comes to occupy the unique place at the center, as befitting the leader: hence the specular structure on which Gracián lingers, involving the need to fill the gaze of the spectator. Ideology takes the form of transforming the masses into a *subjected* or "suspended" population: "*Llevar sus cosas con suspensión.* La admiración de la novedad es estimación de los aciertos. El jugar a juego descubierto ni es de utilidad, ni de gusto. El no declararse luego suspende, y más donde la sublimidad del empleo da objecto a la universal expectación, amaga misterio en todo, y con su misma arcanidad provoca veneración. Aun en el darse a entender se ha de huir la llaneza, así como ni en el trato se ha de permitir el interior a todos" (*Conduct your affairs so as to "suspend."* Admiration of novelty is proof of one's successes. To show one's cards serves no purpose and betrays a lack of taste. A certain guardedness "suspends," above all where the sublimity of action constitutes an object of universal expectation, and through its very mystery provokes veneration. Even in ordinary communication openness should be avoided, so as to preclude free access for all) (151). Inaccessibility, Gracián explains, is the means by which God maintains the admiration of *his* subjects, and other rulers should learn by example.

In sum, "difficulty" consists of stylistic devices through which subjects are dispossessed of the *linguistic* means of production, by rulers who arrogate to themselves control of linguistic circulation. (Needless to say, it is in essence a localized version of that larger process through which the ruling class appropriates the general means of production.) Of course, the victims of the ideological apparatus of the state may be mocked with impunity, once they have been rendered harmless: "Llegaron a una gran plaza, embarazada de infinito vulgo, muy puesto en expectación de alguna de sus necias maravillas, que él suele admirar mucho" (They arrived at a large square, overflowing with a mob all agog for one of those silly spectacles it finds so astounding) (978).

Conclusion

Walter Benjamin offers some intriguing hints on the similarities between the Baroque and the Expressionism of his own day, insofar as both were not so much movements of "genuine artistic achievement" as possessed by a common "unremitting artistic will" (55). He clearly welcomed the fresh immediacy that the Baroque gave to Expressionism, to the extent of hinting at a recursive theory of culture in which eras of decline are characterized by rhetorical effervescence. The time is now ripe, it seems, for a fresh re-evaluation of the Baroque's "relevance." The transition from Renaissance to Baroque traditions will doubtless be found to exhibit an uncanny resemblance to that from modernism to postmodernism. Justification for the analogy will be sought, and found, in the current reinvention of allegory. Critics on the left will also discern, in the reversal of the bourgeois revolution that subsumes the Baroque, prefigurations of socialist defeats in the twentieth century. However legitimate such readings may be, we need to be mindful of Benjamin's further advice to the effect that "so many analogies should not lead us to forget the difference[s]" (56). This is good advice, and to follow it properly, we need to attend to those historical circumstances that are never repeated and that resist absorption by blandly idealist narratives.

Notes

1. References throughout will be to Gracián, *Obras completas*. All the translations are my own.

2. I have in mind, of course, the debate between Benjamin and Theodor Adorno concerning the problem of defining the relation between the base and the superstructure (see Bloch 128–129). Benjamin " 'solves' this problem by suspending it, forcing adjacentist parallels between two realms that leave their true relations entirely unspoken" (Eagleton, *Walter Benjamin* 76).

3. Noam Chomsky's work (*Cartesian Linguistics, Language and Mind*) provoked numerous bourgeois responses, such as those of Salmon, Lakoff, Miel, and Aarsleff. Thompson's Marxist critique was particularly virulent.

4. In order to accommodate Chomsky's technical advances, empiricists have sought to disassociate his linguistics from its philosophical basis in mentalism. See, for example, Palmer 188.

5. It is no coincidence that Bouhours was one of Gracián's staunchest, albeit more critical, admirers (see Hoyo, in Gracián xx–xxi).

Works Cited

Aarsleff, Hans. "The History of Linguistics and Professor Chomsky." *Language* 46 (1970): 570–585.

Benjamin, Walter. *The Origin of German Tragic Drama.* Introduction by George Steiner. Trans. John Osborne. London: Verso, 1985.

Bloch, Ernst, et al. *Aesthetics and Politics.* London: NLB 1977.

Bursill-Hall, G. L. *Speculative Grammars of the Middle Ages.* The Hague and Paris: Mouton, 1971.

Callinicos, Alex. *Althusser's Marxism.* London: Pluto Press, 1976.

Chomsky, Noam. *Cartesian Linguistics.* New York: Harper and Row, 1966.

———. *Language and Mind.* New York: Harcourt Brace Jovanovich, 1968.

Doyle, Brian. *English and Englishness.* London: Routledge, 1989.

Eagleton, Terry. *Walter Benjamin; or, Towards a Revolutionary Criticism.* London: Verso, 1981.

———. *The Ideology of the Aesthetic.* Oxford, Cambridge: Basil Blackwell, 1990.

Gracián, Baltasar. *Obras completas.* 2nd ed. Ed. Arturo del Hoyo. Madrid: Aguilar, 1960.

Lakoff, Robin. Review of *Grammaire générale et raisonnée. Language* 45 (1969): 343–364.

Maravall, José Antonio. *Culture of the Baroque: Analysis of a Historical Structure.* Trans. Terry Cochran. Foreword by Wlad Godzich and Nicholas Spadaccini. Minneapolis: University of Minnesota Press, 1986.

Miel, Jan. "Pascal, Port-Royal and Cartesian Linguistics." *Journal of the History of Ideas* 30 (1969): 261–271.

Padley, G. A. *Grammatical Theory in Western Europe, 1500–1700: The Latin Tradition.* Cambridge: Cambridge University Press, 1976.

Palmer, Frank. *Grammar.* Harmondsworth: Penguin, 1971.

Pelegrín, Benito. Introductory study to Baltasar Gracián, *Oráculo manual y arte de prudencia.* Zaragoza: Guara Editorial, 1983.

Read, Malcolm Kevin. *The Birth and Death of Language: Spanish Literature and Linguistics, 1300–1700.* Madrid: José Porrúa Torranzas, 1983.

———. *Visions in Exile: The Body in Spanish Literature and Linguistics: 1500–1800.* Amsterdam and Philadelphia: Benjamins, 1990.

Rodríguez, Juan Carlos. *Teoría e historia de la producción ideológica: Las primeras literaturas burguesas (siglo XVI).* Madrid: Akal, 1974.

Rosset, T. "Le P. Bouhours critique de la langue des écrivains jansénistes." *Annales de l'Université de Grenoble* 20.1 (1908): 55–125.

Rossi Landi, Ferruccio. *Linguistics and Economics.* The Hague and Paris: Mouton, 1975.
Salmon, Vivian. Review of *Cartesian Linguistics. Journal of Linguistics* 5 (1969): 165–187.
Smith, Paul Julian. *Representing the Other: "Race," Text, and Gender in Spanish and Spanish American Narrative.* Oxford: Clarendon Press, 1992.
Thompson, J. S. "The Reactionary Idealistic Foundations of Noam Chomsky's Linguistics." *Literature and Ideology* 4 (1969): 1–20.
Walton, L. B. Introduction to Baltasar Gracián, *The Oracle: A Manual of the Art of Discretion.* London: Dent, 1953.
Williams, Raymond. *Keywords: A Vocabulary of Culture and Society.* London: Flamingo (Fonatan), 1983.

Chapter 4

Surviving in the Field of Vision: The Building of a Subject in Gracián's *El Criticón*

Luis F. Avilés

It would not be difficult to demonstrate that Baltasar Gracián conceived the first half of the seventeenth century as a conflictive and perilous time for Spain. It was a time when the empire's grandeur was falling apart, when cultural unity was being contested along all fronts (Catalonia and Portugal being the most representative), and when military and maritime superiority was definitely on a downward spiral against the French, Dutch, and British. For the Aragonese author, reality was defined as chaos and crisis.[1] Whenever these conceptions of reality are dominant in a particular culture, there arises a need to articulate new ways of dealing with such realities. Subjects start to question the parameters that have directed actions and behavior up to the same moment of reflection. New answers have to be sought, new ideas are conceived, and a varied productivity of new voices evolves. Social reality and textual productivity intermingle to produce a true chaos of opinions and contrasted discourses that fight each other for hegemony, that look for new spaces of distribution and new readers in positions of power (those who will be able to effectively change the problem situation). With such an understanding of social reality, some of these new responses are characterized by their highly disciplinary and axiologically charged content. A "corrective" stance in many ways predisposes writers toward "commentary,"[2] as a means of deploying educational tools in order to effect change. Texts start to become allegorized, and a search for new alternatives ensues. The written word transforms itself at the level of both content and syntagmatic distribution. Textual reality becomes enmeshed in the constant search for responses to crisis.

Such is the power of crisis as a conceptual framework and an experiential symptom, and it certainly dominates the texture of *El criticón*,[3] one of the most important representatives of the "writing of chaos" in seventeenth-century Spain. The word *crisis* even determines the text's title, its divisions (called "crisi"), and one of its main characters (Critilo). *Crisis* derives from the Greek *krisis* (decision), from *krino* ("yo decido, separo, juzgo" [I decide, separate, judge], in Corominas 179a). The "critical" situation demands a response, a reaction; in other words, it demands discursive productivity in the form of opinions expressed orally and textually, through art, allegory, satire (as a corrective way of putting people and institutions in their right place), new political solutions ("arbitristas," or political commentators), military interventions, and "premáticas" (edicts) of all types (from the regulation of clothing to the expulsion of beggars from cities). In the case of *El criticón*, the response consists, among others, of the construction and the possibility to adequately "socialize" a subject. The text describes a journey from a deserted island toward the center of European civilization (Rome). It is an allegorical voyage undertaken by two characters, Critilo and Andrenio, who contain in themselves a plurality of deictic functions and chronotopic significances: they are respectively father and son, teacher and disciple; they go from youth to maturity, travel through various countries, and encounter multiple obstacles. My purpose here is to study two fundamental mechanisms that construct a semblance of socialization and progress and that are centered on the body as the arena of allegorical significance and spatial distributionality. I will concentrate my analysis on "sight" and "confrontation": vision as a fundamental way of defining one's position in several spaces (familial and societal), and the presence of the other as a conflictual situation that requires new visual and interpretative "technologies."[4] I will also study how mirror images work out to be recognition tools and at the same time modes of positioning, in equal or subordinate terms, for both characters and readers alike.

Before I begin mapping the two mechanisms just mentioned, it is important to remember that for some authors conceptions of crisis in seventeenth-century Spain eroded the parameters that define masculinity and femininity as categories of distinction and separation. The boundaries between these concepts became blurred, often resulting in the contamination of each other. As a consequence, men were seen as insufficient, lacking in those characteristics that once defined the male paradigm. Men suddenly became more feminine, and at the same time women were seen as more powerful:

> —Aguardá, ¿mugeres? —dixo Andrenio—, ¿dónde están?, ¿cuáles son, que yo no las distingo de los hombres? ¿Tú no me dixiste, ¡oh Critilo!, que los hombres eran los fuertes y las mugeres las flacas, ellos hablaban recio y ellas delicado, ellos vestían calçón y capa, y ellas basquiñas? Yo hallo que todo es al contrario, porque, o todos son ya mugeres, o los hombres son los flacos y afeminados; ellas, las poderosas. Ellos tragan saliva, sin osar hablar, y ellas hablan tan alto que aun los sordos las oyen; ellas mandan el mundo, y todos se les sugetan. Tú me has engañado.[5] (1.6, 134–35)

The crisis attacks the male body and deflates its power. The female body, on the other hand, becomes, to the eyes of the moralists, more powerful and free of restraints. This representational mechanism is extremely important because it becomes a distributional narrative tool designed to project a beginning and a sequentiality organized around a recuperation of something perceived as being lost. What is needed then is a narrative that will initially do two things: it must represent the status quo of male deficiency (satire) and at the same time provide an alternative to that state of being (allegory). In the quotation above we encounter a character surprised by the incongruence between what his father taught him and what the body of women and men show him. A kind of satirical mode focused on the body tries to devalue "man" as category. As a supplemental way of representing the "correct" alternative, Gracián starts with a child and proposes an educational development constructed through allegory. Andrenio is abandoned by his mother Felisinda on the island of Santa Elena,[6] where he is raised by a she-wolf. There Critilo encounters him, and the process of *Bildung* starts.[7]

As a child born and raised in a place outside of culture, Andrenio is defined as a tabula rasa, a European out of place, lacking language skills and proper dress (1.1, 68–70). In his first encounter with Critilo, Andrenio immediately assumes a subordinated position because of all the things he lacks. At that same moment Critilo establishes himself as a character with authority, acquiring his functions as father, educator, mentor, and even "master" (in the text, a distinction between these functions is almost impossible). This authoritative position can be perceived in the first linguistic lesson given to Andrenio: "Emprendió [Critilo] luego el enseñar a hablar al inculto joven, y púdolo conseguir fácilmente favoreciéndole la docilidad y el deseo. Començó por los nombres de ambos, proponiéndole el suyo, que era el de Critilo, y imponiéndole a él el de Andrenio, que llenaron bien, el uno en lo juizioso, y el otro en lo humano" (1.1, 69).[8] Andrenio accepts the imposition of his name because he is docile and also because he desires it ("deseo"). At the same time, both names indicate the functions these two characters will play between themselves: one will give advice and be judgmental, and the other will receive these primary messages; in one the ideas and main commentaries will be concentrated, while the other will receive them as part of his development. This passage is surprisingly similar to the one describing the moment when Robinson Crusoe names his newly acquainted native, Friday:

> In a little time I began to speak to him and teach him to speak to me; and first, I made him know his name should be Friday, which was the day I saved his life; I called him so for the memory of the time; I likewise taught him to say "Master," and then let him know that was to be my name; I likewise taught him to say "yes" and "no" and to know the meaning of them.[9] (203)

Subordination to a superior companion is the key in both examples. The communicative model presented here strongly objectifies Andrenio and Friday. We know that Crusoe's name is not Master, but such an articulation is highly motivated and desirable for both Gracián and Defoe. There is an urgent need to establish a hierarchy, because without such *discipline* there cannot be *Bildung* (the need to imitate a paradigm). The imposition of names in both texts is not far from that "yes" and "no" that the master needs to communicate very quickly in order to mark boundaries and limitations. Language, birth, and parenthood are interlaced with power, subordination, and control. "Master" (like "maestro") marks the limitations that are associated consistently with the word "no."

Andrenio even needs a definition of himself through his father: "Tú, Critilo, me preguntas quién soy, y yo deseo saberlo de ti" (1.1, 70).[10] Narrative fills a need to start from the very beginning, from childhood, in the instant when father and son confront each other and immediately assume their prescribed roles. Both Friday and Andrenio become empty bodies that are permitted to start all over again (an authentic rebirth) in the encounter and intercourse with the father,[11] both need to be filled up with new codes, and as we will see, they are restrictive and disciplinary ones.

Andrenio's empty body starts to absorb new and significant information from the moment he encounters Critilo. As a form in space, Critilo's image enters the body through sight. Andrenio says: "Tú eres el primer hombre que hasta hoy he visto y en ti me hallo retratado más al vivo que en los mudos cristales de una fuente que muchas vezes mi curiosidad solicitaba y mi ignorancia aplaudía" (1.1, 70).[12] The "other" functions as a more reliable mirror, an imago that delineates more clearly the contours of the self. Andrenio's own reflection in the water remains unintelligible to him (the image of the "mute fountain" is perfect), until he sees Critilo. The reflection does not respond fully to Andrenio's curiosity about who he is. Sight, in this sense, remains insufficient. Only through social recognition, here represented by means of an encounter with the father, can the answers be found.[13] Sight becomes myopic until a bodily mirror (the paternal "other") appears. Then from sight we arrive at what Norman Bryson has called "visuality": the beginning of socialization and the ideologization of visual perception:

> Between the subject and the world is inserted the entire sum of discourses which make up visuality, that cultural

> construct, and make visuality different from vision, the notion of unmediated visual experience. Between retina and world is inserted a *screen* of signs, a screen consisting of all the multiple discourses on vision built into the social arena.[14] (91–92)

If sight is the physical ability to perceive objects in space, visuality permits us to categorize and reconfigure those objects and to understand them according to distributional (cultural) codes. Even Gracián notes this distinction with surprising accuracy: "Va grande diferencia del ver al mirar, que quien no entiende no atiende: poco importa ver mucho con los ojos si con el entendimiento nada, ni vale el ver sin el notar" (3.4, 611).[15] *Ver* (to see, look) is distinguished here from *mirar, atender,* and *notar* (to observe, to look with attention), the latter defined as a kind of look that is integrated with intellectual thought. The distinction is an important one because children are incapable of visuality; it must be constructed in both society and fiction. Remarkably, Bryson sees exactly what, at a distant past, Gracián perceived as a cultural need to counteract crisis: the building of a new "screen," feeding the body new codes and filters of reality. If we go back to Andrenio, we see that his own image reflected in the water does not explain anything to him because the grid (screen) is lacking in cultural content. Only the other can function as a "provisional screen" through which Andrenio will start recognizing himself and the world. Critilo functions as a new reflection, a feeder of cultural discourses, a taxonomic entity that organizes the world for the child. When Andrenio relates his experience to Artemia (Art), he again goes back to the image in the water: "Acabé de contemplarme en los reflexos de una fuente; cuando advertí era yo mismo el que creí otro, no podré explicarte la admiración y gusto que allí tuve" (1.9, 189).[16] Andrenio recognizes his difference with his pseudobrothers, the wolves, but he is not yet able to *explain* this difference.[17] He needs the substitute mirror of the father. The true beginning of socialization, the entrance into the new order of community and language, needs to be initiated through the body of an other.

The similarities between the passages I have quoted from *El criticón* and what Lacan has called the "mirror stage" are remarkable. If we focus our attention on terms such as "admiration" and the overall sense of joy that Andrenio describes when he sees himself, and the concept of "insufficiency" and "lack" that does not permit him to articulate an explanation of himself, we start to observe some surprising parallels with the Lacanian description of the child looking at itself in the mirror:

> This jubilant assumption of his specular image by the child at the *infans* stage, still sunk in his motor incapacity and nursling dependence, would seem to exhibit in an exemplary situation the symbolic matrix in which the *I* is precipitated in a primordial form, before it is objectified in the dialectic of identification with the other, and before language restores to it, in the universal, its function as subject. (*Ecrits* 2)

He continues by stating the incompleteness of the child:

> The objective notion of the anatomical incompleteness of the pyramidal system and likewise the presence of certain humoral residues of the maternal organism confirm the view I have formulated as the fact of a real *specific prematurity of birth* in man.[18] (4)

In Lacan's narrative, the child sees a kind of "integrity," which in symbolic terms is called an "I" (contrary to "subject," determined by identification with the other and by language).[19] The admiration and joy experienced by Andrenio form part of an idealized construction that recognizes itself as different from and potentially better than the wolves. But at the same time there is a recognition of lack, the inability to work out a definition of himself. This inability is oriented toward a new set of questions: Who am I? Where are my mother and my father? And what can I do in this world with my body? In "crisi nona" of Part 1, after having been introduced to the complexities of the world, Andrenio systematically describes the body as insufficient, stating that some parts could be relocated in order to avoid problems (188–204).[20] The allegorical functions of Critilo (judgment) and Artemia (Art) will start filling up those gaps seen in the bodily configuration, trying to maintain a semblance of anatomical organicism and structure. The title of the *crisi* also denotes the supplementarity of language and culture on the body ("Moral anatomía del hombre," Moral anatomy of man). The *Bildung*, which started with language and names, now tries desperately to keep the body intact.[21]

For Gracián, the place of the other (the father) becomes the possibility of development, the way to acculturation and discipline. The gaze of the father is defined in *El criticón* as an operation of control designed to provide a mold to be assimilated by the child. Visuality starts with the desire to rule the retina. Mothers are effaced from this narrative altogether. Felisinda will not appear in the text either as mother or as happiness (primary and allegorical meaning; see Avilés, *La alegoría* 81–83, and Kassier 12). It is the father who is called to take the child, educate him, and build his cultural screen. This process is constructed in *El criticón* as a journey from the empty space of Santa Elena to the culturally charged center, Rome. The chronotopic distribution of the text also describes a need to change from childhood to "persona" (a crucial concept for Gracián, describing all the essential qualities that a person should have). It is a journey through space and time that promises to solve the major problems confronting Andrenio as lack. Only through spatial movement and the passing of time will he be able to evolve from childhood. But travel and Andrenio's development are not so smooth. The interaction between father and son is drawn by Gracián as a constant battle of resistance and unsupervised experimentation by the character-child. Andrenio as child becomes Andrenio as a grotesque body (Bakhtin 26), a body that does not recognize limits. He wants to experiment with everything, without discrimination (he falls in love with Falsirena, or false siren; he wants to partake of the court of Falimundo; he gets drunk; and he always has to be rescued by a more experienced character). Like a child, he is unable to discern between good and evil and he does not have directionality in his movements; there is no purpose other than gratification of the body. The journey is the process by which narrative tries to cancel out childhood as quickly as possible. Descartes significantly associated some of the major problems of adulthood with the childhood stage: "Since we have all been children before being men . . . it is almost impossible that our judgments should be so excellent or solid as they would have been had we had complete use of our reason since our birth, and had we been guided by its means alone" (in Bordo 97–98). A similar thought crossed Gracián's mind in *El discreto* (The discreet):

> En el vaso frágil del cuerpo se va perfeccionando de cada día el ánimo. No luego está en su punto. Tienen todos los hombres a los principios una enfadosa dulzura de la niñez, una insuave crudeza de la mocedad; aquel resabio a los deleites, aquella inclinación a cosas poco graves, empleos juveniles, ocupaciones frívolas.[22] (*Obras completas* 333)

From the point of view of Gracián and many other writers, childhood tends to overextend its temporal boundaries, and thus must be conquered as soon as possible. The stage is like the grotesque body of Andrenio, surpassing the limits that authors and moralists try desperately to impose on it. Childhood is a stage that needs to be lived in the shortest amount of time. The function of the fifth *crisi,* entitled "Entrada del Mundo" (Entrance to the world, 113–126), is to show the reader the true danger of this stage. In it the allegorical figure of "Inclinación" (inclination), together with her company of beasts, starts eating the children she is supposed to take care of. They are later rescued by Reason. What is important about this *crisi* is the representation of Inclination as a mother who kills children through *coddling.*[23] This attitude toward motherhood is not arbitrary. It is part of an ideological devaluation of motherhood that apparently intensified at the end of the sixteenth and the beginning of the seventeenth centuries (Ariés 130, with a remarkable example from Montaigne).[24] Motherhood is rejected precisely on the grounds that excessive love is localized in the mother. The father's quick intervention and participation in the process of formation seem to indicate the need to substantially reduce the early history of the newly born male.

El criticón starts a process of socialization with an identification with the father and a complete rejection of the mother. The text becomes an assembly line for Andrenio, and delineates a quick de-fetalization of his body, distancing it from the proximity of the mother and also providing him with cultural and social rules, which in this case could be considered as the "supplemental food" for the body. The text, which goes out in search of Felisinda as mother and happiness, in reality strays further and further from her. Gracián states that it is better for children to be raised "con necessidad, y tal vez entre los rigores de una madrastra" (1.5, 119).[25] The gaze of the father is the building block that constitutes the subject into a cultural entity. Gracián and many other writers saw the need to "direct" children toward manhood as soon as possible so the sediments of that initial stage could be conquered and redirected toward more "noble" and virtuous deeds. Speed is the key element for a culture and a representation that lack what is needed to be improved: the effective male. As a manifestation of Baroque culture, this process is similar to what Maravall has called "una cultura dirigida" (a directed culture), a culture that tries to reproduce social subjects that could conform to the particular needs of the state (*La cultura del Barroco* 132).

Visuality becomes the productive picture of an imago that will function as a goal to be reproduced through travel, education, and manhood. The function of Critilo is to introduce Andrenio into sociality. But this entrance to social intercourse articulates another problem: the danger of the other. The exchange with members of the human community becomes the most difficult and dangerous locus, a new chronotopic enclave that necessitates highly developed skills. This encounter is fictionalized in *El criticón* through a series of improvements on sight and vision. The encounter is full of anxiety and paranoia in terms of visual and verbal interaction. Two persons, face to face, start a kind of "battle of wits," a verbal assault combined with a penetrating visual intensity that wants to re-cognize the other to its core. The mechanisms learned by Critilo and Andrenio are transmitted by four fundamental allegorical figures: Argos, the Acertador, the Descifrador, and the Zahorí.

The entrance to maturity (Part 2, *crisi* 1) is described as the passage through an allegorical "customhouse" ("la aduana general de las edades" [299]), which already signals a type of economy and a special filter of the body. Argos, the first of the central characters mentioned above, appears, and a discussion on the importance of vision ensues (289–295). Vision, however, acquires prominence only through the high anxiety produced by the encounter with the other. Argos states:

> Maldito el hombre que confía en otro, y sea quien fuere. ¿Qué digo amigos y hermanos?: de los mismos hijos no hay que assegurarse, y necio del padre que en vida se despoja. . . . Ni aun en los mismos padres hay que confiar, que algunos han echado dado falso a los hijos; ¡y cuántas madres hoy venden las hijas![26] (2.1, 291)

The complete mistrust of the other establishes the norm for every encounter. Even the structural integrity of the family is suspect. Friendship and familial intercourse are represented as eroded by new transactions based mainly on economic terms (*despoja* means to give property away; even mothers "sell" their daughters).[27] Argos thus recommends that "para poder vivir es menester armarse un hombre de pies a cabeça, no de ojetes, sino de ojazos muy despiertos" (2.1, 293–294).[28] In contrast to Andrenio's encounter with his father and the promise of mutual recognition and intelligibility, there is a marked intensification not only of the insufficiencies of the body, but also on a communitary breakdown. It is clear that, for Gracián, the ability to discern quickly what the other person is all about is very important. Again Gracián articulates the distinctions of visual perception discussed earlier when Argos says: "¿Ves o miras?, que no todos miran lo que ven" (290).[29] By positioning Argos in the customhouse and as the main identifier of the residues of childhood, Gracián gives capital importance to sight as a form of surveillance, identification, and control (observation, careful assessment of the other, and the possibility of establishing a link or rejecting dialogue). The customhouse becomes a kind of social filter where the remnants of childhood are held in check by careful observation (surveillance). Childhood traits cannot be smuggled into the space of adulthood; in other words, the danger of childhood surpassing the boundaries imposed on it is represented and maintained in check through an allegory of the power of visual perception activated at a crucial chronotope that combines sight, economics (customhouse), and the transition to another temporal plane (adulthood). Sight becomes a *defense* mechanism (Kassier 141) that in many ways opposes what the body of the picaro does. For the picaro wants to remain unknown, to appear as an other, to subvert his or her social origin and status; it is an aggressive social posture designed to penetrate the "other's" body and social space (houses, court, and so on).[30] Interestingly enough, the vision of the father for the picaro could be described as an imposed status and social positionality that he has to fight against. In other words, there is no reciprocity with the mutual sight between parent and child. The example of Lazarillo and his relation with Zaide, although peculiar for its racial connotations, is remarkable (see Fra Molinero; one should also keep in mind Pablos's case in Francisco de Quevedo's *El buscón*).

If the visual recognition of the father carries with it the need for the child to subordinate himself to him in order to acquire the goods that are lacking for his socialization, the visual encounter with the other becomes a gaze full of doubt, insecurity, and apprehension, and sometimes even an invasion of one's integrity. The other is an enigma that must be deciphered.[31] The body occupying the space in front of these characters appears to behave more and more as a language (a text) of corporeal contours, of gestures and machinations that need to be read correctly. Socialization, consequently, dwindles toward an incapacity to truly socialize. Socialization, as described by allegorical representation, becomes almost an impossibility in a text where communal relations are almost nonexistent. If they exist, narrative defines them as battles carried out with extreme risk. The community described allegorically by Gracián becomes a community of separated members floating around and trying to inflict harm on others.[32] In order to "socialize successfully," Andrenio needs to learn the equivalent of a foreign language—a process dependent upon the ability to internalize new codes of reading the body. This construction of communal interaction and sociopolitical space as a foreign and strange entity is, I truly believe, one of the most interesting aspects of *El criticón*. Crisis thus becomes an estrangement of one's own spatial reality, and also an oneiric reconstitution of social organizations and cultural codifications through allegorical constructs. Allegory in *El criticón* can be defined as an organized assault on language and material culture that tries to regroup what in actuality seems disjointed, but at the same time allegory approaches its own cancellation as an alternative discourse, because there is the latent danger of a new deficiency *in the gaze of the father* as the provider of much-needed processes for self-definition and communication with others.[33] Critilo's insufficiency is apparent when the text needs to supplement his eyes (his ocular competence) with other characters. We could characterize these supplemental actors as *utopic bodies,* as fantasies of hypermasculinity, as I will discuss later on.

The other three characters are designed not only as helpers of these new paternal shortcomings, but also to intensify the idea of the body as text. In the case of the Acertador (3.3, 592), the focus of attention centers on visible expressions and corporeal deformations, as well as on nationality (interpreted through cultural stereotypes): "De un tuerto pronosticó que no haría cosa a buen ojo, y acertó. A un corcovado le ad[e]vinó sus malas inclinaciones, a un coxo los malos passos en que andaba, y a un çurdo sus malas mañas" (593).[34] Stereotype becomes a tool for Gracián, associating dysfunctional bodily parts directly with imminent moral failure. We could state that the assessment of the other's deformed body is possible by means of what we could call an "ethical eye," or the need to see these deformities as a kind of punishment inflicted upon bodies that were destined to sin.

The case of the Descifrador goes even further. The other person's body becomes a "cifra" (cipher)[35] for which one has to find the "contracifra" (its code). This character expresses the true epistemological difficulty that so profoundly preoccupies Gracián: the extreme difficulty of deciphering the other. After concluding that the stars are relatively easy to comprehend (demonstrating the primacy of the other as a human body rather than the objects that constitute the world), the Descifrador states the major problem directly:

> La dificultad la hallo yo en leer y entender lo que está de las tejas abaxo, porque como todo ande en cifra y los humanos coraçones estén tan sellados y inescrutables, assegúroos que el mejor letor se pierde. Y otra cosa, que si no lleváis bien estudiada y bien sabida la contracifra de todo, os habéis de hallar perdidos, sin acertar a leer palabra ni conocer letra, ni un rasgo ni un tilde.[36] (3.4, 611–612)

This character later on complains about the "bad readers" of signs:

> La lástima es que hay malíssimos letores que entienden C. por B. y fuera mejor D. por C. No están al cabo de las cifras ni las entienden, no han estudiado la materia de intenciones, que es la más dificultosa de cuantas hay.[37] (3.4, 614)

Both passages concentrate on the "writing" of the body, a special kind of text that becomes a danger for the character who does not know how to read it correctly. The "technologies of the body" as "self" deploy here new verbal and iconic mechanisms of communication, what Foucault calls the "technologies of sign systems, which permit us to use signs, meanings, symbols or signification" ("Technologies of the Self" 18). Body, interpretation, and language are united in the need to protect the body from any unwanted intrusions. Space becomes the arena where anxiety (in front of the other), agoraphobia (in the open space of the community where dangerous interactions take place), and allegory (the fictional workings of language) unite to form a complex array of cultural responses to crisis. The Descifrador is able to articulate allegorically one of the ideal mechanisms of cultural and societal interaction: the ability to comprehend the other while at the same time protecting the integrity of one's own body from possible contamination and harm.[38] This ability, surprisingly enough, is associated in the text with one of the conditions that have defined the period of the Baroque: "Desengaño" (disillusionment). In Part 3, *crisi* 5, we learn that this character was the son of "la Verdad" (Truth), called "el Desengaño" (637). The association of knowledge, correct reading, and the pain of disillusionment are unquestionably interrelated here as conceptions of critical malaise.

The last of the characters associated with sight and the ability to understand the other is the Zahorí. His new technology transcends reading, because his visual perception does not have mediations:

> Yo llego a ver la misma sustancia de las cosas en una ojeada, y no solos los accidentes y las apariencias, como vosotros; yo conozco luego si hay sustancia en un sujeto, mido el fondo que tiene, descubro lo que tira y dónde alcança, hasta dónde se estiende la esfera de su actividad, dónde llega su saber y su entender, cuánto ahonda su prudencia; veo si tiene coraçoncillo, y el que bravos hígados, y si le han convertido en baço. Pues el seso yo le

> veo con tanta distinción como si estuviesse en un vidrio...
> en viendo un sujeto conozco lo que pesa y lo que piensa.[39]

The Zahorí's capacity goes beyond reading and deciphering. He is able to "penetrate" to the core of the body and analyze the anatomy of its intentions at a safe distance, because he knows right away the sphere of influence in terms of spatial extension. Intimacy becomes a nonbarrier, a permeable surface easily pierced by vision.

The four characters deployed by Gracián's narrative are allegorical projections of a desire to control one's social being in a community severed by hostile intentions. The new technologies are driven by the need to overcome childhood as soon as possible through subordination to the father, and also by a process of learning to "see" by means of a cultural screen, a special kind of filter of intentions. What is done to the body in *El criticón* is a major shift toward visual literacy that will produce the desired social competence. The child Andrenio has to pass through a prophylactic process whereby other characters, together with Critilo as father, will be able to clean "las lagañas de la niñez" (the slime on childhood's sleepy eyes) (2.1, 308) and prepare him to do battle with others.

Bildung becomes not only the imitation of the father and other crucial characters, but also the acquisition of a greater understanding of others. At the same time, however, the text does not show a change in personality in Andrenio (Blanco 28). Changes occurring at the level of character are mainly forgotten by the narrative because allegory, essentially, becomes a kind of outline, a special type of organized writing that does not need to represent evolving beings. What is important in *El criticón* is an "idea of character," as Lennard Davis calls it.[40] Character development in *El criticón*, although nonexistent, is allegorically projected toward the reader. If Andrenio is the receiver of the message (he becomes the manipulation of his father Critilo and his "Father" the author, the supreme *auctoritas*), then it would not be difficult to see readers (specifically those readers situated at the time of writing) as recipients of those messages transmitted throughout Andrenio's "progress." As readers we also become projections of an author's desires to transform through writing our own conceptions of vision and social intercourse. *Bildung* starts to surpass its own textual boundaries, ending up with a text that wants us to look at ourselves (like the ever-present mirrors in *El criticón*) and change our own imago and our cultural filters.[41] Like Andrenio, we become fantasies of what the author wants us to be—children who must be given the lesson for life. Such is the intensity and the monological push of this text. As Nancy Chodorow comments on the discoveries of Dorothy Burlingham:

> Fathers see babies not as babies but as potentially grown-up. . . . they are more likely than mothers to transform their perception of their newborn into fantasies about the adult it will become, and about the things they (father and child) will be able to do together when the infant is much older. (81)

In order to work as a writing of crisis, Gracián's project required an allegorical reconstruction of childhood, the beginning of social intercourse, the subordination to the father's gaze, and the whole array of technologies of the body needed to survive a hostile environment. Crisis for Gracián allows for the possibility of a new writing of a "possible" social subject. Allegory becomes the productive signifier trying to supplement those gaps and insufficiencies perceived in individuals, but at the same time demonstrating its shortcomings and slips. Its historical specificity becomes apparent in the erasure of motherhood, which in our century has become essential for the raising of young men and women into society.[42] Furthermore, it denotes a significant shift toward a radical mistrust of the other as it appears in the visual scene. A destabilizing experience of crisis during the first half of the seventeenth century, combined with the visual misgivings that define Cartesian subjectivity, seems to coalesce in Gracián's allegorical representation. In fact, Gracián's rendering of the visual as constitutive of a desperately needed new technology to be used as a means to control the space characters occupy and the need to dominate that space in terms of an access to the core of the other seem to point toward what Martin Jay describes as a distinct scopic regime, different from the Cartesian model: the Baroque.[43] The geometrical perspective of the "I" positioned at a privileged point seems to be shifting toward an increasing incapacity to truly survey the other in its totality. Gracián's allegory of visual power is certainly the need to rescue and control the Cartesian geometric point, which seems to have lost its efficiency to interpret the other in the social realm of modernity. That is why, within the arena of social interaction, children become possible new subjects that have to be protected and directed by fathers from a very early stage. Gracián delineates the readers as possible fantasies of what he wants for society (as new Andrenios and Fridays). This authorial push toward control and hypermasculinization of the gaze of both the characters and the readers, I think, has kept such a fascinating text from being studied in the way it deserves. There is certainly a need to go back to Gracián and analyze his complex cultural response to seventeenth-century Spain, allowing us to describe the interplay between the writing of fiction and the writing of society through technologies of control, power, and domination, of which vision is only one of its most important manifestations.

Notes

I would like to thank Professor Betty Sasaky for her revision of the manuscript and her insightful comments, Professor Nicolás Wey for his help with the translations, and Professor Ivette N. Hernández for her close reading and suggestions.

1. The philosopher and sociologist Karl Popper has stated that the "agent's conception of the situation is also part of the situation, a component of the problem situation" (in Werlen 46). What Popper establishes is the importance of the agent's assessment of reality, his own conception of the general climate that he experiences, and how this conception participates in the *construction* of that reality.

2. According to Michel Foucault, commentary is a secondary discourse that tries to restore "the great, unbroken plain of words and things" (*Order of Things* 40); he goes on to state that commentary "calls into being, below the existing discourse, another discourse that is more fundamental and, as it were, 'more primal,' which it sets itself the task of restoring" (41). Commentary, then, is a kind of surplus discourse designed to survey existing knowledge. Like allegory, commentary becomes the explanation of images, the *reasoning* behind textual productivity, and at times the most important feature of any word sequence in terms of pedagogical primacy. See Foucault (*Order of Things* 40–43).

3. I quote from Santos Alonso's edition, because of its accessibility. I consulted Romera-Navarro's edition, the best so far. I will indicate the part, the number of the "crisi," and the page in parentheses. All translations of Gracián's works are mine, with the invaluable help of Nicolás Wey.

4. "Technologies of the self," a phrase coined by Foucault, refers to mechanisms that "permit individuals to effect by their own means or with the help of others a certain number of operations on their own bodies and souls, thoughts, conduct, and way of being, so as to transform themselves in order to attain a cer-

tain state of happiness, purity, perfection, or immortality" ("Technologies" 18). The appeal of this phrase is that it permits a conceptualization of modes and strategies of confrontation and self-definition that are deployed through bodily functions. The body, as I will try to show, becomes a conflictive locus, incorporating characteristics shared by language in new and intriguing ways.

5. " 'Hold on. Women?' said Andrenio, 'Where are they? Which ones are they? For I do not distinguish them from men. Did you not tell me, O Critilo, that men were strong and women weak; that men spoke strongly and women delicately; that men wear cloaks and breeches, and women wear loose dress? But I find that it is the opposite, for either all men are already women, or men are feeble and effeminated, and women powerful. Men now swallow their words and dare not speak, and women speak so loudly that even the deaf can hear them; they rule the world, and all are subject to them. You have deceived me [Critilo].' " Quevedo expresses the same anxieties: "Y lo que es más sentir es la manera que los hombres las imitan en las galas y lo afeminado, pues es de suerte que no es un hombre ahora más apetecible a una mujer, que una mujer a otra. Y esto de suerte que las galas en algunos parecen arrepentimiento de haber nacido hombres, y otros pretenden enseñar a la naturaleza cómo sepa hacer de un hombre una mujer" (And what is worse is the way that men imitate women in their dress and effeminate ways; and so it happens that a man is now less compelling to a woman than one woman is to another. And this happens because some men dress as though they were ashamed of having being born men, and others dare teach Nature how to make a woman out of a man); quoted by Deleito y Piñuela (64). See another example by Juan de Mora, quoted by Vigil (117). José A. Maravall defends the idea that there was a deep anxiety toward feminine subversion, which became an integral part of Baroque culture (*La literatura picaresca* 693). As a concern all over Europe, the problem of the strong woman versus the weak man was very popular; see Natalie Z. Davis (124–151). About women in *El criticón,* see Avilés, "La alegoría y la mujer monstruo."

6. The rejection of the mother as a fundamental member of familial intercourse is discussed by Avilés, "La alegoría"; on women in *El criticón,* see Cacho, Kassier (12, 134), Checa (101), and Paul J. Smith (104–108).

7. Herder has defined *Bildung* as "rising up to humanity through culture" (in Gadamer 10). François Jost defines the concept through *Bild* (image, model, picture): "the process by which a human being becomes a replica of his mentor, and is identified with him as the exemplary model" (135). See also Gadamer (11). The idea of a mentor, the construction of the self by means of another exemplary figure, the acquisition of the necessary cultural codes that define the social space to be inhabited through a familial perception of a model—all of these are crucial ideas that we need to keep in mind.

8. "[Critilo] then began to teach the ignorant young man to speak, and easily succeeded thanks to his [Andrenio's] docility and eagerness to learn. He started with both their names, telling him first his own, Critilo, and imposing on him the name Andrenio. Both names were fitting, the first because it indicated the one's judgment, and the second because it signaled the other's human nature."

9. Something very similar happens with Zoraida in "The Captive's Tale," an interpolated novella in *Don Quixote.* Zoraida insists on being called María, reject-

ing her Moorish past and trying to redefine herself in terms of religious transformation. What is even more significant for our own perspective is the way Zoraida tries to construct a new self through a visual encounter: the apparition of the Virgin Mary, who automatically becomes a visual telos to be achieved by means of a rejection of her father and a journey toward Spain (see Cervantes 296–334).

10. "You, Critilo, ask me who I am, and I wish to learn the answer from you."

11. The difference is that Friday is not a tabula rasa. Like Zoraida in "The Captive's Tale," there is a history in these characters that needs to be transformed by means of an alternative model. In a similar way, Friday needs to get rid of his tribal past, his cannibalistic and grotesque nature. Andrenio needs to distance himself from the she-wolf that raised him in the cave (a true allegory of the female body), although he already knows that there was a difference between himself and his young brothers (the cubs).

12. "You are the first man I have seen until this day, and in you I recognize myself more vividly than in the silent crystals of a water fountain, which many a time I sought out of curiosity and applauded in my ignorance."

13. This social recognition is severely restricted in the text. As I will show later on, societal interaction becomes extremely difficult at the level of communitary encounters.

14. The volume in which Bryson's essay is contained has been very useful to me, especially the preface by Hal Foster and the essays by Martin Jay, Jonathan Crary, and Bryson.

15. "A great difference exists between seeing and observing, since he who understands not cannot be heedful. It does little good to see a lot with one's eyes but not with one's intellect, or to see without noticing."

16. "I saw myself mirrored on a water fountain, and then I noticed that I was the one I had thought other. I cannot describe for you the wonder and pleasure I felt then and there."

17. He knows of his mistaken belief that the she-wolf was his mother from the moment he begins to perceive his being (1.1, 71): "¿Soy bruto como estos? Pero no, que observo entre ellos y entre mí palpables diferencias: ellos están vestidos de pieles; yo desabrigado, menos favorecido de quien nos dio el ser" (Am I brutish [an animal] like them? But no, since between them and me I observe palpable differences: they wear fur, and I am uncovered, less favored by he who created us).

18. He goes on to define the Mirror Stage as a "drama whose internal thrust is precipitated from insufficiency to anticipation" (Lacan, *Ecrits* 4).

19. Jacqueline Rose explains: "The [mirror] stage is a fiction because it conceals, or freezes, the infant's lack of motor co-ordination and the fragmentation of its drives. But it is salutary for the child, since it gives it the first sense of a coherent identity in which it can recognize itself" (30). For Lacan, the presence of the mother is crucial because it "guarantees its reality for the child" (Rose 30). In Gracián, this function is articulated by the look of the father and by his own recognition of his difference with the wolves.

20. For my purposes here let me quote one example pertaining to the eyes: "Para tanto ver, poco parecen dos ojos, y éssos tan juntos; de una alhaja tan preciosa lleno había de estar todo este animado palacio [the body]. Pero ya que hayan de ser dos, no más, pudiéranse repartir, y que uno estuviera delante para

ver lo que viene y el otro atrás para lo que queda: con esso, nunca perdieran de vista las cosas" (for so much there is to see in the world two eyes seem so little, and so close together! This animated palace should be all covered with this precious jewel. Since, however, they are but two, no more, they ought to be distributed, such that one stood in front to see what is coming, and the other one in back to see what is left behind: with this, things would never be left out of sight) (192). Andrenio has a certain anxiety toward his own body and his inability to use it properly. Critilo and Artemia's function is to show him how these parts of the body can be used correctly. They answer by describing the body as "sufficient," and at the same time building a map of functions and strategies that they hope will be internalized by the young character.

21. Going back to Lacan, I wish to state that my use of his ideas does not imply a kind of "ahistorical" detour. As part of the ocularcentrism that has dominated descriptions of socialization throughout the West, Gracián and Lacan partake of the same allegorical productive field, centered on "sight" and "vision" as the privileged locus of development and knowledge. It is also interesting to note that Lacan's construction of subjectivity is based substantially on sixteenth- and seventeenth-century authors like Descartes and painters like Dürer, da Vinci, Holbein and others, especially pertaining to vision. See Lacan (*Four Fundamental Concepts* 67–119), where he reconstructs the scopic field by a radical rearrangement of the Cartesian cogito and the "geometral dimension of vision" as constructed by Renaissance perspective. Freud also creates a narrative of development through the visual recognition of the penis (or the lack of it). Gracián sort of narrates his own version. See Martin Jay, where he describes the hegemonic nature of vision as part of modernity (he states that "modernity has been normally considered resolutely ocularcentric" ["Scopic Regimes" 3; see also 4–5]), and David M. Levin's volume on vision, particularly the essays by Judovitz and Martin Jay. Concerning the allegorical construction made by Freud and Lacan, I completely agree with Lennard Davis: "One could argue that Freud gave people a way of thinking about their own lives in novelistic terms—that is, making an organized series of events out of what had previously been seen as random details of life" (112). Likewise Gracián creates his own peculiar fiction of human development.

22. "In the body's fragile vessel, the spirit is perfected day to day. It is not instantly perfected. All men suffer at first from the annoying sweetness of childhood and the indelicate crudeness of youth; from the lust for sensual pleasures and from the inclination toward levity, toward juvenile pursuits, and toward frivolous occupations." There are many examples of this attitude toward children all over Europe, and especially among moralists. See Ariés (131–32), Vigil (127), and Stone (124–126) for comments on this rejection.

23. "Era increíble el agasajo con que a todos acariciaba aquella madre común, atendiendo a su gusto y su regalo, y para esto llevaba mil invenciones de juguetes con que entretenerlos. Había hecho también gran provisión de regalos, y en llorando alguno, al punto acudía afectuosa, haziéndole fiestas y caricias, concediéndole cuanto pedía a trueque de que no llorasse" (It was a wonder to witness the prodigality of this ordinary mother toward all the children. She was attentive to their every whim, and for this purpose carried with her a thousand tricks with which to distract them. She also carried many gifts with her, and when one of the children cried, she would instantly tend to him affectionately, ap-

plauding and caressing him, and granting him all he asked for so that he would stop crying) (1.5, 115). Later on, the carnage begins, but what matters to Gracián is precisely the excessive care and love for children (see 115–119). Critilo summarizes and *comments* on what they have just seen: "Los propios padres, con el intenso amor que tienen a sus hijuelos, condescienden con ellos; y porque no llore el rapaz, le conceden cuanto quiere, déxanle hazer su voluntad en todo y salir con la suya siempre: y assí, se cría vicioso" (Because of their intense love for their children, the parents themselves give in to them, and to stop the fiend from crying they grant him all he wants, and let him do as he pleases, so that he always gets what he wants: thus he grows spoiled) (119). Again we find here that "no" so important for Crusoe as a paternal figure. Contrary to Lacan, Gracián cannot postulate the mother as an informing tool for the child's imago. The face of the mother is the one that cannot be seen.

24. Even Critilo, when recounting his adventures with Felisinda in Goa, rejects his own mother: "Mas yo, de sus rigores [the father's], apelaba a la piadosa impertinencia de una madre que, cuando más me amparaba, me perdía" (But I, escaping my father's rigor, appealed to my mother's pious impertinence. Her overprotection meant my perdition) (1.4, 105).

25. ". . . in want, and tempered perhaps by a stepmother's rigors." Paraphrasing Walter Ong, Ruth El Saffar comments: "Focusing on schooling and the increasingly widespread development of learned Latin as the instrument of academic discourse, [Ong] likens the process to which so many of the major figures of the sixteenth and seventeenth century were subjected in childhood to a rite of passage, one whose result was to produce in boys a second birth, a renaissance, not now out of the womb of the mother but from the father's head" (9).

26. "Cursed be the man who puts his trust in another, whoever he might be. What should I say, friends and brothers? One should not trust one's own children; he is a fool who gives away his property before his time has come. . . . One should not trust even fathers themselves, since some have deceived their own sons; and how many mothers today sell their own daughters!"

27. Friendship in *El criticón* is the only relationship that produces gratification for Gracián. But this relationship must be established between men of equal social and intellectual standing. The "friend" is also one of the most difficult characters to find. See *crisi* 2 and 3 of Part 2. Because of considerations of space, I am unable to pursue a complete analysis of the importance of friendship and visual self-recognition of the other. What I can say here is that the same recognition found in the look of the father is also found in Gerión, the allegorical figure of the friend. Gerión sends to Salastano (anagram for Lastanosa, a powerful noble and friend of Gracián's in Huesca) a *mirror* where all characters see "sus verdaderos retratos, ocasión de quedar declarada y confirmada la amistad entre todos" (their true portraits, where friendship among all of them was finally declared and confirmed) (339). Here the gaze of the other becomes the mirror image of oneself and a self-satisfying reflection of communal equality.

28. ". . . in order to live a man must arm himself from head to toes, not with just eyes, but with wide-open, alert eyes."

29. "Do you see or do you observe? Not everyone observes what he sees."

30. Sebeok discusses anxiety in semiotic terms and quotes Grinker's definition, which I think is pertinent for what I have been saying: "Anxiety is of great

significance as a signal of threat for it precedes or accompanies active preparation for adjustment" (36). Although one could conclude that the picaros' social actions stem from anxiety, too, I tend to think that theirs is centered on aggressive reaction rather than careful "preparation and adjustment," which is the reaction formulated by *El criticón.* Characters in Gracián's fiction are required to behave according to ethical norms associated with certain classes, all identified with either the nobles or the "letrados" (intellectuals and bureaucrats). Characters in the picaresque novel articulate strategies of deception in order to ascend socially or to be recognized by others as legitimate members of a society that continually rejects them. In that sense, picaros are aggressive movers, trying to distort language and the ethical constructs that support society (Lazarillo, for example, describing his final situation as one of triumph). Critilo and Andrenio, on the other hand, want to maintain a moral status that Gracián associates with their class (keep in mind that Critilo's father is an ambassador to Goa). Such status prerogatives include a visual knowledge, and consequently a special power: the capacity to perceive the other's possible actions.

31. This encounter with the other resembles distantly Sartre's conception of the gaze in *Being and Nothingness,* where the subject as viewer realizes that he is a "spectacle to another's sight" (Bryson 89). Sartre's fundamental assertion in terms of a communitary encounter is described as a "hostile contest of wills between competing subjects" (Jay "Sartre, Merleau-Ponty" 155). See Sartre (301–400), Bryson (88–91), and Jay's article on Sartre and Merleau-Ponty (especially 149–160). Lacan, reworking the Sartrean concept of the gaze, develops his own visual map, describing the subject as a being who is "looked at, in the spectacle of the world" (*Four Fundamental Concepts* 75), not only by other human beings, but by all objects occupying the visual field. See Lacan's personal account of an experience within the realm of the gaze, his recollection of the incident with the fisherman Petit-Jean and the sardine can (*Four Fundamental Concepts* 95–96). Gracián seems to be close to Sartre in his preoccupation with individuals rather than with objects as they appear to the characters. But contrary to Sartre's radical rejection of vision, Gracián's response is to increment a kind of visual competence aided by the intellect. In other words, Gracián cannot dispense with the centrality of vision for the deployment of the body in space, although its capacity to interpret the other in visual terms is in constant jeopardy.

32. I could exemplify these ideas with multiple examples, from the dangers in the court of Falimundo to the difficulties that stem from various spheres of influence (Hipocrinda, Mando, Vicios, Vulgo, and others, translated as Hypocrisy, Rule, Vices, and Common People, respectively). One of the most interesting ones would be Falsirena as the monstrous allegory of the female body, and the only danger described in the text as the one that crosses all stages of development, from adolescence to old age.

33. In a forthcoming article, I explain this sense of futility and self-cancellation as part of Gracián's conception of history as temporal entrapment.

34. "Of a squint-eyed man he foretold that he would not have a good eye for anything, and he was right. Of a certain hunchback he guessed his evil inclinations, of a lame man the crooked path he was following, and of a left-handed man his bad habits."

35. *Diccionario de Autoridades* defines *cifra* (cipher or sign) in the following terms: "Modo u arte de escribir, dificultoso de comprehender sus cláusulas, si no es teniendo la clave: el cual puede ser usando de caracteres inventados, o trocando las letras, eligiendo unas en lugar de otras: a que se suele añadir, quitar algunas letras, y suplir su falta con números" (A way or art of writing, difficult to understand unless you know the key; such an art may consist of using invented characters, or switching letters around, using some instead of others: letters are usually added, or subtracted, and replaced by numbers) (1: 347b).

36. "What I find difficult is to read and understand the things of this Earth, for as everything is in code and human hearts are so hermetic and inscrutable, I assure you that the best reader loses his place. And another thing: If you do not know the key to each code you will find yourselves lost, unable to read a single word or to recognize a single letter, a trace or a tilde."

37. "It is a pity that there be poor readers who take a C to be a B where instead they should have taken it for a D. They are ignorant about codes and cannot understand them; they have not studied the subject of human intention, which is the most difficult of all."

38. See the way in which the Descifrador solves the problem of interpretation through the "contracifra" on pages 616–624. It is interesting to note here how the vision of the other is connected systematically to writing instead of orality. Interpretation needs an allegorical construction of bodily presence at the same time that it articulates features of a written text as visual representation (see Jay, "Scopic Regimes" 3). The body as text corresponds to vision as reading and interpretation. It is also interesting to note that this desire articulated through the Descifrador corresponds to one of the major fantasies of Western culture. We can find a recent formulation of such a fantasy in Kaja Silverman's recent book: "If we were in *possession of an instrument* which would *permit us to penetrate deep into the innermost recesses of the human psyche,* we would find not identity, but a void" (4, my emphasis). The desire to "penetrate" the interstices of the other's body is one of the most salient features of psychoanalysis. In Gracián the actualization of such a power is represented in the character of the Zahorí.

39. "With just a glance I come to see the very substance of things, and not just the accidents or appearances that you perceive; I can recognize whether someone has substance; I measure his depth; I discover how far he will go, what his sphere of influence is, how far his knowledge and understanding reach, how great his prudence. I measure the size of his heart and check whether or not his brave liver has been reduced to a mere spleen. I see his brain as clearly as if through glass.... upon seeing someone I know how much he weighs and what he thinks."

40. According to Lennard Davis, "The very idea of character is inseparable from the moral and civilizing lesson to be learned.... The ideological role of character was certainly part of the civilizing or, if you will, the socially indoctrinating aspect of the novel" (117). Although he speaks of the novel in the nineteenth century, the same could be said about the ideological thrust of *El criticón*.

41. The outward projection toward the reader is found at the end of the book, with the last sentence: "Lo que allí vieron [in the Island of Immortality], lo mucho que lograron, quien quisiere saberlo y experimentarlo, tome el rumbo de la virtud insigne, del valor heroico, y llegará a parar al teatro de la fama, al trono

de la estimación y al centro de la inmortalidad" (Whoever wishes to know and experience what they saw there [in the Island of Immortality], the extent of their joy, should follow the path of outstanding virtue and heroic valor, and he shall reach the theater of fame, the throne of high regard, and the seat of immortality) (3.12, 812). The promise of the text is a reenactment of the journey the characters just ended, with the possibility of attaining the same goals described by the narrative.

42. As a matter of fact, the stage of childhood has been extending progressively throughout the ages. Laws prohibiting youths from drinking alcohol and going to certain movies are just some of the known examples we can recall here. There has been an incremental preoccupation with the speed of child development. The array of cultural devices to control young men and women has also been intensified through the media and education.

43. Jay emphasizes the Baroque's "fascination for opacity, unreadability, and the indecipherability of the reality it depicts" ("Scopic Regimes" 17; see also 16–20).

Works Cited

Alvar, Manuel, ed. *Gracián y su época: Actas de la I Reunión de Filólogos Aragoneses.* Zaragoza: Institución Fernando el Católico, 1986.

Ariés, Phillippe. *Centuries of Childhood: A Social History of Family Life.* Trans. by Robert Baldick. New York: Vintage, 1962.

Avilés, Luis F. "La alegoría y la mujer monstruo: El problema de la representación femenina en *El Criticón* de Gracián." *La Torre* 25 (1993): 79–93.

———. "To the Frontier and Back: The Centrifugal and the Centripetal in Cervantes's *Persiles y Sigismunda* and Gracián's *El Criticón.*" *The Worlds of Pilgrimage: Gender, Nationality and the Sacred.* Forthcoming.

Bakhtin, Mikhail M. *Rabelais and His World.* Trans. Hélène Iswolsky. Bloomington: Indiana University Press, 1984.

Blanco, Mercedes. "*El Criticón*: Aporías de una ficción ingeniosa." *Criticón* 33 (1986): 5–36.

Bordo, Susan. *The Flight to Objectivity: Essays on Cartesianism and Culture.* Albany: SUNY Press, 1987.

Bryson, Norman. "The Gaze in the Expanded Field." *Vision and Visuality.* Ed. Hal Foster. Dia Art Foundation. Seattle: Bay Press, 1988. 87–113.

Cacho, María Teresa. "Misoginia y Barroco: Baltasar Gracián." *Literatura y vida cotidiana: Actas de las Cuartas Jornadas de Investigación Interdisciplinaria.* Madrid: Universidad Autónoma de Madrid, 1987. 173–186.

Cervantes, Miguel de. *Don Quixote.* Trans. John Ormsby. Ed. Joseph Jones and Kenneth Douglas. New York and London: Norton, 1981.

Checa, Jorge. *Gracián y la imaginación arquitectónica.* Potomac, Md.: Scripta Humanística, 1986.

Chodorow, Nancy. *The Reproduction of Mothering.* Berkeley: University of California Press, 1978.

Corominas, Joan. *Breve Diccionario de la Lengua Castellana.* 3rd ed. Madrid: Gredos, 1973.

Davis, Lennard. *Resisting Novels: Ideology and Fiction.* New York and London: Methuen, 1987.

Davis, Natalie Z. *Society and Culture in Early Modern France.* Stanford: Stanford University Press, 1975.

Defoe, Daniel. *Robinson Crusoe.* New York: New American Library, 1961.

Deleito y Piñuela, José. *La mala vida en la España de Felipe IV.* Madrid: Alianza, 1987.

Diccionario de Autoridades. 4 vols. Madrid: Gredos, 1979.

El Saffar, Ruth. "Literary Reflections on the 'New Man': Changes in Consciousness in Early Modern Europe." *Revista de Estudios Hispánicos* 32 (1988): 1–23.

Foster, Hal. Preface to *Vision and Visuality.* Ed. Hal Foster. Dia Art Foundation. Seattle: Bay Press, 1988. ix-xiv.

Foucault, Michel. *The Order of Things.* Ed. R. D. Laing. New York: Vintage Books, 1973.

———. "Technologies of the Self." *Technologies of the Self: A Seminar with Michel Foucault.* Ed. Luther H. Martin et al. Amherst: University of Massachusetts Press, 1988.

Fra Molinero, Baltasar. "El negro Zaide: Marginación social y textual en el *Lazarillo.*" *Hispania* 76 (1993): 20–29.

Gadamer, Hans-Georg. *Truth and Method.* Trans. J. Weinsheimer and D. Marshall. 2nd ed. New York: Crossroad, 1989.

Gracián, Baltasar. *El Criticón.* Ed. Miguel Romera-Navarro. 3 vols. Philadelphia: University of Pennsylvania Press, 1938–40.

———. *El criticón.* Ed. Santos Alonso. Madrid: Cátedra, 1984.

———. *Obras completas.* Ed. Evaristo Correa Calderón. Madrid: Aguilar, 1944.

Jay, Martin. "Scopic Regimes of Modernity." *Vision and Visuality.* Ed. Hal Foster. Dia Art Foundation. Seattle: Bay Press, 1988. 2–27.

———. "Sartre, Merleau-Ponty, and the Search for a New Ontology of Sight." *Modernity and the Hegemony of Vision.* Ed. David M. Levin. Berkeley and Los Angeles: University of California Press, 1993. 143–185.

Jost, François. *Introduction to Comparative Literature.* Indianapolis: Pegasus, 1974.

Judovitz, Dalia. "Vision, Representation, and Technology in Descartes." *Modernity and the Hegemony of Vision.* Ed. David M. Levin. Berkeley and Los Angeles: University of California Press, 1993. 63–86.

Kassier, Theodore L. *The Truth Disguised: Allegorical Structure and Technique in Gracián's "El Criticón."* London: Tamesis Books, 1976.

Lacan, Jacques. *Ecrits: A Selection.* Trans. Alan Sheridan. New York and London: Norton, 1977.

———. *The Four Fundamental Concepts of Psychoanalysis.* Trans. Alan Sheridan. Ed. Jacques-Alain Miller. New York and London: Norton, 1978.

Levin, David M., ed. *Modernity and the Hegemony of Vision.* Berkeley and Los Angeles: University of California Press, 1993.

Maravall, José A. *La cultura del Barroco.* Barcelona: Ariel, 1983.

———. *La literatura picaresca desde la historia social.* Madrid: Taurus, 1986.

Rose, Jacqueline. "Introduction II." *Feminine Sexuality: Jacques Lacan and the Ecole Freudienne.* Ed. Juliet Mitchell and Jacqueline Rose. New York and London: Norton, 1978.

Sartre, Jean-Paul. *Being and Nothingness.* Trans. Hazel E. Barnes. New York: Washington Square Press, 1956.

Sebeok, Thomas A. *A Sign Is Just a Sign.* Bloomington and Indianapolis: Indiana University Press, 1991.

Silverman, Kaja. *Male Subjectivity at the Margins.* New York: Routledge, 1992.
Smith, Paul Julian. "The Rhetoric of Allegory in *El Criticón.*" *Conflicts of Discourse: Spanish Literature in the Golden Age.* Ed. Peter W. Evans. Manchester and New York: Manchester University Press, 1990.
Stone, Lawrence. *The Family, Sex and Marriage in England, 1500–1800.* Abridged ed. New York: Harper and Row, 1977.
Vigil, Mariló. *La vida de las mujeres en los siglos XVI y XVII.* Madrid: Siglo XXI, 1986.
Werlen, Benno. *Society, Action and Space: An Alternative Human Geography.* Trans. Gayna Walls. London and New York: Routledge, 1993.

Chapter 5
Gracián and the Emergence of the Modern Subject

William Egginton

In the current discussions concerning the emergence of the modern subject, philosophers, historians, thinkers, and researchers from all disciplines have agreed that something happened around and during the seventeenth century that fundamentally changed European mentality, ushering in what many have chosen to call modernity. Michel Foucault, in the preface to *The Order of Things*, speaks of the two great discontinuities in the episteme of western thought, the first occurring around the middle of the seventeenth century and announcing what he terms the classical, as opposed to the modern, episteme, but which in all other aspects points to the same concept of modernity (xxii). Among the many voices partaking in this discussion, Jacques Lacan and, more recently, his followers have articulated the questions involved in a particularly eloquent manner. From the psychoanalytic perspective, the emergence of modern subjectivity has to do with the Lacanian dimension of the real, or that which always returns to the same place. It is in this time we call the Renaissance that human observation begins to undermine the tangible reality of the real, mainly in the physical sciences, such as physics and astronomy, but consequently and soon thereafter in the human sciences and letters, principal among those philosophy, thereby threatening to dissolve the basic unity of physical and metaphysical certainties characterizing the anthropocentrism of the Renaissance. The ideal example of the real in the premodern world is that of the stars, which were understood to be fixed in their place in an immobile firmament, until observation proved them to be susceptible to the same laws of motion as earthly things (*Ethics of Psychoanalysis* 75). It is in this gap opened in the texture of humanity's symbolic understanding that Lacan, among others, situates the birth of the modern subject, a subject whose frantic search for self-identity is constantly hindered by his need to mediate that search through a society and a language that consistently evade being anchored to any essential reality. As John Rajchman describes it, for the observers of the Renaissance, "an infinite universe of pointless particles supplants the closed, meaningful world of ancient cosmologies. The good for man can no longer be found in that universe; the world can no longer edify us" (46).

If the process of historical inquiry is close to that of archaeology, as Foucault would claim, then we learn of the events that shape humanity through their effects on human mentality, which we may access only through the records of human discourse. Thus, if we are to continue the search for the origins of modernity, and thereby seek to enrich our knowledge of the modern subject, we are bound to hunt among the products that remain for us of the culture of the epoch for the signs of such a cataclysmic turn. It is the contention of this essay that the Spanish Baroque is an indispensable source of such evidence, one example of which is provided by the writings of a seventeenth-century Spanish moralist, a Jesuit author of books on worldly self-improvement named Baltasar Gracián. Gracián, I shall claim, writes from a historically privileged position, from which he witnesses the epistemological traumas marking the dawn of modernity. Psychoanalysis understands the problem of modernity as primarily one of ethics, posited in terms of a search for the Good beyond the facade of social structures (*Ethics of Psychoanalysis* 75), and it is in the realm of ethics that this study retains its focus. My approach is to analyze the thought of Gracián as a coherent moral system, basing my argument largely on his most synthetic work, *El oráculo manual y arte de prudencia*, and to compare that moral system, within the discursive framework established by Lacan, with the moral system that for many represents the apex of modernity, the ethics of Kant. This comparative analysis will enable me to locate in Gracián the crossroads between the universal anthropocentrism of the Renaissance and the transcendental subject of modernity, and to support, perhaps, some of the most recent groundbreaking insight into the nature of the Enlightenment project and the organization of the modern subject.

To begin with, we must show that there is, in fact, a discernible moral direction to the writings of Gracián. This is not so straightforward as it might appear, as there exists at the moment a current of scholarship that sustains the ultimate ambiguity of Gracián's texts. Notable among these is Jorge Checa, who argues that the *Oráculo manual*, which he also takes as a prime example of his work, is a complex tissue of "numerous bifurcations and unassimilable elements that block the establishment of fixed meaning" (270, my translation). Checa's point is that the complex and apparently contradictory manner of Gracián's writing acts as a sort of *mise en abîme* of his philosophy, obfuscating any immediate or clear understanding of meaning in favor of a shifting, intricate style, in order to communicate an eminently relative or contingent code of behavior. Rather than debating this point with Checa, I accept it fully, with the understanding that, behind the "baroqueness" of his style, there is a stable criterion of action, defining for Gracián a vector of desire and a coherent moral system. In other words, the fact that Gracián rates the contingency of action on circumstance above any metaphysical standard of behavior in no way excludes his work from a definable morality, because the morality of that system depends on the motive behind the guiding of one's actions. This motive, this driving desire behind Gracián's discourse in *Oráculo manual*, does not change. As José Antonio Maravall states, "To each one of us Gracián tries to clarify that depth, elemental and simple, *of the man that we have to make of ourselves*, of the man with which each of us is charged to make into a subject" (351, my emphasis).[1] The goal, everywhere in evidence in Gracián, is the creation of a "persona," which, for reasons I will return to, I shall refer to in this essay as subject.[2]

"Everything is now at a crest, and being subject is the utmost" (*Oráculo,* 1).[3] The very first words of this work convey the sense of a world in stasis, or better yet, saturation: "More is needed just to deal with one man these days than with a whole people in the past."[4] The referent to this feeling of saturation is what one might call society, for as we see, Gracián immediately focuses the scope of his first aphorism to the interrelations of humans. Therein he observes a diachronic change in the nature of these relations, resulting in an actual scenario in which the sufficiency of wisdom is measured against its ability to aid the individual in his "dealing" with the other members of society. In this competitive, even hostile, environment conjured by the text's first four lines, we have already the initial problem, a vector of desire and the designation of a solution: the individual is thrown into a saturated, competitive environment; there is a way of "dealing" with this situation effectively; the name of this way is to become a subject.

The defining characteristic of Gracián's subject is his differentiation from the masses. He desires the recognition of others in order to gain power over them, and the greater his recognition, the higher he rises among the echelons of eminence. There is a definite structure to society expressed in the *Oráculo,* one that could be depicted as a series of concentric circles representing ever increasing "reputación" or social eminence as one moves toward the center, and a corresponding increase in the power to wield one's will over those inhabiting the outer rings. On the very outside would be the great majority of beings, those not recognized as individual subjects, but rather signified always as an indiscriminate and undifferentiated mass. They themselves lack the power of discrimination, and correspondingly they are not distinguished, they are not recognized. The result of this implicit structure is the lack of any definable interior to a person. Any interior worth mentioning only appears as differentiated from external appearances by which a subject continues to garner recognition and increase his power, and to the extent that the interior exists at all, it is only knowable through the reflection of its representation in society.

There is, on the other hand, depth, which translates to a relative depth of exterior, or of ostentatious ability. In maxim 48,

Gracián says that "As much depth as a man has, so much is he a subject,"[5] as if to assure us that the status of subject still depends on some essential interior substance. His metaphor, however, draws a different picture: "There are those with nothing but facades, like houses unfinished because funds ran out; they have the entrance of a palace and the bedroom of a shack. There is nowhere to stand, or rather, everything stands still, because, done with the salutations, all conversation comes to a halt."[6] Here as in every case, the supposed interior qualities of a subject are radically contingent on his social, intersubjective skills. A subject is perceived as having a rich interior if he can sustain conversation beyond a mere greeting, if he withstands the interrogation society poses for him, if his facade is deep enough to satisfy the relative discerning capabilities of his peers. We could complete, then, the structure of concentric circles I proposed as representative of Gracián's society by describing the subjects maneuvering within those circles as identical figures in miniature, whose advancement toward the center of society depends entirely on the depth of their facade in relation to the discernment of those around them.

To be sure, the status of "plausibilidad" (signifying both "worthy of applause" and "believable") is a focus of contention among scholars of Gracián, but there can be no doubt that whether it is a question of impressing the many or of impressing the few, in Gracián it is always a question of whom to impress. In fact, it is not difficult to derive a hierarchy of behaviors from the *Oráculo* that in turn responds to the stage that one occupies in the journey toward the societal acme. Clearly, one needs to win the applause of the masses if one is even to compete in the realm of subjects, but once there, it is never sufficient. As a subject what really matters is the recognition of other subjects, while one always tries to keep an impressive face outward toward the vulgar crowds.

One maxim in particular, 92, has been interpreted to council sobriety of action above pleasing the masses. Its translation in the 1992 edition by Christopher Maurer encourages this reading: "It's more a matter of walking surely than of courting vulgar applause. A reputation for prudence is the ultimate triumph of fame." In Spanish, the same maxim reads, "Es un camino a lo seguro, aunque no tan a lo plausible, si bien la reputación de cuerdo es el triumfo de la fama." In its original, the conditional structure of the sentence is maintained, in which it is clear that "sure footing," or prudence, only takes precedence over fame if one realizes that in itself it is the ultimate guarantee of fame. In the last analysis, it is still the "plausibility" of the action that determines its value for the Gracianesque subject.

As yet another instance of the all-consuming drive toward subject-ness in Gracián, let us turn to maxim 97:

> Obtain and conserve reputation. It is the profit of fame. It costs much, because it is born of eminence, which is as rare as the mediocre is common. Once obtained, it is easily maintained. Oblige much and work more. It is a kind of majesty when it becomes veneration for the sublimity of its cause and its sphere; but substantial reputation is that which always had value.[7]

I bring to attention this example because it is another that seems to revere the idea of substance, in apparent opposition to a primacy of pure representation. What we must remember, however, is that substance, in Gracián, is always posited by way of appearance, as in this case, where it signifies that which is the necessary support of true reputation. This "what lies beyond" is, in fact, an essential part of Gracián's morality. The insubstantial substance, this goal lurking behind the contradictions, conceits, and tautologies, is the device that is most instrumental in inciting and sustaining desire. It is correlative, of course, to the Lacanian *objet a,* the object cause of desire that is described as a place of infinite substitutions, as pure form, as the lack in symbolic representation indicating the real of unsymbolizable desire. There is always an irreducible gap at the base of any symbolic construction, a place from which the system is not coherent, or perhaps an element not definable within the system, but only from outside the system to which it belongs. It is there that subjects posit their object of desire, conceiving of it as some special quality, some indispensable form of enjoyment without which they can never be satisfied. Gracián's discourse uses these irreducible gaps to organize desire much as the desire of the modern subject is organized, that is, structured by the symbolic order, as manifested in society and language.

This is, then, the meaning of that "something else" that is always behind appearances. Gracián conjures this specter of desire by means of the very indeterminacy that Checa notes. The interdependency of his key concepts, such as prudence, acuteness, virtue, genius, and so on, form a network of signifiers of positive value that are ultimately undefinable without reference to the very moral system they serve to support. As the object of desire is always that which is directly beyond the reach of symbolic apprehension, these tautologically defined "pure signifiers" would place a considerable attractive force on the subject. Gracián cultivates this attraction even more explicitly when speaking of the qualities of "persona," as in, for example, maxim 6:

> Man at his peak. He isn't born made; from day to day he perfects himself in his person, in his work, until he becomes the consummate being, to the completion of his talents and his eminence: he must know himself as elevated in taste, purified in genius, mature of judgment, purified of will. Some are never complete, they're always missing something; others take a while. The consummate man, wise in his words, sober in his deeds, is admitted to and even desired in the unique commerce of the discreet.[8]

In this remarkable synthesis of almost everything we have discussed to this point, there are several elements on which to focus. The first is the description of those who don't make it, of whom he says that they are missing a certain "something." This unknown something is by definition the *objet a*, and the obvious effect of the manner of its formation is to instill a desire in the reader for the unknown quality. Another point of interest is, once again, the absolute impossibility of expressing what it is these subjects have that makes them special; we know it has to do with the right mixture of qualities or affects, in the excellence of their tastes, of their cleverness, of their judgment, and so on. In other words, the nature of this ultimate "something" is still entirely determined by the symbolic order of interpersonal exchange, in which the desiring subject must play his cards right in order to match his reputation to the shifting tides of opinion. The third point of interest is the implicit recognition Gracián gives to the effects of this quality on other people. The subject possessing this quality is admitted and *desired* by the most selective clique of all, the inner circle of society whom he terms *los discretos*, the discreet ones. Here we see displayed most blatantly Lacan's formula, that desire is desire of the Other, determined by society and the symbolic network.

This special quality animating the Gracianesque subject immediately confers a real political power on him. It is manifested in his prototype hero, Fernando of Aragón, who is "vital, who sees everything, hears everything, smells everything, touches everything" (Hafter 140). Clearly this describes a special intimacy with the objective world, a gaze unlimited by perspective, which is another manifestation of the fantasy object; those in possession of this quality are conceived of as having a secret means of enjoyment, unattainable to the rest of us, which conveys on them the powers of leadership, charisma, and intrinsic authority. As he says in maxim 122, "Mastery in words and deeds. It makes a place for you in all parts and earns respect in advance. It influences everything: conversation, oration, even walking and looking and desiring."[9] By means of their qualities, but really by means of the desire they control, these subjects can influence the minds and actions of those whose recognition and respect they command.

Gracián not only remarks upon this powerful instrument to be found in the manipulation of appearances, he counsels the reader on how to cultivate it and, as Checa notes, demonstrates his method in his own writing. This manner of representation could be called the quintessential trope of the Baroque, the practice of complicating representation so as to augment the receiver's captivation. In maxim 94, Gracián speaks of the "incomprensibilidad del caudal," or incomprehensibility of means, explaining that "greater affects of veneration are inspired by public opinion and doubt as to how deep one's resources go, than by evidence of them, as great as they may be."[10] The nub of his advice is how to manipulate one's discourse so that the receiver always assumes there is more to it than meets the eye. There is an implicit awareness here, as elsewhere, that substance itself is nothing other than a matter of degrees of appearance and that one can cultivate the impression of interior substance through careful attention to the representation of one's exterior.

This awareness of representation in the writing of Gracián is one of the first indications of his ultimately modern status. In many ways, the subject that Gracián describes, and implies, in *Oráculo manual* is already a modern subject. The essential defining quality of the modern subject is the fact that it is split, that somehow subjectivity is not immanent but rather that the subject can only come to know himself through a reflective process, and that there is, perhaps, some inherent gap between the real self and its capacity to be known. This understanding is in evidence in a great expanse of Gracián's work, particularly a passage from *El criticón*, quoted by Hafter in his *Gracián and Perfection*, in which the author says of his characters that by becoming subjects, "they went advancing beyond themselves first, the better subsequently to come to themselves" (107). This observation fits into a general rubric in Gracián in which the individual can only come to self-knowledge by way of identifying with what Lacan calls the ego ideal, the locus of symbolic identification, or that place from which the subject is seen by the big Other. J. A. Maravall also comments on this "need to know one's self; which for Gracián, in an intellectual way, consists in acquiring consciousness of one's position in relation to the world" (353).[11] This development of the ego ideal corresponds to the third logical moment of the development of subjectivity, the entrance into the symbolic order. The fact that this is recognized as a moment in the constitution of self is an extraordinary clue that this text is witness to a historical time between an episteme in which the self was conceived as coterminous with social position and one in which the trauma of its separation has been submerged, displaced by the symptom of transcendental subjectivity.

Another indicator of the advent of modernity, in accordance with the discursive framework we have established, would be the detachment of the social order from any determination by the real, the realization of a certain arbitrariness at the nexus between identity and social position. Maravall emphasizes this rupture, contrasting the medieval mentality in respect to identity with the change more or less completed by the Baroque period, in which individuals "begin to feel loose, disattached; they have broken the frame in which their life played out, and they must organize with their only means the fight to establish their place in society" (364).[12] An individual born into such a world has the experience of being thrown into a world without direction or positive mooring, "el mundo al revés," or the world topsy-turvy, as it was often called, and it is this feeling, dramatized in the Baroque and expressed most clearly in the works of Gracián, that Maravall associates with the beginning of modernity (355).

While one's locus of identification is still connected to one's position in the social sphere, that sphere is no longer tangibly connected to metaphysical truths. Identity has moved from essence to representation, and, as Alban Forcione says, the new social order involves an "unprecedented recognition that beings are constructed by what others confer to images" (683).[13] Such a conception of the constitution of identity has to be imagined within the structure of a society such as we have already described. Of utmost importance for the understanding of this moment is that this hierarchy of representation had achieved a certain autonomy, in which concepts such as Truth were fixed in relation to the social structure of power rather than to any metaphysical certainties.

As Gracián remarks in maxim 43, "Truth belongs to the few; deception is so common as to be vulgar."[14] In no part of this maxim is Truth treated as somehow essential, but, rather, as part of the patrimony of the upper echelons of society, those who corner the market on discernment. Surprisingly, it is precisely this ability to discriminate truth from falsity that give them the power to lie, to show a different face to the indiscriminate masses. This comes remarkably close to yet another criterion that Lacan establishes for subjectivity, that is, the ability to lie. The subject can lie because of the radical split between the subject of his enunciation and the subject of his utterance; he can pronounce the statement "I am lying" without feeling caught up in an inescapable paradox. Gracián's "persona" has the same ability, and for this reason Gracián can council him to "go with the flow" when in the spotlight of vulgar public opinion, and save his true sentiments for the "shade of the few and sober minded."

This concept of truth he proposes is, thus, intimately connected to the hierarchical structure of representation organizing society. When he states, in maxim 175, that "only Truth can bestow true reputation,"[15] Truth joins the rest of the signifiers of quality that are posited behind the skillfully maintained facade. Only a true subject can discern the Truth, and we recognize him as a subject because of his ability to discern the Truth. In the society of concentric circles, then, Truth is guaranteed by the center of the circle, occupied by whoever commands the most respect in the society, in this instance the monarch. What is most important to remember is that the center is not determined by any metaphysical presence; for Gracián, God does not enter the picture; as Maravall says, "What is certain is that Gracián is the first writer to consider life as a radical and inexorable reality, on which everything else depends" (356).[16] Gracián is writing a secular ethics for those desiring success in this world, and he is not concerned with other-worldly matters.

As I have argued elsewhere,[17] the dissolution of previous modes of organizing identification of self opened the space and the need for ideology in the modern sense, in which a subject is interpolated or invested into a particular political reality through the mediation of desire and identification. Gracián's writing clearly functions in this way in respect to the society of his time, a society that was, in fact, new, as Forcione notes, calling it "the recently discovered space of society" (656).[18] For even the idea of some identifiable concept such as society, not rigidly determined by the estatist reality of serfs and nobles, would have been inconceivable only a few centuries earlier. The move to center society as such can itself be understood as a last-ditch effort to retain the security of the medieval episteme, fossilizing social relations against the threatening tides of social change witnessed since the late Middle Ages. This is how both Forcione and Maravall understand Gracián's role, the former referring to his role in supporting the tensions necessary for the maintenance of society, the latter saying that his writing "supposes a support of the society it criticizes" and calling it "powerfully conservative" (341).[19]

The focus of Forcione's analysis is the tension he sees between two currents of thought at the time, that seeking to reground political difference in "society" and that seeking to defuse all tension in a radical return to "la nada," the nothingness at the heart of humanity. Forcione is right in characterizing each as being the logical reaction to the other, but I would also add that both react to a widespread loss of metaphysical certainty. Clearly, Gracián is symptomatic of the first current of thought, fighting against the hole at the center of existence with the cultivation of the "persona" (Forcione 682). As an example of the opposing school, Forcione turns to Miguel de Molinos, whose goal would be to "abolish the tyranny of the other" (685).[20] Molinos, he says, understands man's need to search for himself every time he tries to leave the nothingness of his soul, every time he tries to become someone or something, a description evocative of the Lacanian concept of repetition, by which the subject always reenacts the loss of some primordial object, in the hopes of recovering his lost *jouissance.* In fact, the sort of religious ecstasy that Molinos promises as the reward for the return to the "nada" is clearly an example of total *jouissance,* the radical dissolution of self that is the goal of the death drive.

To describe Miguel de Molinos, the Spanish mystic who developed the philosophy called quietism, a doctrine of contemplation and resignation, as in any way politically radical must strike some as a strange proposition. Yet, if seen historically, in light of the drive by thinkers such as Gracián to justify in moral terms a society of hierarchical differentiation based on the garnering of "opinión," Molinos's doctrine of total dissolution of self seems radical indeed, precisely because it threatens the foundations of this society upon which all power relations now rest. Thus, when we read Molinos, we can see how his discourse attempts to undermine the entire edifice of desire that moralists such as Gracián have constructed, precisely by teaching individuals not to endeavor to become subjects, by importuning them to accept an indiscriminate existence without the recognition of their peers:

> For the soul to make continual progress in its lowering, it must walk to the practice of annihilation, which consists in the abhorrence of honor, dignity and praise; for it is not right to give dignity, and honor to vileness and pure nothingness.[21] (Molinos 167)

While Molinos's writings are infinitely more directed toward the religious life, toward the adoration of God and the dedication of the self to prayerful contemplation, it was he who was ultimately banned by the Catholic institution and who spent the last years of his life in a prison cell (Forcione 688). On the other hand, although Gracián was taken to task for teaching the importance of worldly interests and barely mentioned the realm of religion, "the Jesuits never accused [him] of contradicting Catholic doctrine" (Maurer, in Gracián, *Art of Wordly Wisdom* xiv). The reason for this should be clear; while the teachings of Gracián may have been seen as somewhat inappropriate subject matter for a priest, they were recognized as serving to sustain the system in which the Church institution was grounded. Molinos, on the other hand, had authored a doctrine that, especially in light of its growing popularity, threatened to defuse the tension between individuals that served as that society's last support.

I said at the start, and have tried to demonstrate, that Gracián authored a definite moral system; I did not try to show, however, that it was ethical, in the Kantian sense of "disinterested." Clearly this would be absurd, as the moral doctrine at the heart of Gracián's writing is to act "pathologically," to act in one's interest. By positing the structure of society as a hierarchy of intersubjective relations, in which the individual gains power by way of his skill in representing himself, Gracián clears the way for a self-sustaining sphere of relations, cemented by the very desire that propels his moral system. As Maravall explains, in reference to the cult of the hero developed by Gracián, "the hero is, himself, a stabilizing factor. And his moral justification lies precisely in that he, the hero, the eminent one, brings to light, through his example, the ethical possibilities that society, such as it is, contains" (341).[22] By defining a morality that is inherently pathological, Gracián provides another support for a society structured on the tension of unequally shared power. The breach between social structure and its essential grounding in the observable real was complete, but humanity's identity had not had a chance to relocate its center. The ethical question of what one ought to do was for a time left in limbo between diametrical alternatives, but it would soon be reprised by the Enlightenment project to reground human identity in the real of the transcendental subject.

To best understand how Gracián intersects with the framing in psychoanalysis of the discussion of modernity, we need first to examine Lacan's reading of the epitome of Enlightenment thought, Immanuel Kant. The operative concept here is transcendental constitution, which posits the subject as the subject of a reasoning apparatus that itself transcends his limited physicality. Opposing the subject is the object, whose nature we can never know completely, the absolute reality of it as expressed by the *Ding an sich,* the Thing in itself. This skepticism toward the physical immediacy of the objective world is spawned of the rupture from the real that we have already said marks the end of the previous episteme; its logical conclusion lies with the positing of a subject that is itself beyond knowing. This transcendental constitution can exist, as Slavoj Žižek says, only so long as the gap separating the phenomenal world of things from the noumenal world of ideas persists (217). In other words, the transcendental subject is the symptom that has emerged in modernity, as a symbolic substitution for the traumatic gap in the real.

This shifting of the center of subjectivity can be located between Gracián's basing of ethical reality on the circumstances of phenomenal existence, and Descartes's move to ground existence in reason alone, the cornerstone of Enlightenment thought. (Of course, for Descartes the shift takes place against the backdrop of a God who serves as the *cogito*'s ultimate support, which is only to say that God himself has been thrown a curve, evicted from the real of an ordered physical/metaphysical harmony and deposited in the somewhat cramped quarters of human reason). The time frame here is remarkably tight—as Maravall points out, Descartes wrote his *Discourse on Method* seven years before the first book of *El criticón* was published (355), an overlap that can be explained by the particular historical differences of their respective countries—but it represents the nexus of a far slower, more vast, epistemological shift. Kant built on this first stone in his quest to ground ethics once again in the real. Since he knew objective reality to be unattainable, the subject must look inward for the traces of a universal law, based on a priori, logical reason (Lacan, "Kant avec Sade" 766). The only way of ensuring that the law met these criteria was to efface from the moral act any and all possible pathological motives. In this way, the law could be a direct expression of a universal and transcendental reason, finding its form in maxims that would only be valid if they could be applied universally. Thus, as Žižek tells us, for Kant, the law emerges in the place of a primordially repressed Good, the Good of the pathological objects that must be effaced in order to ensure the ethical nature of the law (230). Psychoanalysis understands this "wiping out" of all pathological interest from morality as the correlate to symbolic castration, wherein the infant's "pathological" enjoyment is replaced by the formal substitute, and implicit prohibitions, of language, the paternal metaphor. I would thus argue that Gracián is the ideal of that very pathological morality that the Enlightenment had to efface in order to institute the symbolic law of modernity. Kantian ethics, then, are the symptom that emerges in the stead of Gracián's morality, in the wake of its necessary repression.

Now, a symptom is the way a subject enacts an unconscious, prohibited enjoyment, or, more precisely, it is a symbolic repetition of the loss of the privileged object. The way of channeling surplus enjoyment that typified Gracián's morality could not be sustained in an episteme that had repressed the rupture between the self and the real of existence, because it contradicted the alleged universality of the modern subject, not to mention its transcendence. But *jouissance*, while completely excluded by the symbolic, will always return or, more precisely, will always be desired, in the gaps and breaks of a symbolic order, for the reigning law of any symbolic order is that it is finite. Thus, when a new symbolic order is formed through a new sequence of repressions, any repressed representations will necessarily return in a revised symptomatic manifestation. In the case of Gracián, enjoyment was posited at the apex of a moral system of self-representation, as we have seen. To the extent that this possibility was quelled by the restitution of the real within the subject, it would have to reemerge within the new moral constitution. This is why psychoanalysis locates at the heart of Enlightenment ethics an irreducible kernel of pure pathological enjoyment. It is by means of this pathological kernel that the subject is able to enjoy, whether by consenting to the moral law or by transgressing it. One part of the subject, the superego, enjoys the malicious implementation of the law; feelings of righteousness in performing actions in the name of duty that go against one's own best interests, or feelings of guilt at having transgressed the law and acted immorally, are both manifestations of the superego's enjoyment. On the other hand, the law is fundamental for the subject's enjoyment because it enables transgression, without which there could be no enjoyment. As Lacan deftly demonstrates in his seminar on the ethics of psychoanalysis, the law and transgression exist in a state of complete mutual dependency, and society as such could not exist without the tension between them and the surplus enjoyment they produce (*Ethics of Psychoanalysis* 78). Thus, the tensions separating subject from nonsubject that animated Gracián's model of society have disappeared, along with the repression of a society unstitched from the real—society in the Enlightenment is now seen as the manifestation of a universal, practical reason, and the fundamental tensions that it still requires to exist have found their expression as symptoms within the modern subject. Gracián's pathological morality is therefore the necessary "vanishing mediator" enabling the emergence of Kant's categorical imperative, all of which might bring us to posit that Gracián is the truth of Kant.

The prohibitions that accompany the new symbolic rendering of Enlightenment philosophy evidence precisely this sort of original repression. A surprisingly common current of Enlightenment thought, as Žižek notes, is the injunction not to inspect too closely the origins of law. Kant's *Foundation for a Metaphysics of Mores* is replete with such imperatives, which emphasize the futility of such investigation while at the same time issuing an injunction against it (Žižek 204). Pascal is more specific, saying of the authority of custom, "The truth of usurpation must not be made apparent; it came about originally, without reason, and has become reasonable" (Žižek 204). Thus, one of the primary purposes of the law is to prohibit the discovery of its own illegality, how it contains within its texture an "ex-timate" kernel of pure contradiction. In the case of Kantian morality, as formalized in the imperative "Act in such a way as to make of your action a universal imperative," such an "ex-timate" kernel would be contained in the maxim, "Act pathologically!"—in other words, that maxim which characterizes the already repressed moral system of Baltasar Gracián.

To conclude, I would propose the following basic structure for the "discontinuity" marking the dawn of modernity:

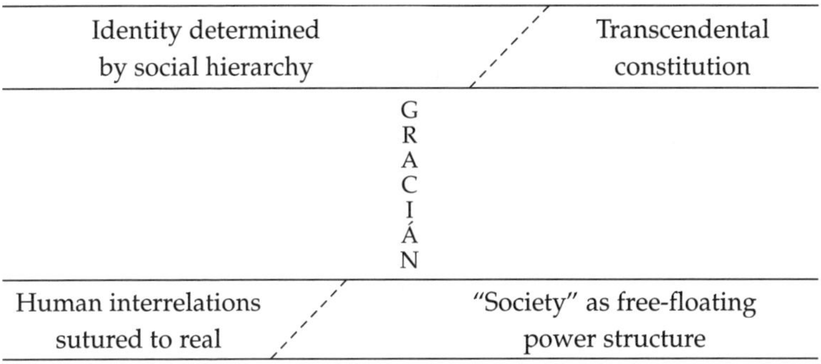

The crucial point of this diagram is that it constitutes an overlapping structure, in which the status of the individual in relationship to the field of human interrelations (preceding the emergence of "society") remains central despite the gradual loss of support in the real. This tension is resolved only later with the move of the Enlightenment to transcendental constitution and its creation of a subject that itself is constituted by the shifting, indeterminate reality at its core. It should be clear by now that Gracián's epistemological context is that of the overlapping time between these epistemes, for, while his moral system conceives of the self as a fundamentally social construction—already repressed in our own modernity—he already posits that social context as an autonomous entity, a society, free from all physical or metaphysical determination. As Žižek tells us, an event is only conceived of as "traumatic" afterward, "with the advent of a symbolic space within which it cannot be fully integrated" (222). In Gracián we have a witness of the modern subject's traumatic birth, before that birth was conceived as traumatic and thereby repressed by the Enlightenment.

Notes

1. "A cada uno trata Gracián de esclarecernos ese fondo, elemental y simple, *del hombre que tenemos que hacernos*, del hombre que cada uno tenemos encargo de llevar a persona."

2. For further evidence of this ethical direction throughout Gracián's work, see David Castillo's essay in this volume, "Gracián and the Art of Public Representation" (chapter 7).

3. "Todo está ya en su punto y el ser persona en el mayor."

4. "Más es menester para tratar con un solo hombre en estos tiempos, que por todo un pueblo en los pasados."

5. "Hombre con fondos, tanto tiene de persona."

6. "Hay sujeto de sola fachada, como casas por acabar porque faltó el caudal; tiene la entrada de palacio y de choza la habitación. No hay en éstos dónde parar, o todo para, porque, acabada la primera salutación, acabó conversación."

7. "*Conseguir y conservar la reputación.* Es el usufructo de la fama. Cuesta mucho, porque nace de las eminencias, que son tan raras cuanto comunes las medianías. Conseguida, se conserva con facilidad. Obliga mucho y obra más. Es especie de majestad cuando llega a ser veneración por la sublimidad de su causa y su esfera; pero la reputación sustancial es la que valió para siempre."

8. "*Hombre en su punto.* No se nace hecho; vase de cada día perfeccionando en la persona, en el empleo, hasta llegar al punto del consumado ser, al complemento de prendas, de eminencias: conocerse ha en lo realzado del gusto, purificado del ingenio, en lo maduro del juicio, en lo defecado de voluntad. Algunos nunca llegan a ser cabales, fáltales siempre un algo; tardan otros en hacerse. El varón consumado, sabio en dichos, cuerdo en hechos, es admitido y aun deseado del singular comercio de los discretos."

9. "*Señorío en el decir y en el hacer:* Hácese mucho lugar en todas partes y gana de antemano el respeto. En todo influye: en el conversar, en el orar, hasta en el caminar y aun en el mirar y en el querer."

10. "Mayores afectos de veneración causa la opinión y duda de adonde llega el caudal de cada uno que la evidencia de él, por grande que fuera."

11. ". . . necesidad de saberse a sí mismo; que para Gracián, en forma muy intelectualista, consistirá en adquirir conciencia de su posición en relación con el mundo."

12. ". . . empiezan a quedarse como sueltos, desvinculados; han roto el marco en el que discurría su vida y tienen que organizar con sus solos medios la lucha para establecer su puesto en la sociedad."

13. ". . . reconocimiento sin precedentes de que los seres están constituidos por lo que los otros confieran a las imágenes."

14. "La verdad es de pocos, el engaño es tan común como vulgar."

15. "Solo la verdad puede dar reputación verdadera."

16. "Lo cierto es que Gracián es el primer escritor en considerar la vida como una realidad radical e inexorable, en que las demás se apoyan."

17. See Castillo and Egginton, "All the King's Subjects: Honor in Early Modernity."

18. ". . . el campo recién descubierto de la sociedad."

19. ". . . supone un apoyo de la sociedad que se critica"; "fuertemente conservadora."

20. ". . . abolir la tiranía del otro."

21. "Haciendo el alma continuo progreso de su bajeza, debe caminar a la práctica de la aniquilación, que consiste en el aborrecimiento de la honra, dignidad y alabanza; porque a la vileza y al puro nada no es de razón que se le dé la dignidad y la honra."

22. "El héroe es, en él, un factor de estabilización. Y su justificación moral está en que precisamente él, el héroe, el eminente, es quien saca a la luz, con su

ejemplo, las posibilidades éticas que en la sociedad, tal como existe, se contienen."

Works Cited

Asensio, Jaime. "Los dictámenes sobre el último capítulo de la 'Guía Espiritual,' de Miguel de Molinos." *Revista de Estudios Hispánicos* 6.3 (October 1972): 345–354.

Castillo, David, and William Egginton. "All the King's Subjects: Honor in Early Modernity." *Romance Language Annual* 6 (1994): 422–427.

Checa, Jorge. "Oráculo Manual: Gracián y el ejercicio de la lectura." *Hispanic Review* 59 (1991): 263–279.

Copjec, Joan. "Vampires, Breast-Feeding, and Anxiety." *October* 58 (1990): 25–43.

Dolar, Mladen. " 'I Shall Be with You on Your Wedding Night': Lacan and the Uncanny." *October* 58 (1990): 5–23.

Forcione, Alban. "El desposeimiento del ser en la literatura renacentista: Cervantes, Gracián y los desafíos de Nemo." *Nueva Revista de Filología Hispánica* 24.

Foucault, Michel. *The Order of Things*. New York: Vintage Books, 1973.

Gracián, Baltasar. *The Art of Worldly Wisdom*. Trans. Christopher Maurer. New York: Doubleday, 1992.

———. *El héroe. El discreto. Oráculo manual y arte de prudencia*. Barcelona: Planeta, 1984.

Hafter, Monroe Z. *Gracián and Perfection: Spanish Moralists of the Seventeenth Century*. Cambridge: Harvard University Press.

Lacan, Jacques. *Ecrits*. Paris: Editions du Seuil, 1971.

———. *The Ethics of Psychoanalysis*. Book 7. *The Seminar of Jacques Lacan*. Ed. Jacques-Alain Miller. New York and London: Norton, 1992.

Maravall, José A. "Antropología y política en el pensamiento de Gracián." *Estudios de historia del pensamiento español*. Serie tercera. El siglo del Barroco. Madrid: Cultura Hispánica, 1984. 335–373.

Molinos, Miguel de. *La guía espiritual*. Madrid: Galo Sáez, 1935.

Rajchman, John. "Lacan and the Ethics of Modernity." *Representations* 15 (Summer 1986): 42–56.

Verbrugge, Rita Maria. "Molinism: 'Fact with Fancy'; Heresy with Truth." *Victorian Poetry* 21.3 (Autumn 1983): 229–240.

Žižek , Slavoj. *For They Know Not What They Do*. London: Verso, 1991.

Chapter 6
Gracián and the Ciphers of the World

Jorge Checa

Cycles and Irregularity in the Wheel of Time

Shortly before they arrive at the Island of Immortality, Critilo and Andrenio contemplate the Wheel of Time from one of the Seven Hills of Rome. Led by the Cortesano, their last guide, both protagonists of *El criticón* then receive what can be considered the culminating vision of their worldly pilgrimage, insofar as the Wheel provides them with a higher degree of wisdom than they have obtained up to this moment. The image not only grants Critilo and Andrenio the possibility of transcending the immediate appearances of reality (as happened in other educational stages); it also raises such intellectual knowledge to a level that encompasses all epochs. Past, present, and future are displayed in the Wheel of Time synthetically and almost simultaneously, and the Wheel proclaims the circularity of history along with the "easy and secure" nature of the predictions derived from it. "Porque has de saber," says the Cortesano when Andrenio manifests his wish to know the future, "que lo mismo que fue, esso es y esso será sin discrepar un átomo" (Because you must know that that which was, is, and will be, without an atom missing) (*Criticón* 3:305).

When Gracián presents in *El criticón* a circular idea of history, based on the principle of recurrence or repetition, he adapts a theory very much alive in his culture, especially in the field of political thought. Numerous early modern authors echo the belief that the lessons of the past have the power to predict, by analogy, the things to come, provided that current situations are similar to those of former times. Being able to efficiently apply the examples of history reveals, in this conception, that one possesses the prudence required to anticipate and meet with success a large number of obstacles.[1]

Nevertheless, several of Gracián's contemporaries do not fail to recognize that historical knowledge is, at most, a necessary but not a sufficient condition for the exercise of political prudence. The novelty of certain situations, the possibility that present "cases," even when they may resemble the past, are almost never identical to it, the influence of fortune: these are factors mentioned insistently during the seventeenth century, and whose consideration motivates the idea that political action must also be grounded in the effective handling of contingencies. Depending on the author, of course, the degree of importance attributed to the circumstantial, the hazardous, or the unexpected varies. Later on I will comment in some detail on the answer given by the *tacitista* Baltasar Alamos de Barrientos to this kind of problem, but for the moment I wish to point out how Diego de Saavedra Fajardo, the most esteemed political writer in seventeenth-century Spain, does not solve them in a conclusive manner. In his *empresa* 28, Saavedra deals with the positive effects that the study of history has on the prince, and the author stresses the idea of repetition: "La historia es una representación de las edades del mundo. Por ella la memoria vive en los días de los pasados. Los errores de los que ya fueron advierten a los que son" (History is a representation of the ages of the world. Through it the memory lives in the days of the past. The errors of those who already were warn those who are) (*Empresas políticas* 1:287). "Y conocidos bien estos dos tiempos, pasado y presente, conocerá también V.A. el futuro; porque ninguna cosa nueva debajo del sol. Lo que es, fue. Y lo que fue, sera. Múdanse las personas no las scenas. Siempre son unas las costumbres y los estilos" (And knowing well these two times, past and present, you will also know the future, because there is nothing new under the sun. What is, was. And what was, will be. The people change, not the scenarios. The habits and styles are always the same) (*Empresas políticas* 1:289).[2] Yet in *empresa* 29 Saavedra warns of the risk of applying too literally the advice provided by past examples, "siendo muy dificultoso, cuando no imposible, que en un caso concurran las mismas circunstancias y accidentes que en otro" (it being very difficult, if not impossible, for the same circumstances and accidents to occur in two different cases) (*Empresas políticas* 1:294). Far from being exceptional, the disparity of points of view manifested in *empresas* 28 and 29 was already incorporated, also within the same book, by sixteenth-century historians such as Francesco Guicciardini.[3] Taking advantage of the indecision characteristic of modern political discourse, Saavedra presents here two conflicting lines of argumentation, in order to suggest that the hypothesis of historical regularity should never be considered a universal law: "Los casos de otros sean advertimiento, no precepto o ley" (The cases of others should be warning, not precept or law) (*Empresas políticas* 1:295).

These considerations might help us to understand properly some interesting peculiarities of the image of the Wheel of Time in *El criticón*. It would be an exaggeration to claim now that Gracián radically undermines or contradicts the cognitive symbolism traditionally ascribed to such a circular figure (whose contemplation indeed emblematizes the prudence attained by Critilo and Andrenio in the final stages of their worldly pilgrimage). The image preserves the prophetic function announced at the outset of the *crisi*, but at the same time (and this is the aspect I want to emphasize), it shows a fracture in the inner logic associated with its geometrical configuration. A "perfect" wheel revolves, of course, regularly; in other words, any given spot on its circumference travels the same distance during each rotation before coming back to the point of departure. The Wheel of *El criticón*, however, does not appear to be subject to regular rhythms; in terms of the symbolic content linked to Gracián's image, the text shows that certain situations repeat themselves later than others, despite the fact that the Wheel never stops rotating.

Although finding differences between allegorical figures and empirical realities should not cause much surprise, we still need to determine in each case the reasons for this lack of correspondence. Regarding the Wheel of Time, the relative incoherence of such an image from an external or mimetic point of view seems to be due to the conflicting nature of the ideas that Gracián presents in his episode. For if the Wheel reveals, on the one hand, an epistemological optimism justified by the belief that it is possible to master or to *regulate* history (making it an instrument for the pre-vision of the future), the figure, on the other hand, simultaneously incorporates less encouraging messages. I do not merely refer to the fact that it recalls the pagan conception of Fortune (also very often symbolized by a wheel in which human beings never occupy stable positions): in the world, says the Cortesano, as Machiavelli did in the Prologue to the Second Book of his *Discorsi,* "no ay cosa que tenga estado, todo es subida y declinación" (there is nothing that has a state, everything is a rise and fall) (*Criticón* 3:308). Nor do I allude only to the explicit contrast between the historical notion of return and the irreversibility of individual lives: as Critilo sadly remarks, when virtue, wisdom, and truth reign again, "ya estaremos nosotros acabados y aun consumidos" (we will all be gone and already consumed) (*Criticón* 3:325).[4] Rather, what I have in mind is that the reluctance to ascribe to history a regular rhythm also functions to introduce in the text the idea of decline: a widely shared perception in seventeenth-century Spain, where it paradoxically competes with the proclamation, equally frequent, that the return to a glorious past is a *necessary* process.[5] The synthesis of these two antagonistic impulses can hardly be conceived in extratextual reality. Within *El criticón,* it is precariously achieved by stating that negative things come back sooner than positive ones, or, in the Cortesano's words: "Detiénense y mucho en bolver los siglos de oro, y adelántanse los de plomo y de hierro. Son las calamidades más ciertas en repetir que las prosperidades" (The golden ages wait a long time to return, and the lead and iron ages hurry back. The calamities are more certain to be repeated than prosperity) (*Criticón* 3:323–324).

With this important modification, Gracián's version of historical return is not identified with the fixed norms of exact laws, but it still retains the approximative or heuristic value of a hypothesis oriented toward prudent behavior in the practical world.

By this I mean that, even though the representation of the Wheel of Time may seem inconsistent by empirical criteria, the figure's imaginary nature does not completely annul its usefulness in adapting history to the mental requirement of order. Cyclical theory, then, operates here as a kind of ordering principle, yet Gracián never dismisses the resistance of human affairs to organizing themselves according to perfect patterns. From the perspective of the epistemological problems posed by Gracián's literature, such is, I think, the sense of the many contingent occurrences that infiltrate the episode of the Wheel of Time. It is important to point out that, together with its parade of illustrious figures and its allusions to memorable events, Critilo's and Andrenio's vision includes references to volatile, inconsequential, and arbitrary phenomena (such as clothing fashions); the episode also presents a curious comment about the capriciousness and, in this case, the irreversibility of linguistic changes.[6] By stressing with these references the haphazard component of historic change, Gracián tends to suggest that not all future events can be anticipated, since not everything fits within the scheme of repetition.

Along the same lines as Saavedra Fajardo's *empresas* 28 and 29, the vision of the Wheel of Time finally corrects and qualifies its initial assumptions. The assertion that all that has been will return "sin faltar un átomo" forsakes its prophetic status to become a guiding motto—never infallible but still valuable when prudently assimilated.

Alamos de Barrientos: *Afectos* and Political Science

In a wider sense, both Gracián and the authors akin to his sensibility transfer to the field of moral and political reflection the exigency of reducing the distance between the thinking subject and the empirical realms where human action takes place. Cassirer's seminal study on Renaissance philosophy confirms that the interest in closing the gap that separates our mind from "objective" reality cannot be said to originate in the seventeenth century, for, much earlier than that, Leonardo da Vinci's artistic theory shows a similar concern. In Leonardo's writings, says Cassirer, the artist's vision achieves a scientific level by discovering the mathematical necessity that presides over the external world, thus adapting such necessity to the formalizing power of the subject's own intellect. According to the process described in Cassirer's work, the path opened by Leonardo leads to the scientific work of Galileo, whose project of bringing to light the mathematical *raggione* underlying the cosmos already seeks to transcend sensorial experience.[7]

It is well known that, to describe the universe, Galileo had recourse to the old metaphor of the Book of the World, yet he modified at the same time the image's customary formulations. Insofar as it is made up of mathematical signs linked to one another by laws of necessity, this universal Book ceases to be an accessible text, and its readers are required to understand the abstract kind of writing that is now postulated.[8] In the exercise of deciphering this writing, the scientist strives to reduce and master the overwhelming multiplicity of nature, in order to reveal its hidden syntax.

When, in the third part of *El criticón,* Gracián expounds his own *moral* version of the Book of the World, he also manifests a clear inclination to reduce multiplicity (even though the differences between Gracián and Galileo are, of course, enormous). But before analyzing this passage of *El criticón,* I should like to emphasize how the generalizing propensity exemplified in very different ways by Gracián and Galileo can also be found in several political writers of the seventeenth century—students of an increasingly complex reality where, as Alamos de Barrientos puts it, "son mas los casos que las leyes" (there are more cases than laws) (*Tácito español* 433). Within the present argumentation, Alamos's name has indeed not been chosen at random, owing to this author's importance in the displacement of some epistemological attitudes from the realms of art and science to the pragmatic field of politics.[9]

Alamos de Barrientos's most pertinent ideas are in the two short pieces preceding his translation and aphoristic commentary of Tacitus's works; pieces consisting of a brief dedication to the duke of Lerma as well as a brief explanation regarding the advantages of aphoristic writing. In the first preliminary text, Alamos outlines his conception of politics as a science; that is, as a discipline that can be systematized by means of general paradigms.[10] The basis of this political knowledge stems from the study of human *affections* ("afectos"), assuming that the origin of the passions and volitions that dominate each individual is usually conditioned (and almost predetermined) by four factors: the country of birth, the *humors* that produce different *complexions*, the family, and the social position. Embracing a position previously defended by Machiavelli, Alamos claims that *affections* tend to remain constant; they not only persist throughout each individual's life, but the behaviors resulting from them are also repeated with few variations whenever two human beings (even if they belong to different epochs) participate in an analogous psychological configuration. Hence Alamos's interest in history; since it is thanks to such a discipline that we can know in depth the *affections* of past figures, by extension, history today allows us to predict the outcome of actions caused by similar predispositions.[11]

In Alamos de Barrientos's theory, history offers, when rigorously written, an *already interpreted* version of any given period. This interpretive (and not merely descriptive) nature explains the enthusiasm for Tacitus that Alamos shares with Gracián and many other seventeenth-century authors, a sentiment substantiated by his belief that nobody has ever surpassed Tacitus in laying bare the *affections* of his characters.[12] Alamos, then, confers on history the potential for becoming a mediated experience—or "una experiencia de segundo grado" (Fernández-Santamaría 178), with the result that Tacitus's works, being the supreme model of their genre, contain "un jardín y seminario de preceptos políticos" (a garden and seminary of political precepts) (*Tácito español* 427). By revealing the *affections* and by showing the *effects* they produce, Tacitus exposes, like no other writer, the hidden motives of human behavior, thus intertwining the tasks of narrating and deciphering past events. The latter idea, however, does not imply that the reader of the *Annals* is condemned to occupy a passive position, for, quite to the contrary, Tacitus's difficult and laconic style is in itself an invitation to carry out hermeneutic activities. In this regard, the *aforismos* written by Alamos in the margins of his Spanish version arise from a new interpretive exercise, performed upon a text that, in turn, interprets historical reality. From the "garden" already cultivated by Tacitus, Alamos seeks to extract, "como un buen distilador" (like a good distiller), "el espíritu y quinta esencia de la Historia" (the spirit and quintessence of history), transforming it into a "universal experience" (*Tácito español* 429).

But we should not forget that, for Alamos de Barrientos and the *tacitista* movement, the universal value of history has to be tested in the practical world, where our inborn affections often compete with other forces. As Gracián would do years later, here Alamos discusses some factors that may question the absolute validity of his model. First, the author deals with the possibility that the kind of *affections* he calls "secondary" (which rather than being natural are occasionally produced by "fortune") might lead the statesman's behavior toward uncharted territory. Alamos refutes this difficulty with an argument probably drawn from Machiavelli's remarks about the supposedly weakening effects brought on humankind by the spread of the Christian religion, and argues that "secondary" or occasional affections are not powerful enough to annul our basic inclinations; because of the decline of present times, such weakness, Alamos continues, is more evident today than in Tacitus's age:

> Las inclinaciones naturales del hombre son tanto más fuertes, y obran mas violentamente, cuando él fuere menos perfecto, porque resiste menos. Y pues nuestros cuerpos son más flacos que los de nuestros pasados, y más que los de aquellos antiguos, y menos saben resistir sus apetitos, más cierto sera el pronóstico y más seguro el consejo que se fundare ahora en el conocimiento de los afectos humanos. (424–425)
>
> [The natural inclinations of man are the stronger, and work the more violently, when he is less perfect, because he resists less. And since our bodies are weaker than those of our ancestors and of the ancient peoples, and know less how to resist their appetites, the more accurate will be the prediction and the surer will be the advice that are established now in the knowledge of human affections.][13]

After dismissing the first objection, Alamos confronts what he considers to be a bigger one, now posited by the undeniable existence of free will. Thanks to it, Alamos says, individuals are sometimes able to control the strength of their permanent *affec-*

tions, and the conclusion is that Alamos is forced to recognize that his theory does not apply to all cases: any given complex of natural *affections* does not always mechanically produce the effects that we anticipate by studying similar examples.

But even Alamos's reluctant admission that political reality cannot be contained within the framework of a theoretical model does not entail a renunciation of his "scientific" project. It is true, he says, that free will precludes the identification of politics with a science based on universal concepts (as Aristotelian tradition requires), yet the alternative remains open of proposing a discipline whose value, rather than absolute, appears to be statistical (Fernández-Santamaría 185), since it allows the prediction of many specific outcomes. Alamos finally arrives at his definition of politics as "ciencia de contingentes" (science of contingents) (*Tácito español* 425), a deliberately paradoxical formula in which the goal of systematizing the varieties of human behavior still leaves a margin to chance.[14] In his application of the impulse to master and regulate an empirical field to the "matters of State," Alamos has to make use of an approximative way of thinking, and this is so despite the author's totalizing ambition to overcome the far greater skepticism shown by several of his contemporaries. The pages of the *Tácito español* devoted to the justification of aphoristic writing indirectly corroborate the difficulties of reducing the practice of government to the rigor of a stable and self-sufficient theory.

Cartographies of Reality

As I have pointed out, the aphorisms that accompany Alamos de Barrientos's translation fulfill the mission of emphasizing the most useful lessons of Tacitus's books, while duplicating and refining the interpretive dimension already present in these prestigious texts. Through his aphorisms, Alamos also seeks to mediate between the ancient world of imperial Rome and the contemporary one of his seventeenth-century readers, all in the best interest of their "bien público" (public welfare) (434). In connection with this altruistic concern, Alamos writes that, in the beginning, he toyed with the idea of giving to his commentary of Tacitus the form of "discursos y lecciones sobre lugares particulares suyos, comparando los sucesos y accidentes que refiere, y los efectos dellos, a los de nuestros tiempos y que hace poco que pasaron" (discourses and lessons about particular topics of his, comparing the events and accidents that he mentions, and their effects, with those of our times which have occurred recently) (*Tácito espãnol* 428), although he finally decided against employing a continuous exposition. After confessing his limited "erudition," and thinking, as Tacitus himself did, that writing the history of the present times is a dangerous endeavor, Alamos opted instead for the use of aphorisms, a "less difficult" enterprise and "con el mismo fruto para los medianamente prudentes" (with the same fruit for the moderately prudent) (*Tácito español* 429). In fact, following Alamos's argumentation, we can even conclude that aphorisms, besides appearing as symptoms of prudence, possess the additional quality of showing, in their very discontinuous configuration, the kind of inductive learning attributed, from Machiavelli on, to politics—a knowledge based (like Hippocratic medicine or astrology in its origins) on the observation of particular cases.[15]

The inseparability of Alamos's method and the genre he adopts also suggests that his aphorisms reveal a type of unfinished reflection, which is open to further developments:

> Póngala en perfección, junte con estos aforismos otros muchos, y a unos y a otros añada sus discursos y comentos el que gustare de semejante trabajo. (*Tácito español* 433)
>
> [Perfect it, put together with these aphorisms many others, and he who would enjoy such work may add to them all his discourses and comments.]

Underlying the inconclusive character of his political maxims, Alamos described them previously as "breves apuntamientos" (brief notes), and later on he illustrates their representative status with images allusive to some synthetic and orienting qualities. Aphorisms, he says, resemble a work of painting that condenses numerous "reglas y doctrinas" (rules and doctrines) extracted from Tacitus's books; next, they are compared to a "mapa y descripción del mundo" (a map and description of the world); and they are finally likened to a "compass" or "aguja de marear," thanks to which statesmen can "navegar y surgir seguramente en el tempestuoso mar desta vida" (successfully sail the tempestuous sea of this life) (*Tácito español* 431).[16] All these images express a double use of the idea of representation: Alamos's alleged fidelity toward Tacitus does not exclude superimposing upon him a new voice ready to bring the contents of the original up to date.

Here, Alamos's cartographic simile seems to me particularly telling, with the comparison of aphorisms to "a map and description of the world."[17] The reason for my preference is that maps purport to be, by design, accurate sketches of geographic realities, but are at the same time obviously conventional objects (among other reasons, because they submit such realities to a reductive process of selection). Maps, in sum, without being postulated as direct copies of a given territory, represent some features of space (those considered relevant by the cartographer) by means of abstract images, thus serving all kinds of practical needs. We then might say that mapping makes the world *legible* by turning certain external data into signs, with the result that, from this point of view, maps can be partially assimilated to those versions of the Book of the Universe that, like Galileo's, aim to transcend the world's immediate appearances.

Having in mind these considerations, it is again time to examine how Gracián's literature addresses the problem of attaining useful knowledge of reality through symbolic representation. One of the best examples in *El criticón* is the *crisi* entitled "El mundo descifrado" (The world deciphered), where the image of the book is related to two opposite contexts. According to the Descifrador (Critilo's and Andrenio's guide at this point in the allegorical novel), the book of the "mundo natural" (natural world) is one thing, and the book of the "mundo civil" (human world) is something very different, for, whereas the divine writing of the former is relatively transparent and easy to read, the human signs of the latter are inevitably fraught with confusion:

> La dificultad la hallo yo en leer y entender lo que está de las tejas abaxo, porque como todo ande en cifra y los humanos coraçones estén tan sellados y inescrutables, assegúroos que el mejor letor se pierde. Y otra cosa, que si no lleváis bien estudiada y bien sabida la contracifra de todo, os avréis de hallar perdidos, sin acertar a leer palabra ni conocer letra, ni un rasgo ni un tilde. (3:118)

> [I find the difficulty in reading and understanding what exists in the sublunar world, because, since everything here is in cipher and human hearts are so well sealed and inscrutable, I assure you that the best reader gets lost. And another thing, if you have not studied hard and learned the countersign for everything, you will surely become lost, without succeeding in reading a word or recognizing a letter, nor a mark nor an accent.]

Certainly, in order to enhance his moral position, Gracián has exaggerated here the interpretive availability of nature (whose marvelous text, in the perspective of an author as close to Gracián as Emanuele Tesauro, also conceals under enigmatic symbols its sophisticated prodigies).[18] However, rather than celebrating Nature's wonders, Gracián's interest is at this moment in guarding his readers against human maliciousness, and such a goal explains the nuanced treatment of the word *cifra* throughout the present episode.[19] In the meaning that corresponds to the passage above, *cifra* seems to refer to an illegible or deceitful message that misleads us by deliberately hiding the truth of certain behaviors. To neutralize such an erroneous way of reading, the Descifrador recommends that Critilo and Andrenio learn and, as he says, carry "muy manual" (at hand) "la contracifra" (countersign) of everything (*Criticón* 3:121); in other words, the key that, properly used, would allow them to find the reality disguised under fallacious appearances. It is very important to point out that in *El criticón*'s episode the notion of *contracifra* is soon identified with a second meaning attributed to the term *cifra*. This alternative meaning also reveals, like the first one, the disorderly and deceitful condition of the *mundo civil,* yet it simultaneously alludes to an artificial kind of writing that enables the Descifrador to organize mentally that chaotic reality. The writing posited by the Descifrador does not then belong to the world itself, but the *cifras* are instead part of a generalizing and nominalistic strategy likened to the subject. If the Descifrador says that the signs of this language are *cifrados,* it is because their appearance does not immediately denote the meaning given to each one of them (with the result that the *cifras,* insofar as they demand to be interpreted, become a simulacrum of their worldly field of reference).[20] Hence the evidently conventional nature of the *cifras* mentioned by Critilo's and Andrenio's guide. Like the graphic representations of human language that they imitate, *El criticón*'s *cifras* are elements of a codified language, whose mastery is imperative to read them correctly (or "al derecho"). Thus, only after assimilating the Descifrador's hermeneutic instructions can Critilo and Andrenio realize, for example, that the *cifra &* stands for the gossiper's malicious ignorance, or that the *quitildeque* points to a form of hollow affectation.

The obviously conventional design of the world's *cifras* tends to suggest, on the other hand, that these signs organize a great variety of moral attitudes in groups that, to a certain extent, are arbitrarily arranged. It is possible to include any individual in more than one category, and, in fact, the number of groupings is limited only by the moralist's lack of ingenuity in distinguishing them. Potentially speaking, the task of constituting the *cifras*' codified language is then an endless one, and this explains why the Descifrador tells Critilo and Andrenio that *cifras* are infinite in number. By naming only "some" (or "the most frequent") of them (*Criticón* 3:125), the Descifrador undertakes a necessarily interminable pursuit, whose possibilities of development can be related to the incompleteness of aphoristic writing (as conceived in Alamos de Barrientos's *Tácito español*). Like Alamos's aphorisms, Gracián's *cifras* subsume our experience in brief and concise formulations and provide us with a key to guide our steps through the world's confusing reality.

Consequently, just as Alamos intends to draw with his aphorisms "a map and description of the world" valuable for statesmen, Gracián's *cifras* set up the criteria to carry out a moral cartography (actually manifested in *El criticón* itself).[21] Both authors give up the illusory attempt to reproduce things the way they appear: since the circumstantial and concrete manifestations of every empirical domain are too complex to be directly represented, Alamos and Gracián appeal to the construction of an abstract *image* of experience. Like a map design, this image is necessarily unfinished and can be modified according to new findings or requirements. When linking Tacitus's text to contemporary issues, Alamos's aphorisms approach reality from a perspective defined by the position of their author. Analogously, the potentially infinite number of Gracián's *cifras*, together with their arbitrary status, signals how moral discourse chooses and defines its interests following a dynamic point of view, which is always prone to readjustment.

Representing an epistemological indecision characteristic of the early modern period, both Gracián and Alamos de Barrientos oscillate between the propensity to integrate their thought within orderly paradigms and the admission of the disruptive power of contingency. Such a conflict can even be detected in the moments when the authors favor the regulating tendency. Thus, whereas in the episode of the Wheel of Time Gracián corrects the perfect symmetry that a cyclical idea of history seems to demand, Alamos's consideration of free will ultimately restrains the universal and mechanist application of his theory.

On the other hand (and leaving aside the stability that still pervades his "scientific" model), Alamos advocates for his exegesis of Tacitus a supplementary writing constituted by aphorisms, whose fragmentary form as well as actualizing function inadvertently collide with the project of creating a systematic model. In this sense, aphoristic comment hampers Alamos's ideal of reducing all possibilities of human behavior to a self-sufficient "grammar," in which our affections would function as minimal units.

In order to justify the viability of his "grammar," Alamos is forced to downplay the importance of what he calls "afectos ocasionales," arguing that most individuals cannot permanently repress their inborn inclinations. Years later, Gracián will claim, on the contrary, that in the *mundo civil*, "la materia de intenciones . . . es la más dificultosa de cuantas ay" (the matter of intentions . . . is the most difficult one) (*Criticón* 3:122), and, observing the increasing preponderance of maliciousness and deceit, he will reject any attempt to attribute primary or natural foundations to ethical thought. Here Gracián also questions the generalizing principles that he himself adopted in the episode of the Wheel of Time, and counteracts (in a more obvious way than Alamos) the normative line of his philosophy.

It is especially in the episode "The World Deciphered" that Gracián suggests that the moralist's task does not consist of "discovering," within ethical reality, a syntax supposedly made up of a limited number of elements. This objective articulation is defended in Galileo's scientific project, and, at another level, still subsists, with modifications, in some cyclical views of history; yet the *mundo civil* requires a continuous rewriting that can transform the world's blurred appearances into the ciphered signs of a dynamic, provisional, and open-ended language.

Notes

1. Hall (372) notes that some cyclical ideas of history were already formulated in Stoic philosophy. In any case, such a principle appears rather frequently in sixteenth- and seventeenth-century political texts, starting with Machiavelli's *Discorsi*. Among the Spanish authors who subscribe to this concept, Maravall mentions Núñez Alba, Páez de Castro, Mariana, Cabrera de Córdoba, and Saavedra Fajardo (*Antiguos y modernos* 394–397). On the connection between prudence and historic repetition, Antonio de Herrera's words can be considered representative: "Y por la estimación en que siempre fue tenida la historia, pintaban los antiguos a Jano, dios de la prudencia, con dos caras: porque mirando en la historia lo pasado se acierta prudentemente lo por venir" (*Discurso* 419).

2. In most seventeenth-century discussions about history's cyclical character, the inclusion of the famous maxim of Ecclesiastes 1:10, which Saavedra incorporates here, seems almost inevitable. Echoes of the same maxim can be perceived in the quote by Gracián reproduced at the beginning of this essay, and more directly, in the following passage: "No acontece cosa que no aya sido, ni que se pueda dezir nueva baxo el sol" (*Criticón* 3:306). The categorical tone of this biblical reference tends to validate an idea usually discussed in nonreligious contexts.

3. We read in Guicciardini's *Ricordi* (76): "Tutto quello que e stato per el passato e al presente, sara ancora in futuro; ma si mutamo e nomi e le superficie delle cose in modo, che chi non ha buono occhio non le riconosce, ne sa pigliare regola o fare giudicio per mezzo di quella osservazione" (Everything that has been in the past and is in the present will again be in the future, but the names and surfaces of things are changed so that those who do not possess sharp eyes neither recognize them nor are able to get a handle on them or come to a judgment through that observation). It is interesting to note that this idea contradicts the dominant principles of Guicciardini's historiographical work, in which the notions of order and system are virtually absent.

4. At the beginning of the episode, the relationship between history and individual life seems to be analogical rather than contrastive. Gracián refers here to the doctrine that divides human life into "seven ages," the last of which somewhat repeats the first: "Acabados los diez años de Saturno, buelve a presidir la Luna y buelve a niñear y a monear el hombre decrépito y caduco, con que acaba el tiempo en círculo, mordiéndose la cola la serpiente: ingenioso geroglífico de la rueda de la vida humana" (*Criticón* 3:302–303). But note how this "cycle" excludes the idea of renovation, therefore anticipating the ambivalent meaning of the Wheel of Time.

5. For the awareness of historical decline in seventeenth-century Spain, see Elliott. About the tensions in the episode between optimism and pessimism, see Hall's considerations.

6. "Hasta en el hablar ay su novedad cada día, pues el lenguaje de oy ha dozientos años parece algaravía" (*Criticón* 3:322).

7. See Cassirer's book, especially chapter 4 ("The Subject-Object Problem in Renaissance Philosophy").

8. For this important transformation in the development of the image of the Book, see Curtius (324).

9. There is little information about Alamos de Barrientos's life. We know that he collaborated with Antonio Pérez and was imprisoned after Pérez's fall. At the death of King Philip II, Alamos was released from jail, and later he supported Olivares's policies.

10. On the problems raised by this question, see Maravall's essay "Empirismo y pensamiento político."

11. For the psychological foundation of the idea of historical repetition, see Machiavelli's *Discorsi* 1.39 as well as 2.43. Here we find formulations quite similar to Alamos's.

12. For a good example of the appreciation enjoyed by Tacitus in seventeenth-century Spain, see Antonio de Herrera's *Discurso.* In *Agudeza y arte de ingenio* (*discurso* 61), Gracián manifests some of the reasons for that enthusiasm: "Porque Cornelio Tácito, aquel que significa otro tanto más de lo que dice, se extremó en las apetitosas crisis, examinando las intenciones y descubriendo el más disimulado artificio" (*Agudeza* 2:236).

13. For Machiavelli's critique of Christianity and his subsequent revalorization of pagan culture, see *Discorsi* 2.2.

14. In opposition to the Aristotelian principle according to which science has to be made up of universal concepts, the paradox of propounding a "ciencia de contingentes" constitutes another Baroque attempt to reconcile two terms commonly perceived as contradictory. For a lucid approach to the role played by early modern political thought in the connection between science and empirical knowledge, see Maravall's "Empirismo y pensamiento político."

15. "De esta manera formó Hipócrates, y los antiguos médicos que le siguieron, los principios de su ciencia por los sucesos de las enfermedades particulares. Lo mismo hicieron Ptolomeo y el resto de los primeros profesores de la astrología" (Alamos, *Tácito español* 430). The tendency to "historize" the birth of any given discipline by remembering its empirical and practical origins is also evident in the prologue to Machiavelli's *Discorsi,* where it is applied to medicine. On this question, see Haydn (especially 149–154).

16. The compass (or *aguja de marear*) image is extremely frequent in many political treatises of the period under consideration. Even certain book titles, such as Juan Pablo Mártir Rizo's *Norte de príncipes* (1645), are inspired by this device.

17. On the development of cartography in early modern Europe, with particular attention to the increasing importance of world maps and atlases, see Bagrow and Skelton (105–140).

18. See the pages in *Il cannocchiale aristotelico* devoted to nature's "argutezze," where Tesauro pays attention to the hieroglyphics, emblems, and, in general "simboliche cifere" of the natural world (*Cannocchiale* 33 ff.). On the other hand, Forcione has recently shown that even the "natural" version of the Book of the World represented in the opening chapters of the *Criticón* appears to be dis-

turbingly contaminated by political and ideological allusions ("La disociación cósmica," esp. 419–431).

19. The *Diccionario de Autoridades* devotes several entries to the word *cifra* and its derivatives, and gives the following definition of the term: "Modo o arte de escribir, dificultoso de comprender sus cláusulas, si no es teniendo la clave." In this episode of *El criticón,* Gracián incorporates three senses of *cifra* included in *Autoridades*: an enigmatic language, an artificial writing, and a sign that condenses a larger message.

20. It should then be noted that, according to this use of the word, a *cifra* is not an immediately visible (yet deceitful) sign; rather, every *cifra* constitutes an enigmatic name that defines an aspect of the world, with the goal of unmasking its seeming normality. See the following example about the *diptongo*:

"—Pues dime —preguntó Andrenio—, estos que vamos encontrando ¿no son hombres en todo el mundo, y aquellas otras ¿no son bestias?

—¡Qué bien lo entiendes! —le respondió en pocas palabras y mucha risa— ¡Eh!, que no lees cosa a derechas. Advierte que los más, que parecen hombres, no lo son, sino dipthongos.

—¿Que cosa es dipthongo?

—Una rara mezcla. Dipthongo es un hombre con voz de muger, y una muger que habla como hombre; dipthongo es un marido con melindres, y la muger con calçones; dipthongo es niño de sesenta años, y uno sin camisa crugiendo seda; dipthongo es un francés inserto en español, que es la peor mezcla de quantas ay; dipthongo ay de amo y moço" (3:122–123).

21. It has often been noticed that, in the brief summary of Critilo and Andrenio's pilgrimage included at the end of *El criticón* (3:411–412), the work's allegorical loci are not mentioned in the order that was previously followed. In my view, this discrepancy emphasizes the "cartographic" dimension of Gracián's masterpiece, whose allegorical settings are now simultaneously displayed (as if they were figures on a map).

Works Cited

Alamos de Barrientos, Baltasar. *Tácito español ilustrado con aforismos.* Madrid, 1613. Dedication to the duke of Lerma and "Discurso para la inteligencia de los aforismos; uso y provecho de ellos." In *Barroco esencial.* Ed. Jorge Checa. Madrid: Taurus, 1992. 421–423.

Bagrow, Leo. *History of Cartography.* Revised and enlarged by R. A. Skelton. Cambridge: Harvard University Press, 1964.

Cassirer, Ernst. *The Individual and the Cosmos in Renaissance Philosophy.* 1927. Trans. Mario Domandi. Philadelphia: University of Pennsylvania Press, 1963.

Checa, Jorge, ed. *Barroco esencial.* Madrid: Taurus, 1992.

Curtius, Ernst R. *European Literature and the Latin Middle Ages.* 1948. Trans. Willard R. Trask. Princeton: Princeton University Press, 1973.

Elliott, John H. "Self-Perception and Decline in Early Seventeenth-Century Spain." *Past and Present* 74 (1977): 41–61.

Fernández-Santamaría, José Antonio. *Razón de estado y política en el pensamiento español del Barroco (1595–1640).* Madrid: Centro de Estudios Constitucionales, 1986.

Forcione, Alban K. "La disociación cósmica de Gracián." *Nueva Revista de Filología Hispánica* 40 (1992): 419–450.

Gracián, Baltasar. *Agudeza y arte de ingenio.* 2 vols. Ed. Evaristo Correa Calderón. Madrid: Castalia, 1969.

———. *El criticón.* 3 vols. Ed. Miguel Romera-Navarro. Philadelphia: University of Pennsylvania Press, 1938–1940.

Guicciardini, Francesco. *Ricordi.* In *Opera.* Ed. Vittorio de Capraris. Milano-Napoli: Riccardo Ricciardi, n.d.

Hall, J. B. "The Wheel of Time: Gracián's Changing View of History." *Bulletin of Hispanic Studies* 52 (1975): 371–378.

Haydn, Hiram. *The Counter-Renaissance.* New York: Grove Press, 1950.

Herrera, Antonio de. *Discurso sobre que Tácito excede a todos los historiadores antiguos, y el fruto que se saca de sus escritos.* In *Barroco esencial.* Ed. Jorge Checa. Madrid: Taurus, 1992. 416–420.

Machiavelli, Niccolo. *Discorsi sopra la prima deca di Tito Livio.* Ed. Sergio Bertelli. Milano: Feltrinelli, 1960.

Maravall, José Antonio. *Antiguos y modernos: Visión de la historia e idea de progreso hasta el Renacimiento.* 1966. Madrid: Alianza, 1986.

———. "Empirismo y pensamiento político (una cuestión de orígenes)." 1947. In *Estudios de historia del pensamiento español.* Serie tercera. *El siglo del Barroco.* Madrid: Cultura Hispánica, 1984. 15–38.

Saavedra Fajardo, Diego de. *Idea de un príncipe político cristiano, representada en cien empresas.* 2 vols. Ed. Quintín Aldea Vaquero. Madrid: Editora Nacional, 1976.

Tesauro, Emanuele. *Il cannocchiale aristotelico.* Ed. Ezio Raimondi. Torino: Einaudi, 1978.

Part III
Representations

Chapter 7

Gracián and the Art of Public Representation

David Castillo

In this study I seek to examine how Gracián's texts inform the redefinition of *public*—public persona, public space, public ostentation—that was taking place in early modern Europe. The essay is structured into three sections: the first explains Gracián's understanding of art and writing as avenues for the public representation of eminent men against the background constituted by the fundamental changes operating in the social function of art in early modernity; the second sets forth a succinct exposition of Gracián's techniques for mastering the supreme art of public ostentation; while the third section reflects upon Gracián's conceptions of knowledge and power as they informed his definition of "persona" as *public subject* in the sociopolitical context of the Baroque absolutist court. It will be my claim that, seen in relation to the sociopolitical changes occurring during the late 1600s in the Spanish state, Gracián's conception of art and the *public subject*—"persona"—appears as commensurate with the interests of the Spanish state's power elites.

Gracián against the Background of the Evolution of Art and Public Representation in Early Modernity

In the feudal stages of the Middle Ages, the art market was ruled by the dictates of official demand. The works of artisans had to correspond to the rigid planning of the official financing institutions. Public contracts always included a series of specific stipulations determining the outcome of works. The particularities of these stipulations were largely based on the existing system of conventions, which, in accordance with the dominant Neoplatonic conception of art, demanded the abstract depiction of objects. Abstract images aimed to capture the soul of the figures represented and in so doing moved the spectator to devotion, pity, and moral perfection. Toward the end of the thirteenth century, but especially during the fourteenth and fifteenth centuries, important changes were taking place in art, just as they were occurring in every other facet of late medieval life. These socioeconomic, political, and cultural changes do not constitute something of a synchronic or lineal program in any manner, but are rather part of a complex—and often contradictory—historical process that can be conceptualized as a period of expansive crisis informed by a barrage of signs: general increase of social mobility; increase of volume and scale of exchange of manufactured products; development of the physical sciences; social rehabilitation of the human individual, of solitude, of intimacy, and of the human body; growth of ornate commodities and clothing; consistent appearance of highly experimental cultural products—such as autobiographies, individual portraits, nudes, still lifes, and landscapes; the appearance of private art clients; and so on.[1] Important sectors of the nobility and clergy resented these changes and actively opposed artistic experiments.

By the end of the fifteenth century and certainly with the preeminence of the Renaissance in sixteenth-century Europe, humanism holds sway. With regard to the representation of principle men, the most representative art treatises of Renaissance humanism do not fail to bring matters of dignity and decorum into intricate connection with the perceived crucial function of art: that of providing, with an adequate avenue, for public ostentation of social status. Thus, chapter 137 of da Vinci's *The Art of Painting* admonishes those who aspire to become good painters to "observe dignity and decorum in the principle figure; such as a King, magistrate, or philosopher, separating them from the low classes of the people" (89).[2] Similarly, Francisco de Holanda's *Diálogos de Roma; da pintura antiga* provides us with insights into the often contradictory crossroads of humanism. The second part of the treatise undertakes the enterprise of sustaining the essential superiority of painting among the artistic disciplines, for it shows greater capabilities for representing and glorifying principle men and their heroic achievements: "Esta nobre arte, mas põenos diante los olhos a imagen de qualquer grande homen, por seus feitos desejado de ser visto e conhenido" (Holanda 29).[3] The emphasis on achievements, as well as on public recognition, is definitely a mark of humanist thought, which postulates fame as the ultimate goal of earthly immortality: "Afirman os grandes engenhos que nenhuma cousa pode o homen achar contra a sua mortalidade, nem contra inveja do tempo, que a pintura" (29–30).[4] The importance of status is not, however, obscured by any means. On the contrary, status and deeds are largely taken as commensurate. The same text contains unambiguous references to the representation of status—what a man is according to his place in society as determined by his lineage—and the fundamental social function of art—painting—to that end. Thus, when speaking of the reasons that drove Emperor Severus Alexander to make use of the art of painting, Holanda asserts: "Pintou ele mesmo a sua genealogia para mostrar que descendia da linhagem dos Metelos" (27).[5]

The proliferation of printed materials[6] and oil paintings, along with the multiplication of private art clients, opened up some room for the appearance of a variety of cultural products that did not—*sensu strictu*—have to carry out public representative functions. That was the case of some of the artistic trends developing in Flanders, Venice, or Seville, which often engaged in experimental practices, including naturalistic reproductions of nature (landscape, still life, nude) and family portraits. Of all these new practices, family portraits—private by definition—are perhaps the best indicators of some of the social changes that were taking place in early modern Europe with the constant growth of money and moneyed groups anxious to see themselves represented, not in terms of their social status, but in terms of their wealth.[7]

Likewise, some written works were produced apart from the official circuits of instrumentalization of art. *El Lazarillo de Tormes* is, for instance, a burlesque treatment of the apparatus displayed by art in providing the medium for public ostentation of principle figures. *Lazarillo* constitutes a powerful satire clearly directed against the paraphernalia used for the ostentation of status as well as deeds, since it proudly narrates in the first person the morally questionable achievements of an individual of obscure social origins.

A paradigmatic case is that of most Cervantian texts, which openly mock conventionalism in writing and vindicate the worth of the text as an artifice. The majority of Cervantes's works make use of a barrage of experimental techniques to expose the essential artificiality of the text, such as providing sudden breaks in the narrative structure, mixing and confronting heterogeneous narrative materials, mocking most successful literary genres, and providing different internal authors and readers.[8]

A similar gesture against the official public representative function of art informs the works of Velázquez, paradoxically a courtly painter. If Cervantes writes about writing, Velázquez paints about painting. Above principle figures, above their heroic achievements, even above royalty, painting becomes for Velázquez the primordial object of painting. By simply looking at any of his royal portraits, any of his mythological and heroic scenes, one is struck by the certainty that *the royal* (royal status), *the legendary,* and *the heroic* are absent from Velázquez's paintings. Instead one finds oneself staring at a spatially and temporally specific pictorial depiction of an individual who happens to be king or a group of individuals engaging in some activity—it could equally be some military activity, some labor activity, or some leisurely activity, such as posing for a portrait or watching somebody doing so. For Velázquez, as for Rubens and other Baroque painters, good painting constitutes an intellectual activity—not craftsmanship—that ought to be awarded with honors regardless of its object.[9]

During the Baroque era, public-representation functions in Spain fell preeminently into the hands of the incipient theatrical institution, largely regulated and controlled by the state. The *co-*

media nueva became the cultural phenomenon that best suited the state's need for the naturalization of the dominant monarcho-seigneurial system of values. Honor, the keystone of the state's ideology, the supreme noble value, constitutes the central thematical basis of Baroque *comedia.* Honorable brave gentlemen, ostentatiously exhibiting capes and swords, are pervasively portrayed as heroic protectors of fragile ladies and honest men and women belonging to all sectors of society under the strict surveillance of the king, supreme fountain of honor whose authority comes from the heavens.[10] The essential role played by the theater in providing an adequate avenue for the ostentation of noble gestures and paraphernalia becomes doubly important if we take into consideration the fact that the nobility had ceased to carry out its traditional military functions as infantry became the heart of the army.[11]

There are fundamental thematical and structural similarities between Gracián's texts and some *comedias,* especially Calderonian *comedias* such as *La vida es sueño.* Both the central characters of *El criticón*—Andrenio and Critilo—and Segismundo constitute appropriate allegories of courtly life as individual success is shown to be achieved through the apprenticeship in techniques in courtly behavior.

El criticón refers to Lope de Vega as an eminent man in connection with his ability to attract the common people (*vulgo*): "el buen político suele echar buena esquila que guíe el vulgo a donde el quiere" (*El criticón* 2.5). It also becomes clear, however, in *El criticón* that Gracián detests the *corrales,* insofar as they are enclosures massively attended by the lowest human urban masses. In fact, Gracián explicitly condemns a long list of manifestations of cultural production for favoring vulgar (*chavacanos*) objects. This is the fortune of "todo género de poesía en lengua vulgar, especialmente burlesca y amorosa, letrillas, jácaras, entremeses, follaje de primavera" (2.1),[12] and also the case of picaresque, chivalry, and Cervantes's *Don Quixote.* Thus, when addressing the need for disposing of chivalry books, *El criticón* reads:

> Replicaron algunos, que para pasar el tiempo se les diese facultad de leer las obras de algunos otros autores que habían escrito contra estos primeros, burlándose de su quimérico trabajo, y respondióles la Cordura que de

> ningún modo, porque era dar del lodo en el cieno y había sido querer sacar del mundo una necedad con otra mayor.[13] (*El criticón* 2.1)

Of all the wrongdoings of modern writers—*plumas modernas*—Gracián explicitly blames the printing press, which has made possible the proliferation of books written for a wider and more heterogeneous market: "Tanto libro inútil (¡Dios se lo perdone al inventor de la estampa!)" (*El criticón* 2.1).[14] According to Gracián, the essence of the problem is that modern writers have forgotten the true soul of history, engaging instead in material, mechanical, vulgar discussions:

> Las más de estas plumas modernas son chavacanas, insulsas, y en nada eminentes. Veréis muchas maneras de historiadores: unos gramaticales, que no atienden sino al vocablo y a la colocación de las palabras, olvidándose del alma de la historia. Otros cuestionarios, todo se les va en disputar y averiguar puntos y tiempos. Hay anticuarios, gaceteros, relacioneros, todos materiales y mecánicos, sin fondo de juicio ni altanería de ingenio.[15] (*El criticón* 2.4)

So where can that forgotten soul of history, that natural object of writing, be found? This question has to be answered in connection with Gracián's defense of the superiority of writing over painting and sculpture. According to Gracián, painting and sculpture can only represent the exterior; the materials they use are futile and the glory they provide limited, since only a few men will be able to contemplate such works. Writing, on the other hand, proves to be of great service to eminent men for it creates long-lasting, accurate, universal, and complete accounts of princely virtues and heroic achievements, providing them with immortality. The mundane and practical side of Gracián's defense of writing finds expression in his consideration of the honors and stipends that are at stake:

> Los príncipes se pagan más y les pagan también a un excelente pintor, a un escultor insigne, y los honran y premian mucho más que a un historiador eminente, que al más divino poeta, que al más excelente escritor, pues vemos que los pinceles sólo retratan el exterior, pero las plumas el interior. Y va la ventaja de uno a otro que del cuerpo al alma. Exprimen aquellos, cuando mucho, el talle,

> el garbo, la gentileza y tal vez la fiereza, pero éstas, el entendimiento, el valor, la virtud y las inmortales hazañas. Aquellos les pueden dar vida por algún tiempo, mientras duraren las tablas o los lienzos, ya sean bronces, mas estas otras por todos los venideros siglos. Aquellos los dan a conocer, digo a ver a los pocos que llegan a mirar sus retratos, mas éstas a los muchos que leen sus escritos, yendo de provincia en provincia, de lengua en lengua, y aun de siglo en siglo.[16] (*El criticón* 3.6)

The value of writing, painting, and sculpture is, according to Gracián, entirely contingent upon the value of the object they choose to reproduce. Only one object is of highest value, that of the excellent virtues and heroic achievements of eminent men. Art and public representation are, in Gracián's perception, inextricably bound together to the point that one can not exist without the other. Art and history exist, in Gracián's terms, to provide eminent men with the means for their public recognition. But how can a man attract the precious, immortalizing gaze of history?

Being in Public Reputation, or the Art of Public Ostentation

Gracián seems to distinguish very sharply between existence and being: existence is futile, belonging to the domain of nature, while being is eternal, and belongs to the domain of history. Existence is a collective given; its meaning lies beyond the self, in the whole of nature. Being is a dynamic and self-creating process, and thus its meaning lies in the individual self. Earthly life takes, in Gracián's texts, the form of a most difficult voyage, an endless search for reputation. Its destiny, immortality, can only be achieved in the eternal fame assured by History—"la maestra de la vida, la vida de la fama, la fama de la verdad y la verdad de los hechos" (*El criticón* 3.12).[17] A single drop of the precious ink of history is enough to provide eminent men with true life: "Es tal la eficacia de este licor, que una sola gota basta para inmortalizar a un hombre" (*El criticón* 3.12).[18]

One's existence is independent from others, for I exist even if no other knows of my existence. One's being, on the other hand, is entirely contingent upon others, since true life is founded upon reputation, which naturally depends on public recognition: "Depende [la estimación] del respeto ajeno, y así, no se la puede tomar uno, sino merecerla de los otros y aguardarla. . . . No se vive de un voto solo, ni de un uso, ni de un siglo" (*Oráculo* 106).[19] A man becomes eminent by cultivating all the noble arts, ancient and modern languages, history, poetry, natural philosophy, moral philosophy, cosmography, astrology, and theology; by living in princely courts among principle men; by enjoying prodigious paintings, statues, tapestries, and jewelry (*El discreto* 25); but, more important, a man becomes immortal by mastering the ultimate mundane wisdom, the art of public ostentation, for all the talents in the world are nothing if they remain hidden from the public eye—the eye of history: "Lo que no se ve es como si no fuese" (*El discreto* 13).[20] Public ostentation gives heroic talents their true brightness:

> Hay sujetos bizarros en quienes lo poco luce mucho, hasta admirar, hombres de ostentativa, que, cuando se junta con la eminencia, forman un prodigio; al contrario, hombres vimos eminentes que, por faltarles realce, no parecieron la mitad. . . . De suerte que la ostentación da el verdadero lucimiento a las heroicas prendas y como un segundo ser a todo.[21] (*El discreto* 13)

Gracián speaks of wise ostentation as a superior art. The majority of his texts are series of lessons and prescriptions regarding the manner in which eminent men ought to construct their public self, manipulating appearances as to best suit the exigencies of public opinion. To that end, it is fundamental to escape isolation,[22] regularly visiting the houses of most principle courtly heroes;[23] to think and act in very practical terms;[24] to accommodate to current circumstances;[25] to observe and understand objects and subjects;[26] to dominate the art of conversation, carefully choosing novel, varied, tasteful topics and agreeable sides;[27] to rationally measure and fulfill one's own convenience;[28] and to either repress one's passions or keep them hidden from the public eye.[29] All the above-mentioned talents will, according to Gracián, provide a man with the necessary skills to perform a moderate, wise self-representation. But once he has become an excellent actor this aspirant to historical character must find a principle role, a popular play, a large audience, and thus he should dedicate himself to the most famous occupations, those that are exposed to the maximum degree of publicity,[30] namely art and letters, or war. War is the perfect occasion for a prince to earn eternal fame, for a man of letters to narrate most heroic achievements, and for both to make history: "¿Qué príncipes ocupan los catálogos de la fama, sino los guerreros? A ellos se les debe en propiedad el renombre de magnos. Llenan el mundo de aplauso, los siglos de fama, los libros de proezas, porque lo belicoso tiene más de plausible que lo pacífico" (*El héroe* 8).[31]

Gracián knows, just as well as Calderón, Lope, or Tirso, that "son los aprietos lances de reputación" and that "puesto el noble en contingencias de honra, obra por mil" (*Oráculo* 265).[32] The honor Gracián is lecturing about, however, is not that collective honor of noble status, or that intimate "patrimony of the soul" embraced by rich peasants in plays such as *El alcalde de Zalamea*, but the individual honor of being, that is, of being public. The relevance of this observation will become clear in the next section, as I try to explain the historical logic behind Gracián's conception of the public subject.

Knowledge, Power, and Courtly Elites: The Historical Logic behind Gracián's Conception of the Public Persona

Gracián's moralistic thought shares some of the principal concerns of metaphysical and political early modern philosophy. Descartes, Leibniz, Hobbes, Machiavelli, Bodin, Montaigne, and Locke all deal in different, and sometimes opposing, ways with the problem of uncertainty in the early modern world. In estatist societies men were, since their birth, fixed into a very particular estate, which performed well-defined social functions according to a static vision of the universe. The constant erosion of estatist barriers, along with the crisis of their sustaining values, originated, during the sixteenth and seventeenth centuries, a vacuum zone that came to be widely perceived, all across Europe and especially among representatives of dominant social groups, as a sign of the emergence of a chaotic world. Thinkers, men of letters, statesmen, economists, scientists, and artists had to redefine the place of men within the fast-changing environment of the modern state.

The 1600s witnessed an unprecedented wave of public debates seeking to explain the nature of the crisis of Spanish society. Outstanding participants in these debates were the *arbitristas* who proposed general socioeconomic reforms. A different response came from those who adopted mystical attitudes, some of which seem to have presented an effective threat to the structure of society.[33]

In dealing with the crisis situation, the state tried to increase its control over its subjects by using repression as well as religious education and public forms of entertainment—the theater—to strengthen necessary social myths, such as the myth of honor, with its code of conduct firmly rooted on those noble values inherent to the system of authority, the myth of world as stage, and the myth of the moral superiority of the countryside life, all of which aimed to stop and reverse the processes of social mobility reinforcing collective subjugation to societal structures.

Gracián elaborates on the topic of the topsy-turvy world—*mundo trabucado*—in several sections of *El criticón*. In *crisi* 6 of the first part entitled *Estado del siglo*, Gracián describes the present state of the world as an absolute chaos in which the beasts have come to the cities and women, slaves, and blind men are in charge. In the second part, *crisi* 5, Gracián points to the heart of the problem, the erosion of the estatist barriers: "Barajados los estados, metiéndose los del uno en el otro, saltando cada uno de su coro."[34]

Gracián detests the *arbitristas* and reformers, whom he calls "vulgo en corrillos,"[35] for eminent men do not waste their lives attempting to change the world, instead they learn how to accommodate to its current circumstances.[36] Knowledge of the world is power over it, and it is this power that provides a man with public recognition. True knowledge is the power to conquer the will of others: "Poco es conquistar el entendimiento si no se gana la voluntad, y mucho rendir con la admiración la afición juntamente. . . . Conseguir esta gracia universal algo tiene de estrella, lo más de diligencia propia" (*El héroe* 12).[37]

Knowledge is power in Gracián's texts. Here lies the fundamental difference between Descartes's metaphysics and Gracián's morals: For Descartes, true knowledge is the result of speculative thinking; for Gracián, it is a praxis inseparable from life, from man's struggle for power.

El criticón is an allegory of man's peregrination from animality to humanity, from nothingness to true life, from savage ignorance to courtly wisdom. Gracián himself explains *El criticón* as life's journey toward the court of crowned wisdom ["el viaje de su vida hacia la Corte del saber coronado"] (*El criticón* 3.6). Andrenio and Critilo become personas as they move through the pages of the text, as they master the knowledge that distinguishes them from the indiscriminate mass of the common people, as they acquire power over hearts. This is life's individual victory over collective nothingness: "Es gran victoria coger los corazones; no nace de una necia intrepidez, ni del enfadoso entretenimiento; sí de una decente autoridad, nacida del genio superior y ayudada de los méritos" (*Oráculo* 122).[38] The pairing of nature and art is everywhere present in Gracián's texts. Nature provides the condition of possibility of man's eminence and art its actuality: "Es el arte complemento de la naturaleza y un otro segundo ser que por extremo la hermosea y aun pretende excederla en sus obras. Préciase de haber añadido un otro mundo artificial al primero. Suple de ordinario los descuidos de la naturaleza, perfeccionándola en todo, que sin este socorro del artificio, quedará inculta y grosera" (*El criticón* 1.8).[39]

Certainly the common people remain inside the margins of what Gracián calls ignorant and vulgar nature. But this taxonomic categorization also includes ignorant noble men: "Tan vulgares hay algunos y tan ignorantes como sus propios lacayos.... Porque vulgo no es otra cosa que una sinagoga de ignorantes" (*El criticón* 2.5).[40]

Gracián explicitly defines *El criticón* as courtly philosophy for wise, judicious readers. The earliest French and Italian translations of *Oráculo manual* were entitled *L'homme de Cour* and *L'uomo di Corte*. Manuél de Salinas y Lizana, the church official who approved the publishing of *El discreto*, makes sure to underline the fact that Gracián's texts address a very exclusive minority:

> Gracián dió las primeras luces de su idea a la enseñanza de un príncipe en El Héroe y Político. . . . Forma ahora de política general a un Discreto. . . . Enseña a un hombre a ser perfecto en todo; por esto no enseña a todos. . . . Todo conseguirá la aprobación de los entendidos, que no acredita el aplauso de todos, cuando son tan pocos los doctos.[41] (*El discreto,* "Aprobación del doctor don Manuél de Salinas . . .")

The quotation suggests that the addressee of Gracián's works must have been the courtly man. Furthermore, toward the end of *crisi* 11 of the first part of *El criticón,* Critilo is looking for a book that could guide him through the courtly labyrinth. A complete scrutiny of courtly manuals immediately takes place, including *El galateo español* by Lucas Gracián Dantisco, *La instrucción de don Juán de Vega a su hijo cuando le enviaba a la Corte, La instrucción del conde de Portalegre quando envió a su hijo a la Corte,* and so on. In the context of the discussion, the courtly man—*el cortesano*—refers to *El galateo* as an outdated book, for "en los tiempos que alcanzamos no valen [sus reglas] cosa."[42] The courtier goes on to ridicule each of the maxims contained in *El galateo* and to suggest some new rules, more commensurate with the circumstances of present courtly life. Not surprisingly, all the new maxims coincide with the ones contained in *El oráculo manual, El discreto,* and *El héroe.* Gracián is fully aware of the ever-changing nature of the space in which public representation is negotiated. In effect, being able to calibrate day by day current circumstances is, in his view, the most secure guarantee of success and hence, the ultimate manifestation of worldly wisdom.

Maravall has documented the nature of the changes that were taking place in the Spanish absolutist court since the end of the sixteenth century. By the mid-1600s the Spanish absolutist court still lodges an important sector of the traditional nobility, but it also includes significant groups of bureaucrats, public management professionals, and new moneyed nobles. Although lineage is still a factor in acceding to the highest public offices, it is not the decisive one any more, insofar as organizing and governing functions constitute technical disciplines requiring a high degree of specialization.

In a passage of the second part of *El criticón,* referring to Luis Vives's *De conscribendis epistolis,* a manual about the art of writing letters, one of the characters manages to highlight the importance of mastering the language of power to achieve success in court: "Este sí que es el práctico saber, esta la arte de todo discreto... esta la que del polvo de la tierra levanta un pigmeo al trono del mando.... ¡Oh, qué lección esta del valer y del medrar! Ni la Política, ni la Filosofía, ni todas juntas alcanzan lo que ésta con sola una letra" (*El criticón* 2.12).[43]

Maravall explains the sociopolitical changes taking place in Spanish society as a transformation of the nobility, which is—in responding to the increasing complexity of the modern state's governmental apparatuses—gradually abandoning its estatist structure to become a power elite. As the century goes on, the process of aristocratization tends to eliminate the lowest noble strata including instead moneyed groups and public management professionals.[44] In their process of self-construction, power elites have to extend the classic monarcho-seigneurial discourse of legitimization beyond the appeal to superiority of the noble estate, insofar as the very definition of their limits depends on a complex network of excluding mechanisms.

This is, in my view, the historical logic behind Gracián's conception of the public persona. Gracián elaborates a new concept of the public man based on criteria of individual superiority, while reconfiguring the space and necessary apparatus for his public representation. Gracián's courtly philosophy is commensurate with the interests of public individuals belonging to the new elites at several levels: (1) by justifying the exclusion of some noble strata and the inclusion of new social elements; (2) by rationalizing attitudes of public cynicism, rethinking the public space as a battlefield in which to pursue power and individual success; (3) by elaborating and legitimizing a definition of art and writing as instruments for the achievement and naturalization of power; and (4) by equating knowledge, moral superiority and humanity with power.

To conclude, Gracián uses the word *subjects*—*sujetos*—to refer to a particular kind of animal entity, while reserving the term *persona* for a social construct whose meaning, whose being, comes about within the sphere of art, the sphere of public representation, as a never-ending process of becoming. Since the final realization of a person can only be achieved in writing, in the immortalizing gaze of history, human life takes the form of a race against the clock—the time of one's biological existence—and against others, in the pursue of reputation and power. There is only one rule in this life-or-death game, that of identifying and obeying one's own interest—*conveniencia*—for "that is virtue and sin to go against it" ("es virtud y pecado el ir contra ella" [*Oráculo* 64]). What distinguishes a *persona* from the indiscriminate animality of other subjects is his public character. If for Descartes what distinguishes the I of the subject is his faculty of reason, for Gracián it is his public nature that constitutes the ever-changing I of the persona. In identifying knowledge, power, and being with the public man, Gracián's courtly philosophy legitimizes the authority of the incipient courtly elites that emerged from within the monarcho-seigneurial alliance as a much-needed response to the crisis precipitated by the modern process of dissolution of the estatist barriers.

Notes

1. See Duby, "Solitude: Eleventh to Thirteenth Century," 509–534; Braunstein, "Toward Intimacy: The Fourteenth and Fifteenth Centuries," 535–630; and Maravall, *Estado moderno y mentalidad social*.

2. Several pages later, da Vinci formulates the same prescription in a more extensive manner: "Observe decorum in every thing you represent, that is, fitness of action, dress, and situation, according to the meanness of the subject to be represented. Be careful that a King, for instance, be grave and majestic in his countenance and dress; that the place be well decorated; and that his attendants, or the by-standers, express reverence and admiration, and appear noble, in dresses suitable to a royal court. On the contrary, in the representation of a mean subject, let the figures appear low and despicable" (97).

3. "This noble art puts in front of our eyes the image of any great man desired to be seen and known for his achievements."

4. "Great minds assert that a man cannot find anything better than painting in defending himself against his mortality, and against time."

5. "He painted his own genealogy to show how he descended from the Metelo lineage."

6. See Eisenstein, *The Printing Press as an Agent of Change*, especially part 1.

7. Berger's *Ways of Seeing* elaborates on the existing relation between the appearance of new pictorial practices and the emergence of a prebourgeois mentality: "Works of art in earlier traditions celebrated wealth. But wealth was then a symbol of a fixed social or divine order. Oil painting celebrated a new

kind of wealth—which was dynamic and which found its only sanction in the supreme buying power of money. Thus painting itself had to be able to demonstrate the desirability of what money could buy. And the visual desirability of what can be bought lies in its tangibility, in how it will reward the touch, the hand, of the owner" (90). For a detailed exposition of the processes of dissolution of the order of traditional wealth in relation to the emergence of the precapitalist mentality, see Maravall, *Estado moderno y mentalidad social*, vol. 2, part 3.

8. For a reading of most Cervantian texts as a constant dialogue with literary and social conventions, see Spadaccini and Talens, *Through the Shattering Glass*, especially chapter 2. For a treatment of Cervantes's rural *entremeses* as a direct confrontation against the Baroque theatrical institution, see Castillo and Egginton, "The Rules of Chanfalla's Game."

9. See Brown, *Images and Ideas in Seventeenth Century Spanish Painting*, and especially Maravall, *Velázquez y el espíritu de la Modernidad*.

10. See Castillo and Egginton, "All the King's Subjects."

11. See Maravall, *Poder, honor y élites en el siglo XVII*.

12. "... every genre of poetry in vulgar [romance] language, particularly burlesque and love poetry, *letrillas, jácaras*, interludes, spring foliage."

13. "Some asked that license be given to them to read the works of those authors who wrote against the former books of chivalry mocking their chimerical exploits. But Wisdom replied that in no way should those readings be permitted, for they run away from mud only to sink in a bog, as they attempt to remove from the world a nonsense by way of a greater stupidity."

14. "So many useless books—God forgive the inventor of the printing press!"

15. "Most of these modern pens are vulgar, tasteless, in no way eminent. You will see many kinds of historians: some grammarians, who pay attention to nothing but words and their location, thus forgetting the soul of history; some polemicists who are always engaged in disputes over meaningless details. There are antiquarians, gazetteers, story tellers, all of them material workers without judgment or wisdom."

16. "Princes most appreciate and remunerate an excellent painter, an illustrious sculptor, and so they honor and award them much more greatly than they do the most eminent historian, the most divine poet, the most excellent writer, and all that in spite of the fact that the brush solely represents the exterior, unlike the pen, which represents the interior. The advantage of the one over the other being that of the soul over the body. The former [brush] expresses, at the most, appearance, grace, and bravery, while the latter [pen] expresses wisdom, valor, virtue, and immortal deeds. The former [brush or burial] endows achievements with transitory life, as long as panels and canvas, even bronzes endure, but the latter [pen] gives them life for centuries to come. The former makes them known to those few who happen to gaze on such portraits, but the latter to the many who read its writings, from province to province, from language to language, from century to century."

17. "The master of life, the life of fame, the fame of the Truth, and the Truth of the facts."

18. "Such is the power of this liquor, that a single drop suffices to make a man immortal."

19. "Reputation depends on the respect of others and so it can not be taken, but awaited and earned . . . One does not live on a single opinion, nor on a single fashion, nor on a single century."

20. "That which cannot be seen is as if it were not."

21. "There are gallant subjects who make their precarious qualities visible and admirable; prodigious men capable of ostentation and eminence. On the contrary, we saw eminent men who, lacking representational skills, shone very little. . . . Thus, ostentation endows heroic qualities with true brightness and it generates something like a second being for everything."

22. "Háse de vivir con otros" (One must live with others) (*Oráculo* 133).

23. "Las casas de aquellos héroes cortesanos que son más teatros de la heroicidad que palacios de la vanidad" (The households of those heroic courtiers, which are more like theaters of heroism than palaces of vanity) (*Oráculo* 11).

24. "¿De qué sirve el saber si no es práctico? Y el saber vivir hoy es el verdadero saber" (How useful may wisdom be if it is not practical wisdom? And knowing how to live is the true wisdom) (*El discreto* 232).

25. See *Oráculo* 20, 107, 120, 194, 203, 288; and *El héroe* 7.

26. See *Oráculo* 37, 39, 48, 157; and *El discreto* 5.

27. See *Oráculo* 22, 63, 81, 118, 148; and *El discreto* 4, 5, 7, 18.

28. To act according to one's own convenience is virtue and sin to go against it ("Virtud y pecado el ir contra ella" [*Oráculo* 64]). See also *Oráculo* 35.

29. "Atienda, pues, el varón excelente, primero, a violentar sus pasiones; cuando menos a solaparlas con tal destreza, que ninguna contratreta acierte a descifrar su voluntad" (The excellent gentleman must first aim to repress his passions; and otherwise he must hide them so skillfully that no maneuver would be able to disclose his will) (*El héroe* 2).

30. "Empleo plausible llamo aquel que se ejecuta a vista de todos y a gusto de todos, con el fundamento siempre de la reputación" (I call a dedication plausible when it is carried out under public scrutiny and it pleases everyone so as to grant good reputation) (*El héroe* 8). Gracián admonishes eminent men to prefer celebrated occupations: thus, "los célebres empleos que todos perciban y participen todos, y a sufragios comunes quede inmortalizado" (famous occupations perceived by everyone and in which everyone could participate, so as to be immortalized by the common opinion) (*Oráculo* 67); and "hidalgo asunto expuesto al universal teatro" (noble subject exposed to the universal theater) (*El héroe* 8).

31. "What princes occupy the catalogs of fame, but warriors? Only they deserve the renown of Great Ones. They elicit the applause of the world, centuries of fame, books of exploits, for war exploits elicit greater admiration than peaceful enterprises." In fact, the mechanics of war had changed considerably during the previous century. Infantry had appropriated most of the historical functions of noblemen. We should remember that war had been for a long time the very reason for nobility to exist. Gracián does not speak favorably of these changes insofar as they prevent eminent men from being able to adequately display their eminence in the battlefield. This explains his diatribes against gunpowder, the invention that instituted the anonymous war: "Que no puede ser otra una invención tan sacrílega, tan execrable, tan impía y tan fatal, como es la pólvora. . . . Ya ninguno puede lucir ni campear" (There has not been a more sacrilegious, more

execrable, impious, and fatal invention than the invention of gunpowder.... No one may now shine in triumph) (*El criticón* 2.7).

32. "Quandaries are strokes of reputation.... When a nobleman's honor is at stake, he is capable of more than a thousand men."

33. See Forcione, "El desposeimiento del ser en la literatura renacentista, 34; and Egginton's "Gracián and the Emergence of the Modern Subject" in this volume (chapter 5).

34. "Shuffled the estates, intervening those of one estate into the other, going everyone beyond the limits of his own sphere."

35. "Villains in huddles"; see also *El criticón* 2.4, 2.7.

36. Maravall clearly perceived the conservatism of Gracián's thought when he wrote: "Ni en el pensamiento de Gracián se contiene una fórmula de transformación de la sociedad.... El culto gracianesco del héroe tiene un carácter conservador: el héroe es, en él, un factor de estabilización" (Gracián's thought does not contain a formula for the transformation of society.... Gracián's cult of the hero has a conservative character: The hero is a stabilizing factor) ("Antropología y política en el pensamiento de Gracián," *Estudios del pensamiento español* 197–222).

37. "Conquering minds has little value if wills are not subjugated. Much has been accomplished, however, when the will has been rendered along with admiration.... This universal grace can be achieved through good fortune but most of all through personal diligence." There are a wealth of considerations on this subject in Gracián's texts. See, for instance, *El discreto* 19, 22; *Oráculo* 4, 26, 40; *El criticón* 2.6.

38. "It is great victory, that of capturing hearts; it does not originate from foolish intrepidity, or from annoying entertainment, but from that decent authority proper to the superior genius with the assistance of his merits."

39. "Art is the complement of nature, a second being which embellishes it, and it even aims to surpass it in achievements. It has added to the world another artificial one. It ordinarily covers the mistakes of nature, perfecting it in such a way that without this aid of the artifice, it [nature] would remain rustic and uneducated."

40. "There are some as vulgar and ignorant as their own servants.... For *vulgo* is nothing but a congregation of ignorant people."

41. "Gracián dedicated the first light of his idea to teaching a prince in *The Hero* and *The Politician*.... He now educates a Discrete in general politics.... He teaches a man to be perfect in all; and thus, he does not speak for everyone.... Everything will conceal the approbation of the initiated ones, for it does not seek everyone's applause, the wise being so few."

42. "Its prescriptions are of little value at the present time."

43. "This truly is the practical wisdom, the art of every discreet man... that which raises anyone from the dust to the throne.... Oh, what a lesson of worthiness and prosperity! Neither Politics, nor Philosophy, nor all of them reach what this one does with a single letter."

44. See Maravall, *Poder, honor y élites en el siglo XVII* (173–251).

Works Cited

Braunstein, Philippe. "Toward Intimacy: The Fourteenth and Fifteenth Centuries." *A History of Private Life*. Vol. 2. Ed. Georges Duby. Cambridge: Harvard University Press, 1988.

Brown, Jonathan. *Images and Ideas in Seventeenth-Century Spanish Painting.* New Jersey: Princeton University Press, 1978.

Berger, John. *Ways of Seeing.* London: British Broadcasting Corporation and Penguin Books, 1972.

Castillo, David, and William Egginton. "The Rules of Chanfalla's Game." *Selected Proceedings from the Fourteenth Spanish Golden Age Theatre Symposium.* Ed. Luis Suárez. El Paso: University of Texas at El Paso, 1994.

———. "All the King's Subjects: Honor in Early Modernity." *Romance Language Annual* 6 (1994): 422–427.

Da Vinci, Leonardo. *The Art of Painting.* Ed. Alfred Werner. New York: Philosophical Library, 1957.

Duby, Georges. "Solitude: Eleventh to Thirteenth Century." *A History of Private Life.* Vol. 2. Ed. Georges Duby. Cambridge: Harvard University Press, 1988.

Eisenstein, Elizabeth. *The Printing Press as an Agent of Change.* Cambridge: Cambridge University Press, 1979.

Foucault, Michel. *The Order of Things: An Archaeology of the Human Sciences.* New York: Vintage Books, 1973.

Forcione, Alban. "El desposeimiento del ser en la literatura renacentista: Cervantes, Gracián y los desafíos de Nemo." *Nueva Revista de Filología Hispánica* 34 (1986): 654–690.

Gracián, Baltasar. *Obras completas.* Madrid: Aguilar, 1944.

Holanda, Francisco de. *Diálogos de Roma; da pintura antiga.* Lisboa: Livraria sá da Costa Editora, 1955.

Maravall, José Antonio. *Velázquez y el espíritu de la Modernidad.* Madrid: Guadarrama, 1960.

———. *Estado moderno y mentalidad social.* Vol. 2. Madrid: Alianza, 1972.

———. *Poder, honor y élites en el siglo XVII.* Madrid: Siglo XXI, 1979.

———. "Antropología y política en el pensamiento de Gracián." *Estudios de historia del pensamiento español.* Serie tercera. El siglo del Barroco. Madrid: Cultura Hispánica, 1984.

Spadaccini, Nicholas, and Jenaro Talens. *Through the Shattering Glass: Cervantes and the Self-Made World.* Minneapolis: University of Minnesota Press, 1993.

Chapter 8

Symbolic Wealth and Theatricality in Gracián

Francisco J. Sánchez

Within the society of the court and among the aristocratic-bourgeois groups of seventeenth-century Spain, there arises a concern for the role and place that literature and writing have in politics. In this context, I first analyze the notion of *caudal* as symbolic wealth, a notion that brings to light the close relationship that Gracián establishes between *prudencia* and *agudeza* (prudence and wit). His description of an essentially strategic conception of social performance also has, in my view, aesthetic implications. Courtly society becomes a theatrical stage for the public display of economic and cultural attributes of the subject.

On the one hand, this process may be called theatrical because it is an attempt to build a scenic movement on the basis of a sociopoetic description of society. On the other hand, the iconological function of poetic imagery and ideas in the Baroque allows for an understanding of literary devices, such as the *concepto*—literary "conceit"—as producers of visual effects.

Deception and Symbolic Wealth

One of the notions that run through Spanish Baroque texts is that of "deceit." It is the basic motif of the picaresque, the theme with which love is often treated in poetry as well as in narrative, the subtext of a large part of theater, and a basic assumption underlying all political writing. If Cervantes plays with illusion, his characters are often forced to probe the limits and interrelationships between appearances and reality, between deception and truth.

Particularly during the first quarter or so of the seventeenth century, the depiction of society, especially the depiction of urban populations, is marked by the impossibility of trust, social solidarity, moral justice, or economic stability. Thus, if Campuzano—in Cervantes's *El casamiento engañoso y coloquio de los perros* (1613)—gets sick because of his sexual contact with Estefanía, is robbed by her, and thus becomes a dreamer or a writer, this is because in the first instance he thought that Estefanía was a "lady" and therefore that he could improve his social status by marrying her. Some years before, Justina, a female rogue in *Pícara Justina,* declares without shame that love equals money. Elena, in *La hija de Celestina* (1612), is a prostitute who receives punishment by death. Around 1620, the rogue and the criminal are often undifferentiated, as in *La desordenada codicia de los bienes ajenos, Lazarillo de Manzanares,* and some of the stories of Liñán y Verdugo. In sum, even love and love relations become the place for disaster, economic pitfall, and moral dissolution in most of the stories of Liñán, in Céspedes y Meneses's *Historias peregrinas y ejemplares* (1623), and a few years later in the writing of María de Zayas. Likewise, it is well known that Quevedo's *Buscón* and *Sueños* are a vision of humanity that is in an irreversible state of deception.

The moral decadence of society portrayed in this literature is in most cases related to fears of loss of social and economic privileges or even to threats to the social order in its entirety. This literature belongs, therefore, to a cultural discourse that attempts to produce a social understanding of the conditions of social cohesion and ethical unbalances and of the ways in which symbolic value affects appearances; that is, the ways in which symbolic value affects the perception of reality. One of the key elements of this understanding has to do with an inquiry into the nature of illusion as the characterization of the way that the social subject collaborates in the reproduction of deceit.

No matter how hard Spanish Catholic political writers fought to counteract the legacy of Machiavelli, the awareness of a political dimension that did not deal with moral or religious truths but that was essentially involved with a technology and a strategy of social appearances helped to invigorate an inquiry into the consequences and the profitability of deceit.[1] We find in this period that deception is one of the expressions connecting individual struggle and competition to a particular perception of moral codes and social norms. Deception appears to belong to both the actual social exchange and to the symbolic apprehension of reality; it is a product of social relations and, at the same time, a belief that most people hold to be true about any social relationship. In this sense deceit and deception are notions that refer to the conditions of a social practice and are also symbols that express the way in which the subject perceives his or her participation in society.

Both these conditions and these symbols are in many cases condensed in the idea of *caudal,* wealth. In Spanish picaresque narratives, the term covers both economic wealth and the skills to convey an appearance, a representation aimed at deceiving individuals who are rich—or at least those who would seem to be. In *Guzmán de Alfarache,* the protagonist arrives in Madrid and strategically interacts with many people to amass a large fortune with "caudal poco" (a small amount of money) (Alemán 259). Years later, after acquiring a knowledge of business, Guzmán says that "la ostentación suele ser parte de caudal por lo que al crédito importa" (ostentation is usually part of wealth because it grants credit) (Alemán 762).[2] He receives a great deal of "credit" from a woman for whom he works, because she has "abundante caudal" (an abundance of wealth) (Alemán 863). This reconfiguration of *caudal* from merely a supply of coins to the actual work of capital in credit will take on a religious-mercantile twist in Guzmán's conversion, as I will show later. In *Pícara Justina,* the female is portrayed as leading a life of pragmatism; when she decides that it is time to choose a husband, she affirms that love resulting from contemplation does not imply wealth:

> Creer que en mirar ventanas echa el amor su caudal, es creer que sin fundamento pintaron al amor con los ojos vendados. (Francisco López de Ubeda 711)
>
> [To believe that loves wastes its wealth by gazing at windows is like thinking that there is no reason to portray love blindfolded.]

Justina is already touching upon a notion of *caudal* in which social interaction has a representational side that affects the goals of individual interest. In the same vein, Jerónimo de Salas Barbadillo treats *caudal* as economic wealth in *El caballero puntual*,[3] yet he depicts a symbolic conception of *caudal* in *La hija de Celestina*. Elena, the female rogue, deceives an old rich man by playing the role of a raped lady. She thinks of her own crying and her tears as *caudal* (capital) and *moneda* (coin, money) respectively (Salas Barbadillo 36). In *Vida y hechos de Estebanillo González* the same notion is continuously related to economic wealth in plain terms, just as it is in Castillo Solórzano's novels.[4]

With María de Zayas, one encounters once again a symbolic understanding of *caudal*. In this case it refers to the sociointellectual status of the individual. Debating the reasons that women have not achieved a prominent position in the field of knowledge, she says, "La verdadera causa de no ser las mujeres doctas no es defecto del caudal, sino falta de la aplicación" (the fact that women are not wise is not due to a lack of talents/wealth, but to a lack of training) (Zayas 48).

In *La esclava de su amante*, the main character describes her social and cultural origins, and mentions that she writes poetry—an action that angers many people because they are afraid of losing their own imagination. With this in mind she then exclaims, "¡Bárbaro, ignorante! ¡si lo sabes hacer, hazlos, que no te roba nadie tu caudal!" (Brute, ignorant! if you know how to do it, do it [poetry], for nobody is stealing your wealth!) (Zayas 210).

In Gracián the term *caudal* refers to the level of wealth and to the skills inscribed in a practical performance; it also means the capacity to produce a symbolic field within which the subject performs a strategic behavior. This strategy embodies a conceptualization of social exchange. Such a description entails the hypothetical introduction of the subject's performance within the other's sphere (which is configured in a similar way):

> Excuse el varón atento sondearle el fondo, ya al saber, ya al valer, si quiere que le veneren todos: permítase al conocimiento, no a la comprensión. Nadie le averigüe los términos de la capacidad, por el peligro evidente del desengaño. Nunca dé lugar a que alguno le alcance todo: mayores afectos de veneración causa la opinión y duda de

> adónde llega el caudal de cada uno que la evidencia de él, por grande que fuere. (*Oráculo* 172)[5]
>
> [The prudent person—if he wants to be revered by others—should never allow them to judge the extent of his knowledge and courage. Allow yourself to be known, but not comprehended. No one will discern the limits of your talent, and thus no one will be disappointed. You can win more admiration by keeping other people guessing the extent of your talent, or even doubting it, than you can by displaying it, however great.] (Maurer 53)

Although Christopher Maurer uses the word "talent" in his translation, I think that even here "wealth" is a closer translation of *caudal*. Gracián means not only mental attributes, but material and symbolic attributes, as well; moreover, *caudal* is a good that may be augmented or diminished within social exchange and competition. In another work, Gracián says, "Arguye eminencia de caudal penetrar toda voluntad ajena, y concluye superioridad saber celar la propia" (To know how to penetrate the other's will is the discourse of a superior wealth; to know how to defend one's will is the highest conclusion) (*El héroe* 9).

The defense of *caudal* is the goal of a practical knowledge that is both an action and a theoretical reflection on the position of oneself among deceiving signs. This defense is produced only by concrete activity within a cultural place that is, in turn, a construction, a representation: "Sea ésta la primera destreza en el arte de entendidos, medir el lugar por su artificio" (This must be the most important skill for those who want to know: one must measure the place according to its craftiness) (*El héroe* 7).

This space is defined by its reference to both the means of acquiring knowledge and the term's signification. The place is, above all, a moment of exchange and a movement of wealth; the conception of the craftiness or artfulness of the place, the artfulness of the socioeconomic and symbolic exchanges, implies the idea of a place that properly belongs to cultural production. In this space, *caudal* is represented with all the markings of a game with its own arbitrary—nonessential—regulation.

The inseparability of the physical and linguistic aspects of *caudal*, the continuity of social and material wealth, with discursive and political wealth, has to do with one's awareness of a "symbolic capital" that conducts the social exchange at the level of language, status, and culture. In this sense *caudal* is both the amount of cultural and material wealth and also the dialogic sign of social struggle, knowledge, and deception.

For Bourdieu symbolic capital allows the distribution of goods and ideas to enlarge the profit of socioeconomic exchange by means of the investment made on "credit," "trust," "images," "status," "authority," and "beliefs."[6] In this sense, I will argue that Gracián articulates the conditions of social exchange as being engendered through a process of symbol formations. The connection between social and symbolic formation is facilitated because the topology of social exchange is meaningful and is regulated according to its own symbolic value—a value created and realized in the process of exchange. This exchange is discourse. He says that "las juiciosas calificaciones participan igualmente de la prudencia y de la sutileza" (good judgments partake both of prudence and of subtle wit) (*Agudeza* 2:7).

Since the beginning of the debate on "razón de Estado," *prudencia* is the realm of practical political knowledge; *sutileza,* however, is one of the particular and sometimes idiosyncratic expressions of *agudeza,* which is the working of *ingenio,* wit. *Juicio* is the capacity for political and moral judgment. Within the context of Gracián's book, the quoted sentence clearly states that symbolic production participates in a practical activity.

Social strategy is a performance in which the process of symbol formation unveils its dramatic visual imagery. In the *Oráculo manual y arte de prudencia,* Gracián writes:

> Pelea la sagacidad con estratagemas de intención: nunca obra lo que indica; apunta sí para deslumbrar; amaga al aire con destreza, y ejecuta en la impensada realidad, atenta siempre a desmentir. Echa una intención para asegurarse de la émula atención, y revuelve luego contra ella, venciendo por lo inesperado; pero la penetrante inteligencia la previene con atenciones; la acecha con reflejas: entiende siempre lo contrario de lo que quiere que entienda, y conoce luego cualquier intentar de falso: deja pasar toda primera intención y está en espera a la segunda, y aun a la tercera. (*Oráculo* 146–147)

> [Cunning arms itself with strategies of intention. It never does what it indicates. It takes aim deceptively, feints nonchalantly in the air, and delivers its blow, acting upon unforeseen reality with attentive dissimulation. To win the attention and confidence of others, it hints at its intention. But immediately it turns against that intention and conquers through surprise. The penetrating intelligence heads off cunning with close observation, ambushes it with caution, understands the opposite of what cunning wanted it to understand, and immediately identifies false intentions. Intelligence allows the first intention to pass by, and awaits the second one, and even the third.] (Maurer 7–8)

Social exchange and competition are seen as processes of uncovering meaning in the other's behavior. These are thus social as well as textual processes; they participate in a dialogic sphere of discourse and they attempt to unveil *caudal,* to reveal the quality and quantity of the other's hidden assets, and as such to leave them open for evaluation.

In his book on *agudeza* (wit), Gracián offers a similar description of the way "truth" should be expressed under the deceitful conditions of discursive exchange:

> Abrió los ojos la Verdad, dio desde entonces en andar con artificio, usa de las invenciones, introdúcese por rodeos, vence con estratagemas, pinta lejos lo que está muy cerca, habla de lo presente en lo pasado, propone en aquel sujeto lo que quiere condenar en éste, apunta en uno para dar en otro, deslumbra las pasiones, desmiente los afectos, y, por ingenioso circunloquio, viene siempre a parar en el punto de su intención. (*Agudeza* 2:192)

> [Truth opened its eyes; since then, it began to walk with artfulness; it uses inventions, comes by roundabout ways, wins by means of strategies, paints far away what is actually nearby; it speaks about today through the past, proposes something on that subject which it actually condemns on this other, aims at this one to target at another; it blinds passions, refutes affections, and, by an ingenious circumlocution, it always arrives at the matter of its intention.]

At the level of linguistic articulation the topology of social exchange becomes a description of the subject's actions to defend and increase *caudal.* Such actions coincide with the description of the self-regulation of discourse in order to establish not the criterion of its "truth" but rather the condition of its existence. This is something that resembles what Foucault has proposed in order to understand discourse as "a field of strategic possibilities" (Foucault 37).

In Gracián social reality is a sign that needs to be decoded in terms of the subject's success in the imposition of its own meaning and in its increase in symbolic capital, or *caudal.* Thus, social performance is also a discursive exchange. Political behavior (*prudencia*) and symbolic production (*agudeza*) are places for the subject to emerge. Substantially strategic attributes are translated to the symbolic activity, and, vice versa, the signifying capacity of the subject constitutes the very strategy of performance. This synthesis establishes the identity of social and symbolic orders insofar as they produce relations of signification; they are given in equal terms and are, using Foucault's terminology once again, positivities, moments and places for the emergence of the subject of discourse.

Subject and Theatricality

The identification, in Gracián's writing, of these two sociotextual places reaches an important point in his description of the supreme attribute of both the *prudente* (prudent) and the *agudo* (a person with wit): the *despejo.* He defines it as

> alma de toda prenda, vida de toda perfección, gallardía de las acciones, gracia de las palabras y hechizo de todo buen gusto, lisonjea la inteligencia y extraña la explicación. . . . es perfección de la misma perfección, como trascendente beldad, con universal gracia. Consiste en una cierta airosidad, en una indecible gallardía, tanto en el decir como en el hacer, hasta en el discurrir. . . . Sin él la menor ejecución es muerta, la mayor perfección, desabrida. . . . No sólo sirve al ornato, sino que apoya lo importante. Porque si es alma de la hermosura, es espíritu de la prudencia. . . . hasta en la cátedra da bizarría a la agudeza. (*El héroe* 29–30)

> [... the soul of every attribute, life of all perfection, elegance of actions, gracefulness of words, and spell of good taste; it pleases the mind and refuses explanation.... It is the perfection of perfection, like a transcendent beauty, a universal gracefulness. It consists in an ethereal grace, in an unspeakable elegance of what is said as well as of what is done, even of thinking.... Without it, every performance is dead, the biggest perfection is with no color.... It is not only an element of ornament, but it also supports what is important. For being the soul of beauty, it is the spirit of prudence.... It even gives grace to wit in the very same school of learning.]

Despejo is an element of both sides of the subject's activity, and it is properly an attribute of its expression at the moment of practice. It shows the strategy of subjectivity to be a complete identification between action and representation. This identification is, in turn, the production of a game by which the subject's identity is assimilated to the image of its performance. A subjectivity formed essentially by means of the images of representation is a paradoxical one.

A subjectivity gained through a strategic performance also reveals an awareness of a political dimension of culture. The political side of linguistic (symbolic or poetic) activity is articulated within the notion of symbolic exchange (*caudal*). The conflation of these two dimensions of human action, which had for a long time remained apart, becomes a fundamental reason for the debates in seventeenth-century Spain on the illusory features of reality, for the conception of society as representation, and for the ontological status of fiction and deception. Gracián's straightforward identification of representation and social action, symbolic production and social exchange, is a turning point for these debates. Already in his writing one finds a conception of cultural production as a signifying practice and thus a sociopoetic notion of the subject of that practice.

This writing must not be understood in merely rhetorical terms. Anthony Cascardi has suggested that it is precisely in the society of the court that the emergence of the modern subject can be detected. This author considers that the outcome of the process of disenchantment through which modern subjectivity is born relates to a "psychological subject" (Cascardi, *The Subject of Modernity* 254). It should be added that this psychological effect is the result of the transmission of discourse within a dialogic field. In this field, the "self" understands his or her social and linguistic performance as an ongoing answer, virtual, real, or implicit, to the other's move. The metaphor of this relationship is the game, a game that is, essentially, a dialectics between that unknown other that is always there within the moment of "my" practice, and the social and symbolic activities of that other as far as "I" am able to respond to them. *Caudal,* sociosymbolic (poetic) wealth, is the factor at stake. The other's intentions and actions are implicit within the subject's activity.

The connotations of the Spanish word *caudal,* the flow, that elusive element that runs without ever stopping at any particular moment (and even the literary and mythical connotations of the river that flows on), creates an image of an ongoing process of transformation from physical and material attributes of wealth to its symbolic status in the order of language—a process that constitutes a dialogic subjectivity by and through linguistic creativity.

To this extent, it is appropriate to recall Bakhtin's characterization of the relations between culture and language and his description of the phenomenon of "answerability": "I have to answer with my own life for what I have experienced and understood in art" (Bakhtin 1).

The unity of answerability is the unity of a subject not in itself but in language, understood dialogically, that is, in the field of what is always "inhabited" by the other. This "answerability" characterizes, in my view, the courtly space as a game of strategic oppositions. Maravall has even considered the function of the you-I relationship as a basic structure in some of Gracián's works.[7]

This dialogical strategy also involves courtly narratives by engendering broader games between verbalizing and listening, between fiction ("tales," "fables," "stories") and context ("dialogue," "advice," "entertainment," "gathering," "celebration"), between text and its own exterior, its receptor's locus. This is a narrative strategy that seems to be reproduced endlessly. The scenario of an infinitely expected answer, a continuously unresolved conflict, a game that never ends, is central to this sociosymbolic wealth.

This is a configuration that also pertains to other narrative genres and in particular to picaresque literature. At the time of Gracián's literary production, a cultural dimension of the formal device of an "answer" to an implicit, repressive framework had already been expressed in *Lazarillo de Tormes*.[8] The subjectivity here expressed is necessarily born out of a strategic relationship between social and institutional orders. The narrative process of picaresque literature is a good example of Bakhtin's answerability, the fusion of the social sphere into the poetic realm. Within this process *caudal*, wealth, constitutes itself as a fusion of economic needs in a representational practice.

In *Guzmán de Alfarache*, the character performs a mercantile-religious conversion by means of an internalization of a "voice" that gives him advice about the infinite *caudal* of God:

> Buscaste caudal para hacer empleo: búscalo agora y hazlo de manera que puedas comprar la bienaventuranza. Esos trabajos, eso que padeces y cuidado que tomas en servir a ese tu amo, ponlo a la cuenta de Dios. Con eso puedes comprar la gracia. . . . Sírvelo con un suspiro, con una lágrima, con un dolor de corazón, pesándote de haberle ofendido. Que dándosele a él, juntará tu caudal con el suyo y, haciéndolo de infinito precio, gozarás de vida eterna. (Alemán 890)

> [You were looking for wealth to make a living: look for it now and do it in a way that you can afford to be blessed. The troubles that you suffer for and the care that you take to serve your master must be placed in God's account. You can buy, then, the grace. . . . Serve Him with a sigh, with a tear, with the suffering of your heart. In this way, giving it to Him, He will join your wealth with His own and, doing it of an infinite price, you will enjoy eternal life.]

Elena's *caudal*, in Salas Barbadillo's *La hija de Celestina*, allows her to successfully enact her robbery. Here and in many other picaresque texts, *caudal* is maintained and increased by the initiation of the symbolic order. A dialogic narrative textualizes the you-I relationship as a game of oppositions that obtains a sociopoetic synthesis, which is the understanding of social exchange, competition, and aggression by means of their characterization as strategic, theatrical representation.

Gracián's hero and picaresque antiheroes are, thus, textual spaces to exemplify a worldview in which essence and representation are not clearly differentiated:

> Las más de las cosas no son las que se leen.... Donde pensaréis que hay sustancia, todo es circunstancia.... De modo que es menester ser uno muy buen lector para no leerlo todo al revés. (*Criticón* 3:98)
>
> [Most of the things are not the way they read.... Where you would think that there is an essence, it is rather a circumstance.... Thus, one must be a very good reader if one does not want to read everything backwards.]

This conflation of spheres might be said to belong to a postmodern stage in which the aesthetic-representational realm "invades" all other supposedly autonomous areas of knowledge and action.[9] Within this configuration one might recognize the importance of the following paradox suggested by Gracián:

> Las contingencias son la ordinaria materia de los misterios, porque como pudieron variarse, el consumir éstas más que otras, ocasiona luego el reparo. (*Agudeza* 1:92)
>
> [Contingencies are the usual stuff of mysteries. For as they are subject to change, their use rather than others later obliges us to rectify.]

Language plays and deceives; it creates reality by means of the imagery that it sets in motion and by the translation of circumstantial relations to purposive ideas. The discovery and interpretation of those ideas, or *misterios,* is the product of an intellectual relation that is also at work in the social strategy of courtly games.

This strategic conception of the subject in language and in performance was seen by eighteenth-century writers as the function of a "taste of social life."[10] Later, Croce, working on a history of a "modern" concept of aesthetic taste, even said: "The word 'taste,' in the sense of a special faculty or attitude of mind, appears to have been used for the first time in Spain in the middle of the seventeenth century by Gracián" (Croce 191). We may also give credit to Croce and his eighteenth-century predecessors if we are willing to see in social taste—or tact—an institutional dimension of answerability. Taking the notion of "public" in Habermas's sense,[11] this social strategy or social tact would be the public function of courtly society at the level of symbolic exchange. The identification between mask and essence, between reality and representation, coupled with the programmatic sense of performance—that is, a logic of appearances[12]—allows one to see this public space of the court as a theatrical space.

A theatrical subject is one who emerges in play, struggle, and the enactment of strategies. The nondifferentiation between strategy and representation makes courtly society appear as a staging site in which spectators and actors exchange their respective roles. This spectacle, however, must be deciphered carefully because it hides deception itself; that is, it hides the other's self-interest, the other's intention to reduce the subject's wealth (*caudal*). The subject must carefully translate to conceptual terms the images that the stage produces.

This theatricality is mediated therefore by an imagery, by the visualization of performance. Theatricality implies a dialogue within the text—a dialogue built upon the plastic, spatial, and conceptual dimensions of poetic creativity.[13] From the privileged position that books occupy in courtly society, Gracián's writing proposes right performance by the deciphering of the right vision. It is from the consideration of books as things and monuments, from the idea of an architecture of the letter,[14] that both symbolic exchange and the movement of *caudal* become a sociopoetic image. In other words, symbolic production and the transfer of wealth become, in the process of writing, an image that builds up the idea of a public regulation of self-interests.

The radical conception of *social* reality as an essentially linguistic reality suggests, of course, that the world itself is a text. There are implicit connections between images and letters. Those connections are the result of the major role of writing (and of books) in the production and transmission of ideas and knowledge. Then the writing in the book may be conceived as an intellectual instrument to materialize images in the form of letters; in other words, writing is an intellectual instrument to transform the image into a graph. This is the process that the aesthetic of the *concepto*—or linguistic "conceit"—reveals.

Gracián defines the *concepto* as "un acto del entendimiento que exprime la correspondencia que se halla entre los objetos" (an act of understanding that expresses the correspondences among objects) (*Agudeza* 1:55). The *concepto* is, above all, activity, production;[15] this is an activity that results in a deepening of correspondences, of relations; the *concepto* opens the very possibility of signification by a permanent differentiation of qualities and attributes; the *concepto* is bifurcation, diversification; in other words, the *concepto* is a production of new structures for the practical and for the symbolic spheres of the subject's strategy.

The sociopoetical function of *concepto* confirms, in my view, that Gracián's writing is at the same time both a literary and a cultural journey. It is a literature that talks about its own participation in a social knowledge; it is a description of society and individual competition achieved by a textualization of social performance.[16]

Croce observed the influence of seventeenth-century writing in the work of Giambattista Vico.[17] This influence might also be sustained by the sociopoetic trend that particularly Gracián has to offer. Moreover, the sociocultural imprint that Raymond Williams has also detected in Vico might relate to the acknowledgment in that writing of a public dimension of literary creativity.[18] This is especially clear in Gracián's synthesis between *prudencia* and *agudeza*.

Furthermore, Vico's work is an attempt to apprehend social evolution by means of a history of the formations of institutions. He wrote this history by means of an explanation of the symbols created through poetic images. Within this system of thought, images and institutions are ultimately language: "There must in the nature of human institutions be a mental language common to all nations, which uniformly grasps the substance of things feasible in human social life and expresses it with as many diverse modifications as these same things have diverse aspects." (Vico 67).

The *New Science* is a large *concepto*—"linguistic conceit." It is the *writing* of "correspondences" that are implicit in an emblematic figure of social evolution; these correspondences are, broadly speaking, the social function of poetry and, at the same time, the symbolic function of institutions.

In seventeenth-century Europe, emblematic literature, icons, theater, and spectacles had an important role for the transmission of ideas and messages. Relations between them have long been studied as a particular area of the relationship between literature and the visual arts.[19] In this context, we may talk of an intertextuality between narration and vision that informs the way people thought and understood many different issues of a political relevancy.

Diego de Saavedra Fajardo, a high-ranking diplomat involved in the European conflicts of the Thirty Years' War and a member of the Consejo de Indias, shows in one of his *empresas* (emblems with a political message) a pen and a ruler coming from the mouth of a cannon; he then comments:

> Para mandar es menester sciencia, para obedecer basta una discreción natural, y a veces la ignorancia sola. En la planta de un edificio trabaja el ingenio, en la fábrica la mano. (Saavedra Fajardo 1:105–106)
>
> [Science is needed to rule others, while, to obey, a natural discretion and at times ignorance alone is enough. The mind works in the planning of a building, while the hand works in the making of it.]

Physical reality is mysteriously embodied in emblematic reality. It would seem that the image establishes a meaning that functions as the "graph" of the idea developed in writing. Writing is related to the image by means of the pen, which, in turn, connects the graphic idea with a technological medium. The pen, this medium, is visualized as one of the elements of power (the cannon). The important thing is that the story portrayed in the emblem is a "conceptualization" of an imagery. The idea is here the product of a textualization of reality by means of the connections between seeing and reading.

The notion that ideas have a graphic base is also related to the central position that writing has in the construction of a differentiated political praxis.[20] In this sense, the *concepto* is an intellectual device to express the feeling that a symbolic (literary) field is always present in social exchange. Symbol, graphic design, idea, image, and thing are not, in this period, completely understood as separated entities;[21] a good deal of Baroque literature states one way or another that dream, illusion, and reality are sides of the same coin; the consciousness of the major role that writing and books play in courtly society is a symptom of an increasing identification between social order and the practical means in the formation of meanings. The symbolic field that the *concepto* pervades is the image of a theatrical conception of society.

Gracián mentions *emblemas* many times in his description of *agudeza*. It has been argued that the interplay between doctrine and exemplum in *El criticón* is reminiscent of emblematic literature.[22] I would even say that the aphoristic style of *Oráculo manual* and of *El político* participate in the intertextuality created by the relations between imagery and reading, sight and thinking. This intertextuality was, in turn, further developed by the emergence of printed books during the Renaissance;[23] by the seventeenth century it has become an inquiry into the status of vision in the acquisition of knowledge.[24]

To this extent, Saavedra Fajardo's work on the *idea* of the perfect prince also figuratively portrays the idea of this thinking:

> A nadie podrá parecer poco grave el asunto de las empresas, pues fue Dios el autor dellas. La sierpe de metal, la zarza encendida, el vellocino de Gedeón, el león de Sansón, las vestiduras del sacerdote, los requiebros del Esposo, ¿qué son sino empresas? (Saavedra Fajardo 1: 66–67)
>
> [Nobody should think that emblems are not a serious issue, because God was the author of them. The metal snake, the burning bush, the Golden Fleece, Sampson's lion, the priest's clothes, the flattering of the Husband, are they not emblems?]

The image is the literal, graphic support of a conceptual value. Gracián's definition clarifies that the *concepto* refers more to "correspondences" about objects than to objects themselves.[25] This is something that allows him to speak of intellectual relations of reality. His *prudencia* and *agudeza* are "conceptual" in the sense that they establish relations between signs; these correspondences configure a symbolic field in which social performance occurs.

This is why literature and society are so closely interrelated in Gracián's subject. His writing opens, in Baroque Spain, a literary or aesthetic approach to society that is, paradoxically, part of our present debates on culture.

Notes

I want to acknowledge the time, work, and talent that Jennifer Cooley has devoted to this article throughout the editing process.

1. See Fernández Santamaría for a comparative study of the major political writers of the period.

2. Unless otherwise stated, all translations are mine.

3. The character of this novel is a crude example of an attempt at social mobility, and of the consideration of status and economic wealth as indivisible phenomena.

4. Castillo Solórzano's *Las harpías en Madrid o coche de las estafas* deals with the investment of deceit and representation in the acquisition of money and well being, something that he repeats in his major picaresque stories, for example *La garduña de Sevilla*. Estebanillo's *caudal* gives an unambiguous conception of wealth; see *Vida y hechos de Estebanillo González* 1:151, 247, and 2:323, 437, 441, 456, 483, 502. Although without mentioning the notion of *caudal*, Tierno Galván wrote that "en ningún país europeo ha habido tan clara conciencia del proceso capitalista, sus elementos y sus consecuencias" (*Sobre la novela picaresca y otros ensayos* 88).

5. I give in parentheses the titles of Gracián's works.

6. See Bourdieu, *The Logic of Practice* (112–120) for a description of symbolic capital in the organization of values and ideas. For the relations between linguistic and cultural capital, see also "The Production and Reproduction of Legitimate Language."

7. Writing about *El criticón*, Maravall suggests that the work is configured toward a "you": "Con el fin de intensificar la repercusión de su obra, esto es, con objeto de seguir la pretensión barroca de involucrar al lector en el drama humano que la obra entraña, Gracián presentará su historia de Andrenio y Critilo como historia de la segunda persona. *El criticón* es la patética aventura del tú." ("Antropología y política en el pensamiento de Gracián" 351). Later, Maravall says that Gracián's intention is "organizar el comportamiento recíproco de los individuos, incomunicables como mónadas" (367).

8. Gómez-Moriana considers this answer to be the outcome of a rhetorical device by which "the speaking subject is here but the vicar of the true subject.... [It] is the voice of the other marked with an 'I' of referential ambiguity" (*Discourse Analysis as Sociocriticism* 56).

9. This is what Lash proposes in order to understand the postmodern process. The "aesthetic turn" would be, thus, a consequence of a dedifferentiation of spheres that is functionally complementary to the exhaustion of a rationalization of social exchanges. See his *Sociology of Postmodernism*.

10. Croce (*Aesthetics* 192, 200) describes the reception of seventeenth-century "conceptual" writers, Gracián among them.

11. See Habermas, *The Structural Transformation of the Public Space*, chapters 1 and 2.

12. See Cascardi, "The Subject of Control" 251.

13. Maravall has acutely analyzed the visual component of art, literature and communication in general as the major feature of Baroque culture. This is something that can be said of many European countries in the seventeenth century. See the last chapter of *The Culture of the Baroque*.

14. Compare the following: "De la arquitextura a la arquitectura final de la agudeza, el jesuita aragonés levanta un templo grandioso a su más profunda religión: el Libro" (From the architexture to the final architecture of the *agudeza*, the Aragonese Jesuit constructs a grandiose temple to his most profound religion: the Book) (Pelegrín, "Arquitextura y arquitectura del *Criticón*: Estética y ética de la escritura graciana" 66). The relation of Gracián's writing to architecture had already been seen by Correa Calderón, *Baltasar Gracián: Su vida y su obra* 155.

15. There are, *grosso modo*, two approaches to the study of *concepto*. On the one hand, a literary approach would consider it to be an expression of either satire or the Baroque's conception of difficulty. In that line, May already saw the *concepto* as a result of the interpenetrating game of "disorder" into "order" and of a cynic mentality; see "An Interpretation of Gracián's *Agudeza y arte de ingenio*." It could also be seen as the aesthetic product of normative constraints imposed upon writing; see Pozuelo Yvancos, "Sobre la unión de teoría y praxis literaria en el conceptismo." On the other hand, from a linguistic approach Hernández understands the *concepto* as the work of rhetorical "disposition" and the result of a "consciencia didáctica," which is engaged in "la búsqueda ingeniosa de correspondencias intelectuales en la realidad"; see her "La teoría literaria del conceptismo en Baltasar Gracián" (19, 42). Hilary Smith has even analyzed the *concepto* as a condensed *sermón* and as the consequence of Gracián's concern for "the analytical and organizing capacity of the mind," in "Baltasar Gracián's Preachers: Sermon-Sources in the *Agudeza*" (336). For a comparative study on the notion, as a rhetorical device that tends to be different from metaphor, see Woods, "Conceit versus Metaphor in Tesauro and Gracián."

16. Beverley considers that "the study of literary conceits (*conceptos*) could be seen as a prerequisite for the formation of the Baroque man of affairs, the *político*" ("On the Concept of the Spanish Literary Baroque" 220).

17. "It may well be granted that Vico was more in sympathy with the seventeenth-century rhetoricians, in whom we have detected a premonition of aesthetic science"; this is so, because for Vico and for them, "wit" was "the father of all invention" (Croce 230). Croce meant by rhetoricians the writers of conceits.

18. In *The Sociology of Culture*, Williams affirms that Vico's work may be considered the "first theory of culture" (Williams 15).

19. For the iconological meanings of imagery, see Panofsky, *Studies in Iconology*. Argan has analyzed these iconological structures of artistic meaning as being relevant to a study of ideologies; see his "Ideology and Iconology." For an analysis of the topic of "ut pictura poesis," see Praz, *Mnemosyne: The Parallel between Literature and the Visual Arts* 3–27. For the conceptual relations between "conceit" and *emblema*, see Praz's *Studies in Seventeenth Century Iconography* and, from a social approach, Maravall's "La literatura de emblemas como técnica de acción sociocultural en el Barroco." A semiotic description of poetic and imagery meaning can be found in García-Berrio and Hernández, "The Semiotics of Discourse and of the Plastic Text: On the Textual Scheme and Imagery Constitution." González-Echevarría, studying Calderón's *La vida es sueño*, develops an iconographic interpretation of Baroque metaphors; see *Calderón: Códigos, Monstruos, Icones* 27–58.

20. Goody has analyzed the anthropological value of writing in the division of labor and the consequences for a hierarchy of both knowledge and society; see Goody, *The Logic of Writing and the Organization of Society*.

21. See Fernando R. de la Flor, *Atenas castellana* 59–66. Bouzy, in "El *Tesoro de la lengua castellana o española*: Sebastián de Covarrubias en el laberinto emblemático de la definición," discusses the ambiguities in the attempts to differentiate notions such as *emblema* and *símbolo.*

22. See Darst, "Gracián's Structural Method of Philosophy and Experience" 53–55. Selig, years ago, saw the relationship between Gracián's writing and the literature of emblems ("Gracián and Alciati's *Emblemata*"). Sánchez Pérez has a survey of this kind of literature in Spain (*La literatura emblemática española*). It is worthwhile to navigate through Henkel and Schöne's *Emblemata* to see that the relations between image and writing covered many different topics and narrations.

23. See Ong, *Orality and Literacy,* for a discussion on the role of printing in the formation of a new mentality.

24. Jay develops a critical inquiry on the place of vision in modernity; see his *Force Fields,* especially "The Rise of Hermeneutics and the Crisis of Ocularcentrism" and "Scopic Regimes of Modernity."

25. Parker wisely saw that with "objects," Gracián means qualities and attributes as well as physical "things"; see *Polyphemus and Galatea: A Study in the Interpretation of a Baroque Poem* 21.

Works Cited

Alemán, Mateo. *Guzmán de Alfarache.* Ed. F. Rico. Barcelona: Planeta, 1983.

Argan, Gulio Carlo. "Ideology and Iconology." *The Language of Images.* Ed. W. J. T. Mitchell. Chicago: University of Chicago Press, 1980. 15–23.

Bakhtin, Mikhail. *Art and Answerability.* Ed. Michael Holquist and Vadim Liapunov. Austin: University of Texas Press, 1990.

Beverley, John R. "On the Concept of the Spanish Literary Baroque." *Culture and Control in Counter-Reformation Spain.* Ed. Anne J. Cruz and Mary Elizabeth Perry. Hispanic Issues 7. Minneapolis: University of Minnesota Press, 1992. 216–230.

Bourdieu, Pierre. *The Logic of Practice.* Stanford: Stanford University Press, 1990.

———. "The Production and Reproduction of Legitimate Language." *Language and Symbolic Power.* Cambridge: Harvard University Press, 1991.

Bouzy, Christian. "El *Tesoro de la lengua castellana o española*: Sebastían de Covarrubias en el laberinto emblemático de la definición." *Criticón* 54 (1992): 127–144.

Cascardi, Anthony. "The Subject of Control." *Culture and Control in Counter-Reformation Spain.* Ed. Anne J. Cruz and Mary Elizabeth Perry. Hispanic Issues 7. Minneapolis: University of Minnesota Press, 1992. 231–254.

———. *The Subject of Modernity.* Cambridge: Cambridge University Press, 1992.

Castillo Solórzano, Alonso de. *La garduña de Sevilla.* Madrid: Ediciones La lectura, 1922.

———. *Las harpías en Madrid o coche de las estafas.* Ed. P. Jauralde. Madrid: Castalia, 1985.

Correa Calderón, Evaristo. *Baltasar Gracián: Su vida y su obra.* Madrid: Gredos, 1970.

Croce, Benedetto. *Aesthetics as Science of Expression and General Linguistic.* New York: Noonday Press, 1953.

Darst, David H. "Gracián's Structural Method of Philosophy and Experience." *Studies in Honor of Gerald E. Wade.* Ed. Sylvia Bowman et al. Madrid: José Porrúa Turanzas, 1979. 49–56.

Fernández Santamaría, J. A. *Reason of State and Statecraft in Spanish Political Thought, 1595–1640*. Lanham: University Press of America, 1983.

Flor, Fernando R. de la. *Atenas castellana: Ensayos sobre cultura simbólica y fiestas en la Salamanca del Antiguo Régimen*. Salamanca: Junta de Castilla y León, 1989.

Foucault, Michel. *The Archaeology of Knowledge*. Translated by A. M. Sheridan Smith. New York: Pantheon Books, 1972.

García-Berrio, Antonio, and Hernández, M. Teresa. "The Semiotics of Discourse and of the Plastic Text: On the Textual Scheme and Imagery Constitution." *Dispositio* 10.27 (1985): 127–160.

Gómez-Moriana, A. *Discourse Analysis as Sociocriticism: The Spanish Golden Age*. Minneapolis: University of Minnesota Press, 1993.

González-Echevarría, Roberto. "El monstruo de una especie y otra: *La vida es sueño* III, 2, 725." *Calderón: Códigos, Monstruos, Icones*. Montpelier: C.E.R.S., 1982. 27–58.

Goody, Jack. *The Logic of Writing and the Organization of Society*. Cambridge: Cambridge University Press, 1986.

Gracián, Baltasar. *Agudeza y arte de ingenio*. Ed. E. Correa Calderón. 2 vols. Madrid: Castalia, 1969.

———. *The Art of Worldly Wisdom*. Trans. Christopher Maurer. New York: Doubleday Currency, 1992.

———. *El criticón*. Ed. E. Correa Calderón. 3 vols. Madrid: Espasa-Calpe, 1971.

———. *El héroe. El discreto. Oráculo manual y arte de prudencia*. Ed. Luys Santa Marina. Barcelona: Planeta, 1990.

Habermas, Jürgen. *The Structural Transformation of the Public Space: An Inquiry into a Category of Bourgeois Society*. Cambridge: MIT Press, 1993.

Henkel, Arthur, and Albrecht Schöne. *Emblemata: Handbuch zur Sinnbildkunst des XVI. und XVII Jahrhunderts*. Stuttgart: Metzler, 1967.

Hernández, M. Teresa. "La teoría literaria del conceptismo en Baltasar Gracián." *Estudios de Lingüística de la Universidad de Alicante* 3 (1985–1986): 7–46.

Jay, Martin. *Force Fields: Between Intellectual History and Cultural Critique*. New York: Routledge, 1993.

Lash, Scott. *Sociology of Postmodernism*. New York: Routledge, 1990.

López de Ubeda, Francisco. *La pícara Justina*. Ed. A. Rey Hazas. Madrid: Editora Nacional, 1977.

Maravall, J. A. "Antropología y política en el pensamiento de Gracián." *Estudios de historia del pensamiento español*. El siglo del Barroco. Madrid: Cultura Hispánica, 1984. 333–373.

———. "La literatura de emblemas como técnica de acción socio-política en el Barroco." *Estudios de historia del pensamiento español*. El siglo del Barroco. Madrid: Cultura Hispánica, 1984. 197–222.

———. *The Culture of the Baroque*. Translated by Terry Cochran. Minneapolis: University of Minnesota Press, 1986.

May, T. E. "An Interpretation of Gracián's *Agudeza y arte de ingenio*." *Hispanic Review* 16.4 (1948): 275–300.

Ong, W. *Orality and Literacy: The Technologizing of the Word*. New York: Routledge, 1982.

Panofsky, Erwin. *Studies in Iconology*. New York: Harper and Row, 1967; Icon Editions, 1972.

Parker, Alexander A. *Polyphemus and Galatea: A Study in the Interpretation of a Baroque Poem.* Austin: University of Texas Press, 1977.

Pelegrín, Benito. "Arquitextura y arquitectura del *Criticón*: Estética y ética de la escritura graciana." *El mundo de Gracián.* Ed. S. Neumeister and D. Briesemeister. Berlin: Colloquium Verlar, 1991. 51–66.

Pozuelo Yvancos, J. M. "Sobre la unión de teoría y praxis literaria en el conceptismo: Un tópico de Quevedo a la luz de la teoría literaria de Gracián." *Cuadernos Hispanoamericanos* 361–362 (1980): 40–54.

Praz, Mario. *Studies in Seventeenth Century Iconography.* Rome: Edizioni di Storia e Letteratura, 1964.

———. *Mnemosyne: The Parallel between Literature and the Visual Arts.* Princeton: Princeton University Press, 1967.

Saavedra Fajardo, Diego de. *Idea de un príncipe político cristiano representada en cien empresas.* Ed. V. García de Diego. 3 vols. Madrid: Espasa Calpe, 1927.

Salas Barbadillo, Jerónimo de. *El caballero puntual.* Madrid: Tipografía de la Revista de Archivos, 1909.

———. *La hija de Celestina y la Ingeniosa Elena.* Ed. J. Fradejas. Madrid: Instituto de Estudios Madrileños, 1983.

Sánchez Pérez, Agustín. *La literatura emblemática española (siglos XVI–XVII).* Madrid: SGEL, 1977.

Selig, Karl-Ludwig. "Gracián and Alciati's *Emblemata.*" *Comparative Literature* 8 (1956): 1–11.

Smith, Hilary D. "Baltasar Gracián's Preachers: Sermon-Sources in the *Agudeza.*" *Bulletin of Hispanic Studies* 63.4 (1986): 327–338.

Tierno Galván, Enrique. *Sobre la novela picaresca y otros ensayos.* Madrid: Tecnos, 1973.

Vico, Giambattista. *The New Science.* Trans. T. Goddard Bergin and Max Harold Fish. New York: Cornell University Press, 1984.

Vida y hechos de Estebanillo González. Ed. N. Spadaccini and A. Zahareas. 2 vols. Madrid: Castalia, 1978.

Williams, Raymond. *The Sociology of Culture.* New York: Schocken Books, 1982.

Woods, M. J. "Conceit versus Metaphor in Tesauro and Gracián." *Hispano-Italian Studies* 2 (1979): 1–19.

Zayas, María de. *Tres novelas amorosas y tres desengaños amorosos.* Ed. A. Redondo. Madrid: Castalia, 1989.

Chapter 9

Gracián and the Scopic Regimes of Modernity

Oscar Pereira

(*translated by Evelyn R. Phillips*)

It seems that in academic circles, iconoclastic attitudes are on the rise. In a recently published article, D. M. Levin goes so far as to state that a change has taken place in our cultural paradigm, "from (the normativity of) seeing to (the normativity of) listening" (3). Some years earlier, Martin Jay already had noted that the iconoclastic tendencies present in Wagner, Nietzsche, and Heidegger are renewed and strengthened in the work of Richard Rorty, as well as by the acceptance of hermeneutics favored in Hans-Georg Gadamer's work (Jay, "Hermeneutics" 309). In his latest book, *Downcast Eyes,* Jay has noted that a discourse hostile to sight penetrates French thought, from Henri Bergson to Jean-François Lyotard. At the present time, then, we would be witnessing the appearance of a discourse that throughout the twentieth century has been substituting the preeminence of the eye for that of the ear, observation for interpretation.

Furthermore, given the centrality of sight in the project of modernity—"Ilustración" (Enlightenment) means "iluminación" (illumination), hence its main objective: to clear away the shadows of tradition with the light of reason—it is evident that the emergence of postmodern attitudes has accentuated preexisting antiocular currents. While postmodern thought cannot be totally identified with the denigration of vision, it is clearly marked by a rejection of what Jay calls "ocularcentrism." This convergence between postmodernity and antivisual discourse opens up the possibility of an analysis that simultaneously attempts to clarify the role that the eye and ear play in the constitution of a cultural product, and sheds light on the debate regarding modernity and postmodernity.

The Baroque perhaps is one of the phases of modernity most suited to this type of analysis, if only for the apparently contradictory tendencies that run through it. On the one hand, during this period there appears a modern science governed by a zeal to think clearly.[1] On the other hand, as an artistic style as described by Heinrich Wölfflin, the Baroque denotes not only the abandonment of line, symmetry, clear backgrounds, the roundness of objects, and Renaissance characteristics, but also the replacement of these features by chiaroscuro, movement, concealment, and displacement. The Baroque, according to Wölfflin, thereby gives rise to "the radical antithesis of the plastic sensibility" (Wölfflin 34).[2]

The extent to which this double tendency of the Baroque coincides, respectively, with a defense or a rejection of sight and the relevance of the opposition between light and darkness to a description of Baroque culture are subjects that must be analyzed. In this vein, the objectives of this essay are (1) to explain the function of sight in Gracián's thinking; (2) to establish the relationship of sight to hearing and writing; and (3) to indicate the relevance of previous research to the modernity-postmodernity debate.

If the subject of sight in Gracián were reduced simply to a matter of establishing its status relative to the other senses, there would be little to investigate, for the author takes it upon himself to point out the primacy of the eye. Thus, in *El criticón,* Gracián notes through Critilo that sight is the "noblest" of senses (1.3, p. 87). Later, the same character states that the eyes are divine members that "act with a certain universality that seems like omnipotence" ("obran con una cierta universalidad que parece omnipotencia" [1.9, p. 191]), while another character, Artemia, adds soon afterward that the eyes "make up for all the other senses, for all of them together do not suffice to make up for their absence" ("suplen todos los demás sentidos y todos juntos no bastan a suplir su falta" [1.9, p. 193]). Previously, in *Oráculo*, Gracián already had written that the ear is the "second door to the truth" ("la puerta segunda de la verdad") meaning that the eye is the first, because the "truth is seen in an extraordinary way, and is infrequently heard" ("la verdad extraordinariamente se ve, extravagantemente se oye" [80, p. 168]).

Nevertheless, the matter is more complex, as can be seen from the opinions of a number of experts on Gracián's work. Jorge Checa, for example, pointed out that the "*reading* of reality"[3] is a topic having utmost priority for Gracián (*Gracián* 121).[4] Benito Pelegrín, for his part, contravening the statement "seeing as living" ("ver como vivir"), which Gracián insistently propounds, writes that "reading equals living" ("Arquitextura" 62). Finally, in his analysis of *El criticón*, Aurora Egido concludes that hearing is "the noblest and worthiest of the senses," whereas "sight and the rest of the senses are relegated to lesser planes" (58–59). A more detailed analysis of sight in Gracián's writings may permit us to judge simultaneously the opinions of the authors mentioned and to understand why Gracián gives preeminence to sight.

The enormous richness of the vocabulary connected with sight in Gracián's work derives from the intertwining of words and expressions related to the eye and to light. My intention is not to inventory the various forms of this lexicon,[5] but rather to emphasize its relation to the theory of knowledge and the structure of subjectivity. That is, the nuclei around which my analysis will turn are the sense of sight, vision as a metaphor for understanding, the observer's point of view or perspective, and the metaphor of light with respect to reason.

The way in which Gracián conceives of knowledge coincides with representational theories of the mind, which originate in Aristotle and are developed by Descartes, Hobbes, Locke, and Hume. On the one hand, the path to knowledge begins in the senses and ends in understanding. Hence, in *El discreto*: "Whatever enters through the doors of the senses . . . will end at the customhouse of understanding; there everything is registered" ("Todo cuanto entra por las puertas de los sentidos . . . va a parar a la aduana del entendimiento; allí se registra todo" [25, p. 135]). In *El criticón*, the eyes produce "in the soul as many things as there are images and species" ("en el alma todas cuantas cosas hay en imágenes y especies" [*Criticón* 1.9, p. 191]).[6] On the other hand, in order for the mental image to represent the actual object in the understanding, the mind must be thought of as a kind of mirror, a camera obscura, a surface on which to draw or print, or the like.[7] Gracián in particular tends to think of the mind as a mirror and in some instances as a register. The use of the term "reflection" ("reflexión") as applied to the activity of the mind implies its mirrorlike quality.[8] Thus, Gracián recommends reflection on oneself (*Discreto* 14, p. 95; *Oráculo* 69, p. 164) or on things through inner "contemplation" ("contemplación") (*Discreto* 25, p. 135); and given that literally there are no mirrors of understanding (*entendimiento*), understanding metaphorically must be a mirror of itself: "Oh, if only there were mirrors of understanding, as there are of countenance! It has to be it [understanding] of itself" ("¡Oh, si hubiera espejos de entendimiento, como los hay de rostro! El lo ha de ser de sí mismo" [*Héroe* 9, p. 22]).[9] For its part, the idea of the mind as a register is implied in the use of the verb *to register* ("registrar"), as in the quote given earlier in this paragraph, or in the following: "to see and to register everything good in the world" ("ver y registrar todo lo bueno del mundo" [*Oráculo* 229, p. 212]). With regard to its being a register, the mind is a surface on which are imprinted the images that enter through the senses, where they remain for their later re-view (*re-visión*).[10]

What has been described up to this point—the moment of the subject's passivity—is only halfway there, however. The mental images of objects capture the "outside" of things, and although "through the outside one reaches knowledge about what is inside" ("por lo exterior se viene en conocimiento de lo interior" [*Discreto* 22, p. 213]), given that what "is not seen is as if it did not exist" ("no se ve, es como si no fuese" [*Discreto* 13, p. 90]), in the knowledge of things as much "circumstance as substance" ("la circunstancia como la sustancia" [*Discreto* 22, p. 213]) is required. If the external appearance of things were to coincide with its internal truth, it would be unnecessary to labor mentally over the information received through the senses. However, the optimism that Alfonso de Baena would express at the outset of modernity, in asserting that "by sight alone all things are known and better understood" ("por la sola vista se conosçen e se saben mejor e más ayna todas las cosas" [34]), is turned into a warning by

Don Quijote during the Baroque period: "It is necessary to touch appearances with the hand in order to bring about enlightenment" ("es menester tocar las apariencias con la mano para dar lugar al desengaño" [Cervantes 117]).

This distrust of the appearance of things can be found in the origins of modern science, at least in its rationalistic vein. Blumenberg has pointed out that in Descartes, "appearance" means "possible deception," because "the apparently true (or probable) is only something that looks like the true and must therefore be methodologically 'bracketed'" (61 n. 101).[11] The truth must be discovered actively by the mind, penetrating the barrier of appearances that the senses, and above all sight, transmit. Out of this attitude there emerges the questioning of verisimilitude as a standard for gaining access to the truth: "There is no greater enemy of truth than verisimilitude" ("no hay mayor enemigo de la verdad que la verisimilitud" [*Criticón* 3.4, p. 615]).[12]

This aspect of Gracián's thought has been noted by several authors. Miguel Batllori, for example, has stated that with Gracián the path is cleared from a rhetoric based on the "classical principles of 'mimesis'" to another one based on the "exaltation of wittiness" (110–113). Nevertheless, it would be erroneous to conclude that Gracián no longer considers sight as the privileged instrument for access to reality. Yet the eye must not be equated ingenuously with a photographic camera.[13] I do not think it necessary to go as far as Umberto Eco in asserting that "the iconic sign . . . is completely arbitrary, conventional and unmotivated" (32). What is clear, as Baroque painting demonstrates, is that the level of sophistication reached during the sixteenth and seventeenth centuries in the analysis of sight leads to the abandonment of the idea that the eye is limited to the passive copying of reality.

Thus, according to Maravall, in Velázquez's paintings, one never finds a "determined objective reality faithfully copied" ("Velázquez" 483). For that reason, Maravall contrasts the ideal of the "classicistic" painter—who would not want us, upon approaching the painting, to see the canvas or brush strokes, but rather a piece of leather, ceramics, or wood—to that of the Baroque painter, who concerns himself with the visibility of things as painted, that is, with their conditions of perception: "For the classical painter, things must be well done and completed, so that they may appear as such from afar and up close, because their presence could not depend on the conditions under which their contemplation will be undertaken" ("Velázquez" 482).[14]

If the "smudges" and "thick brush strokes" that Velázquez put on his canvas are perceived as objects, such can be due only to the "active function of the eye in vision" (ibid.), to a reconstruction in the beholder's mind of what is perceived. Paradoxically, though, the strides made in the knowledge of the actual functioning of sight further empower the painter to produce illusionistic effects more efficiently. As a result, what could appear to be a liberation of the eye with respect to appearances could turn out to be its complete opposite, that is, a greater ability to deceive the eye.

Gracián shows keen awareness of this problem and emphasizes the importance of the circumstances affecting both subject and object in visual perception. Thus, concerning the colors of the objects, he will assert that they are the effect of "the different dispositions of the surfaces" ("las diferentes disposiciones de las superficies") and of the "light" that bathes them (*Criticón* 3.4, pp. 651–652). In addition, lighting affects not only the coloring of the object but overall appearance as well: "The same thing has very different appearances if it is looked in different lights" ("Hace muy diferentes visos una misma cosa si se mira a diferentes luces" [*Oráculo* 224, p. 210]). On the other hand, the position and distance of the subject with respect to the object determines what is perceived, a phenomenon that is the basis of the perspectivist construction. Thus, Gracián observes that when someone is in the middle of a staircase, that person perceives those in front as being larger than those behind (*Criticón* 2.6, p. 408). Gracián would even come to agree with Cervantes in pointing out the role of prejudices in the perception of reality. I am referring to *El criticón*'s passage regarding the mirror, which is "a spectacle of marvels" ("expectáculo de maravillas" [3.4, pp. 630–631]) and which has so many parallels with the *El retablo de las maravillas*. If one sought to bring together all of these aspects—which influence as much the observer as the object observed—in a single example, there would be no better example than those paintings "that, if you look at them from one side, appear to you to be an angel, from the other a demon" ("que si las miráis por un lado os parece un ángel y si por el otro un demonio" [*Criticón* 3.11, p. 773]). This is so because in the hands of an experienced artificer, detailed knowledge of the functioning of sight can be turned into an instrument for creating illusions.

In conclusion, the rejection of verisimilitude by Gracián should be understood not as a questioning of sight, but rather as the emergence of a new model of vision that attempts to incorporate the advances in the knowledge of the functioning of sight. To suggest the contrary, namely, that the rejection of verisimilitude necessarily implies the rejection of vision, can only be attributed to an identification between ocular vision and "photographic" vision, and a reduction, therefore, of vision to mere passivity.

That this is not the model that Gracián follows is clear from both his emphasis on an active use of the eye and his use of vision as a metaphor for the workings of the mind. For, once the eye is made to coincide with understanding, sight becomes the privileged instrument for the analysis of the functioning of appearances. Therefore, against appearances such as those created by artificers, which take into account the active character of the eye, Gracián suggests an increase in peoples' ability to distinguish and clarify. Thus there arises the seeing-looking-contemplating (*ver-mirar-contemplar*) gradation and the distinction between the external and the internal eye. In general, in Gracián "to see" refers to the act of the outer eye, whereas "to look" and "to contemplate" are properly activities of the inner eye. The difference between "looking" and "contemplating" depends on the degree of temporal and spatial distance between the subject and the experience that is the object of observation. Amid the bustle of life it is unthinkable to go beyond looking, while "contemplating," as D. G. Cañas has pointed out, "carries a burden of mental and panoramic looking to the past" (58). Nevertheless, that panoramic looking can also consist of a figurative spatial distance, such as when Andrenio states that "there I looked at it [the world] from afar and here up close; there contemplated, here experienced" ("allí lo miraba [al mundo] de lexos y aquí tan cerca; allí contemplado, aquí experimentado" [1.5, p. 126]).

The distinction between internal eyes (of understanding, or of the soul) and external eyes (of the body)[15] allows Gracián to contrast a superficial seeing with a looking within ("mirar por dentro"). The difference lies in the ability of the observer to discover how surfaces and appearances (artificial or natural reality as phenomena) are constructed or produced. Gracián is interested only in social reality, whereas natural reality would become the object of natural sciences. K. A. Blüher argues that in Gracián, "looking within" refers to self-knowledge and the knowledge of others (205), that is, to reflection upon oneself and upon others, and specifically consists of having "eyes within the eyes themselves" ("ojos en los mismos ojos"), of "looking as they [the eyes] look" ("mirar como miran [los ojos]" [*Criticón* 2.1, p. 294]), of "seeing oneself" ("verse" [*Discreto* 21, p. 212]), and of "seeing" that "people look [at you] or that they will look [at you]" ("mirar [que te] miran o que [te] mirarán" [*Oráculo* 297, p. 229]). I have no doubt that because of its reliance on self-reflexivity, "looking within" is at the origin of scientific attitudes and modern conceptions of subjectivity, which in Descartes, for instance, go hand in hand.

If we had to condense the importance that Gracián gives to an active mental looking into a single concept, it would be "perspicacity" ("perspicacia"), a term that the *Diccionario de Autoridades* defines as "sharpness and strength of sight" ("agudeza y fuerza de la vista") and, "metaphorically," as "sharpness and insight of wit or understanding" ("agudeza y penetración del ingenio u entendimiento"). Gracián further specifies its meaning by describing "keenness of perspicacity" ("agudeza de perspicacia") as an attaining of "difficult truths" (*Agudeza* 3, 1:58) through an act of understanding that "squeezes out the correspondence that is found among objects" ("exprime la correspondencia que se halla entre los objetos" [*Agudeza* 2, 1:55]). Whenever Gracián wants to emphasize the mind's ability to discover what is hidden, to establish the relationships between apparently different objects, or to project sight beyond the appearance of things, he reaches for that term. Expressions emerge such as "perspicacity of wit" ("perspicacia del ingenio" [*Agudeza* 8, 1:111]) and "perspicacity of discourse" ("perspicacia de discurso" [*Agudeza* 38, 2:93]). The Gracianesque figure who incarnates by antonomasia this highest quality of understanding is Zahorí (Seer),[16] who in the *El discreto* "looks with a telescope" ("mira con cristales de larga distancia" [19, p. 113]) and who in *El criticón* is the "Seer of all" ("Veedor de todo" [3.5, p. 640]). Zahorí's perspicacity is characterized, à la

Descartes, as a seeing with clarity and distinction.[17] In fact during the pilgrimage of Critilo and Andrenio he is the main guide, for once truly in possession of his ability, it only remains for them to arrive in Rome and contemplate with "divine perspicacity" ("perspicacia divina")—thanks to the "crystals" that the Cortesano lends them for the "eyes of the soul"—the present, the past, and the future (3.10, pp. 744–745).

The journey that brings Critilo and Andrenio to a perspicacious contemplation of the world, *sub specie aeternitatis,* is also the conquest of a point of view that is compared with the divine gaze. This means that the passage from "seeing" to "contemplating" demands an exercise of distancing with respect to the objects upon which the gaze falls. Gracián thus identifies "seeing" with looking up close and "contemplating" with looking from afar (*Criticón* 1.5, p. 126). In other words, "seeing" means submerging oneself in reality, whereas "contemplating" means observing it in a detached manner.[18] Moreover, given the fact that the images that will become the objects of contemplation are taken from experience, the two points of view are required to attain mastery of what Gracián calls "experimental science" ("ciencia experimental"), which consists of an exercise of reflection upon what is seen.[19]

An analysis of perspective in Gracián must distinguish between the gaze of an incarnate eye and that of an eye that we can term disembodied or angelic.[20] The embodied eye is immersed in the earthly world, where "continuous mutability in all things" reigns (*Discreto* 17, 108). The angelic eye, for its part, is the one that speculates, because it is located virtually beyond the moon, in a region without "change" (*Discreto* 6, p. 68).[21] Therefore, the constitution of subjectivity, according to Gracián's writings, consists of a learning to look as well as to distance oneself. Hence, the self is an eye in search of a transcendent perspective, a "center"—which, to the greatest extent possible, should be "fixed"—from which to order the chaos of life (*Discreto* 17, p. 108).[22] A description of Critilo's pilgrimage, and especially Andrenio's, exemplifies this assertion, for Andrenio, beginning his journey amid the shadows of a deep "cavern," will end it by contemplating the "Wheel of Time" ("la Rueda del Tiempo") from one of the hills of Rome.

Critilo and Andrenio's trip can be described as a climb undertaken in order to occupy the best position from which to see, to look, and to contemplate. Thus, Andrenio, abandoning the cave and leaning out from the "balcony of seeing and living" ("el balcón del ver y del vivir"), makes contact with reality. From there he could spread his sight for the first time over "this great theater of earth and sky" ("este gran teatro de tierra y cielo" [*Criticón* 1.2, p. 76]). At first Andrenio thinks that this experience provides an adequate model for facing not only nature but also the world of human beings and social reality. For that reason, he suggests to Critilo that they sit on a "hill" ("alto") in order to be able to see the world "safely and with dominion" ("con seguridad y señorío" [1.6, p. 131]), but Critilo refuses. Previously this same character had described Andrenio's first sight as a "contemplation" of the "works of God" (1.5, p. 114); now he points out that this model is not adequate for contending with a human reality full of appearances. First it is necessary to learn how to look.

That is what Prudente teaches Andrenio to do at Falimundo's court. Deceived by appearances, Andrenio had succumbed to the lies of the court. In order to enlighten him, Prudente takes him to an "eminence" ("eminencia"), for he claims that "lifted up from the earth I know that we will discover much" ("levantados de tierra yo sé que descubriremos mucho"). Next he hands a "mirror" to him to look at the reflected image of the palace. From this passage we can conclude that "to look" ("mirar") means *to reflect* [reflexionar] from a privileged *perspective,* and thus obtain knowledge of the truth (1.8, p. 182).

Further on, in the passage in which Critilo and Andrenio have Argos of the hundred eyes as their guide, they end up at the top of a "mountain pass" ("puerto") from which both characters are allowed to "tower over" ("señorear") human life. Here life is a map, and "Courage," "Knowing," "Virtue," "Honor," and other such qualities are "countries" that are within the scope of their vision. Nevertheless, at this point in their ascent, the perspective they acquire does not permit them to overcome their individual perspectives, because "what appeared white to some, appeared black to others" ("lo que a unos parecía blanco, a otros negro" [2.2, p. 312]).

The arrival of Andrenio and Critilo to the palace of Sofisbella is facilitated by the intervention of the "winged one" ("alado"), who suggests that they climb to the "highest regions" with the "wings" of "wit" (2.4, p. 358). On their way through the palace of Virtelia, a maiden of Fortune advises them to continue in their "ascent" (2.7, p. 419). The climb is completed when Virtelia "transforms them from men into angels" ("los transforma de hombres en ángeles"), rising so high that they "were lost from sight" ("se perdieron de vista" [2.10, p. 484]).

What they saw from there will remain suspended until the end of the third part of *El criticón* when, guided by the Cortesano, they climb into Rome's watchtower (*atalaya*)[23] to "tower over... the world throughout the centuries" ("señorear... todo el mundo con todos los siglos" [3.10, p. 744]). This is the purely angelic perspective, for it is likened to "divine perspicacity" and it surpasses all the individual perspectives. Furthermore, it is the perspective that the narrator uses systematically throughout the text, in such a way that in the end Critilo's and Andrenio's gazes come to be identified with that of the narrator.[24]

Without a doubt, parallels exist between the angelic eye that Gracián proposes in *El criticón* and the transcendental Cartesian self. In both cases an attempt is made to overcome individual perspectives by means of a gaze located in a position that cannot be considered relative. Moreover, the result is similar: an abstract vision. Concerning Descartes, Karsten Harries has pointed out that "the search for a secure foundation leads to an attempt to lift the self out of this world.... But far from leading to reality this ascent to angelic heights leaves only the emptiness of abstraction" (40).[25] Checa has written that *El criticón* makes use of an "allegorical technique based on abstraction and on the use of some protagonists who, like personifications of fixed mental instances, are characterologically static or semistatic" (*Gracián* 100). Checa also establishes a connection between this technique and the use of the "panoramic perspective" that came from the tradition of Lucian (ibid. 76–79). José Montesinos has judged the same phenomenon to be the "denovelization" of the novel through the imposition of a "moral totalism" on human life (146). In this sense, Gracián's model is *Guzmán de Alfarache*, a book to which he repeatedly refers by its subtitle: *Atalaya de la vida humana* (Watchtower of human life).

I will conclude the study of vision in Gracián's work with an analysis of the function of light in his writings. This analysis will provide us with a new perspective from which to consider both his questioning of verisimilitude and the importance he assigns to the active role of the mind. It is worth noting that metaphors of light generally form a system with those of darkness to create a collection of oppositions. The most basic of them arises from the identification of light with truth and of darkness with falseness. Plato's myth of the cave customarily is considered the origin of this tradition. In this myth, the absence of sunlight inside the cave brings about a world of shadows. The departure from the cave, which involves an encounter with the light of the sun, is an allegory for the arrival in the world of ideas, of eternal truths. This model, which can be called the model of *natural light*, is present in Gracián's work according to the inflection that the Middle Ages gave to this classical tradition. Thus, the first thing God created was light (*Discreto* 13, p. 92), while the sun is the creation that best depicts divine power:

> It is called sun because in its presence all other lights retreat: it alone abounds. It is among the celestial orbs as if in the center. . . . It influences and converges with the rest of the causes to give being to all things, even man himself.
>
> Llámase sol porque en su presencia todas las demás lumbreras se retiran: él solo campea. Está en medio de los celestes orbes como en su centro . . . influye y concurre con las demás causas a dar el ser a todas las cosas, hasta el hombre mismo. (*Criticón* 1.2, pp. 78–79)

In the Platonic-Christian view, light comes from outside and "man" is limited to gathering it, for which reason knowledge of truth is reached by means of a change in attitude: either one is or is not ready to receive the truth. Because of this emphasis on the subject's passivity, it is impossible to force parallels between the model of natural light and the treatment of light in Gracián's writings. As Maravall has suggested, upon comparing Plato's cave with that of Gracián, contrary to the ideal world that awaits those who abandon the Platonic cave, the world that Andrenio faces is permeated with deceptive appearances ("Un mito" 378–379).[26] In his treatment of light, Gracián will keep the light-truth and darkness-lie association, while distinguishing between natural and artificial illumination. As a result, what apparently is clear, illuminated by the natural light of the sun, could hide darkness in its bosom. This is the problem of the water coming from the "fountain of illusions" ("fuente de los engaños"), whose clearness hides a lie (*Criticón* 1.7, p. 155). The same thing is affirmed regarding Falimundo's court, for when they arrive at the city, "what seemed clear on the outside was confused within" ("lo que parecía clara por fuera, era confusa dentro" [1.7, p. 160]). For the same reason, Vulgacho's arrival in full daylight reduces the square to "horrible darkness," a darkness that would go back to light only when the square was lit by the "torch" carried by a "Wiseman" ("Sabio") (*Criticón* 2.5, pp. 398–399).

Blumenberg describes this treatment of light as an inversion of medieval metaphors of light and notes that its origin is found in Bacon and Descartes, because for them, "phenomena no longer stand in the light; rather, they are *subjected to the lights of an examination* from a particular perspective" (53).[27] The inversion is complete in the Enlightenment period, a time during which the medieval notion that the truth reveals itself because it is "self-luminous" is totally reversed: "The truth does not reveal itself; it must *be revealed*. 'Natural' luminosity cannot be relied on; on the contrary, truth is of a constitutionally weak nature and man must help it back on its feet by means of light-supplying therapy" (52, Blumenberg's italics).

That extra light that is capable of illuminating the darkness hidden behind apparent light, or of discovering the light hidden behind apparent darkness, comes from inside the individual himself; it is the "light of reason" ("la luz de la razón" [*Oráculo* 91, p. 171]). Once again it is a matter of the active role of the mind, but now expressed, for example, as the "sun of the intelligence" ("sol de la inteligencia" [*Agudeza* 63, 2:257]); the sun of the wit (*Discreto* 1, p. 49); the light of discretion (*Discreto* 19, p. 116); the light that spreads "rationality" (*Oráculo* 298, p. 298); and reason as the "queen of light" (*Criticón* 1.5, p. 119). Gracián incarnates this capacity for illumination in Lucindo, the "man of lights" ("varón de luces"), who is able to emit "light from himself, especially amid the greatest shadows" ("luz de sí . . . especialmente en medio de las mayores tinieblas" [*Criticón* 2.10, p. 470]). Also possessing this quality is Zahorí, who by means of thinking, opened up a crack through which a "ray of light, a glimmer of truth" ("rayo de luz, una vislumbre de verdad") entered to light up the palace of Caco (*Criticón* 3.6, p. 655).

In conclusion, the questioning of verisimilitude in Gracián's writings, far from suggesting a weakening of vision, becomes a reinforcement of its role, but this time in terms of a metaphor for mental activity. Thus, seeing clearly and distinctly is the result of a perspicacious looking or contemplating realized from a privileged perspective from which the light of reason is projected.

On the level of explicit statements, Gracián subordinates the ear to the eye. Furthermore, we will not find the development of the metaphorical system of the ear with a complexity and richness comparable to that of the eye; for example, there are no *ears* of the soul. With the term "ear" Gracián refers to the receiving of the spoken or written word, the first being in the heart of a real conversation, the second as a metaphorical conversation with those who are not present: "The first day of beautiful living is spent in talking with the dead . . . , and books faithfully make us into persons" ("Gástase la primera estancia del bello vivir en hablar con los muertos . . . , y los libros con fidelidad nos hacen personas" [*Oráculo* 230, p. 212]). In Gracián's educational ideal, conversation with wise men and the dead occupies an important role, since it constitutes the first step toward wisdom. This step, however, must be complemented by life experience—"seeing" and "inspecting" ("registrar")—and by philosophizing—"contemplating" (ibid.).

The emphasis on personal experience derives from the inadequacy of a knowing based on authority and tradition: "One lives mainly from information [what is received through the ear], but less from what we see: we live by other people's faith" ("Vívese lo más de información [lo recibido a través del oído], es lo menos lo que vemos: vivimos de fe ajena" [*Oráculo* 80, p. 168]).[28] The eye-experience and ear-tradition associations arise from the active character of the eye and the passivity of the ear, since the eyes "search for things how and when they want" ("buscan las cosas cómo y cuándo quieren"), whereas the ear "is sought for by them [e.g., things]" ("[al oído] ellas le buscan" [*Criticón* 1.9, p. 195]); hence the need for having "eyes in the ears" ("ojos en las orejas" [*Criticón* 2.1, p. 294]). What never will be found in Gracián, therefore, is a metaphor of the ear that expresses the active nature of the mind, a necessary activity in a world of deceiving appearances and the problematic of verisimilitude.

On the other hand, in a mind conceived of on the basis of visual metaphors, the image is primordial with respect to the word. That is, words, in the simplest case, refer to images and images to reality, or they refer to relationships between images when dealing with concepts. This explains why Gracián shows us Andrenio acquiring awareness of himself and of reality before acquiring mastery of language. Self-consciousness, therefore, is a "flash of light" ("golpe de luz") that generates inner "reflection" ("reflexión"), and Andrenio's perception of things precedes Critilo's act of naming them (*Criticón* 1.1). In this way, the questioning of the image as proposed by Gracián—namely, that it represents reality in a verisimilar manner—is strengthened when the problem of representation is observed from the level of words. For these have their own life and establish relationships among themselves, not necessarily between images and, therefore, between objects.

That words have their own life is attributed by Gracián to their rhetorical dimension, which is the product of "verbal wit" ("agudeza verbal" [*Agudeza* 3, 1:58]). When writers emphasize this dimension and neglect the conceptual content, they create an "affected, mongrel, and showy style" ("estilo culto, bastardo y aparente") that lacks the "soul of insight" ("alma de agudeza" [*Agudeza* 62, 2:243]). Verbal wit, therefore, must be accompanied by "insight of concept" ("agudeza de concepto"), that is, by a content that refers to the relationships between objects. Starting from these considerations, Gracián distinguishes between styles that are clear, difficult, and obscure. The first two have a conceptual content, while the last one does not. The criterion that separates both groups is the ability, or lack of same, to generate a "mental concept" ("concepto mental") in the readers or listeners (*Oráculo* 216, p. 208). Gracián equates this ability with the translatability of the style (*Agudeza* 3, 1:58). Clear style is described as "the most suitable one for the purpose of speech, which is to make us understand" ("el más apto para el fin del habla, que es darnos a entender"), and difficult style as the most pleasant one, "because it joins what is sweet with what is useful" ("porque junta lo dulce con lo útil" [*Agudeza* 62, 2:243]). This distinction seems to indicate that for Gracián, the same concept can be expressed in a clear style as well as in a difficult one. For this reason the latter would consist of an artificial obscuring of a mental concept through the manipulation of words. Thus, Gracián's classification of styles would differ from the most systematic classification proposed by the painter and poet Juan de Jáuregui, for whom the difficulty must derive only from the concept and not from the words (136). In some places, however, Gracián seems to move toward Jáuregui's position, as when he asserts that what distinguishes fifteenth-century *cancionero* poems from "modern" poems is that in the former everything "was invested into the concept" ("echaban en concepto"), while in the latter, "everything goes to the words, to the obscurity of the phrase" ("su eminencia ponen en las hojas de las palabras, en la oscuridad de la frase" [*Agudeza* 25, 1:253–254]).[29] Nevertheless, this cannot hide the fact that for Gracián the same "truth can be dressed in many ways" ("la verdad puede vertirse de muchos modos"), and that the "light that rightfully injures tortures the eyes" ("la luz que derechamente hiere atormenta los ojos" [*Agudeza* 55, 2:192]). Finally, the style that is properly obscure is the affected style that relies exclusively on words and hides no concept and is, therefore, only a little bit of air.[30]

Although the distinction between the three styles can be described in terms of a gradual loss of transparency, the relationship of words to things is not mimetic. In other words, the clear style is not more verisimilar than the obscure style, but rather the complete opposite. That is so, because the clear style does not express so much the result of a passive perception as the activity of the mind. That is, words communicate what the mind, in its illuminating ability, previously has clarified; whereas the obscure or affected [culto] style results from a mind lacking that ability.

Under ideal conditions there is no doubt that the clear style is the one most suitable for transmitting the truth, given that this style is characterized repeatedly as transparent and luminous.[31] Nevertheless, in the context of conflictual social relationships, writing, as other public activities, must be subject to the requirements of control of the outward appearance, requirements that constitute the main feature of the ideal of conduct suggested by Gracián. There are, then, two arguments that explain the importance given by Gracián to difficult style. On the one hand, it is pure strategy for social interactions, since it is unacceptable to allow oneself to be understood by all. On the other, it is the style that best reproduces the *process* that leads to knowledge of the truth. The emphasis on understanding connects both arguments. Thus, by means of it truth is reached, and only those who possess it will have access to the circle of people who deserve to enter the Island of Immortality.

Hence, the importance given by Gracián to the difficult style does not imply a favoring of the ear, but rather of understanding. Moreover, given that the mind's functioning is based on visual metaphors, words will be subjected to their system. Writing, like images, must be submitted to mental illumination, since understanding eliminates "all obscurity in the concept" ("toda oscuridad en el concepto" [*Criticón* 1.9, p. 190]), and "perspicacity" is capable of conquering the "labyrinths of discourse" ("laberintos del discurso" [*Agudeza* 45, 2:133]). This conclusion is implied in the use of the terms "clear" and "obscure" to refer to style, since, as Lázaro Carreter has noted, the artificial darkening of writing suggests that the "direct vision [of the object represented in it] has been substituted by a reflected vision" (15).

Nevertheless, when an author such as Aurora Egido points to the importance of the ear, the argument revolves around Gracián's use of the term "to decipher" ("descifrar"). "To read" and "to decipher" are related to each other in the same way as "to see" and "to look." Namely, "to read" is superficial and "to decipher" profound: "Things are not those things which are read" ("las cosas no son las que se leen"); thus reading must be supplemented with the "art of deciphering" (*Criticón* 3.4, p. 614). Without a doubt, this approach creates a metaphorical system different from the strictly visual one: the world is a book; people are (alphabetical) letters or codes (*cifras*) (ibid. 611–619); the soul is decoded or deciphered. What is unclear, however, is whether for this reason Gracián gives the ear preeminence. On the one hand, the art of Descifrador is inferior to the art of Zahorí, which consists of "looking within" (*Criticón* 3.5, p. 639). On the other, Gracián does not subordinate this metaphorical system to the ear, for the ear is a passive organ that never gives rise to metaphors of the mind. Moreover, it must not be forgotten that reading is an activity in which the eyes are involved. Thus, when Gracián emphasizes the element of passivity in reading, books illuminate (*Criticón* 1.1, p. 69), and when the matter pertains to deciphering, wit is the "sun . . . of this world in code" ("sol . . . de este mundo en cifra" [*Héroe* 3, p. 11]).

W. J. T. Mitchell has written that the history of culture is partly the history of a struggle between linguistic and pictorial signs (43). The coordinates of this struggle change over time. Up until G. Ephraim Lessing's *Laocoonte,* the use of expressions such as "blind painting" to refer to poetry, or "mute poetry" to refer to painting, indicated the close connection seen between the two. Beginning with Lessing's book, the debate shifted, since the distinction that he established between arbitrary sign—word—and motivated sign—image—implied the drawing of clear boundaries of separation.[32] Baroque experiments with images—such as emblems or hieroglyphics—based on a more or less arbitrary use of the image to mean something more than what is referred to by resemblance were exposed as an improper use of the expressive capacity of the visual. However, certain developments in the twentieth century, especially the appearance of semiotics and its affirmation of the arbitrariness of all signs, came to question the pertinence of Lessing's distinction. It should not be surprising, then, that there may be a renewed interest in Baroque techniques from a semiotic perspective.[33]

The analysis that I have offered in these pages questions both the radical separation established by Lessing and the linguistic reductionism that supports semiotics. The identification between looking and deciphering that Gracián suggests makes a sign, a code, of the image, but also sets off the inseparability of the concept with respect to the image. Finally, if sight is the main sense for Gracián, that is because it provides the materials for the constitution of the mind and of subjectivity.

Recently, Martin Jay has classified Western modalities of the visual into three "scopic regimes:" "cartesian perspectivalism," "baconian art of describing," and "baroque vision." The first, which Jay considers the hegemonic visual model of the modern era, joins the rationalized and three-dimensional space of perspectivist vision with the Cartesian subject, transcendent and disembodied, to give rise to a static, distant, and ahistorical gaze. The second, exemplified in seventeenth-century Dutch painting, is characterized by its descriptive impulse, the careful inspecting of objects and surfaces. The latter shuns the mathematical ideal and the attempt at abstraction of Cartesian perspectivalism, instead proposing to us the gaze of the incarnate eye. Finally, Baroque vision rejects clarity and transparency. Fascinated by the opaque, the illegible, and the indecipherable, it conceives of space as heterogeneous and calls attention to the conventionality of vision.

If we project onto this background the results of the analysis of Gracián's thought effected in this essay, some interesting conclusions emerge. In the first place, given that Gracián customarily is considered a Baroque writer par excellence, what draws one's attention is the presence in his texts of elements common to the three scopic regimes. As I have mentioned, the so-called Cartesian perspectivalism not only is present in his thought, but furthermore can be considered as the structuring form of *El criticón.* The difference with respect to Descartes is that what in him is a scientific method in Gracián is a projection of an abstract moral plan. On the other hand, Gracián would share the emphasis on the incarnate eye with the Baconian art of description in texts such as the *El discreto* and *Oráculo.* Nevertheless, whereas Dutch painting offers us a world of objects to see and possess in the privacy of a bourgeois home, Gracián sees instead a purely Baroque world: changing, blurry, obscure. Once again there emerges here the moral preoccupation, the theme of *desengaño,* since that world presents itself to us as hostile and, at times, in decadence. The combination of elements indicated explains, finally, his position regarding the Baroque regime. The rejection of verisimilitude and, with it, the questioning of transparency do not presume a rejection of clarity, at least as an ideal of understanding. For that reason, what is obscure generally is connoted negatively in Gracián's work. Furthermore, what is encoded is meant to be decoded, not to remain as it is. All things considered, the aspects that characterize the Baroque regime do not constitute an ideal for Gracián, but rather the other side of utopia represented by the "city of truth" ("la ciudad de la verdad"), that is, a world penetrated by conflicting relationships in which what is at stake is who has the power to dominate.

According to Jay, the Baroque scopic regime, although having its origin in the sixteenth and seventeenth centuries, "has finally come into its own in our time" ("Scopic" 189). This would have been possible through modern criticism's rejection of the enlightened ideal of a transparent model of representation, on the level of both words and images, going on to propose in its place, as Mitchell has pointed out, the idea that words and images are enigmas, prisons of language that keep knowledge of the world away from us (8). From among the modern scopic regimes, postmodern discourse would be favoring the purely Baroque one, the one that Gracián tried to balance with his utopian "city of truth" and that cultural historians such as Maravall have described as suitable for the exercise of power: "When a society... shows itself to us to be more adapted to a Baroque culture, when we consider in it its Baroque content to be so much richer, we will contemplate accurately that the future of that society will be that much more closed" (*Cultura del Barroco* 524).

Notes

1. In Boileau's neoclassical poetics, this eagerness is expressed in the dictum that what is well understood is clearly stated.

2. Translation of secondary sources in Spanish are not followed by the original quotation.

3. Checa's italics.

4. See also by Checa, "*Oráculo manual*: Gracián y el ejercicio de la lectura" 267–269.

5. Cañas, Cacho, and Blüher give abundant information on the vocabulary of the eye.

6. The *Diccionario de Autoridades* defines "especie" as "the image or representation of itself that the object gives" ("la imagen o representación de sí que envía el objeto").

7. Mitchell (115–117) presents in a very clear outline the common elements of representational theories of the mind.

8. The *Diccionario de Autoridades* defines "reflection" as the "inflection of the ray of light or species that is made on the clear surface of an opaque body, turning back" ("la inflexión del rayo de luz o especies que se hace en la superficie tersa de un cuerpo opaco, retrocediendo") and "metaphorically" as "consideration or second look that is made of the matter or subject being treated or thought about" ("consideración o segundo reparo que se hace sobre el assunto o materia que se trata u discurre").

9. A similar idea is found in *Oráculo*: "There are mirrors of the countenance, but there are none of the mind; it must be discreet reflection on itself" ("Hay espejos del rostro, no hay del ánimo: séalo la discreta reflexión sobre sí" [89, p. 171]).

10. The *Diccionario de Autoridades* defines *to register* as "to look at something carefully and diligently" ("mirar con cuidado y diligencia alguna cosa"). The word *inspection* ("revista") also forms part of Gracián's vocabulary.

11. Judovitz also has called attention to this aspect, connecting it with the Baroque obsession for illusions: "From Descartes's earliest writings... to his more elaborate philosophical disquisitions... the same concern continues to be reiterated in different ways: that of the danger of illusion. This invocation of illusion is invariably tied to deception and the problem of the unreliability of the senses" (64–65).

12. As Blumenberg has written, this change in the valuation of verisimilitude is also found in Descartes. Hence, the "original" meaning of "verisimile," "appearances as pale reflection of the *proximity* of truth," is no longer valid with Descartes, given that the apparently true can be false (61 n. 101). This changes the emphasis from a knowledge of essences through the verisimilitude of appearances to a knowledge of how appearances are produced. Maravall has noted this tendency in Gracián on affirming that, in the latter, appearance is the "form of the true being of the world" ("Un mito platónico" 380); hence his description of the world as one of "phenomena," a world in which the "how" of relationships between things is what must be investigated.

13. This is what Pring-Mill does in the following assertion: Gracián "do[es] not observe the rules of... ocular or *photographic* verisimilitude—namely, fidelity to the surface appearance of things as perceived by our physical eyes" (270). Gracián's distrust of appearances does not imply necessarily the identification of ocular looking with photographic looking, if only because most people perceive with two eyes that are normally in constant motion. Gracián, who customarily writes "the eyes" thus, in plural form, considers sight as an active sense.

14. An aspect that Eco recognizes distinguishes the iconic sign from all others: "A closer inspection of the data... leads us at once to a concession: iconic signs reproduce some of the conditions of perception, correlated with normal perceptive codes" (32).

15. For example: "The eyes of the soul perceive inner beauty, just as those of the body perceive outer beauty" ("Llévanse los ojos del alma bellezas interiores, así como los del cuerpo la exterior" [*Discreto* 6, p. 68]).

16. It appears as a common name in *El político* (57) and in *El discreto* (19, p. 113), and as a character in *El criticón* (3.5).

17. "There are Seers as accurate as perspicacious: I am one of them. I see extremely clearly... and with much distinction" ("Zahoríes hay tan ciertos como perspicaces: por señas, que yo soy uno de ellos. Yo veo clarísimamente... con tanta distinción" [*Criticón* 3.5, p. 640]). Later on: "I see and distinguish extremely clearly" ("Veo y distingo clarísimamente" [3.5, p. 642]). The citations recall, obviously, the activity of the mind as guided by Descartes's method: to think clearly and distinctly.

18. "Seeing makes one learned, but contemplating makes wise people. All of those ancient philosophers journeyed, wandering or thinking first with their feet

and sight, in order to do so afterward with their intelligence" ("Hácese noticioso el ver, pero el contemplar hace sabios. Peregrinaron todos aquellos antiguos filósofos, discurriendo primero con los pies y con la vista, para después con la inteligencia" [*Discreto* 25, p. 135]).

19. "That experiential knowledge is acquired . . . when the one who is inspecting is attentive and knows how to think, examining everything with admiration or enlightenment" ("Adquiérese aquella ciencia experimental . . . cuando el que registra atiende y sabe reparar, examinándolo todo o con admiración o con desengaño" [*Discreto* 25, p. 134]).

20. These two perspectives do not agree exactly with the two "fundamental perspectives" of *El criticón* that Baquero Goyanes assigns to the respective gazes of Critilo—"experience"—and Andrenio—"thoughtless impulse" (15). It is in agreement, however, with the distinction between the narrator's perspective and the combined Critilo-Andrenio perspective. For their part, Critilo and Andrenio represent two ways of confronting life experience, for which reason the difference between their gazes has to do, instead, with the distinction between seeing and looking. To the extent that, at the end of *El criticón,* the Critilo-Andrenio perspective coincides with that of the narrator, it can be asserted that the journey of both characters consists of a learning to see (which is properly to look) that ends in contemplating.

21. Both eyes are necessary, since, as is asserted in *El discreto,* it does not "suffice to give the biggest speculation dominion in doing and saying; continuous experience is required, for from the continuity of actions the aristocratic habit is born" (no "basta la mayor especulación para dar este señorío [en el hacer y en el decir]; requiérese el continuado ejercicio en los empleos, que de la continuidad de los actos se engendra el hábito señoril" [*Discreto* 2, p. 54]).

22. See also chapter 1 of *El discreto* (p. 51).

23. Gracián derives the verb "atalayar" (to watch, to observe) from "atalaya" (watchtower, observation tower) (See *Criticón* 3.10, p. 744).

24. Perhaps it can be stated that in *El discreto* and *Oráculo* emphasis is placed on the incarnate eye, whereas in *El criticón* it is subordinated to the requirements of the angelic eye. Hence, we may interpret *El criticón* as an attempt to transcend the experience of that multifaceted reality that we see reflected in *El discreto* and *Oráculo.* That difference in emphasis on one or the other eye derives from a dissimilarity between the objectives of the texts. Whereas *El criticón* allegorizes the process of formation of an individual perspective or subjectivity, *El discreto* and *Oráculo* are more concerned with the clash of individual perspectives. In other words, *El criticón* is more interested in how to come to be the "master of oneself" ("señor de sí"), while the other two texts center on how to come to be the "master of others" ("señor de los demás") (*Discreto* 3, p. 59). It is a matter of a difference in emphasis, since in Gracián's project both aspects are identified.

25. Unamuno had noted it previously in *Del sentimiento trágico de la vida*: "The bad thing about Descartes's discourse is not its methodical doubt . . . it is that he wanted to start doing away with himself, Descartes, the actual man . . . in order to be a mere thinker, that is, an abstraction" (35).

26. Gracián's cave derives from that of Cicero (*De natura Deorum* 2.37.95), since in Cicero, as Blumenberg has pointed out, the cave is "a thought experiment for hypothetically reducing the factor of being accustomed" (37). Compare the fol-

lowing quote: "[Critilo to Andrenio:] the only privilege of the first man, and yours: to come to see with newness and awareness the greatness . . . of this great created machine. . . . Admiration commonly is lacking in us because newness is lacking" ("privilegio único del primer hombre y tuyo: llegar a ver con novedad y con advertencia la grandeza . . . desta gran máquina criada. . . . Fáltanos la admiración comúnmente a nosotros porque falta la novedad" [*Criticón* 1.2, p. 77]).

27. Blumenberg's italics.

28. Ynduráin extends this opinion in an analysis of the subject of "falling in love by hearsay": "The supporters of sight trust in the personal, individual ability to discover the truth. Those supporters of hearing, on the contrary, prefer established doctrine, authority" (598). Blumenberg has noted the same opinion in connection with the emergence of modern science: "Metaphors of 'hearing' are also significant for grasping the phenomenon of *tradition*. 'Seeing' is oriented toward the *repetition* of eyewitness experience. . . . The demand for the *presence* of the object under study is the point of departure for the modern idea of science, and in Bacon and Descartes, this demand is formulated in opposition to the validity of *auctoritas*" (48). The same idea, with further implications, is found in Jay ("Rise of Hermeneutics" 312).

29. The same idea is in *El criticón*: "The words have more or less profundity, depending on the subjects" ("Tienen más o menos fondo las palabras, según las materias" [*Discreto* 8, p. 76]).

30. Thus, as a character says after drinking of the "fountain of illusions," "I am nothing but one of those who, because of speaking affectedly, speaks in the dark" ("No soy sino uno destos que, por hablar culto, hablo a escuras" [*Criticón* 1.6, p. 157]). Also, in *Oráculo* it is stated that "without facts the voice is nothing but a little [bit of] air" ("sin los hechos no es más la voz que un poco de aire" [203, p. 204]).

31. Thus, the "city of truth" is described as open, symmetrical, rectilinear, with crystal houses, a very clear sky and a cloudless horizon (*Criticón* 3.3, p. 607).

32. "If it is true that painting . . . uses means or signs that are completely different from those which poetry uses . . . then juxtaposed signs [painting] cannot express more than juxtaposed objects . . . , whereas successive signs [poetry] cannot express more than successive objects" (Lessing 165). Later on: "These signs which poetry uses are not only successive, they also are arbitrary" (175).

33. For example, Mercedes Blanco notes that a text such as Gracián's *Agudeza* represents "an attempt . . . to reduce the novelty, the beauty, the interest of any discourse to a series of procedures subject to definition and classification." She continues: "Perhaps only modern semiotics has a comparable ambition, given that it considers transversally the most heterogeneous manifestations of culture, from gestural constructs to the sciences, as generators of meaning" (18). This procedure is possible through a reduction of all production of meaning to a code.

Works Cited

Baena, Alfonso de. "Prologus Baenensis." In *Las poéticas castellanas de la Edad Media*. Ed. Francisco López Estrada. Madrid: Taurus, 1984.

Baquero Goyanes, Mariano. "Perspectivismo y satira en *El Criticón*." *Temas, formas y tonos literarios*. Madrid: Prensa Española, 1972. 13–60.

Batllori, Miguel. *Gracián y el Barroco.* Roma: Edizioni di Storia e Letteratura, 1958.

Blanco, Mercedes. "El mecanismo de la ocultación: Análisis de un ejemplo de agudeza." *Criticón* 43 (1988): 13–36.

Blüher, Karl Alfred. "'Mirar por dentro': El análisis introspectivo del hombre en Gracián." In *El mundo de Gracián (Actas del Coloquio Internacional Berlín 1988).* Ed. Sebastian Neumeister and Dietrich Briesemeister. Berlin: Colloquium Verlag, 1991. 203–217.

Blumenberg, Hans. "Light as a Metaphor for Truth: At the Preliminary Stage of Philosophical Concept Formation." In *Modernity and the Hegemony of Vision.* Ed. David Michael Levin. Trans. Joel Anderson. Berkeley: University of California Press, 1993. 30–62.

Cacho, María Teresa. "*Ver como vivir.* El ojo en la obra de Gracián." *Gracián y su época (Actas de la I Reunión de Filólogos aragoneses).* Zaragoza: Institución Fernando el Católico, 1986. 117–135.

Cañas, Dionisio G. "El arte de bien mirar: Gracián." *Cuadernos Hispanoamericanos* 379 (1982): 37–60.

Cervantes, Miguel de. *El ingenioso hidalgo don Quijote de la Mancha.* Vol. 2. Ed. Luis Andrés Murillo. Madrid: Castalia, 1978.

Checa, Jorge. *Gracián y la imaginación arquitectónica: Espacio y alegoría de la Edad Media al Barroco.* Potomac, Md.: Scripta Humanistica, 1986.

———. "*Oráculo manual*: Gracián y el ejercicio de la lectura." *Hispanic Review* 59.3 (1991): 263–280.

Eco, Umberto. "Critique of the Image." *Thinking Photography.* Ed. Victor Burguin. London and Basingstoke: Macmillan, 1982.

Egido, Aurora. "El arte de la memoria y *El Criticón.*" In *Gracián y su época (Actas de la I Reunión de Filólogos aragoneses).* Zaragoza: Institución Fernando el Católico, 1986. 25–66.

Gracián, Baltasar. *Agudeza y arte de ingenio.* 2 vols. Ed. Evaristo Correa Calderón. Madrid: Castalia, 1969.

———. *El criticón.* Ed. Santos Alonso. Madrid: Cátedra, 1984.

———. *El héroe. El discreto. Oráculo manual y arte de prudencia.* Ed. Luys Santa Marina. Introduction and notes by Raquel Asun. Barcelona: Planeta, 1984.

———. *El político don Fernando el Católico. Obras completas.* Ed. Arturo del Hoyo. Madrid: Aguilar, 1967. 35–71.

Harries, Karsten. "Descartes, Perspective, and the Angelic Eye." *Yale French Studies* 49 (1973): 28–42.

Jáuregui, Juan de. "Discurso poético." In *La teoría poética en el Manierismo y Barroco españoles.* Ed. A. Porqueras Mayo. Barcelona: Puvill Libros, 1989. 126–138.

Jay, Martin. "The Rise of Hermeneutics and the Crisis of Ocularcentrism." *Poetics Today* 9.2 (1988): 307–326.

———. "Ideology and Ocularcentrism: Is There Anything behind the Mirror's Tain?" *Intellectuals and Politics: Social Theory in a Changing World.* Ed. Charles C. Lemert. Newbury Park: Sage, 1991. 143–156.

———. "Scopic regimes of modernity." *Modernity and Identity.* Ed. Scott Lash and Jonathan Friedman. Oxford: Blackwell, 1992. 178–195.

———. *Downcast Eyes: The Denigration of Vision in Twentieth-Century French Thought.* Berkeley: University of California Press, 1993.

Judovitz, Dalia. "Vision, Representation, and Technology in Descartes." *Modernity and the Hegemony of Vision*. Ed. David Michael Levin. Berkeley: University of California Press, 1993. 63–86.

Lázaro Carreter, Fernando. "Sobre la dificultad conceptista." *Estilo barroco y personalidad creadora: Góngora, Quevedo, Lope de Vega*. Salamanca: Anaya, 1960. 11–59.

Lessing, G. Ephraim. *Laocoonte, o sobre las fronteras de la poesía y la pintura*. Ed. and trans. Eustaquio Barjau. Madrid: Editora Nacional, 1977.

Levin, David Michael. Introduction to *Modernity and the Hegemony of Vision*. Ed. David Michael Levin. Berkeley: University of California Press, 1993. 1–29.

Maravall, José Antonio. *La cultura del Barroco: Análisis de una estructura histórica*. Barcelona: Ariel, 1975.

———. "Un mito platónico en Gracián." *Estudios de historia del pensamiento español*. Serie tercera. El siglo del Barroco. Madrid: Cultura Hispánica, 1984. 375–383.

———. "Velázquez en el horizonte intelectual de su época." *Estudios de historia del pensamiento español*. Serie tercera. El siglo del Barroco. Madrid: Cultura Hispánica, 1984. 467–483.

Mitchell, W. J. T. *Iconology: Image, Text, Ideology*. Chicago and London: University of Chicago Press, 1986.

Montesinos, José F. "Gracián o la picaresca pura." *Ensayos y estudios de la literatura española*. Ed. Joseph H. Silverman. Madrid: Revista de Occidente, 1970. 141–158.

Pelegrín, Benito. "Arquitextura y arquitectura del *Criticón*: Estética y ética de la escritura graciana." *El mundo de Gracián (Actas del Coloquio Internacional Berlín 1988)*. Ed. Sebastian Neumeister and Dietrich Briesemeister. Berlin: Colloquium Verlag, 1991. 51–66.

Pring-Mill, Robert D. F. "Some Techniques of Representation in the *Sueños* and the *Criticón*." *Bulletin of Hispanic Studies* 45 (1968): 270–284.

Rorty, Richard. *Philosophy and the Mirror of Nature*. Princeton: Princeton University Press, 1979.

Unamuno, Miguel de. *Del sentimiento trágico de la vida*. New York: Las Américas, 1965.

Wölfflin, Heinrich. *Renacimiento y Barroco*. Trans. Alberto Corazón's editorial team. Barcelona: Paidós, 1986.

Ynduráin, Domingo. "Enamorarse de oídas." In *Serta Philológica a Fernando Lázaro Carreter. Tomo II*. Madrid: Cátedra, 1983. 589–603.

Chapter 10
Gracián and the Authority of Taste

Anthony J. Cascardi

In the opening chapter of *Truth and Method* (1960), Hans-Georg Gadamer described the work of Gracián as standing at the very beginning of the modern discourse on aesthetics, which concerns itself primarily with the question of taste.[1] Typically, the problem of taste in its modern form has been understood in the following more or less Kantian terms: if knowledge involves establishing a relationship between the objects of cognition and the categories of reason we bring to bear on them, then how can we validate the claims we customarily make about beauty and sublimity, which are based on feelings of pleasure and pain and so do not conform to reason's categories? How can we show that the judgments of taste we make about the beautiful and the sublime do in fact constitute knowledge?[2] As Gadamer goes on to say, and as Kant is well aware, it might initially seem doubtful that one could speak of "knowledge" with respect to aesthetic judgments at all, since these are not made according to a priori concepts, but it remains nonetheless clear that aesthetic judgments do indeed contain the idea of universal agreement or assent, even if this agreement is sensuously and not conceptually grounded. Perhaps for this reason, Gadamer locates the most instructive aesthetic claims in the form of judgments about "tasteless" objects, or in claims about objects offensive to "good taste":

> Taste really seeks, not what is tasteful but what does not offend it. . . . Taste is practically defined by the fact that it is offended by what is tasteless and thus avoids it, like anything else that threatens injury. Thus the idea of "bad taste" is not an original counter-phenomenon to "good taste." The opposite of the latter is to have "no taste." (35)

To be sure, the idea of aesthetic judgment as rooted in the fundamental sensuous experiences of pain and pleasure, aversion and preference, is not in itself at odds with the views put forward in modern critical theory. The grounding of taste in the sensuous experiences of pleasure and pain is nowhere more apparent than in Freud, who describes the originary identification of the ego as taking the form of an aesthetic judgment on the corporeal plane:

> Expressed in the language of the oldest—the oral—instinctual impulses, the judgment is: "I should like to eat this," or "I should like to spit it out"; and, put more generally: "I should like to take this into myself and to keep that out." . . . The original pleasure ego wants to introject everything into itself that is good and to eject from itself everything that is bad.[3]

Freud's observations represent a reversal of Aristotle's idea of a categorical distinction between the human and the animal and, within the human, the idea of an ascent from sensation to the intellect; in the *De sensu et sensato* (443b) Aristotle had said that only human beings are sensible to the differences between agreeable and disagreeable odors, noting that animals do not shun the disagreeable, properly speaking, but only the noxious, which harms them physically or taints their food (445a).[4] Along with Freud more recent social theorists like Pierre Bourdieu have argued that the experiences of pleasure and pain form the very basis of modern aesthetic theory, even if it is a basis that such theory would prefer to renounce: " 'Pure taste,' " writes Bourdieu, "purely negative in its essence, is based on the disgust that is often called 'visceral' (it 'makes one sick' or 'makes one vomit')"; "Kant's principle of pure taste is nothing other than a refusal, a disgust—a disgust for objects which impose enjoyment and a disgust for the crude, vulgar taste which revels in being represented comfortably to nature without destroying all aesthetic delight, and consequently artistic beauty, namely, that which excites *disgust*."[5]

For Gadamer, however, the phenomenon of taste as rooted in the individual ego is immediately (and, I would add, proleptically) subsumed into a phenomenon of the collective, social body—the community. Gadamer maintains that writers beginning with Gracián show us that "the true sense of community... is taste" (*TM* 33). And yet it seems that it is not enough simply to identify the sense of community or the "community sense" (*sensus communis*) with taste *tout court*. As in Kant, the validation of taste as a "foundational" concept for the community requires also *limiting* the concept to judgments about what is beautiful or not.[6] In other words, the community's foundational need can be addressed not just by restricting the concept of the sense of community to that of taste—as if what were at stake were simply the movement from the empirical singularity of the individual's corporeal experiences of pleasure and pain to the supposedly reasoned generality of judgments that could be validated by everyone—but also limiting the application of taste itself to the objects we would judge beautiful, that is, to works of art, which come to define an independent realm within the social. Accordingly, it is not just that aesthetic judgments serve "foundational" ends for the community; it is also that the founding of community in taste is dependent on the (prior) existence of works of art. But if this is the case, then it is not surprising to find that we can uncover a residue of the transition from the physical reactions of the sensuous and material body to the reasoned response of the "social body" or the "body politic" in the aesthetic judgment, whose strict delimitation to works of art was the concern of French neoclassical theorists.[7]

By the same token, artworks came eventually to be seen as sublimating or subsuming the particularity of sensuous aesthetic experience into occasions of universally acceptable and communicable judgments. Taste has its origins in the sensuous experiences of pleasure and pain, but the exercise of taste can appear to hide the genealogy of the aesthetic in sensuous reality, just as the development of culture by and through taste can seem to conceal the animal origins of human nature. This situation is duplicated in the notion of the *sensus communis,* which like taste has sometimes seemed not really to be a sense at all, or to be only a sense of form: it is neither the particular nor the general, but rather is what makes it possible to assimilate the particular to the general, an individual to a pattern, the self to the social or political world. Precisely in order to recover the sensuous moment of taste and of the *sensus communis,* Gadamer relies on Gracián. Indeed, Gadamer quotes Gracián to say that the development of taste represents a "spiritualization of animality."[8] In his view, Gracián helps us modify the prevailing Enlightenment view that the concept of taste was of a piece with the rationalism that came to dominate ethics, politics, and philosophy in the seventeenth and eighteenth centuries. For the most part, critics have wished to see theories of aesthetic judgments of beauty in art as supported by the same combination of arguments that were advanced in favor of universal rational law and natural justice, and have in turn wished to see these as establishing an ideal of ethical necessity that followed the same kind of laws as direct physical or material causal relations. In the view of at least one recent critic, it was thus assumed that the aesthetic pleasure provoked by beauty, and especially by beauty in literature, was essentially rational and could at least initially be opposed to the pleasure of the sublime, which was viewed as irrational.[9] But insofar as the formation of the "sense of community" requires not just the laws of reason, but the existence of artworks around which to develop judgments of taste, the Enlightenment understanding of this issue hides the problematic role of taste in "raising" mankind out of sensuous reality, for clearly if such artworks exist then humanity is no longer in an uncultured state.[10] (As we also shall see, it similarly obscures the aporia of the social education of taste.) Gadamer suggests that Gracián's understanding of the problem of taste can be of particular importance nonetheless, for he seems to suggest that if we can recover from Gracián's work an understanding of the civilizing role of taste with respect to sensuous, material reality, then presumably we can move from an understanding of political community as founded directly in sensuous reality—not on the basis of desire, but of need—to the notion of politics as founded on judgments, even if these, like aesthetic judgments, do not necessarily conform to a priori concepts.

In assessing Gadamer's account of the origins of taste in Gracián, it must first be said that the history of taste he has proposed favors the notion of the beautiful at the expense of the sublime. Moreover, Gadamer's attempt to recuperate aesthetic pleasure for social ends does not sufficiently take into account the ways in which communities may constitute and transform themselves by the systematic exclusion of what they cannot represent, and, in Kant at least, it is the fear of exclusion and unrecompensed sacrifice that is so strongly rendered in the sublime. Moreover, if taste is in principle founded on agreement, then artworks are bound to be pressed into the service of recognition at the expense of historical transformation. Where then is the possibility for the kinds of resistance to agreement that works of art so often provoke? Where is the residue of materiality such works may contain? Furthermore, Gadamer asserts that the origins of taste lie in sensuous reality, but he begins his discussion with the claim that Gracián demonstrates how taste was originally a moral concept. To say the very least, the route from sensuous reality to morality in Gracián—where taste is deemed to play a crucial role—is unclear. In Gadamer's view, Gracián configures taste itself as an "ideal of genuine humanity" whose broad accessibility is nothing short of remarkable when compared with the philosophical Scholasticism whose earlier prudential ideals were the province of the privileged few.[11]

Gracián starts from the view that while the sense of taste may be the most animal and inward and in this respect the most common of our faculties, it nonetheless contains the beginnings of the discriminations we all can make in our "higher" reflective and moral judgments (see Gracián: "No hay perfección donde no hay delecto"; "There is no perfection without discernment").[12] The sensuous judgment of taste, by which we seem to accept or reject things as if by instinct, is not *merely* an instinct, because it subordinates our instinctual reactions to the "freedom" of reflective judgment: "*Cultura y aliño.* Nace bárbaro el hombre; redímese de bestia cultivándose. Hace personas la cultura; y más, cuanto mayor" (*OM*, sec. 87, p. 395) ("*Culture and refinement.* Man is born a barbarian. Culture raises him above the beast. Culture turns us into true persons: the more culture, the greater the person" [*Art of Worldly Wisdom*]). Taste begins in instinct, but, as Gracián seems also to say, taste is itself instinctual. In this respect, it is the mark of a "natural" refinement, whose cultivation is therefore rather difficult to explain. As Andrée Collard observed, "en su aplicación crítica, *buen gusto, gusto* designa la reacción espontánea de un individuo frente a tal o cual obra, e implica cierto natural refinamiento, cierto sentido innato del decoro."[13] At the same time, it is through the exercise of choice and judgment that taste is conceived as being able to gain us a "humanizing" distance from the natural world. Perhaps this is why the exercise of taste would appear to be a moral faculty of the spirit or soul; indeed, there are moments in Gracián when its relationship to a perfectionist ethics would seem to be all but direct.[14] The overcoming of instinct by aesthetic judgment is said to provide evidence that there is cultivation (*cultura*) not only of the faculties of the mind (*ingenio*), but of *gusto* itself. As Gracián remarks in *El héroe,* "Hay cultura de gusto, así como de ingenio" (*El héroe, primor* 5, p. 122). He takes up the theme again in the *Oráculo manual,* under the heading "*Gusto relevante*": "Cabe cultura en él, así como en el ingenio" (sec. 65, p. 385) ("*Elevated taste.* You can cultivate it, as you can the intellect" [*Art of Worldly Wisdom* 36]).

Gadamer's interpretation of Gracián's importance for the history of the concept of taste follows more or less in the line of Romantic notions about the formation of an "aesthetic state." His account of the role of taste in society can be located as part of a tradition that goes back at least as far as Schiller's *Letters on the Aesthetic Education of Man.* By implication, Gadamer positions Gracián as the forerunner of this same line. As Gadamer claims, the notion of *gusto* is the starting point for Gracián's ideal of an education that is itself aesthetic, even if it is not directly controlled by works of art. For Gracián, "good taste" (which is also to say, educated taste) is seen as essential to the constitution of "good society." As we shall also have occasion to discuss, Gracián's ideal of education (*Bildung*) is that of preparation for life in the social world; as such, it may be understood as a more modern version of the ideal of the Christian courtier, one that looks forward to the reorientation of taste not according to virtue but according to the values of social class. It represents an overtly sociological interpretation of the prudential ideals characteristic of Scholastic thought. Perhaps with reason, Hannah Arendt credits Gracián in her lectures on Kant's political philosophy as having been instrumental (along with Cicero) in developing the sense of taste as a faculty of judgment.[15]

On Gadamer's account, however, the ideal of aesthetic education is understood as occurring independent of the class construction of social reality. In his view, Gracián's educational ideal is "remarkable in the history of Western ideals of Bildung for being *independent of class.* It is the ideal of a society based on Bildung" (*TM* 34, my emphasis). But at the same time Gadamer remains convinced that taste is a historical idea, and that the particular notion of taste that emerges in Gracián has its roots in a process of social change that can be tied to the question of social class. As he goes on to say, "The ideal of social Bildung, while independent of class, seems to emerge everywhere in the wake of absolutism and its suppression of the hereditary aristocracy. Taste is not only the ideal created by a new society, but we see this ideal of 'good taste' producing what was subsequently called 'good society.' Its criteria are no longer birth and rank but simply the shared nature of its judgments, or, rather, its capacity to rise above the narrowness of interests and private predilections to the title of judgment" (ibid.).[16]

In what follows here, I want to suggest not only that Gracián's notion of taste must be historicized in relation to the question of the formation of the psychology of the "individual," as a relatively new social phenomenon in early modern Spain, but that the "historicization" of taste can in turn provide access to an understanding of taste's social genesis, even if this is not the genesis that a thinker like Gadamer imagines for it. This is to say that the historical specificity of Gracián's notion of taste must be located in relation to the ways in which the individual, bodily experiences of pleasure and pain were subsumed as part of the social structuring of experience in early modern Spain. This process can best be understood in terms of the displacement of the hierarchical and hereditary values of social caste, founded on the principles of purity of blood, by a system of values that would eventually consolidate themselves around the principles of social class, which entails a suppression of the corporeal basis of social value.

In Alasdair MacIntyre's view, the essentialist principles of traditional society are reflected in the organization of human relations within it. In traditional societies "it is through membership in a variety of social groups that the individual identifies himself or herself and is identified by others. I am brother, cousin and grandson, member of this household, that village, this tribe. These are not characteristics that belong to human beings accidentally, to be stripped away in order to discover 'the real me.' They are part of my substance, defining at least partially and sometimes wholly my obligations and my duties. Individuals inherit a particular space within an interlocking set of social relationships; lacking that space, they are nobody, or at best a stranger or an outcast."[17] It is on the basis of a direct contrast with the principles of traditional society that the problem of taste can in the end be understood. Gadamer's assertion notwithstanding, Gracián's notion of social *Bildung* is not at all "independent" of notions of social class; on the contrary, Gracián's notion of taste points in the direction of the psychology of "good sense" and "common sense," which formed one of the philosophical foundations by which the primacy of lineage was suppressed by the emerging middle class. (See Descartes, whom we shall have occasion to cite at greater length below: "Good sense is the best distributed thing in the world: for everyone thinks himself so well endowed with it that even those who are the hardest to please in everything else do not usually desire more of it than they possess.")[18] In response to Gadamer, it would be more accurate to say that Gracián's notion of taste marks a formative moment in the history of the values of social class—a moment at which the notions of social relations as fixed and the capacity for judgment as inborn were displaced by the notion of aesthetic judgment as socially formed. The invention of "good taste" served the aims of a society that could no longer adequately legitimize its ethical and moral projects (not to speak of its aesthetic ones) according to the aristocratic criteria of rank, while at the same time it served the continuing need for discrimination among those whose interests had formerly been characterized as illegitimate or "vulgar" ("el gusto del vulgo"). In a period of dramatic social change, taste (and especially "good taste," *buen gusto*) emerged to ground that particular form of social distinction that was crucial for the redefinition of "good society." In this way, Gadamer's "enlightened" understanding of taste as a faculty that operates at a distance from social interests must be set beside the sociopolitical understanding of taste, which sees the exercise of taste as a necessary means for maintaining distinctions within the modern world, for it is through the process of distinction, and not just identification, that societies are formed.

And yet the question of taste as posed by Gracián presents an additional problem for an understanding of the changing socio-historical order of which it is so symptomatically a part. For while taste proves essential for the (re)constitution of social order within a period of historical change, it turns out that the constitution of society seems always to *precede* the formation of judgments of taste. As we shall in conclusion see, this presents a particular problem for the authority of taste, which would seem to be without foundations.[19] In one respect, the problem of taste with respect to early modern Spanish society is a version of the "foundational" problem common to the question of judgment in all political societies and states. Already Aristotle recognized that education in political life required possession of the same virtues that participation in political life would cultivate; in the *Nicomachean Ethics,* for instance, he wrote that "any one who is to listen intelligently to lectures about what is noble and just and, generally, about the subjects of political science must have been brought up in good habits."[20]

Gracián's understanding of the education of taste mirrors this same problem, but does so more dramatically, because it is articulated during a period of radical social change. Insofar as Gracián's understanding of this problem centers around the cultivation of the individual's distinctive individualism, it may itself be seen as "modern," for it offers a way to *resist* the tendency of the preconstitution of social reality to dictate the limits of political life. But since the preexisting social world cannot be rejected *tout court,* Gracián comes to regard the *differential* exercise of taste as one of the ways in which the individual can best achieve success in social and political life. The exercise of taste, which requires the assertion of individual differences within the context of universal agreement or assent, comes to represent not just a historical shift of preferences, but a "moral" correction of modernity's universalizing aims. In this respect, taste joins dissimulation as a means to preserve and protect individual identity, which is taken as a moral project. As Gracián wrote: "*Entrar con la ajena para salir con la suya.* Es estratagema del conseguir; aun en las materias del Cielo encargan esta santa astucia los cristianos maestros. Es un importante disimulo, porque sirve de cebo la concebida utilidad para coger una voluntad" (*OM*, sec. 144, pp. 416–417) ("*Enter conceding and come out winning.* This is a strategy for getting what you want. Even in heavenly matters, our Christian teachers recommend this holy craftiness. It is an important sort of dissimulation and you use it to capture someone else's will" [*Art of Worldly Wisdom* 81]).[21]

As the foregoing remarks will have made clear, I believe that Gracián's concept of taste (*gusto*) marks a complex set of relations between the individual and society, involving judgments not just of artworks but of social values as well. At the same time, taste marks the project of founding the community as one of establishing internal differences and distinctions, rather than simply one of asserting common identities. In what follows here I want to consider the more specific claim that Gracián's ideas of taste and of the education (*cultura*) of taste emerge in the context of the crisis of values created by the weakening of the hereditary aristocracy in Spain, one of the consequences of which was a corresponding crisis in the authority of judgments of all kinds. The notion of a crisis in early modern Europe is familiar enough from the work of social historians, but it has not been sufficiently noted that this crisis had direct consequences for the system of social values in terms of which judgments of taste were articulated. As Norbert Elias and others have amply noted, the crisis of the hereditary aristocracy was widespread throughout Europe and may help account for the extraordinary resonance of Gracián's work outside of Spain. As Elias points out, the *Oráculo manual* went through approximately twenty editions in France alone during the course of the seventeenth and eighteenth centuries under the title *L'homme du cour*; it came to be regarded as the first handbook of courtly psychology in the same way that Machiavelli's *Il principe* was recognized as the first handbook of courtly-absolutist politics.[22] On the account I would propose, the context for the emergence of Gracián's notion of taste was that of an encompassing shift from a world in which judgments of value (including, increasingly, judgments of moral and aesthetic value) were supported by the notion of a fixed social hierarchy to a world in which grounds for discrimination among values could no longer be aligned with the notion of an inherent hierarchy of social ranks. As the social basis of the hereditary aristocracy weakened, it became increasingly difficult to sustain the idea that "good taste" was aligned in any fundamental way with a privilege guaranteed by nobility of birth or purity of blood. And yet, as is all too clear from the literary controversies of the late sixteenth and early seventeenth centuries, as it is from a work like the *Oráculo manual,* the need to provide a grounding for social values like taste remained urgent.

One can read Gracián's work as a sign of the continuing need to assert the possibility of making discriminations of taste in the absence of a hierarchical social basis for such judgments. And yet, to complicate matters further still, it seems that the need to articulate the principles of such new values was systematically precluded within the framework provided by Gracián. While Gracián puts forward a series of generic figures who represent recognizable character ideals (e.g., the man of "good taste," "el hombre de buena elección," "el discreto," "el hombre en su punto"), he never quite succeeds in laying bare the sources of the ability to choose well. It is clear that "good taste" cannot be cited directly as confirming evidence of one's incorporation into "good society." This is because one must first be educated into good taste. And yet it remains unclear just how society can accomplish this task. A critic like Gadamer simply does not notice that the antinomy of taste yields a paradox in which society requires for its foundation a process of education that it must at the same time presuppose. Likewise, he seems not to notice that taste is a faculty that requires an education that is always insufficient to it and that it is always required to surpass. (Gracián: "Supone el buen gusto y el rectísimo dictamen, que no bastan el estudio ni el ingenio" [*OM,* sec. 51, p. 380]; "You need good taste and an upright judgment; intelligence and application are not enough" [*Art of Worldly Wisdom* 29].)[23] This paradox is especially sharp where Gracián rejects the imitation of models as a paradigm of cultural education.[24] In the case of "el discreto," for instance, Gracián holds as an ideal that of someone who, on his own, achieves the proper freedom and distance from life and society, and who is thus able to make choices and distinctions from a superior position. But Gracián does not (or perhaps cannot) say whether it is distance that enables good judgment or whether such distance is itself already the result of having been educated into the habits of good judgment. So too for the man who "knows how to choose," the "hombre de buena elección":

> *Know how to choose.* Most things in life depend on it. You need good taste and an upright judgment; intelligence and application are not enough. There is no perfection without discernment and selection. Two talents are involved: choosing and choosing the best. There are many people with a fertile, subtle intelligence, rigorous judgment, both diligent and well informed, who are lost when they have to choose. They always choose the worst, as though they wanted to show their skill at doing so. Knowing how to choose is one of heaven's greatest gifts.[25] (*Art of Worldly Wisdom* 29)

The cultivation of the faculty of taste is essential to the development of the personality of each of the figures Gracián imagines. And yet the cultivation of taste seems also to indicate the prior completion of the moral development it initiates. One must exercise taste in order to reach perfection, and yet the exercise of taste is also seen as providing evidence of perfection achieved:

> *Reach perfection.* No one is born that way. Perfect yourself daily, both personally and professionally, until you become a consummate being, rounding off your gifts and reaching eminence. Signs of the perfect person: elevated taste, a pure intelligence, a clear will, ripeness of judgment. Some people are never complete and are always lacking something. Others take a long time to form themselves. The consummate person—wise in speech, prudent in deeds—is admitted to, and even desired by, the singular society of the discreet.[26] (*Art of Worldly Wisdom* 3–4)

To say that the social context for Gracián's understanding of *gusto* is one in which the privilege of making discriminations of taste was no longer guaranteed by claims of nobility of birth is not to say that Gracián writes out of a context where the traces of social difference had been eradicated. Rather, it is to suggest that the authority of those making such distinctions could no longer be explained in terms of lineage, heredity, or other "natural" traits. Indeed, even when Gracián recognizes the ordering principle of distinction that seems to be fundamental to most conceptions of social reality, he avoids any explanation that would rely on the criteria of inborn rank:

> There are some subjects who are good for carrying out orders, because they do so with pleasure and diligently, but they are not good for giving orders, because they do not think well and make worse judgments, always making mistakes. There are all kinds of men, some who lead and some who follow.[27]

It is clear that social distinctions remain in place even after the erosion of the hereditary nobility. Indeed, some of these distinctions are seen as categorical, and some are as unfathomable in Gracián's mind as the distance that separates man from beast: "Hay, a veces, entre un hombre y otro casi otra tanta distancia como entre el hombre y la bestia; si no en la substancia, en la circunstancia; si no en la vitalidad, en el ejercicio della" (Sometimes there is as much distance between one man and another as there is between man and beast; if not in substance, then in circumstances; if not in vital power, then in the exercise of it) (*El discreto* 240). But since it was not immediately clear just how distinctions could continue to be made in the absence of criteria that depended solidly on the principles of lineage, there arose a need to "invent" the (aesthetic) circumstances within which they might occur. The emergence of the styles of *culteranismo* and *conceptismo*, which were purposefully difficult and so served to create a social elite, can be understood in this light. So too Gracián's own aesthetic, where the capacity to produce and comprehend difficulty is valued as a sign of the ability to make discriminations: "*No allanarse sobrado en el concepto.* Los más estiman lo entienden y lo que no perciben lo veneran. Las cosas, para que se estimen, han de costar; será celebrado cuando no fuese entendido" (*OM*, sec. 253, p. 460) ("*Don't express your ideas too clearly.* Most people think little of what they understand, and venerate what they do not. To be valued, things must be difficult: if they can't understand you, people will think more highly of you" [*Art of Worldly Wisdom* 143]).

If difference is ineradicable—indeed, if the need to recognize and mark difference is the constitutional basis of the social—the question then becomes how to sustain the authority required by a notion like *buen gusto,* which is at the heart of Gracián's understanding of social differentiation. Similarly, one might ask how the different levels of accomplishment or perfection in evidence in society could be judged (Gracián: "Hay perfecciones soles y perfecciones luces" [Some perfections are like suns, others like stars] [*El héroe, primor* 5, p. 122]). In one respect, the answers to all these questions are to be found in Gracián's concept of the individual—perhaps one should say, in the *individualism* that underwrites Gracián's conception of the individual—especially if one considers the fact that the notion of the "individual" and the principles of social differentiation based on such a notion are categories that could only have emerged after the weakening of the value base of the hereditary aristocracy had taken place. But since Gracián also thinks of taste as a quality that must be cultivated through social action, and not as something that is simply exhibited as a function of social status, it might be more accurate to say that the "individual" is for him the name for that set of calls to social action generated by the erosion of the notion of authority as hereditary.

It is no great surprise to find that Gracián's conception of the individual is subject to the same paradox that marks the social education of taste. On the one hand, "individualism" is a quality that is necessary for achieving the right relationship to the praxis of life, while on the other hand individualism is the quality that results from having successfully achieved such a relationship. Ideally, individualism describes a kind of self-sufficiency that would be independent of social reality: "Bástese a sí mismo el sabio" (*OM*, sec. 137, p. 413) ("The Wise are sufficient unto themselves" [*Art of Worldly Wisdom* 76]). And yet the individual who exercises "good taste," such as the "hombre de buena elección," must by definition also validate social norms. Insofar as taste occupies a central place in the ethos of the individual cultivated by Gracián, it is at once the occasion of a certain independence from the social body and also a confirmation of the primacy of the social body. Ideally, it is the sign of an ability to establish and reproduce one's own standards. In principle, it marks an ability to fashion oneself as free from the practice of imitation, which appears to be inextricably bound up with the aporias of social education described above. The "individual" sets his own standards and goals: "Grande excelencia en una intensa singularidad, cifrar toda una categoría y equivalerla" (Great excellence in an intense singularity, to mark off an entire category and be equal to it) (*El héroe, primor* 6, p. 125). Imitation, by contrast, is seen as a thanklessly difficult and doomed procedure, one that threatens to absorb and exhaust the individual: "Son tenidos por imitadores de los pasados los que les siguen; y por más que suden, no pueden purgar la presunción de imitación" (They who follow past examples are deemed imitators of the past; and no matter how hard they might work, they cannot purge the presumption of imitation) (*El héroe, primor* 7, p. 127). And yet it remains equally true that the individual's individualism, especially as it is achieved through the exercise of taste, would have no standing were it not for the validation offered by society. "Taste" is the mark of the individual, but it also marks the incorporation of the individual into the social body.

In a recent study of the aesthetics of individuation, Frances Ferguson identifies a closely related paradox in the eighteenth century. Referring to the work of Edmund Burke, she writes that

> even if [his] is a "scientific" account of taste, an analysis of the kinds of social testimony that people give in expressing what looks like individual preference, it describes taste not by explaining individual tastes as relationships toward aesthetic objects but rather by redefining what it might mean to give an explanation of taste. Explaining taste turns out to be pointing to other tastes like this one, admitting, that is, that one cannot give a very good explanation of individual taste but can show that there is more (i.e., collective taste, in the form of the social, the class, the local, etc.) where it came from. . . . Individual taste appears merely a mystification of the social. (*Solitude and the Sublime* 63)[28]

In Gracián, however, where the historical context is quite different, the cultivation of the individual's individualism is also a sign and substitute for a certain kind of social prestige that, under other circumstances, could be guaranteed by claims to nobility of birth. Similarly, taste is a quality of character whose principal trait is itself the ability to make judgments of quality: "Tanta diferencia e importancia puede caber en el cómo" (Just as much difference and importance can depend on the "how") (*El discreto, discurso* 22, p. 125). It is of particular importance to members of social groups whose economic means were substantial, and who could thus enjoy the luxury of pretending to have overcome their "natural" needs. According to the account proposed by Elias,

> a compulsive desire for social prestige is to be found as the primary motive of action only among members of classes whose income under normal circumstances is substantial and perhaps ever growing, and at any rate is appreciably over the hunger threshold. In such cases the impulse to engage in economic activity is no longer the simple necessity of satisfying hunger, but a desire to preserve a certain high, socially expected standard of living and prestige. This explains why, in such elevated classes, affect-control and self-constraint are generally more highly developed than in the lower classes: fear of loss or reduction of social prestige is one of the most powerful motive forces in the transformation from constraints through others into self-restraints. Here, too, as in many other instances, the upper-class characteristics of "good society" are particularly highly developed in the courtly aristocracy of the seventeenth and eighteenth centuries, precisely because, within its framework, money was indispensable and wealth desirable as a means of living, but certainly not, as in the bourgeois world, the basis of prestige as well. Membership of courtly society means to those belonging to it more than wealth. (*Power and Civility* 268)

If Elias is right, then it is no surprise to find that the category of *gusto* emerges in its full aesthetic sense in the debates surrounding *conceptismo* and *culteranismo* in poetry,[29] as well as in discussions of the aesthetic principles underlying the *comedia* as a form of entertainment designed for the *vulgo,* and not just in the writings of Gracián, for it was in all these areas that one could witness the suppression of "natural" needs by the "social" refinements of culture. Earlier, in a work like the *Lazarillo,* where the "natural" passion of hunger is figured as standing at the root of all desire (including the preeminent social desire for prestige that dominates the Escudero and, presumably, "Vuesa Merced," as well), the concept of "taste" did not yet have the aesthetic standing it acquired later in the Golden Age. This is because "nature," and natural needs, had not yet been conclusively overtaken by the new configuration of social values evident in seventeenth-century Spain; needs (e.g., the need to satisfy hunger) and desires (e.g., for social standing) are equally forceful factors in that work. But already by 1615 things had changed in radical ways. Sancho Panza's experiences in governing the island of Barataria in *Don Quixote,* part 2, are determined by the need to temper his "natural" inclinations and appetites so that he might "civilize" himself. But since Sancho's experience on Barataria is, of course, staged by the duke and the duchess, it seems reasonable to assume that the "civilizing" desire to overcome nature was also quite self-consciously felt among the courtly aristocracy.[30]

Although Elias is certainly right to suggest that the desire for social prestige was intensified at court, it would be mistaken to think that the validity of the concept of taste was limited to this context. Especially in debates surrounding the legitimacy of "vulgar taste" (*el gusto del vulgo*), it is clear that the newly emergent notion of taste played a decisive role in establishing a basis for discrimination among works of art where the "natural" (read as hereditary) basis for distinction had been eroded. Consider in this regard the positions of Cervantes and Lope de Vega on the role of the *vulgo* in fashioning taste. In *Don Quixote,* part 1, the canon of Toledo inveighs against the *novelas de caballerías* insofar as they cater to the *gusto del vulgo,* whose uneducated interest in reading for pleasure is said to outweigh the intellectual interests of learned readers. Regarding the contemporary *comedias,* he says that taste is not in itself sufficient to guarantee the quality of the works being judged. This is because, while taste must be educated, the *vulgo* brings uneducated opinion to bear on these works:

> The crowd enjoy seeing them, and approve of them and reckon them good, when they are so far from being so; and if the authors who write them and the managers who put

> them on say that they must be good, because the crowd likes them like that and not otherwise, and that the authors who observe a plan and follow the story as the rules of drama require only serve to please the three or four men of sense who understand them, while all the rest are left unsatisfied and cannot fathom their subtlety.[31] (Trans. Cohen 427)

For Don Quixote, the issue of taste is somewhat more difficult to resolve. Especially in part 2 of the novel, Don Quixote rejects both the "progressive" view of taste as the forerunner of social change and the "conservative" view of taste as requiring the confirmation of preexisting social groups. He represents the view that there is a nobility of taste that reaches "beyond" conservative and progressive postures, a "true nobility" that cannot be defined in any social terms, a nobility that produces a hierarchy of taste all its own and that is not determined by social standing at all. His defense of poetic taste in response to the Caballero del Verde Gabán would seek to "overcome" the traces of both the individual and the social body in the work of art. But rather than simply reject the affiliation of taste with the individual body, he interprets good taste as a form of bodily purity. And once the body is introduced it seems that even an idealizing defense of poetry is bound to be the defense of *particular* literary tastes; in the case at hand, it amounts to a rejection of modernizing tendencies in art in favor of more traditional poetic values:

> Poetry... is like a tender, young, and extremely beautiful maiden, whom other maidens toil to enrich, to polish and adorn. These maidens are the other sciences; and she has to be served by all, while all of them have to justify themselves by her. But this maiden does not care to be handled, or dragged through the streets, nor to be shown at the corners of the market place, or in the antechambers of palaces. She is formed of an alchemy of such virtue that anyone who knows how to treat her will transform her into purest gold of inestimable price. Her possessor must keep her within bounds, not letting her run to base lampoons or impious sonnets. She must be exposed for sale only in the form of heroic poems, piteous tragedies, or gay and artificial comedies. She must not let herself be handled by buffoons, nor by the ignorant vulgar, who are

> incapable of recognizing or appreciating her treasures. Now do not imagine, sir, that by vulgar I mean only the common and humble people; for all who are ignorant, even if they are lords or princes, can rightfully be included under the name of vulgar.[32] (Trans. Cohen 568–569)

For Gracián, by contrast, the *vulgo* is scorned for its lack of wisdom and independence; in *El criticón,* part 2, *crisi* 5 ("Plaza del populacho y corral del vulgo"), it is said that "los sabios son pocos, no hay cuatro en la ciudad, los ignorantes son los muchos, los necios son los infinitos" (wise men are few, there are not four in the city; the ignorant are many, the fools are infinite).[33] But in *El criticón,* at least, it is not the *taste* of the crowd that is at stake. Indeed, Gracián elsewhere sees the exercise of taste as itself a sign and symbol of modernity. Taste does not just rely for its validity on the fact that there are other tastes like it, as in the case of Burke. The power of taste is validated because it is a forerunner of social change, which it in turn validates. As Gracián writes in *El discreto,* "Siempre va el gusto adelante, nunca vuelve atrás; no se ceba en lo que pasó, siempre pica en la novedad; pero puédesele engañar con lo flamante del modillo," (Taste always runs ahead, it never turns back; it does not feed on what has already happened, it always snacks on novelty; but it can be bedazzled by the latest fashion) (*El discreto, discurso* 22, pp. 334–335).[34]

In contrast to the quixotic understanding of the unchanging aristocracy of certain tastes, Gracián's conception of taste is more closely allied to notions of common sense. On the one hand, his notion of *gusto* as a form of judgment represents a transformation of the Scholastic ideal of prudence:

> *Good common sense.* It is the throne of reason, the foundation of prudence, and by its light it is easy to succeed. It is a gift from heaven, highly prized because it is first and best. Good sense is our armor, so necessary that the lack of this single piece will make people call us lacking. When least present, most missed. All actions in life depend on its influence, and all solicit its approval, for all depends on intelligence. It consists of a natural inclination to all that conforms most to reason, and to all that is most fit.[35] (*Art of Worldly Wisdom* 53–54)

But perhaps more important than its scholastic affinities, taste, as a form of "common sense," bears striking resemblance to the modern, Cartesian notion of "good sense." When seen in relation to "good sense," what Gracián calls *gusto,* and especially *buen gusto,* is not at all a form of reason *manqué.* Rather, it represents a kind of judgment that, conceptually and structurally, mirrors the form of critical reason that was systematized in modern philosophical discourse.[36] For Descartes,

> good sense is the best distributed thing in the world: for everyone thinks himself so well endowed with it that even those who are the hardest to please in everything else do not usually desire more of it than they possess. In this it is unlikely that everyone is mistaken. It indicates rather that the power of judging well and of distinguishing the true from the false—which is what we properly call "good sense" or "reason"—is naturally equal in all men, and consequently that the diversity of our opinions does not arise because some of us are more reasonable than others but solely because we direct our thoughts along different paths and do not attend to the same things. For it is not enough to have a good mind; the main thing is to apply it well. The greatest souls are capable of the greatest vices as well as the greatest virtues; and those who proceed but very slowly can make much greater progress, if they always follow the right path, than those who hurry and stray from it.[37]

The problems faced by Descartes in moving from the "good sense" that is plentiful in the world, but so often insufficient or simply wrong, to critical reason, which is far less common but unimpeachable, are not so different from those encountered by Gracián in formulating the notion of *buen gusto.* What links Gracián and Descartes is the need to account for the authority that is invested in the judgments of "good taste," even if the answers suggested by these two writers take somewhat different forms. The question, What is the authority of taste in Gracián? is parallel to the question, What is the authority of critical reason in Descartes? because both are derived from a common basis in a form of "good sense" that purports to validate itself. As is well known, the confirmation of the authority of reason for Descartes involves a derivation of the truth of pure self-reflection through the overcoming of skepticism that calls mere "good sense" into question; it relies on and confirms a categorical distinction between the individual, corporeal self and the disembodied rational subject. Indeed, Descartes formulates the authority of the subject through an overcoming both of the errors of sense experience and of the social authority of commonly distributed "good sense." Accordingly, the voice of authority that speaks in the *Meditations* and the *Discourse on Method* is taken to represent more than the voice of authority of René Descartes; it achieves a "generalization" of the authority of that voice by "calling away" all the particularities of body that might locate it in physical, social, or historical space and time.

For Gracián, the problem of the authority of taste is likewise "resolved" through the qualities of voice, which lend authority to the maxims that govern conduct. Especially in the *Oráculo manual,* where matters of taste seem to move us directly from the arena of social conduct to the moral domain, Gracián's maxims present themselves as authoritative insofar as they are spoken by an anonymous, generalized, and disembodied voice: "Don't outshine your boss"; "associate with those you can learn from"; "don't make yourself disliked"; "don't talk about yourself"; "be known for your courtesy"; "live practically." These and many other maxims like them are articulated by a voice that refuses to be positioned exclusively either on the side of the individual or on the side of society. Indeed, its authority stems from its ability to refuse either of these positions, as if to suggest that its authority does not derive either from society or from the individual, even though it presupposes society and is exercised by (and over) the individual. Specifically, this is a voice that effects the socialization of the individual and the subjection of the subject. Its authority seems to extend from judgments of taste to judgments of morality. In Gracián's maxims, it is no longer the voice of the individual or of society that speaks, but rather the voice of conscience, which is to say, the voice of that peculiar, internal form of authority that governs conduct where no "external" authority is in sight.[38] It is a surprisingly short step, then, from Gracián's aesthetically oriented maxims to Kant's conception of what a moral "maxim" is (that is, one that could be willed as a universal law).[39] If it is true, as Alasdair MacIntyre claims, that Enlightenment morality as configured along Kantian lines requires on the one hand a stock of maxims and on the other hand a conception of just what a rational test for a maxim must be,[40] then Gracián's importance is to demonstrate the relevance of judgments of taste for the history of morality insofar as the internal, inner voice of the individual, the voice that internalizes and reproduces society's "universal" commands, provides an anticipatory semblance of what Kant will later indicate as the "rational" bases of morality, that is, the strict universalizability of its commands.

In addressing the question of the foundations of the social community in relation to the authority of judgments of taste, however, we encountered the structural dilemma wherein judgments of taste and social community seem at once to create and to presuppose one another, such that the idea of a social education into "good taste" seemed at best aporetic. While the aporia of taste may be widespread within the culture of modernity, the solutions for it are historically specific; they become especially apparent at moments of social change, when the principles by which society is ordered are themselves called into question. In the instance of a social world governed by the traditional principles of caste, for instance, the solution to the aporia of taste takes the form of an assumption that there is something inborn but nonetheless transmissible, something prior to the social and prior to any faculty of judgment—something, indeed, that is prior to the individual itself—that is constitutive of social values and that authorizes judgments of taste. In such a context, judgments, including those of taste, can be seen to derive from and reflect back directly upon the existing social order, reconfirming it and conferring upon it the authority of moral commands. Within the changing social climate of early modern Spain, however, where the hereditary aristocracy had grown weak and where the principles of *limpieza de sangre* were beginning to be placed in doubt, it began to appear that the authority of taste was no longer supported by social norms and no longer carried its former moral force; indeed, if the literature criticizing the principles of caste can be taken as any indication, it would seem that aesthetic practice had long been running considerably ahead of the authority of social norms. It was such a dilemma that the quasi-moral notion of "good taste" was meant to resolve. Like the notion of the *sensus communis*, "good taste" was not conceived of primarily as a physical "sense," but rather as a supplementary sense, a sense of form, and especially for Gracián a sense of "good form." As such, it was a particularly powerful tool in forming social cohesion while preserving the need for social distinction. Moreover, taste was not itself conceived as having an authority in the conventional sense; it was the indication, more accurately, of a social authority that was absent or displaced. In part by appropriating the problem of authority, the discourse of taste made it possible for the newly emergent individual, as a particular body, to imagine himself or herself as standing in relation to a social body that was in the process of reconstituting itself. As Gracián's writings suggest, social authority was not dissolved in the process; rather, it was displaced by the workings of a seemingly anonymous voice onto subjects who accepted its insistent self-commands.

Notes

1. Hans-Georg Gadamer, *Truth and Method* (hereafter cited as *TM*). See Joan Corominas, *Diccionario crítico etimológico castellano e hispánico,* s.v. "buen gusto": "sentido estético justo parece haber nacido en España, donde ya lo empleaba Isabel la Católica." Gracián's importance for the eighteenth-century conception of "taste" is developed in Karl Borinski, *Baltasar Gracián und die Hofliteratur in Deutschland* (Halle an der Saale: Nachdruck Tübingen, 1971). See also Emilio Hidalgo-Serna, *Das ingeniöse Denken bei Baltasar Gracián: Der 'concepto' und seine logische Funktion* (Munich: Wilhelm Fink Verlag, 1985), especially chapter 5, "Die Vorrangstellung des ingeniösen 'guten Geschmacks'—*buen gusto*: Seine Bedeutung und Funktion." To be sure, there are contrary views. Concerning the priority of Gracián in the history of the concept of "taste," in *A History of Modern Criticism,* René Wellek, for instance, cites passages from Guez de Balzac (1645) and Ludovico Zuccolo (1623)—by way of Benedetto Croce—and draws the conclusion that "the widely held view that 'taste' comes from Spain and particularly from Balthasar Gracián is thus untenable." He grounds his claim in a passage of a letter by Guez which includes the phrase "Puisque vous *goutez* mes derniers Ecrits, et que vous avez *le gout* extrémement bon..." (reproduced in Borgerhoff, *The Freedom of French Classicism* 14). Croce cites Zuccolo on *buen gusto* as "una certa potenza superiore, unita insieme con l'occhio e con l'orecchio, forma un cotal giudicio: la qual potenza tanto meglio conosce, quanto ha più d'accutezza nativa o più di perizia nell' arti, senza pero valersi di discorso" (*Dialoghi,* Venezia, 1625, 67–68), in *Storia dell' Età barocca in Italia* 166. I should thus clarify that the question is not so much one of priority as of the particular inflection Gracián gives to the notion of *gusto* in relation to questions of social change. But there is a second challenge as well, which concerns the distinction between taste and aesthetics. In a recent study, Frances Ferguson claims that "the aesthetic, in the process of becoming defined as something distinct from taste as a particularly demanding

version of consumption, becomes less important as a social and sociological phenomenon and more important for representing a distinct kind of experience. The aesthetic, as Kant outlines it, prefigures and justifies Heidegger's later suggestion (in *Kant and the Future of Metaphysics* [*sic*]) that the imagination should be promoted to the standing of a separate faculty, on the order of reason or the understanding" (*Solitude and the Sublime* 6). Her reference to Heidegger is meant to be to *Kant and the Problem of Metaphysics* (*Kant und das Problem der Metaphysik*).

2. The Kantian formulation, drawn from the opening of the *Critique of Judgement*, is as follows: "If we wish to discern whether anything is beautiful or not, we do not refer the representation of it to the Object by means of understanding with a view to cognition, but by means of the imagination. . . . we refer the representation to the Subject and its feeling of pleasure or displeasure. The judgement of taste, therefore, is not a cognitive judgement, and so not logical, but is aesthetic—which means that it is one whose determining ground *cannot be other than subjective*" (Kant, *Critique of Judgement* 41–42).

3. Freud, "Negation" 237. As Freud goes on to say, "Judging is a continuation, along lines of expediency, of the original process by which the ego took things into itself or expelled them from itself, according to the pleasure principle" (239).

4. See Summers, *The Judgment of Sense* 56.

5. Bourdieu, *Distinction* 486, 488. Compare Hannah Arendt, who reminds us that for Kant "the true opposite to the Beautiful is not the Ugly but 'that which excites disgust.' " She goes on to remind us that "Kant originally planned to write a Critique of Moral Taste" (i.e., instead of a *Critique of Judgement*) (Hannah Arendt, *The Life of the Mind* [New York: Harcourt Brace, 1978], 2: 266). Kant's remarks on disgust (*Ekel*) can be found in sec. 48 of the *Critique of Judgement*.

6. For Kant, of course, the question is one of delimiting and thereby purifying judgments of taste (judgments of the beautiful and the sublime) by excluding everything that is not sufficiently pure.

7. In Kant, the application of judgments of taste extends equally to nature and to art. In the preface to the *Critique of Judgement* Kant writes that "it is chiefly in those estimates that are called aesthetic, and which relate to the beautiful and sublime, whether of nature or of art, that one meets with the above difficulty about a principle [of judgment]." Caygill, *Art of Judgment*, argues that the adaptation of taste constituted a gesture of aristocratic dissent against the Royal Academy (39). See also Remy G. Saisselin, *The Rule of Reason and the Ruses of the Heart: A Philosophical Dictionary of Classical French Criticism, Critics, and Aesthetic Issues* (Cleveland: Case Western Reserve University Press, 1970).

8. It would perhaps be more accurate to say that the development of taste *preserves* the contradiction implicit in the notion of a "spiritualized animality." Bourdieu offers a fascinating commentary on the "overcoming" of barbarism by "pure" taste: "If one follows through all the implications of an aesthetic which, in accordance with the logic of Kant's "Essay on Negative Magnitudes," has to measure virtue by the magnitude of the vices overcome and pure taste by the intensity of the impulse denied and the vulgarity refused, then the most accomplished art has to be recognized in those works which carry the antithesis of civilized barbarism, contained impulse, sublimated coarseness, to the highest degree of tension" (*Distinction* 490).

9. Reiss, *The Meaning of Literature* 179. See also my critical review of Reiss in *Modern Language Quarterly* 54 (1994): 393–404.

10. Pierre Bourdieu provides a forceful critique of the Enlightenment's rejection of the sensuous basis of taste: "'Pure' taste and the aesthetics which provides its theory are founded on a refusal of 'impure' taste and of *aisthesis* (sensation), the simple, primitive form of pleasure reduced to a pleasure of the senses, as in what Kant calls 'the taste of the tongue, the palate and the throat,' a surrender to immediate sensation which in another order looks like imprudence. At the risk of seeming to indulge in the 'facile effects' which 'pure taste' stigmatizes, it could be shown that the whole language of aesthetics is contained in a fundamental refusal of the *facile,* in all the meanings, which bourgeois ethics and aesthetics give to the word" (*Distinction* 486).

11. Gracián frequently makes reference to "la sindéresis," or "law of understanding which contains the precepts of natural law, which are the first principles of human action" (*Summa Theologica,* I-II, q. 94a, I ad 2). See the note in *El héroe* 116.

12. Gracián, *Oráculo manual,* sec. 51, p. 380 (hereafter cited as *OM*); *The Art of Worldly Wisdom* 29.

13. "In its critical understanding, 'good taste,' taste designates the spontaneous reaction to a given work, and implies a certain natural refinement, a certain innate sense of decorum" (Collard, *Nueva Poesía* 63–64).

14. On the question of perfection in Gracián, see Hafter, *Gracián and Perfection.*

15. Hannah Arendt, *Lectures on Kant's Political Philosophy,* ed. Ronald Beiner (Chicago: University of Chicago Press, 1982); see esp. 64, 66.

16. As readers of *Truth and Method* are apt to be aware, Gadamer tends to sacrifice the social and historical understanding of taste to a theoretical interest in locating a type of agreement that is sensuously, rather than conceptually, grounded.

17. Alasdair MacIntyre, *After Virtue,* rev. ed. (Notre Dame: Notre Dame University Press, 1984), 33–34.

18. Descartes, *Discourse on the Method,* I, in *The Philosophical Writings of Descartes,* trans. John Cottingham, Robert Stoothoff, and Dugald Murdoch, 111.

19. Howard Caygill—who likewise places Gracián in the line that leads up to Kant's aesthetics—relates the question of such nonfoundational judgments to the paradigm of production: "Like Hobbes, who saw productive judgment as the creation of illusion, Gracián resolved the formative moment of taste into the production of appearance. In the *Oráculo manual y arte de prudencia* (1647) taste finds itself between reticence and dissemblance, applying judgment to the shaping of appearances. It is an unknowable faculty, present in the subject in an inexplicable way, and exercised intuitively. The object of its formative activity is the subject as appearance, the prudent one 'who realises that he is being observed, or will be observed' (1647 Sec. 297). Much of the pathos of Gracián's writing arises from the necessity of the prudent to dissemble, to represent themselves as appearance, to 'Cultivate a happy spontaneity.' But what if the object of taste is not the subject itself, but a different object? A similar conclusion follows: the object exists only as appearance, only in so far as it has been produced by taste. And yet this formative activity of taste cannot know itself; it is only discernible through the pleasures of producing and manipulating appearances" (*Art of Judgment* 39).

20. Aristotle, *Nicomachean Ethics,* I.4, 5.

21. In moments such as these, Gracián approaches La Rochefoucauld; nonetheless La Rochefoucauld's *Maxims* often lack impulse toward the moral command that runs through Gracián. For example, La Rochefoucauld states as if it were a fact that "in order to succeed in the world people do their utmost to appear successful." La Rochefoucauld, *Maxims,* trans. Leonard Tancock (Harmondsworth: Penguin Books, 1959), no. 56, p. 44. Or again, La Rochefoucauld states that "hypocrisy is a tribute vice pays to virtue" (no. 218, p. 65). Emilio Hidalgo-Serna comments briefly on the relationship between Gracián and both La Rochefoucauld and Madame de Sablé in *Das ingeniöse Denken bei Baltasar Gracián* 24. See also G. Hough, "Gracián's *Oráculo manual* and the "Maximes" of Madame de Sablé, *Hispanic Review* 4 (1936): 68–72.

22. See Elias, *Power and Civility* 358.

23. The ideal of "social education" must at the same time be considered in relation to Gracián's sometimes quite unsocial understanding of human nature. See, for example, *OM,* sec. 167, on "self-reliance" ("saberse ayudar").

24. This is yet another instance in which Gracián prefigures Kant in the *Critique of Judgement.*

25. "*Hombre de buena elección.* Lo más se vive della. Supone el buen gusto y el rectísimo dictamen, que no bastan el estudio ni el ingenio. No hay perfección donde no hay delecto; dos ventajas incluye: poder escoger, y lo mejor. Muchos de ingenio fecundo y sutil, de juicio acre, estudiosos y noticiosos también, en llegando al elegir, se pierden, cánsanse siempre con lo peor, que parece afectan el errar. Y así este es uno de los dones máximos de arriba" (*OM,* sec. 51, p. 380).

26. "*Hombre en su punto.* No se hace hecho; vase de cada día perfeccionando en la persona, en el empleo, hasta llegar al punto del consumado ser, al complemento de prendas, de eminencias. Conocerse ha en lo realzado del gusto, purificado el ingenio, en lo maduro del juicio, en lo defecado de la voluntad. Algunos nunca llegan a ser cabales: fáltales siempre un algo; tardan otros en hacerse. El varón consumado, sabio en dichos, cuerdo en hechos, es admitido, y aun deseado, del singular comercio de los discretos" (*OM,* sec. 6, p. 362).

27. "Hay sujetos que son buenos para mandados, porque ejecutan con felicísima diligencia, mas no valen para mandar, porque piensan mal y eligen peor, tropezando siempre en el desacierto. Hay hombres de todos géneros, unos para primeros y otros para segundos" (*El discreto, discurso* 21, p. 330).

28. Cf. Gracián, who elevates *gusto* to the level of a "science": "Un modo de ciencia es éste que no le enseñan los libros ni se aprende en las escuelas; cúrsase en los teatros del buen gusto y en el tan general tan singular de la discreción. Hállanse unos hombres apreciadores de todo sazonado dicho y observadores de todo galante hecho. . . . Estos son los oráculos de la curiosidad y maestros de la *ciencia del buen gusto*" (*El discreto, discurso* 5, p. 63, "Hombre de plausibles noticias: Razonamiento académico"; this title duplicates that of the *Oráculo manual,* sec. 22, which nonetheless does not mention the "ciencia del buen gusto").

29. Andrée Collard writes that "aside from arguments about changes in practice and custom that cause change in art, the notion of *good taste* becomes generalized, which occupies a preeminent place in the criticism of culteranism and in critical language in general. Herrera uses it already with reference to the pleasure that is derived from the reading of some beautiful pages: the ancients 'travajaron por el gusto y aprovechamiento de todos' " (*Nueva poesía* 20). The reference to

Herrera is to the *Anotaciones* to the poetry of Garcilaso de la Vega, in Antonio Gallego Morell, *Garcilaso de la Vega y sus comentaristas*, 581.

30. At the same time, one must recognize that Sancho's abandonment of his governorship represents a rejection of these "civilizing" pretenses and a "return" to the "natural" world of needs.

31. "El vulgo las oye con gusto, y las tiene y las aprueba por buenas, estando tan lejos de serlo, y los autores que las componen y los actores que las representan dicen que así han de ser, porque así las quiere el vulgo, y no de otra manera, y que las que llevan y trazan y siguen la fábula como el arte pide, no sirven sino para cuatro discretos que las entienden, y todos los demás se quedan ayunos de entender su artificio, y que a ellos les está mejor ganar de comer con los muchos, que no opinión con los pocos" (*Don Quixote* 1.48, p. 568).

32. La poesía . . . es como una doncella tierna y de poca edad, y en todo extremo hermosa, a quien tienen cuidado de enriquecer, pulir y adornar otras muchas doncellas, que son todas las otras ciencias, y ella se ha de servir de todas, y todas se han de autorizar con ella; pero esta tal doncella no quiere ser manoseada, ni traída por las calles, ni publicada por las esquinas de las plazas ni por los rincones de los palacios. Ella es hecha de una alquimia de tal virtud, que quien la sabe tratar la volverá en oro purísimo de inestimable precio; hala de tener, el que la tuviere, a raya, no dejándola correr en torpes sátiras ni en desalmados sonetos; no ha de ser vendible en ninguna manera, si ya no fuere en poemas heroicos, en lamentables tragedias, o en comedias alegres y artificiosas. No se ha de dejar tratar de trujanes, ni del ignorante vulgo, incapaz de conocer ni estimar los tesoros que en ella se encierran. Y no penséis, señor, que yo llamo aquí vulgo solamente a la gente plebeya y humilde; que todo aquel que no sabe, aunque sea señor y príncipe, puede y debe entrar en número del vulgo" (*Don Quixote* 2.16, p. 155).

33. Gracián, *El criticón* 179. From Gracián's scorn of common ignorance to Flaubert's great fear of *bétise*, which culminates in a work like *Bouvard et Pécuchet*, is but a short step.

34. But compare the following passage from *El discreto*: "Es lisonja la novedad, hechiza el gusto, y con solo variar de sainete, se renuevan los objectos [*sic*], que es gran arte de agradar" (*El discreto, discurso* 22, p. 335).

35. "*De la gran sindéresis.* Es el trono de la razón, basa de la prudencia, que en fe della cuesta poco el acertar. Es suerte del cielo, y más deseada por primera y por mejor: la primera pieza del arnés, con tal urgencia que ninguna otra que le falte a un hombre le denomina falto; nótase más su menos. Todas las acciones de la vida dependen de su influencia y todas solicitan su calificación, que todo ha de ser con seso. Consiste en una conatural propensión a todo lo más conforme a razón, casándose siempre con lo más acertado" (*OM*, sec. 96, p. 398).

36. See Robert Klein, "Judgment and Taste in Cinquecento Art Theory," in *Form and Meaning: Writings on the Renaissance and Modern Art* (Princeton: Princeton University Press, 1981), 161–169. In *The Judgment of Sense* David Summers provides a succinct conceptual genealogy of "common sense" in which there are striking connections between ancient philosophy and early modern thought: "The modern notion of common sense retained its connection with spirit, embracing the Stoic notions of *oikeiosis* [an implanted feeling or affinity, not a product of custom or habit], the self-evident principles of human society and of *koinos nous*, common reason undisfigured by sophistication, combining them with the Stoic

koinai ennoiai (or common notions, which Locke rejected as 'innate'), and 'common conceptions of the mind,' as writers of the Middle Ages had called the axioms of Euclidean geometry. The philosophy of the common sense school incorporated these traditional elements.... The 'common conceptions' were supplemented by the newly self-evident principles of modern natural science, which in turn magnified and solidified the authority of the common sense as a criterion. In these ways common sense grew closer to reason, from which reason might proceed" (328–329).

37. Descartes, *Discourse on the Method,* I, p. 111.

38. Several recent studies point out the ways in which various forms of interior speech came into play in the *asujetissement* of New World subjects. See especially Jorge Klor de Alva, "Colonizing Souls: The Failure of the Indian Inquisition and the Rise of Penitential Discipline," in Mary Elizabeth Perry and Anne J. Cruz., eds., *Cultural Encounters: The Impact of the Inquisition on Spain and the New World* (Berkeley: University of California Press, 1991), 3–22. Some of this work has recently been brought to bear on Peninsular texts, such as Cervantes's *El celoso extremeño.* See James D. Fernández, "The Bonds of Patrimony: Cervantes and the New World," *PMLA* 109 (1994): 969–981.

39. Kant, *Foundations of the Metaphysics of Morals,* trans. Lewis White Beck, ed. Robert Paul Wolff (Indianapolis: Bobbs-Merrill, 1969), 23.

40. See MacIntyre, *After Virtue* 44.

Works Cited

Aquinas, Saint Thomas. *Summa Theologica.* Trans. Fathers of the English Dominican Province. New York: Benziger, 1947–48.

Aristotle. *The Nicomachean Ethics.* Trans. David Ross; Rev. J. L. Ackrill and J. O. Urmson. New York: Oxford University Press, 1980.

Borgerhoff, E. B. O. *The Freedom of French Classicism.* Princeton: Princeton University Press, 1950.

Bourdieu, Pierre. *Distinction: A Social Critique of the Judgement of Taste.* Trans. Richard Nice. London: Routledge and Kegan Paul, 1984.

Cascardi, Anthony J. "Poetry as Political Foundationalism; or, The Dangers of Discursive Dominance." *Modern Language Quarterly* 54.3 (September 1993): 393–404.

Caygill, Howard. *Art of Judgment.* Oxford: Basil Blackwell, 1989.

Cervantes Saavedra, Miguel de. *Don Quixote de la Mancha.* Ed. Luis Murillo. Madrid: Castalia, 1986. Trans. J. M. Cohen. Harmondsworth: Penguin Books, 1950.

Collard, Andrée. *Nueva poesía: conceptismo, culteranismo en la crítica española.* Madrid and Waltham, Mass.: Editorial Castalia and Brandeis University, 1967.

Corominas, Joan. *Diccionario crítico etimológico castellano e hispánico.* Madrid: Gredos, 1954–57.

Croce, Benedetto. *Storia dell' Eta Barocca in Italia.* Bari: Laterza, 1957.

Descartes, René. *Discourse on the Method.* In *The Philosophical Writings of Descartes.* Cambridge: Cambridge University Press, 1985.

Elias, Norbert. *Power and Civility.* New York: Pantheon, 1976.

Ferguson, Frances. *Solitude and the Sublime: Romanticism and the Aesthetics of Individuation.* New York: Routledge, 1992.

Freud, Sigmund. "Negation." In *The Standard Edition of the Complete Psychological Works of Sigmund Freud.* London: Hogarth Press, 1953–74.
Gadamer, Hans-Georg. *Truth and Method.* New York: Continuum, 1975.
Gallego Morell, Antonio. *Garcilaso de la Vega y sus comentaristas.* Granada: Publicaciones de la Universidad de Granada, 1966. 2nd ed., Madrid: Gredos, 1972.
Gracián, Baltasar. *El criticón.* Ed. P. Ismael Quiles. Madrid: Espasa Calpe, 1964.
———. *El discreto.* Ed. Luys Santa Marina. Barcelona: Planeta, 1984.
———. *El héroe.* Ed. Arturo del Hoyo Martínez. Barcelona: Plaza y Janés, 1986.
———. *Oráculo manual.* Ed. Arturo del Hoyo Martínez. Barcelona: Plaza y Janés, 1986. Trans. Christopher Maurer. *The Art of Worldly Wisdom: A Pocket Oracle.* New York: Doubleday/Currency, 1992.
Hafter, Monroe. *Gracián and Perfection.* Cambridge: Harvard University Press, 1966.
Heidegger, Martin. *Kant and the Problem of Metaphysics.* Trans. Richard Taft. Bloomington: Indiana University Press, Studies in Continental Thought, 1990.
Kant, Immanuel. *Critique of Judgement.* Trans. James Meredith. Oxford: Oxford University Press, 1986.
Reiss, Timothy. *The Meaning of Literature.* Ithaca: Cornell University Press, 1992.
Summers, David. *The Judgment of Sense: Renaissance Naturalism and the Rise of Aesthetics.* Cambridge: Cambridge University Press, 1987.
Wellek, René. *A History of Modern Criticism.* New Haven: Yale University Press, 1955.
Zuccolo, Ludovico. *Dialoghi.* Venezia, 1625.

Part IV
Politics of Everyday Life

Chapter 11
The Art of Worldly Wisdom as an Ethics of Conversation

Carlos Hernández-Sacristán
(translated by Paul Derrick)

In this essay I aim to show how Gracián's *Oráculo manual y arte de prudencia* can be read in the light of a sociology of everyday life, such as that developed by Erving Goffman and his followers.[1] This is not, of course, to say that the conceptual world of Gracián's work is comparable to that of Goffman's. Nevertheless, they do address the same objective, as both of them analyze the social encounter from the point of view of the subject involved in it. This shared objective also leads to several other common issues: what kind of practical knowledge guides our interaction with others, how another's knowledge comes to form a part of our own knowledge, how this knowledge is, as well, part of the reality of the social encounter, and how this reality, finally, determines another, that of the subject—Goffman's "self" or Gracián's "persona"—which does not exist apart from the social encounter it participates in.

It should be stressed that this kind of interpretation of Gracián's work is in no way meant to be exclusive. It is not my purpose to deny other possible readings that may even contradict my own. I hope, however, that the interpretation here proposed is not merely an "ad hoc" attempt to force Gracián's thinking into compliance with modern sensibility. Certainly, it does seem necessary to explore the implicit meaning of Gracián's text, even though that meaning may not always agree with what is literally expressed. But then, isn't that the aim of a hermeneutic approach? Not only *what* is said is significant, but also how and when, and in Gracián these two levels of signification can often be contradictory.

A similar idea was expressed in García-Gibert and Hernández-Sacristán (1991), where we concluded that in his *Criticón,* Gracián combines a literalness that manifests the gnoseological framework of realism, that is, an essentialist philosophy, with a type of discourse and an implicit sense that are nominalist. What the spirit of Gracián's exposition least resembles is a scholastic treatise. The nonessential and merely occasional nature of all reality is clearly manifested in his argumentative form, particularly in the treatises. The reader of these works is never allowed to discover any kind of thematic organization. Since individual objects do not really constitute global structures, since they are determined by their circumstances, there cannot really be thematic structures either, but only a pure and simple discursive praxis. Something similar to this can be found in Goffman's procedure of anecdotal exposition.

Especially in *El criticón,* expressions of censure and pessimism before a changing world dominated by the perspective of individuals can be understood as a subterfuge we use to be able to speak precisely of this kind of world, perhaps the only terrestrial world whose existence we believe in. It is paradoxical that the more irremediable the supposed "perversion" of the world appears to be, the more the unavoidable reality of this world is implicitly confirmed, and to this must be added the fact that Gracián's hero does not withdraw from the world but adopts, instead, a clear worldly vocation.

The moral treatises, and particularly the *Oráculo,* which are less pessimistic in tone than *El criticón,* speak of a kind of dialogical knowledge that is relative to specific social encounters, especially to conversations, which are paradigms of social encounters. This dialogical—and therefore relativistic and antidogmatic—knowledge is clearly opposed to the framework of realism, that is, to the framework of revealed truth. Even so, Gracián respects this framework when he represents relativistic knowledge only as a defense mechanism that the wise man would employ against the strategies of the enemy. This is, however, another subterfuge, as

I shall try to demonstrate, since the alleged enemy is rather a subject with whom we are obliged to maintain a cooperative attitude in the cultivation of our practical knowledge and on whom our realization as persons finally depends.

The implicit sense of Gracián's texts contradicts, to some extent, their literal sense. The pessimistic tone may be understood as a way to conceal what is really being stated; the enemy may actually be a subject we cooperate with in order to discover a hidden or veiled knowledge. But none of this necessarily implies that Gracián was aware of these contradictions, or that his contemporary readers were. It should be pointed out, however, that there was at least a suspicion of such contradictions, as the well-known reservations against Gracián's work and the author's cautions clearly reveal. In any case, more important for us as modern readers is the fact that these contradictions are expressed in Gracián's text and, further, that they open up the text to a hermeneutic approach that should augment and enrich our understanding of it.

When, well into the *Oráculo,* the reader attempts to imagine a referent for the thoughts and actions being described, that is, to connect them with some kind of real space, he naturally thinks about specific social encounters in which the subjects to whom these thoughts or actions are attributed exchange words or gestures. Undoubtedly many, if not all, aspects of Gracián's knowledge and ethics are decided within the confines of the social encounters that we know as conversations. On several occasions Gracián refers to conversation as the generating matrix, or palestra, in which the rules of discrete action, or doing, are discovered:

> Sabiduría conversable valióles más a algunos que todas las siete, con ser tan liberales. (Aphorism 22)[2]
>
> [Conversable wisdom was more useful for some than all the seven arts, no matter how liberal.]

> *Tener el arte de conversar*: en que se hace muestra de ser persona. En ningún ejercicio humano se requiere más la atención, por ser el más ordinario del vivir. (Aphorism 148)
>
> [*To have the art of conversation*: in which one shows himself as a person. No other human exercise requires more attention, precisely because it is the most common thing in life.]

Conversation is the basis not only of knowledge, but of a pleasurable form of knowledge, as Gracián makes clear from the first passages of the *Oráculo*:

> Sea el amigable trato escuela de erudición, y la conversación enseñanza culta; un hacer de los amigos maestros, penetrando el útil del aprender con el gusto del conversar. (In aphorism 11)
>
> [Let your dealings with your friends be a school of erudition, and conversation a cultured teaching; to make teachers of your friends, suffusing the usefulness of learning with the pleasure of conversation.]

How should we understand that "conversable wisdom" ("sabiduría conversable") that Gracián speaks of? It could be, first of all, a knowledge relative to the rules of conversational exchanges, the observance of which permits individuals to preserve or improve their social image. Certainly, the central interest of microsociological studies is the defense of a social image that is always potentially vulnerable in any social encounter and, in particular, in any conversational exchange. Most of those rules that supposedly represent the kind of knowledge that is implicit in conversational praxis have to do with the notion of preference,[3] which, in turn, has to do with the notion of courtesy. Everything seems to center on those mechanisms that operate for the purpose of avoiding the introduction of conversational turns that might damage the social image of the interlocutors.

This defensive concept of conversational technique also holds for Gracián, but it is complemented by another, more belligerent concept of conversation.[4] Gracián designs a technique that would, more than preserve the social image, improve it, and this by means of a sort of militant attention that allows us to emerge victorious from the social encounter conceived as a theater of operations. It should, however, be pointed out that the existence of a victorious party does not necessarily imply the existence of a defeated one. To win, for Gracián, normally means to obtain the applause and respect of others. Only rarely does he construe the interactive strategy as a direct attack on someone.

The social encounters Gracián describes would be a kind of "podium" (cf. Goffman, "Footing") from which the social, and in most cases, verbal activity of a subject, although directed to a specific participant, is observed and evaluated by other nonratified, occasionally present participants. An awareness of the evaluation of these nonratified persons clearly determines one's own performance. What Gracián refers to as discretion must surely be understood as a discrete exhibition.

Gracián deals explicitly with diverse aspects of conversational technique. Aphorism 164 clearly formulates the equivalent of the strategy known in conversational analysis as the introduction of presequences:[5]

> *Echar al aire algunas cosas.* Para examinar la aceptación, un ver cómo se reciben, y más las sospechosas de acierto y de agrado. Asegúrase el salir bien y queda lugar o para el empeño o para el retiro. Tanteánse las voluntades desta suerte, y sabe el atento dónde tiende los pies: prevención máxima del pedir, del querer y del gobernar.
>
> [*Casting a few things into the air.* To examine the acceptance, seeing how they are received, and especially those suspicious of being appropriate and pleasing. This assures a good result and leaves room either for insistence or retreat. The intentions are assayed in this way, and the attentive man knows where his feet are: maximum caution before requesting, willing, and governing.]

Presequences are described in conversational analysis as turns with a prospective function that a speaker might launch (as Gracián puts it, "casting a few things into the air" ["echar al aire algunas cosas"]) to avoid the later introduction of unwanted turns, which, to a greater or lesser degree, could damage her or his social image. Before offering an invitation, for example, we assure ourselves through the conversational mechanism of the "preinvitation" that certain conditions for the acceptance of the offer are met. On the basis of the response to a preinvitation, the "inviter" can opt, in Gracián's terms, for "insistence" ("empeño") or "retreat" ("retiro"). By "empeño" he means proffering an invitation that we expect to be accepted, and by "retiro" he means avoiding the invitation or framing it in the conditional if we expect it to be turned down. In this way the interlocutor is spared the embarrassment of having to refuse the invitation.

The fundamental effect of "casting a few things into the air," like that of "presequences," is double. They can be considered simply as a preventive measure that allows us to proceed more securely in social life, but they are, at the same time, a way to avoid forcing another's will. Gracián is fundamentally concerned with winning the applause of others and not with forcing their will, a way of acting proper not only to someone in a subordinate position, who needs to ask for a favor, but also to someone in the position of a prince. To govern, in effect, is to move wills; it is not a matter of imposing oneself on others. To force others, even if they may not be impolite in their reply, is to lose credit before them.

Another's will can be forced in the very domain of his or her verbal activity. In aphorism 141 Gracián criticizes those who continually solicit the approval of their listeners as they embark on relating something. For while it is normal for the speaker to make brief pauses to seek the listeners' approval, the forcing of such signs by the narrator is a clear pathway to being discredited:

> Achaque de señores es hablar con el bordón del "¿digo algo?" y aquel "¿eh?" que aporrea a los que le escuchan; a cada razón orejean la aprobación o la lisonja, apurando la cordura. También los hinchados hablan con eco, y como su conversación va en chapines de entono, a cada palabra solicita el enfadoso socorro del necio "¡bien dicho!"
>
> [An ailment of gentlemen is to speak with pet words like "Am I making any sense?" and that "eh?" which pummels the listener; they hang on approval or flattery with every sentence they say, draining good sense. Swell-heads also speak with an echo, and since their conversation walks on resounding clogs, every word solicits the maddening aid of a foolish "well said!"]

On more than one occasion, Gracián also turns his attention to the interlocutor who is obliged to give an unwanted (nonpreferred) response and also manages to suggest how this kind of conversational turn can be "softened." Such is particularly the case with aphorism 70: "Know how to refuse" ("Saber negar"). Any refusal should be wisely administered, since the act of negation is essential to anyone's credit. A circumspect refusal, one that postpones the concession of what is requested without completely denying it, is the wise man's response. In this way, the petitioner's self-esteem is preserved and, thus, the fundamental social relationship is not threatened, enabling the request to be made again at some later date:

> No se han de negar de rondón las cosas; vaya a tragos el desengaño; ni se ha de negar del todo, que sería desahuciar la dependencia.
>
> [Do not simply refuse things; mete out disappointments in small sips; nor refuse completely, which would kill all dependence forever.]

When some concrete transaction between individuals fails, the wise man is asked to make use of some mechanism to repair or preserve the foundation that makes other transactions possible. It is observed in conversational analysis that the introduction of an unwanted turn is a marked linguistic operation. The denial of a request or the refusal of an invitation are preceded by an initial pause, which is meant to indicate either real or feigned awkwardness, or by explanations and postponements. All of this serves as a warning, permitting the petitioner or inviter to correct their turns, phrase them in the conditional, or search for an honorable withdrawal from the situation. The refusing party should make it possible for the petitioner or inviter to retire with as much dignity as possible. In any case, directing the social encounter such that the social image of the other is preserved is a way to gain credit. This is particularly true in those cases where a subordinate is obliged to refuse the prince's request or invitation. But the prince would also diminish his own credit by "discouraging the dependence" of his subordinates with categorical refusals.

When circumstances require it, the tactic of misunderstanding may be used as a signal to the attentive petitioner or inviter to desist. Misunderstanding or misinterpreting become, in this way, a kind of cooperative understanding that allows the social relationship to continue even though a specific transaction fails. This tactic is explicitly described in aphorism 73:

> Cortés treta del negar mudar el verbo, ni hay mayor atención que no darse por entendido.
>
> [Courteous ruse of refusal to change the subject, and there is no greater form of attention than not willing to understand.]

In a different sense, "conversable wisdom" would also be a knowledge that is necessarily expressed either from the perspective of a speaker or from the perspective of a listener. Although this kind of knowledge is relative to one of these two perspectives, it can be transposed from one to the other, thus being continually enriched. In other words, we can also say that it is a knowledge that always has the others' knowledge as a reference. This is undoubtedly not a monological knowledge that a transcendent source reveals to the individual. One's knowledge can only be constituted and perform its basic function of improving one's condition as person, in the light of another intelligence. If anything terrifies the author of the *Oráculo manual,* it is precisely the thought of having to cope with passive spectators or listeners in the world. It is most probably true that the less intelligent our interlocutors or competitors are, the higher our chances of social triumph, and surrounding oneself with mediocrities is a well-known method of maintaining or even augmenting a position of power. But this is not the kind of triumph that interests Gracián. Although it may be paradoxical, Gracián seems to fear the common and mediocre spectator/listener more than the active and keen one. The presence of a keen spectator and his or her perceived power of interpretation constitute a dynamic stimulus to a knowledge that is in a constant process of redefinition, a knowledge that is not "ergon" but "energeia," one that is continually adapting itself to the particular occasion or social encounter in which it operates.

Although most of the aphorisms take the viewpoint of the actor/speaker, there are also those that deal specifically with the viewpoint of the spectator/listener, like number 215: "Beware of the man with hidden intentions" ("atención al que llega de segunda intención") (we might say the same of aphorism 73, cited earlier). Now as I have already pointed out, Gracián's knowledge can move from one perspective to the other. The interpretive rule that I use as a spectator/listener in one encounter can determine my activity as an actor/speaker in another, and vice versa. Aphorism 13, "To act with a purpose, sometimes covert, sometimes overt" ("Obrar de intención, ya segunda y ya primera"), clearly expresses how the strategy we suppose another to assume comes to form a part of our own strategy, how the artifice of one's own behavior increases to the degree that one perceives the artifice in another, and, finally, how this dialectic game, which has its inevitable limits (as seen by Goffman, *Strategic Interaction*; cf. also Wolf 58–61), ends up turning naturalness itself into another artifice:

> Auméntase la simulación al ver alcanzado su artificio, y pretende engañar con la misma verdad. Muda de juego, por mudar de treta, y hace artificio del no artificio, fundando su astucia en la mayor candidez.
>
> [A pretense is augmented if its artifice is discovered, and attempts to deceive with the truth itself. By changing ruses, it changes games, making artifice from nonartifice and founding its cleverness in the greatest ingenuousness.]

Concealing a strategy with natural behavior is, of course, essential to the strategy's success, but the dialectic between my own knowledge and that of the other sooner or later forces the natural behavior to exhibit rather than conceal the strategy.

An important aspect for evaluating the attitudes of the participants in all social, and especially conversational, encounters is the kind of power relationships they establish among themselves. A decisive part of our common social knowledge is the recognition of our position of power with respect to other participants in the social encounter and what bias the rules of interaction assume as a result. Many of Gracián's aphorisms explicitly adopt one or the other of these two perspectives, either that of the subordinate or that of the prince. But it should also be pointed out here that the art of prudence is a dynamic form of knowledge that grows as it shifts from one perspective to the other. One can be prince or subordinate, depending on the particular encounter, and it is prudent to be prepared to take on either role and, above all, to make good use of what one knows as a subordinate when acting as prince, and vice versa. The inability to transfer roles also leads to discredit (compare in this respect aphorism 74).

The essentially dialogical foundation of Gracianian knowledge, which demands a conjunction of the perspectives of both actor/speaker and spectator/hearer, also demands the joint evaluation of the perspectives of the prince and the subordinate. This allows the development of an ethics based on cooperation between different social ranks. Power is never unidirectional, because its exercise is based on personal credit, and personal credit is always granted by others. The individual can and should continually look for the kinds of social encounters or occasions that facilitate the concession of credit, but must never explicitly demand it. This obliges one who holds power always to exercise it from the perspective of the subordinate.

In reality, the basic role of "person" in the social sphere neutralizes the roles of prince and subordinate. How to behave with a prince and how to be one, although they correspond to two different perspectives, are two kinds of practical knowledge that interpenetrate to form a unified framework. In any case, though, if any one of these two terms can be considered to be unmarked, it is undoubtedly that of the prince. In other words, in the basic role of "person" the art of prudence always emphasizes the condition of prince over that of subordinate. All of a person's social activity is directed toward augmenting his or her credit and thus, as well, augmenting his or her moral authority over others, even when a particular occasion requires that he or she act as a subordinate.

The princely model of action should, according to Gracián, suffuse all social activity. The courtly situation is paradigmatic for all kinds of social encounters, as we can see in aphorism 103:

> *Cada uno la majestad en su modo.* Sean todas las acciones, si no de un rey, dignas de tal, según su esfera.
>
> [*To each his own kind of majesty.* All actions, if not those of a king, should be worthy of a king, according to one's own sphere.]

Or in aphorism 122:

> *Señorío en el decir y en el hacer.* Hácese mucho lugar en todas partes y gana de antemano el respeto. En todo influye: en el conversar, en el orar, hasta en el caminar y aun en el mirar y en el querer.
>
> [*Lordliness in speaking and doing.* It makes itself a place wherever it goes and earns respect in advance. It influences everything: conversation, prayer, even walking and looking and willing.]

Gracián is referring here to the whole range of social encounters, from the encounter with the divinity in prayer, to more common conversational situations, to, finally, nonverbal encounters based on physical presence itself and its symbolic values. In this sense, Gracián is clearly a sociologist of everyday life, or a microsociologist "avant la lettre," although his theoretical position is more normative than descriptive. Even so, what the sociologist of everyday life describes are internalized norms of action by which the subject preserves in any social encounter his own or another's condition as person. The fundamental difference between Gracián's theoretical position and that of the modern sociologist of everyday life is not really that between a normative and a descriptive science. In both cases, knowledge is expressed by describing norms, and it can be said that the description of a norm is a norm for whoever chooses to take it as such. The fundamental difference lies in the fact that, as already mentioned above, Gracián describes norms that not only preserve one's condition as person, something of central interest for everyday life sociologies, but also permit the improvement of this condition.

Authors like Goffman are concerned with the study of repair mechanisms that come into play when the social image has deteriorated, or strategies that permit us to avoid the dangers that the social image is subject to in social encounters. Gracián also deals with all this, but his fundamental concern is those strategies that would improve the social image. It is possible, however, to see the question otherwise: Goffman's strategies and Gracián's are essentially the same, although their effect for the sociologists of everyday life would be to preserve the quality of the person, while for Gracián their effect would be to augment it.

This difference is related to another essential difference in the assumptions used to describe social encounters. I have already pointed out that Gracián recognizes a paradigm of the social encounter that serves as a criterion for the evaluation of any other encounters. This paradigm can be initially understood as the courtly encounter, that established between the sovereign and his or her subordinates. Social knowledge would be amplified in the courtly space, where the highest levels of social credit, as well as the lowest levels of discredit, would be obtained. The wise man and the fool are wiser and more foolish in the court.

One might come to think that Gracián situates the divine above this mundane courtly space and that, in this sense, the relationship between man and the divinity could also offer a paradigm of social encounters. But this relationship lacks obviously any interchangeability of perspectives and, therefore, it is not easy to think of it as such a paradigm. In any case, it is certain that for Gracián the experience of the social encounter is teleologically guided by some model, either mundane or transcendental. This kind of orientation explains the person's continuous drive to improve his or her condition or to augment his or her credit, and differs considerably from the common assumptions of sociologies of everyday life. In these, the most trivial daily situation seems to be able to explain itself without any paradigm. For Gracián, the subject is physically and mentally involved in his or her social encounters, but at the same time transcends them, experiencing them from the perspective of the courtly (perhaps divine) encounter.

The conceptualization of power is closely related to that of the practice of justice. Here we can say that both Goffman's and Gracián's conceptions are quite similar, if not identical. The errors committed in the interactive scene (Gracián is not interested in private vice) convert it into a kind of court of law where the transgressor is summarily tried and receives discredit as his or her punishment (Goffman, *Relations in Public* 137; cf. also Wolf 85–90).

Morality and justice are the same for Gracián and Goffman: both are founded on the believability of the self or person, understood as a subject involved in the construction of social reality. Both authors affirm that a cooperative attitude is required for the construction of this reality, which, although it may be a fiction, is the only one there is. Those errors or failures of attention, whether voluntary or not, that can leave us simply without reality, are a result of the inability to maintain this cooperative attitude, and they are punished with discredit and the social isolation of the transgressor.

For Gracián, the subject and his or her knowledge are dialogical realities, that is, they are constructed out of the specific social encounters in which they are involved. This is evidenced, as well, in some common formulas for conceptualizing the person and his or her art of prudence. Prudence has to do with the analysis of the transactional capacities of all participants in a social encounter. The subject must be aware of what he or she can give and receive from another in order to be able to offer or request in the proper measure. The value of both material and spiritual goods is not intrinsic, but is, instead, and from an apparently mercantile point of view, obtained in the transaction itself and, therefore, relative to the social encounter they are involved in.

> *Saber vender sus cosas.* No basta la intrínseca bondad dellas, que no todos muerden la substancia ni miran por dentro. Acuden los más a donde hay concurso; van porque ven ir a otros. Es gran parte del artificio saber acreditar. (Aphorism 150)
>
> [*Know how to sell your things.* Their intrinsic value is not enough; not everybody bites the substance or looks inside. The most people go where there is hustle and bustle; they go because they see others go. A large part of artifice is knowing how to give credit.]

Given that the value of any particular good depends on the transaction in which it is involved, it is also fundamentally the product of a certain dialogical or interactive strategy. Veiling one's own goods, making them seem scarce, whether abundant or not in reality, is an indispensable means of augmenting their value.

> *Incomprehensibilidad de caudal.* Excuse el varón atento sondarle el fondo, ya al saber, ya al valer, si quiere que le veneren todos: permítase al conocimiento, no a la comprehensión. Nadie le averigüe los términos de la capacidad, por el peligro evidente del desengaño. Nunca dé lugar a que alguno le alcance todo: mayores afectos de veneración causa la opinión y duda de adónde llega el caudal de cada uno que la evidencia dél, por grande que fuere. (Aphorism 94)
>
> [*Unfathomable store.* The wise man must not sound the depths of his knowledge or his value, if he wants to be venerated by all: let himself be known but not comprehended. He must not let the terms of his capacity be ascertained, because of the evident danger that others may be disillusioned. He must never permit anyone to reach everything he has. The opinion and doubt as to the

> limits of each one's store cause greater effects of veneration than the evidence of those limits, no matter how extensive they may be.]

But veiling one's goods can also be understood as a polite form of exhibiting oneself to another, and even something more than a polite form. This is not such a selfish ruse as it might at first glance seem, but, in a certain sense, a means of acknowledging that the value of one's own goods, spiritual as well as material, ultimately depends upon the other. The fact that our spiritual goods, our "knowing" and "valuing," are negotiated is, either thanks to or in spite of the mercantile metaphor, a clear expression of antidogmatism. Gracián's antidogmatic attitude in the sphere of knowledge corresponds to a clearly antidespotic attitude in the sphere of power: my power, as we have already seen, also derives from the fact that others recognize it as such.

What may at first sight appear to be the simple astuteness with which one protects his own interests is, in reality, a clear recognition of the role of the other, of his or her intelligence or will. In aphorism 3 Gracián says:

> El jugar a juego descubierto, ni es de utilidad, ni de gusto. El no declararse luego suspende, y más donde la sublimidad del empleo da objeto a la universal expectación, amaga misterio en todo y con su misma arcanidad provoca la veneración.
>
> [To play at an open game is neither useful nor pleasurable. Not declaring oneself creates suspense and, especially where the sublimity of the office causes universal expectation, gives the impression of a pervasive mystery, and its very arcaneness provokes veneration.]

Although a hiding that misleads may surpass the limits of the ethically acceptable, veiling the truth is the mechanism that makes the truth valuable. The veiled is always intrinsically attractive. The interlocutor will always be willing to accept a certain truth when it is somewhat concealed, that is, when some amount of intellectual activity is required to discover it. In this way, we can manage to make others believe that a truth we formulate is really theirs. Plainly to offer a truth is to deny the interlocutor any active role in the encounter and thus to belittle his or her intellectual capacity and condition as person. Veiling, understood as one of the virtues of prudence, would therefore have a double dimension: respect for the referred reality, which we can thus come to venerate, and respect for the other participant in the social encounter, whose intellectual capacities and condition of person are thus implicitly recognized.

The improvement of both my own social image and the social image of my interlocutor, the exercise of the rules of interaction, demands a margin of maneuver that can only be obtained on the level of the implicit. Literalness nullifies the interlocutor's ability to maneuver and, at the same time, the real progress of an interactive praxis such as a conversation. The existence of the implicit is what truly justifies a cooperative attitude among the interlocutors and maintains their interest, thus creating a real conversational dynamism.

There exists in Gracián, although it is not literally expressed, what can be called a proposal of cooperative construction of social reality. The assumption that this reality is dialogically constructed clearly situates Gracián in the nominalist gnoseological framework, as opposed to the realist one. Since the only literalness Gracián admits is that of realism, or philosophical essentialism, he must literally express disillusion or pessimism before the negotiable character of all-that-is. But through this formula he can also suggest antidogmatism, antidespotism, or, in general, a cooperative attitude in the construction of all social realities. Another question—as I have already pointed out—is whether the author or his contemporaries could have made this reading of Gracián's text. If the value of goods is not intrinsic, if it is negotiated in social encounters, this circumstance can only be conceptualized as a protest in an essentialist gnoseological framework. But a protest that recognizes the irremediable character of the situation it denounces presupposes, to some extent, the acknowledgment that the censured reality is very different from anything an essentialist framework can describe.

The "disqualification of innocence," as Wolf (19) characterizes Goffman's work, also becomes in Gracián's work a critical attitude that helps us to understand the social reality. The set of fictions and strategies employed cooperatively by the participants in a social encounter should be properly considered as a set of instruments for a critical approach to reality (cf. Wolf 65). Instruments of knowledge are as well, for Gracián, a part of the very reality that they apprehend, in that they permit us to construct that reality. What enables us to speak of Gracianian reality as dialogical is precisely the fact that the kind of knowledge that constitutes it is also dialogical.

But not only knowledge is conversable; the very reality of the subject involved in a social encounter is, as well. The subject of knowledge discovers himself as a reality that must be constructed in his dialogical relationship with the other. The "person" of the *Oráculo* can be defined, on the basis of the etymological sense of the term, as a subject that speaks, that speaks naturally with another and to whom, as a consequence, another directs his or her speech. In other words, the person is not only a subject who participates in social encounters, but is also a product of them. What is submitted, therefore, to negotiation with the other is not only material or spiritual goods, but also one's own identity, which does not exist beyond the confines of the social encounters.

If some essential subject exists beyond or outside of social interactions, it is of no interest to Gracián, in that it is not cooperative and there is no reason to exhibit it. Goffman clearly shares this point of view (see Wolf 62). Whenever Gracián alludes to the solitary subject, he qualifies it as superhuman or monstrous. If the subject is beyond the control that social interaction exercises, it is either mad or attended by the divinity.

That the person has no true psychological base, that his or her reality is problematical, "in fieri," none of this necessarily denies the person, at least on the metaphorical level, the aura of a sacred reality, which demands sincere veneration from others (see Lenz 281 for the Goffmanian point of view). The power he or she holds or fights for is extremely spiritualized, in the sense that it is based on the acknowledgment by others of a moral authority and is not the result of any imposition. The sacred, or potentially sacred, character of a person is confirmed in many of Gracián's passages. See, for example, aphorism 3, mentioned earlier.

Gracián does not, however, think of the legion of adorers as merely passive subjects, but as very attentive and worthy of attention. A person does not simply possess sacred qualities; rather, they are continually subject to debate in conversation with others, who are also persons. The sacred is also constructed, preserved, and emphasized through cooperation. This is the ultimate meaning of Gracián's elitism.

Notes

1. I am referring here to works such as Goffman's. Goffman's followers in a large sense are the scholars who developed Conversational Analysis, although they are also directly connected with the epistemological framework of ethnomethodology promoted by Harold Garfinkel. Many of these scholars, such as Harvey Sacks, Emanuel Schegloff, Roy Turner, and Matthew Speier, were students of Goffman. (See Bergmann for detailed information about the relations between Goffman and his disciples.)

2. The quotations used here are from *Obras completas.*

3. A preferred conversational turn among several other possibilities in a conversational position is the most frequent and least linguistically marked solution and the one that preserves to the greatest degree the social image of the interlocutors. See Levinson for the basic concepts of conversational analysis and for later references.

4. Such a belligerent concept is undoubtedly present in the metaphors we use to describe conversational strategies and is, in this sense, a common way to experience conversation, as seen by Lakoff and Johnson.

5. See Levinson for a basic introduction to this concept.

Works Cited

Bergmann, J. "Goffmans Soziologie des Gesprächs und seine ambivalente Beziehung zur Konversationsanalyse." *Erving Goffman: Ein soziologischer Klassiker der zweiten Generation.* Ed. R. Hettlage and K. Lenz. Bern and Stuttgart: Paul Haupt, 1991. 301–326.

García-Gibert, J., and Carlos Hernández-Sacristán. "El razonamiento etimológico como procedimiento discursivo en Baltasar Gracián." *Archivo de Filología Aragonesa* (Zaragoza) 41 (1988): 153–172.

Garfinkel, Harold. *Studies in Ethnomethodology.* Englewood Cliffs, N.J., Prentice-Hall, 1967.

Goffman, Erving. *Strategic Interaction.* Philadephia: University of Pennsylvania Press, 1969.

———. *Relations in Public: Microstudies of the Public Order.* New York: Basic Books, 1971.

———. *Frame Analysis: An Essay on the Organization of Experience.* New York: Harper and Row, 1974.

———. "Footing." *Semiotica* 25 (1979): 1–29.

———. *Forms of Talk.* Philadelphia: University of Pennsylvania Press, 1981.

Gracián, Baltasar. *Obras completas.* Ed. A. del Hoyo. Madrid: Aguilar, 1967.

Hettlage, R., and K. Lenz, eds. *Erving Goffman: Ein soziologischer Klassiker der zweiten Generation.* Bern and Stuttgart: Paul Haupt, 1991.

Lakoff, G., and M. Johnson. *Metaphors We Live By.* Chicago: University of Chicago Press, 1991.

Lenz, K. "Goffman—ein Strukturalist?" *Erving Goffman: Ein soziologischer Klassiker der zweiten Generation.* Ed. R. Hettlage and K. Lenz. Bern and Stuttgart: Paul Haupt, 1991. 243–297.
Levinson, S. *Pragmatics.* Cambridge: Cambridge University Press, 1983.
Wolf, Mauro. *Sociologías de la vida cotidiana.* Madrid: Cátedra, 1988.

Chapter 12
Gracián in the Death Cell

Michael Nerlich
(translated by Michael Shandley)

Gracián and Werner Krauss: A First Possible Discussion

On Gracián Scholarship in Germany

Sebastian Neumeister has recently pointed out that if German Gracián scholarship is particularly solid it is because of Werner Krauss and Hugo Friedrich. Of Krauss he says the following: "In 1943 he was to write the first monograph on Gracián after Borinski.... He [Krauss] understands Gracián as a court psychologist, with a humanistic culture but at the same time as very modern in his pragmatic philosophy. Krauss's book ... is among the best studies of Gracián's work" (121–125, 123). The importance that Neumeister grants to Werner Krauss for the further development of Gracián scholarship in Germany is surprising. For while it is indeed true that his book *Graciáns Lebenslehre* (Gracián's worldly wisdom) is mentioned in every bibliography for reasons of completeness, one has to register a certain degree of doubt regarding its decisive influence on German Gracián scholarship. As unbelievable as it may sound, this unique book received but a single review in Germany, in *Romanische Forschungen* (1950), three years after its appearance in 1947. This sort of neglect was underscored recently by Helmut Lethen (1994), who remarks that in researching his chapter on *Graciáns Lebenslehre* as part of his work on anthropological-philosophical texts and political engagement in the period between the two world wars, he was unable to find further German literature on Krauss (Lethen 54–70).

Lethen was not able to find it because it does not exist. From any perspective this fact is astonishing not only because Neumeister's positive critique is actually justified, but also because we do not have many books on Gracián of equal stature in Germany. Moreover, it could be argued that because of its political and philosophical perspectives Krauss's book is perhaps the most amazing work written on Gracián to date. I would argue further that the story surrounding Krauss's work represents one of the most shameful chapters in reception history. And, since the history of reception—according to modern understanding—is an integral part of the text itself, it is necessary to retrieve what was omitted at the time of its 1947 publication: an appropriate introduction and discussion.

In order to measure the importance of *Graciáns Lebenslehre,* we must take a brief look at German studies on Gracián prior to Werner Krauss. After all, in Germany Gracián had, in Schopenhauer and Nietzsche, two not unimportant readers. All the more astonishing is the fact that this work has been left largely to foreign commentary. Except for Karl Borinski's *Baltasar Gracián und die Hofliteratur in Deutschland* (Baltasar Gracián and courtly literature in Germany, 1894), no other substantial study before Krauss's is to be found. It is also the case that one-third of Borinski's small but thorough book is devoted to Gracián's work. Borinski introduces him as an important stage in the history of political thinking and as the founder of a modern aesthetics based on the emancipation of taste (*gusto*)—a prelude to Kant. It is telling that Borinski's book itself attracted less interest in Germany than elsewhere (with Arturo Farinelli and Benedetto Croce, among others) and was quickly forgotten.

In 1919 Ludwig Pfandl, a German Hispanist in a narrower sense, entered Gracián scholarship with a work on the catalog of the Lastanosas library. He published his study in 1925 in the *Historisches Jahrbuch der Görres-Gesellschaft* (Historical yearbook of the Görres Society), a first attempt at a short general view of Gracián's works, which was later published unchanged in his *Geschichte der spanischen Nationalliteratur in ihrer Blütezeit* (History of Spanish national literature in its Golden Age, 1929). Pfandl tries to distinguish Gracián from Cervantes and Quevedo, viewing him as an unsystematic philosopher and, despite his heterodoxical, pragmatic worldly wisdom, as a "devout Spaniard." He rightly polemicizes against a premature identification of Gracián's hero with the "Führer" or with the superhuman concept à la Carlyle or Nietzsche; he also polemicizes against an identification of Gracián's pessimism with Schopenhauer's "Quietive of the Will," the withdrawal from the world into nonbeing (defined by Pfandl a bit too simplistically as striving toward suicide). Pfandl attempts to lay bare the internal developmental cohesion of Gracián's work and pleads for a study of its reception beyond Borinski's: "Gracián's works," according to Pfandl, "branch themselves off in two directions. The one has as its goal human perfection. The other leads through the painful purification of a pessimistic worldview to greater heights of hope in the beyond" (554). The stylistic analysis of the "means of expression" that Gracián puts forward as a technique of speaking and writing by the ideal human being constitutes the most important part of Pfandl's thoroughly subtle discourse. Pfandl argues against the trend of literary history to project modern definitions of *cultismo* and *conceptismo* onto Gracián's work, countering that *cultismo* and *conceptismo* are eclectically and inseparably bound together in Gracián (551–552).

A year after the publication of Pfandl's important *History,* Leo Spitzer addressed the issue of proper names in Gracián (see his essay in *Romanische Literatur und Stilstudien,* 1931). In 1935 Karl Vossler published an essay in which he praised Gracián for having freed the most uncompromising *conceptismo* from the sterility of rhetoric and turned it into a natural and necessary tool of thinking. This tool, according to Vossler, heaps powerful rhetorical scorn onto earthly affairs while at the same time thoroughly supporting technologies of the moral arts and of the effects on the "quotidian." Yet Vossler also argues that Gracián's apparatus treats otherworldliness as something unnameable, to be approached with respectful silence. After a brief view of Gracián's life, Vossler turns to his reception by Schopenhauer, whose "German answer to the *Oráculo manual*" he called "the most congenial and allocutive" of all time (330–348, 345). In his *Poesie der Einsamkeit in Spanien* (Poetry of loneliness in Spain), which he first published in 1935–38 in the *Sitzungsberichten der Bayerischen Akademie der Wissenschaften* (Proceedings of the Bavarian Academy of Sciences) before publishing it as a book in 1940, Vossler turns to the "solitary man," who is implied in Gracián's scorn and who is explicitly named in *El criticón*. In the society of like-minded intellectuals, the "solitary man" achieves harmonic union. That is, the "solitary man" ascends out of the disillusionment of earthly existence into "the individuality of the rising man." Vossler cannot help but state in this solitude the loss of traditional utopian thinking in idylls. He writes, "The tendency toward solitude belongs to the Renaissance individual's joy in his uniqueness, which eventually wanes into general moralism." Besides this, Vossler denies any assumed dependence of Gracián on Descartes: "For the most part, Gracián slips back into the Averroistic and old Spanish position of dual truths. The dual notions, a temporal one and an eternal succession, stand next to one another and dissolve into a unity in the beyond" (315).

This rather forced tension—due to the problematic larger conceptualization of Vossler's work—between a political philosophy of life and Gracián's harmonizing interlacing of religious flight from the world and backward-thinking Spanish tradition, met with the protest of Fritz Schalk, whose essay from 1940–41, "Baltasar Gracián und das Ende des siglo de oro," begins with the first German inventory of research up to that point. While Schalk hardly brings anything new to Gracián scholarship apropos the evaluation of his significance in the history of political ideas, of psychology, and of aesthetics, he does examine briefly the reception of Gracián in the French Enlightenment and also goes on to expand upon newer studies, such as Adolphe Coster's Gracián biography of 1913, Américo Castro's essay "Gracián y España" (1929), and Miguel Romera-Navarro's introduction to his edition of *El criticón* (1938). Finally he emphatically calls into question Azorín's thesis from his famous 1919 essay, according to which Gracián's teachings of "the world as an eternal battle" ultimately lead to an un-Christian and skeptically anti-Spanish "inadmissible Epicurean intellectual ethics."

In light of this background, Schalk undertakes what for German scholarship is a thoroughly innovative analysis of the stylistic and rhetorical forms of Gracián's thinking. He argues revealingly and convincingly that the often-made accusation against Gracián's writing as empty and repetitive rhetoric is unfounded, because the formal material used by Gracián continually masters new dimensions of thinking in ever new variations: "What is at stake is the pouring of the same experience into another form out of the fable, the emblem, the dialogue, and so forth, of *Héroe* and *Discreto* into *Oráculo manual,* compiled solely of maxims. A sentence from one dialogue, bordered by maxims, contains another resonance and gains another level of intuition" (273). Schalk carries out a cataloging of Gracián's forms of thought and style, from the *sentencia* and the popular and (Erasmian) scholarly *refranes,* to the *exemplos,* Adagia, and Apophtegma; from hieroglyphics to emblematics; from the epigrams and jokes to the allegories and wordplays. He thereby shifts into the heart of his arguments the direct exchange of Gracián—due in great part to the mediation of Lastanosa—with Seneca, Martial, and Tacitus (an exchange whose significance Farinelli had already insisted upon).

But even if Schalk's analytical inventory shows brilliantly and convincingly that Gracián understands language "not as form but rather as forming, as an expression of constantly developing energy" that is "adequate to the tensions and contradictions of the reality" (121), it is difficult not to see that this analysis substitutes, on the one hand, the reflection upon the (philosophical) cohesion of Gracián's cognitive system and its function by an inventory of stylistic structures, which ultimately has little to do with content. On the other hand, it deviates from the network of questions that up to that point had occupied Gracián scholarship without having come up with a satisfactory answer. Those questions concerned Gracián's place in his own time, his contribution to the history of political ideas, the founding of scientific psychology, and the foundations of modern aesthetics—a question that still troubled (after Borinski) even Croce in his *Estetica.* His essay, which deepens Pfandl's reflection upon the significance of rhetoric and stylistics in Gracián, leads to a nontemporal description of internal textual structures, a movement that Schalk tries to complete ideologically in his concluding chapter, "Die Selbstbehauptung der Weltklugheit" (The self-assertion of worldly wisdom). He places Gracián within the group of humanist authors who tried to raise the national cultural consciousness through the integration of ancient heritage. But, as the "tablets of humanist value began to shatter" at the end of the Golden Age (Schalk 122), this group fell to the margins of societal interest and thus broke up. According to Schalk, the consequences of this marginalization led Gracián to develop, from a humanistic point of view, a strategy of "resistance to the hostile world." Such a strategy is held up on one hand by "trust in the transforming powers of the 'virtue,' of the moral-philosophical teaching of the Stoics and of Christianity" (Schalk 123). On the other hand, it is supported by the consciousness that "ancient philosophy can no longer be paradigmatic for others," that is, that the era of the decline of humanist education (*Bildung*) and moralism had dawned; the laws of movement of such decline depend upon the powers of ignorance (*Unbildung*) and contingency. Gracián shares this insight with the picaro, according to Schalk. Thus, Schalk is struck by a parallel between the picaresque artifice and "rules of *Oráculo*" for the "worldly wise." The *Oráculo* is "nothing but a handbook of tactics, of lies through which one protects oneself from society, in that one speaks only to the appearance of the language of the society" (126). Of course, "the other-worldly goals are . . . not forgotten" but appear to be "utterly absorbed in the struggle against worldly contingencies": "Worldly wisdom, the ideal of the intelligent, cunning, and tyrannical human [subject], moves into the position that the humanistic educational ideal had once occupied" (127).

Contrary to the mentioned studies of Borinski, Pfandl, or Vossler, Schalk's own scholarly interests are no longer explicit. This could be attributed to at least two reasons: first, that the research on Gracián was being conducted for its own sake (a reason that seems to be belied by the meagerness of that research in Germany up to that point and by Schalk's own research inventory). The second reason could be that the questions posed, explicitly and out of individual and overriding societal interests, lead to a depersonalized and detemporalized relationship to the objects and discourses in question and subsequently turn in on themselves. In any case, the questions that moved Borinski, Farinelli, Azorín, Pfandl, or Vossler are abandoned in favor of text-immanent (descriptive) approaches that at best can be placed, as a kind of history of ideas, in the Latinist humanism tradition and by some topoi linked with Gracián's epoch and a general attitude toward the world. Explicitly, Schalk attacks only the theses proposed by Vossler and especially by Pfandl of the world-fleeing and other-worldly-longing individual: the Catholic Gracián. Even the question, so energetically posed against Azorín, of whether or not Gracián provides the "nourishment for a profound anti-Spanishness" remains—in an ahistorical perspectivelessness—unanswered.

Graciáns Lebenslehre

Contrary to Schalk, Werner Krauss does not treat history as a *decorum* added to the texts, but rather as the productive societal context out of which Gracián's work springs. Such a context is something one must be familiar with in order to understand the political, moral, literary, aesthetic, and theoretical function and significance of Gracián's texts, or, for that matter, the interests that led to their later reception. In his first chapter, which he, in characteristic reversal of the general norm, names "Work and Life," he masterfully situates Gracián and his work not only in the sociopolitical collective context of the period, but also in the geographical, intellectual, and cultural coordinates of the Spanish regions. He shows how, in opposition to Madrid, Toledo (where Gracián, born in Aragón, spent his youth) becomes an element of eclecticist thinking and writing, in which—according to (Spanish) neo-Aristotelian tradition—prose can and does take the rank of poetry. Moreover, Gracián does not hesitate to place his own family as literary authorities next to the great authors of world literature. The fact that he was born at the end of the *siglo de oro*—something that in Schalk is taken out of the text-immanent perspective—is Krauss's natural starting point for understanding Gracián, who produced his first work, *El héroe,* quite late. While paying tribute to the memory of the past and of origins, the work is a monument to the will to self-determination of the individual who knows himself to have been born too late and too old, recognizing at the same time that only the aging man achieves the maturity that man needs at birth. Age, or for that matter, finality itself is for Gracián of even less negative value since his *patria*, Aragón, is an old Spanish province and thus rich with *entendimiento*, that is, with cultural knowledge from Italy. And if Aragón is the formative grounding of the Spanish character, "Gracián is the first Spanish intellectual (*Geist*) of truly conscious European orientation," writes Krauss, and adds (defining thus a double program), "a forerunner of the Enlightenment, insofar as he praises the national as a special circumstance of individual disposition and leads it to a higher synthesis of intellectual life" (Krauss, *Lebenslehre* 13).

Krauss reports on Gracián's life and intellectual development, drawing upon seldom discussed topics such as, for example, his critical and intellectual distance to his mentor and patron, Lastanosa, thus modifying the appreciation of Farinelli, Vossler, and Schalk. Analyzing that relationship, Krauss concludes that Gracián was in very little need of belonging to groups or cliques. Taking as a point of departure Gracián's brief stay in Madrid, made easier by the friendly reception of his *Politico: Fernando el Católico* by Philip IV, and following with the leadership of the Jesuit college in Tarragona and the dissension caused by the publication of *El criticón* with his religious order, Krauss shows the periods of Gracián's short life with a minimum of facts and figures in order to better elucidate his intellectual status with the help of precise analysis of the texts and their development. A prominent place in this analysis is given to *Agudeza y arte de ingenio*, a work in which—according to Krauss in agreement with Schalk—Gracián sought to find "the elements of style that the living spirit had at its disposal in regards to speech": "an idiosyncratic logic arises, that does not get bogged down in abstract grammatical categories. Rather, it stylistically seizes upon the vitality of language. The lessons of style basically show... a special case in the lessons of life that are set forth in the *Discreto* (1646) and in the *Oráculo manual* (1647)" (Krauss, *Lebenslehre* 18–19). What Gracián had still introduced in his early writings as the "privileges of a blessed nature" are generally presented as "attributes of worldly wisdom." Life is a battlefield from which there can be no flight into idyllic fields; rather it is one on which man must develop into a *persona*: "Because life completely unfolds its combative character, morality is entirely reduced to the tactical rules of self-assertion amid a general threat" (19). In fact one could draw parallels between Gracián's combative morality and the picaro's morality of provision (as did Schalk, to whom Krauss alludes in this context). The difference is, however, that the picaro "will never get ahead," whereas the prospects of success for Gracián's "worldly wisdom" are very good—a fact that finds its explanation in the society of the time. As universal as the man whom Gracián is addressing would be, Krauss says that neither the "working class" nor the members of "mechanical" vocations belong to it, and neither can they rise. For this reason the ideals of life that Gracián preaches become privileges that only "Jesuitic wit" could present as pleasing to God.

What Gracián had transformed into a system in his theoretical writings, he tries to illuminate in *El criticón* (1651–58) "with the broad strokes in the painting of the moral world." Krauss reads this as a consequence of Gracián's experience of life, which had seen Spaniards ruined by wars that "had been paid for at the expense of every last bit of the people's strength": "The construction of the novel allows the exclusive manner of the maxims to achieve a broader effect. This is a tremendous inventory of the intellectual world and not the cool and forced balance of lessons for life.... The extremes are juxtaposed in their breadth: vice and virtue, truth and deception. The hero, who must reach perfection, is not spared the stages of madness and foolishness as touchstones of their work" (Krauss, *Lebenslehre* 22–23). Thus, Gracián, a man with infinitely vast reading, can mobilize a range of appropriate forms, from the Byzantine novel to Lukian's "Work of Wonder"; from Alciati's and Boccalini's allegories to Vélez de Guevara's humorous, Romanesque *Diablo cojuelo*; and, above all, from the visions and magical scenes of exorcism in Quevedo's "nocturnal pieces" to the allegorical novels of the Middle Ages such as *Le roman de la rose* and *El libro de buen amor*. According to Krauss, they all serve Gracián's purpose of putting on a "collective display of the intellectual and moral world through the developmental tendencies of the novel" as "no one had dared to attempt with such scope since Dante" (24). "For Gracián, all artistic representation served only to make visible the anatomy of thought" (27).

Herein lies the decisive difference between Gracián and the other giant of Spanish prose, the Cervantes of *Don Quixote* and

Persiles. Krauss works through this in a brilliant analysis of *El criticón*, whose pair of protagonists anticipate Fénelon's *Télémaque* and, simultaneously, refer back to Don Quixote and Sancho Panza. Cervantes, Krauss states, "calls for the reconciliation of man with his fate," which makes him reach moments of existentially harmonious balance despite all of the adversities and unavoidable struggles, "unsuccessful identifications, failed attempts of self-consciousness." "The poetic form of this state is the idyll. The stormy waves of events break on the shores of its contained peace. The movement in Cervantes's narrative is interspersed with idyllic pauses, with experiences and encounters with those people who have found peace in the transfiguration of the everyday. Coming and going are not only phases of calm in the narrative technique, but also all essential states in which all dynamics endeavor to sublate themselves" (Krauss, *Lebenslehre* 27).

In opposition to Vossler's thesis, Krauss argues that "Gracián hates and is suspicious of all idyllic states, all quiet lingering." Since not only is the world broken, decaying and ruined, not only is there in this world—apocalyptically—no point from which a "renewal of the human soul" would be possible, neither is there "happiness that can be bracketed off." Formulated differently, to feign this parenthetical happiness would be to strive toward false goals. What grants consistency to man "is nothing but the unrelenting tension of the struggle.... that which we desire escapes us like a shadow." That raises its worth and our desire and makes it such that our "happiness... lies not in our renunciation, but in the tension of the striving toward a higher goal, which comes from every disappointment." Of these goals the highest can be nothing but the posthumous fame of "having survived one's self": "It is no accident that tension occupies such a basic position in Gracián's aesthetic" (Krauss, *Lebenslehre* 28).

The "tension" is the point at which practical life's experience, the development of a theory for a pragmatic lifestyle, and aesthetic experience and production meet. This expresses itself in artistic representation through uninterrupted changing of perspective, always to something new (29–30). Here we see both schematic forms, Critilo and Andrenio. Through these forms, Gracián guides the perspective of the reader to the "plan of the phenomenon" out of which the "steps of the sciences, as Gracián conceived them" can be read: from practical knowledge resulting from sensual perception toward "political science." The "art of inquiry into the soul" should mediate between these sciences and all other forms of (scientific) thinking. One needs this inquiry in order to unmask the "betrayer of the people" who (in *Criticón*) "makes his mischief in public." But inquiry should also go beyond this service of unmasking and must lead to the science of thinking, and to the enthroning of reason, that is, of "*seso*." Even reaching this stage of insight nevertheless does not protect the individual from falling back into error and delusion. For not only the world of real appearances but also the allegorical figures of value, virtue, and the categories of thought of all types of wisdom from *virtus* to *Fortuna,* seen from close up, show other faces and figures than the familiar emblems from allegory and mythology.

Once again Werner Krauss insists upon the recognition that Gracián strives not toward the past but toward an unknown future that contains all potentials, including the most positive. Wandering through the unmasked world of the *engaños* not only destroys one's comforting certainties and beliefs but also tends to constantly lay bare the way to growing knowledge: "Gracián finds himself here on the way to enlightened demystification. The figures of destiny are monstrosities of man's unknown. Their riddles are the riddles of the human breast" (Krauss, *Lebenslehre* 35). No divine will shows man the way through the "river of life," "in which vice stagnates." Like the protagonists of *El criticón,* man must find the judgments in the dialectic of (sensual) experience and the critique of reason. At best man has learned on his "lifelong journey" that there are "many points of view" and that "truth itself can appear dependent from points of view endangered by falling apart into multitudinal perspectives and different opinions." Man learns that everyone has the right (and the duty) to derive the truth from the experiences of the real world and from the manifold of opinions (including from within "every literary work of art"). This does not allow anything but contradictory truth. That this is valid even regarding the life wisdom of the people, which, in Spain, expresses itself in the *refranes* and stands in contradiction to the higher learned knowledge, according to Krauss, reveals a deep tragedy in Gracián, namely the loss of an irreplaceable societal balance: "Cervantes set the wisdom of the people in a fruitful polarity to the creative production of educated reason . . . [whereas] Gracián finds himself in sullen intellectual resistance to the confused manifold of an arbitrary dogmatism. . . . The situations of the maxims are not empirical. They orient themselves not in the manifold of life, but in its stages" (37–38). In other words, the dialectical unity of people and spirit, of Sancho Panza and Don Quixote, has been lost. In its place has stepped the lone man who makes decisions for himself, and for whom the rights of reasons are placed above the rights of the people.

In the second chapter of his book, "Gracián and the Psychologists" (39–44), Krauss pursues the question as to what right (asserted by, among others, Farinelli) nineteenth- and twentieth-century psychology has to call upon Gracián. He starts with the assumption that psychology as a science is concerned with the "leftover objects of the soul" (or rather, it incorporates these leftovers "into the nexus of the sciences"), which "remain in the midst of a reified and specialized culture" insofar as they have not been co-opted by a sociology based on Comte. Krauss makes it no secret that he is skeptical of the "immeasurably increased claims of knowledge" of depth psychology as an alternative to "technicism" and "maladjustedness" of the sciences. He distrusts the "inflation of the psychological" based on the belief in its growing universalist claim as much as he distrusts its twin sister, the life philosophy of Schopenhauerian and Nietzschean orientation (39–40): "Psychology believes itself to have the key to decipher the world's secret code. That is the way to a schematic typology, which, in any crazed and superstitious empirical system, flatters the desire for knowledge and demand for power" (41). For he who knows the souls of others and understands how they are stirred, also possesses the power over others who are unfamiliar with this science. Actually the *descifradores* and *zahoríes* in Gracián seem to provide assistance to such desires. "It is no wonder that psychologists here smell the morning air," cries out Krauss and thereby points to the fact that Machiavelli was already possessed by the "passion of analysis." But rather than the manipulation of others, Machiavelli as well as Gracián stood for empowering the "analyzed" individual to come to know himself in "pedagogical practice": "Man has it in his own hands to free himself. For Gracián, analysis is not the final word (that may become the key word of an angry or a gracious God). His lessons for life attempt to make man... capable of surviving his own weakness, and that means: by his own power.... Gracián posits the soul onto itself." His "psychology" belongs in the context of an "emancipation of the powers of the human soul," which, historically seen, is connected to the emancipation of political existence. These are the political stakes that Machiavelli had first dared to set" (44). As such, they have nothing to do with psychology as a science of supremacy.

Logically connected to these considerations is the chapter "Gracián and the Psychology of the Nations" (45–71), in which Krauss determines that, with his presentation of the character of the peoples in *El criticón,* Gracián is "ultimately at the end of a tradition with great ramifications," of a tradition that expressed in the Renaissance "boundless joy in the richness of being." This coincided with the development of nations and national culture as well as with the development of the "triumph of the new consciousness of language," which is "the starting point of modern philology as a whole" and which succeeded without rupturing the feelings of "universal belonging and community," which was "an inseparable part of humanistic national consciousness" (50). The latter slides into narrow-minded nationalism and hostile folk psychologism in late humanism—in the bellicose relationship of nations and especially in religious wars. This also appears in Gracián's work, albeit in thoroughly contradictory ways. For even if for Gracián the regional or the national character serves as a contributing factor in the construction of the individual—which is why he assembles catalogs of characteristics that are heavily informed by stereotypes—the national or regional within Gracián's system of the construction of the individual must be reconciled with the transnational and nonregional aspects of the system, all of which are sublated into the individual. This reconciliation leads Krauss to the conclusion that the theses regarding the insurmountable nature of national characteristics contradict the enlightened side of Gracián's thought. The theses, as his dream of the symbiosis of the Italians and Spaniards shows, are unstable: "Critilo's and Andrenio's travels through the nationally articulated civilized world is at once a journey through human life, the developmental history of the natural human being to universal perfection" (71).

In the chapter entitled "Gracián's Consciousness of Time," Krauss takes up the relationship of the order of the Jesuits in general and of Gracián in particular to Machiavelli, whose breakthrough in anthropological thought he sees as every bit as epochal as the "shake-up of the anthropocentric worldview" (72–74). Working out the divergences and agreements of Machiavelli and Gracián in their common veneration of Fernando el Católico, Krauss underlines the meaning that Gracián's writings possessed in the epoch of Jansenian critique of the Jesuit order with their own borrowing of the Machiavellian notion of "moral 'empirismus' " and "probabilism." Nevertheless, Krauss specifies that the full explosiveness of Gracián's writing would prove itself "in light of the modern notion of labor," because Gracián's introduction to successful action still remains primarily limited "to the courtly political existence." Gracián's commentaries upon the *demystified Fortuna* (74–78) also belong within the context of a tendency toward desecularization of earthly matters according to the pragmatic maxims of the "probabilism" (72–74). Indeed, in Dante's terms, *Fortuna* appears again to be tied to the role of mediator between Christian providence and practical matters. Nevertheless, even here Krauss sees the path having been taken toward a "process of rationalist demasking" of mythical thought, a path toward planning and calculating action, that may still appear marginally in courtly society, but that will unfold in the context of bourgeois ethics. This also holds true for the notion of the political that Krauss analyzes ("Die höfische Sphäre" [The courtly sphere], 78–81) in the period of transition from the courtly ideal of civilization and statecraft to Gracián's "applied human knowledge." In so doing, Krauss pays close attention to the specifics of Spanish power relations and the dialectic of the Madrid court and the provinces, with their retarding effects on the development of a modern state in the eighteenth century. Regarding the realm of politics, he also remarks a growing extension of the circle of addressees for the new forms of societal strategic action. "In fact," he writes in the following section, entitled "Life and Truth" (81–86), "Gracián seeks to assist his readers toward success." This is only possible through cunning, pugnacious, and pragmatic relinquishment of action according to Christian notions of morality. Such a relinquishment includes "sympathy and the (senseless and functionless) Christian-Stoic asceticism." "The new science is a science of life" in which one must also acquire the taste of fine society (*buen gusto*) as a means of success. In this respect, the production of appearance, of "verisimilitude" is afforded greater significance than action according to the criterion of ethically motivated veracity (a development that Krauss associates with Kant's aestheticization of the practice of life): "This world is no place for the 'anima naturaliter christiana.'"

Naturally, action that is aimed at the development of the individual and the changing of society is always tied to a finality. In other words, naturally, Gracián's philosophy of pragmatical action poses the question concerning the underlying conception of history. Krauss situates it, in the section entitled "The Historical Perspective: Fall and Cultural Growth" (87–92), "between both poles of the belief in progress and in the teachings of the gradual fall of the world," between an optimism influenced by the Erasmian Renaissance and an apocalyptic Christian pessimism. Indeed Gracián knows the Stoic historical conception of the eternal cycle, which expresses itself in the image of the Wheel of Fortune (*la rueda de la Fortuna*). But, although he is conscious of late-born *modernus* in relation to the necessarily innovative *antiquus* and, consequently, does not have a high opinion of the inventiveness of the "novi," the later-borns, he does not collapse into epigonistic melancholy. Rather he perceives history as a continuum determined by ebb and flow. Everything in this continuum is subjected to change and decay, but also increasing growth of knowledge; because of this, innovations or new self-realizations are therefore possible. While such possibilities of innovation will diminish in regard to the general growth of knowledge, the possibilities expand when it comes to grasping that which has already been worked out. On the other hand, the growing difficulties constitute an incitement for the "novi." In short, the *Querelle des anciens et des modernes* also takes place in Gracián's work and, regarding activities for the future, may be said to open early Enlightenment and historical progressive thought, however critically it might be shaded.

Nevertheless, if in France early Enlightenment optimism also focused on discovering untapped energies and the corresponding historical analysis (as Krauss shows already in 1936 in his *Corneille as a Political Thinker),* Gracián ends up in a dangerous dead end with regard to history. "The Struggle with the Vulgar" (92–96) is the heading of the next chapter, in which Krauss portrays Gracián's fear of the people, who are disqualified as "vulgo." It is in this "vulgo" however, that Lope de Vega and Cervantes placed their epistemological and/or aesthetic confidence. Krauss writes, "Because Gracián dared to place his teachings in the realm of life, he shares a common basis with the truth of the people, which is indeed life itself. But precisely this commonality unleashes the most brutal competition. . . . Gracián fears the people as much as he has contempt for them." He places a protective barrier between himself and them in the form of *conceptismo,* which is incomprehensible for the *vulgo.* This weakens the hero, however, who can no longer—as in Lope—support himself with the community of people, although even on this point there is never a permanent certainty in the dialectical thought of Gracián. Since Gracián's critical reason probes all forms of idiocy, it does not escape him that idiocy transcends class and is represented equally as often in the court as in the common man: "Thus, the use of the term 'vulgo' is extended to man in general." This, of course, means that the inverse must then also be true—that it is not impossible for the common man to rise to *persona.* Naturally, the barriers he must overcome in the epoch of the declining Spanish Empire appear overwhelming, especially because he must find an entrance to "cultura," which, as Krauss shows in the section entitled "The Process of Culture" (97–99), is basically possible only for members of the privileged class. But, in the dualistic sense of class privilege and the natural system, one may be born to the "varón culto" of the *ingenio;* one will not, however, be able to achieve this quality without work, which opens up again in this crazy dialectic at the end of which yet another answer may be possible: "He who understands, rules. Culture [*cultura*] not only makes men out of beasts, but also, out of men, individuals. It is the condensation, the work on man's internal being. The word 'work' makes company with new sound, with the word of '*cultura.*' "

In chapter 5 ("The Stages of the Intellect and the Gradation of Education" [100–106]), Krauss takes up in a somber tone the dialectic between the growing birth of man and death, which occupies Gracián over and over again, but above all in *El criticón.*

Of course, the masses (regardless of class) are destined to remain uneducated and without access to reason. Yet, where the process of the development of individuality begins, it is necessarily a process of developing a path from imbecilic youth ("necedad"), through the lesson of the dead determined by will (of those before us who left their experiences and their books), to the wise age. The process goes through "praxis" (the phase of the "cordura," in which the relationship of the "ingenio" and the "genio" develops) to the wise age, which finally possesses reason ("juicio"). It is at this age, however, at the very moment when the individual would begin a truly human existence, that man lacks energy. At this age all action lies already within the horizons of death. Krauss, who associates this vision of maturing with death to the Kantian notion of the development of the critique of judgment, lays bare the coordinates in which the maturing process is carried out in the interplay of "memoria" and "imaginación," "juicio" and "trabajo." He concludes by presenting the educational program—with its gradations and ramifications of poetry, history, the conceptual textual and thinking strategies of archaeology, mathematics, architecture and painting, natural philosophy, moral philosophy, and politics, above which only philosophy stands—that Gracián introduced in the *Museo del discreto* in *El criticón*, and which must serve to convert theology into societal action. "Civilization is not the compilation of knowledge, but an education that reaches into life, the contest of the new in a lively tension with existing values."

The sixth chapter of *Graciáns Lebenslehre* has the most complicated but most carefully constructed structure. Entitled "The Situation and Task of Man" (107), it is divided into two sections, "The Contemporary" and "Lifestyles," which are each again divided into two subsections. The first is entitled "Self-Recognition and the Understanding of Others" (107). In this chapter, Krauss suggests that Gracián, in what is close to an inversion of traditional procedures, shows "the way to knowledge" as leading "from the external to the internal." As opposed to other conceptions of individuality of the Renaissance and the epoch of the declining *siglo de oro*, Krauss reveals in the next section, "The Individual with His World" (108–113), that this implicit preponderance of self-recognition through recognition of the other also determines Gracián's conception of the individual. Contrary to the traditional definitions of the integrity of introspection, Gracián presents the individual as a "bearer of connections to the contemporary world" and even as a product of communicative action: "The dialogical character and the dependency of man in relation to his equals is affirmed through individuality. Gracián sees individuality as a product of experience and education." In light of this background, the next section, "The Value Tensions in Things" (113–119), is especially important. Krauss analyzes the motivations of the individual who is grounded in inescapable communicative interaction. Validity (i.e., significance in action) and the increasing, corresponding appearance are the decisive stimuli that derive from "lack" and "loss." "Only with some distance from want and need, only through lack or loss does the value of things become apparent and tangible," writes Krauss, proving to the astonished reader that Gracián already thinks in the language of commodity exchange and surplus value.

Gracián takes into consideration the shortage of commodities, the investment of labor determined by increasing use and trade value, and the guidance of consumer behavior through recommendation (advertisement), thereby defining the basis for an "aesthetic of commodities": "An aspect of reification creates a surprise in his discussion of worldly laws, a reification in which Gracián transposes even incommensurable quantities: Values are something like marketed and accounted for." In the first section of the subchapter "Method and Strategy" (119–121), Krauss reveals how in Gracián concrete social action also is understood according to the model of economical legitimacy, and the next section, "The Validity of Language and Linguistic Style" (121–126), shows that this is even the case in the realm of the language arts: "When things are seen platonically as shadows of ideas, then words are the shadows of deeds. But deeds are rare. Therefore, words as more or less covered treasury bonds get their special value." Formulated differently, the dialectic of labor and market laws also prevails in the realm of the language arts. This is particularly visible in the *conceptos*: "to make oneself valuable" and "to create tension" are the premises under which language must be produced and distributed, from which the question follows as to the limits of the "makable" and the "marketable." In other words, to what extent is mankind, dependent on the use value of "natural language," disposed to accept and receive linguistic rarity and eccentricity? This is a question that requires equilibristic acts in the production of texts. "The breeding of a conceptual style does not tend to repudiate entirely Spanish freedom [for example, the *refranes*], rather it seeks to bind itself to this freedom. Gracián's philosophical linguistic style fascinates, while speech rushes forward. The author is always ahead of the reader." He continually delivers to the surprised reader, desirous of news, uninterrupted aesthetic excitement. But, as Krauss shows, the danger of exaggeration and weariness of the reader exists. "Tension here is not collectedness, which—generated in the calm—leads to a solution. It is not a moment in the linguistic movement, but a principle of conviction, a durability in which one plays until the last reader has been trumped." The conclusion that Krauss draws from Gracián's model of an art of thinking, speaking, and writing aiming at successful action is surprising and convincing: "In a certain way conceptual prose stood *before* a philosophy, which did not attain Spain anymore."

The previous quote provides an occasion to determine that which can and should be noted on every page, sentence after sentence, in Krauss's Gracián monograph, namely the immense density of this text, in which there is—using Krauss's judgment on Gracián—"no hollow ground, no silent interval, no comfortable distance from the observation," and which fascinates and impresses the reader. *Graciáns Lebenslehre* is in every way an unusual text, which, without sliding into self-indulgent wordplay, keeps pace with Gracián. This also holds true for the seventh chapter, "The Art of Living" (127–137). In its first section, "The Fertile Land" ("The Beginning and End" [127–129]), the parallels of Gracián's notion of success are introduced in relation to practical life and the production of texts. Both are determined by their successful conclusion. Spontaneity is not called for, since the reflectedness of action (i.e., the caution in the editing and reworking of a text) must dominate. Only results count. The next section, "The Opponent and the Will" (129–134), begins with an original connection to this basic rule. The will of the others achieves the greatest resistance in striving toward success, wherein, among other things, the embattled nature of existence is revealed. Logically, it is imperious to study the will of the others in order to overcome them. In such study, it is necessary to understand the "genio" of one's opponent, that is, "the determinate power that hangs over life and imposes upon it the laws of its particular inclination." The genio is the driving power (derived from demonology) that inspires man (and according to Gracián even entire nations) and drives them forward. It also determines his propensities in taste. It stands in opposition to *ingenio,* the innate potential for reasonable guidance of one's driving impulses. "The higher powers of the will impose themselves upon the impulse tendencies," writes Krauss, who (following Gracián) places *entendimento, juicio, voluntad, brío,* and *destreza* in the realm of the *ingenio*: "The higher force of the intellect expresses itself in this functional nature of the will." If the inclinations (strengths and weaknesses) of one's opponent are studied so that finally the arms of the *destreza* can be used with *entendimiento* and *juicio,* the concrete carrying out of the struggles remains to be thought out. Therefore, one must be familiar with the "Rules of the Game," as Krauss prescribes in the last section of the chapter (134–137): "But one cannot blindly follow the rules. A zigzag course is advisable." In short, the struggle with one's opponent reminds one of a chess game, in which one also must take into account the intelligence of one's opponent in order to anticipate his intentions. This is best performed with fakes and bluffs, with artistic deception according to the rules of probability: "The victorious life struggle not only brings forth the truth of man through the dialectic of being and appearance [*Sein und Schein*], it also discloses the nature of human existence itself. The embattled character that, at first, showed a face of incalculable resistance, then develops the capacity for a coexistence in which one's own life takes part. The battle turns to a competition." And the competition, one might add, takes place in all realms of human life, including the production of art and literature.

The penultimate chapter, "The Crown of Virtue and the King's Virtues," likewise divided into subsections, begins with the consideration of the "Myth of Perfection" (138–139), in which Krauss, in an attempt to clarify what Gracián's rules of life are meant to accomplish, even takes up Nietzsche's notion of an *Übermensch* (superman). The *Übermensch* has to learn to put himself on the stage, an art to which keeping distance and the naturalness of appearance belong as well. The labor of becoming an individual—not unlike the dance parable in Kleist's *The Puppet Theater*—must, in the end, be invisible and, as an appearance of ungroundedness and incalculability, stir feelings of infiniteness (greatness). That does not mean that the perfection (of appearance) achieved by work would not be assembled from the most varying and analyzable factors, as the section "Gemination and Competition" (139–142) explains. Perfection is achieved precisely in the combination of varying qualities and virtues, which Gracián catalogs in *El discreto*—similar to modern linguistics' parts of speech: "The distribution of attributes in double columns acquires a fundamental standing through the idealizing manner of its composition." This fundamental standing can be attained by the extraordinary virtues, the *eminencias,* which are generated from the dualistic system of virtues and combined according to value criteria ("Eminencies and Perfections" [142–143]): "The soul is . . . a hierarchically ordered nexus, in which the perfections have submitted themselves to the guidance of an eminence." The *eminencias* encompass all other qualities ("The Transcendent Qualities" [144–145]) to which above all others "the untranslatable *despejo*" belongs: gracefulness. This, along with *entereza* (the intact, the whole) and *capacidad,* provides the functional context of the psychological and the physical qualities themselves, from which perfection develops. Thus it is incumbent upon "The Relation to the Admixture" (146–147) to bring that certain inexplicable "je ne sais quoi" to perfection: "Thus, the structure of the human character no longer appears harmoniously determined through the balance of its elements, rather in the incalculable way it is determined by an infinity that occasionally impels happiness of perfection or the loss of the cohesive powers through a slight addition of a dangerous supplement."

The precariousness of the network of connections out of which perfection (never closed, always needing defense) emerges, the acknowledged and feuding greatness, this precariousness also draws upon itself the loss of a centrally cataloged Western morality, that is, the *mesotes* as defined in Aristotle: the *aurea mediocritas* ("Gracián's Concept of Standards" [*Maßbegriff*] [148–154]). For when even Gracián claims that "all virtue . . . [lies] in the middle," then this middle of the virtue system of the exceptional man must reside far above the masses: "The middle value is not the average value, rather it steps forward as the highest value, the unique and extraordinary achievement of concentrated intellectual energy." Thus a value is dismissed that once appeared to guarantee social equality. "Gracián's worldly wisdom," writes Krauss, "marks an important incision in the history of the concept of measure." At this point, Krauss allows himself a rare digression into contemporary conceptualization in order to clarify his intentions: "One only need listen to common language usage. New creations in this area prove how completely the concept of measure has lost its mediating powers. One is reminded of the new German idiomatic construction 'from measure [orders, law] giving authority'—'this is not measured [standard] giving' " ("von maßgebender Seite erfahre ich" or "das ist für mich nicht maßgeblich"). In short, out of a harmonious equalization of virtues, but also out of a communicative equality with the other, which translates into intellectual and social behavior, a norm imposed from above has developed, which must be respected and obeyed as a command or duty. This is a development anticipated by Gracián, yet still bound to a Renaissance substratum and not yet entirely bound to the "Herrenmoral," the morality of the Master, which will be represented by a more or less singular person (or unquestioned state authority).

The powerful analysis of Gracián's complete works, which reaches its end here, allows Krauss in his last chapter, "Perspective: The End of Humanism" (155–161), to address the reception of Gracián in France, which is tied to the notions of "génie" and "goût," and to trace the comparative differentiation of Gracián's moralistic position with the basic tendencies of the French. In so doing, Krauss defines Gracián's singular position—once again in comparison to Cervantes—with regard to the Spanish context of epoch, a singular position that manifests itself above all in a turning away from "the reality of the people": "The 'hero' of Gracián's mintage is far from one raised in the deep 'rootedness' in the folkloric Mother Earth. A rootedness on which Goethe once had said 'Plants go from knot to knot, ... in the animal world it is no different ... what happens to individuals also happens to whole corporations. The bees ... as a unity produce something ... a queen bee. . . . Thus does a people produce its heroes.' " Such a conception is naturally the opposite of Gracián's worldview; he entered "with his creation into a reactionary countercurrent against the popular foundation of Spanish literature." This popular foundation of Spanish literature was particularly familiar to Krauss since he had completed a dissertation, directed by Karl Vossler, entitled *Das tätige Leben und die Literatur im mittelalterlichen Spanien* (*The active life and the literature of medieval Spain*). Gracián's heroism of "Señorío," Krauss concludes, is an authority "created by the forces of time and will, without connection to the deep roots of existence, but in cooperation and openness to all suprasensible powers, which radiate the luster of infinity in the mirror of an exalted humanity."

After our long course through the work of Werner Krauss we can say that it is in every way unique. It is so because of its breadth and scope, as it comprises a social analysis and the analysis of the context into which Gracián's text comes into existence, based on a history of mentalities; the analysis of form; the philosophical, stylistic, and concept-historical survey of the text; and the analysis of its meaning for posterity. Without any doubt, it is one of the most important German works on Spanish literature in general and one of the most significant on Gracián in particular. It is the work of a philosopher, who out of a masterful knowledge of Spanish literature in its historical development is able to enter as an equal into a dialogue with Gracián, a dialogue that is linguistically grandiose, overall stylistically refined, and never redundant or sloppy. He enters this dialogue in order to question Gracián about his motivations and intentions and also perhaps to put Gracián face to face with his responsibility toward his contemporaries and toward posterity. Above all, however, he enters the dialogue in order to inform us, his contemporaries, of what we can learn from Gracián and where we must contradict him. In the future it will be impossible to speak or to write about Gracián without crossing the royal path paved for the understanding of Gracián by Krauss; without Krauss's information about the development of Gracián's philosophical or protophilosophical system, about the reasons that his work came into existence, about the goals it set and its dialogue with other philosophical and theological systems; without Krauss's function-genetic imbedding of Gracián's formulae in a tradition that extends back to the ancients, to the international and national manifold of forms of the epoch; in short without paying a visit to Krauss's stylistical concept-historical analyses of Gracián's complete works.

A Second Possible Discussion

Werner Krauss's Communist Castration of Gracián

Of course, many readers may ask what good it is to so completely introduce a text that appeared almost fifty years ago. In 1993, Hans Robert Jauß called *Graciáns Lebenslehre* Krauss's "authentic and unmatched contribution to the history of European moralism" (208). Since Werner Krauss is not an unfamiliar figure, one must also assume that the state of scholarship is also well acquainted with this obviously fundamental work and has been appropriately influenced by it. As stated at the beginning of this essay, it is perplexing that *Graciáns Lebenslehre* has left hardly any traces in (German) research on Gracián, although it remains unmatched by any other (German) work on Gracián. Yet, if one observes the works that have been presented on Gracián by (West) German Hispanists since 1947, one is astonished to note how often the *studiosi,* if they quote Krauss's work at all, do not know that the author's name is not "Kraus," "Krauß," or "Krause," or how often they have merely leafed through his book in order to quote a sentence with indignation, the message of which they are able to rebuff as dogmatically wrong within the framework of their own investigation.

We may find an explanation for this in the only German book review on Krauss, which is presented by Ludwig Flachskampf in *Romanische Forschungen.* Flachskampf reports in three pages the contents of *Graciáns Lebenslehre,* thereby allowing himself to be enraptured into high praises that are not shy about using formulations such as "masterful," which, I might add, are wholly justified. His judgments contain such comments as "Werner Krauß [*sic,* even then], in a number of places, treats . . . Gracián's relationship to Christianity and to the Jesuit order and he does so much more significantly than most of the French biographers (Hazard, Coster, Rouveyre) and on the Spanish side more so than Américo Castro"

(*Flachskampf* 261). The review's tone then turns immediately from a positive philological discussion to a current political discourse:

> We get an idea in Gracián . . . occasionally of the frightening departure from means and end, of the absolutization of the means that is radically affirmed, and of the goal placed on such a distant altar, that the autonomy of the means does not disturb any longer. In our time the means often enough become the goal. The means dangerously satisfy themselves and move, therefore, into the "fatal circulation of the godless." And, instead of Christianity, something entirely different could end up on the throne, some of its secularizations, for instance, the communist Messianism. Reading Gracián undoubtedly should bring great pleasure to a Marxist, if for no other reason than because certain of Gracián's formulations invite him to free his [Gracián's] doctrine out of its "mystical veil" and to take out its useful kernel. This is similar to what the prophet himself [Marx] had done with Hegel's dialectic. Such a castration—and that is what every secularization of Christianity is—would have very much astonished Gracián. Here it becomes clear, I think, how little is said of Gracián when one asks whose predecessor or disciple he might be. There is absolutely nothing that, "with historical necessity," stems from Gracián's work in his particular place in intellectual history. It is therefore problematic to speak in regard to Gracián of an "End" of an epoch—"End of Humanism" is the perspective of Werner Krauß's book. . . . To what time an author belongs, and whether or not that "time" is irretrievably gone ("fortunately," one often believes to understand) is a frequently intentional interpretation from the outside that ignores the autonomy of literary history vis-á-vis the history of "that which is happening and has happened." . . . Spanish history knows the uninterrupted continuity of the Middle Ages up to the end of the seventeenth century. That is, it knows the history of an older Europe, in which no gate is "forever" slammed shut, in which and out of which everything could yet come. "To this universal Europe, enriched also by the tremendous impulses of the Orient, given through Spain" (Schalk), Gracián belongs, too—as a figure of peculiar intellectual range to whom the modern interpretation of a forerunner of, what would have been to him, foreign goals would

> have been unintelligible. Just as Erasmus would have shaken his head when Américo Castro calls him no longer Christian." (*Flachskampf* 264)

What was wrong? What did *Graciáns Lebenslehre* do to earn the assessment of a communist usurpation, even of a communist "castration," where even a jubilation by Krauss about the "end of humanism" can only be read between the lines because that is the point from which the reviewer wrote it? Obviously Krauss's diagnosis that Gracián had advanced himself with a worldly wisdom, oriented exclusively toward success, to the utmost limit of Christian ethics on the verge of a fall into the loss of faith, is enough for Flachskampf. Although Krauss shows that this fall does not take place, Flachskampf denounces Krauss's diagnosis as an attempt to usurp Gracián as an atheistic comrade of the communist Krauss. This is all the more curious, in that the witness Fritz Schalk not only completely agrees with Krauss on this point, but also concurs in the diagnosis that the era of humanism is here drawing its last breaths. In any case, the decisive and dominant condemnation of the Cold War had been made, and Krauss as the communist enemy of humanist education and agent of Communist historical and cultural liquidation was to be pilloried. German-German dialogue was never to recover from this and thousands of other such cases. It was not only a dialogue of which, despite the differences in worldview, Krauss always dreamed, but also one that he actually practiced through his powerful critical activities. His work always proved to be open to new methodological directions and was never polemical.

As indicated by the foreword to *Graciáns Lebenslehre,* which was recently found by Jauß and documented in *Lendemains*—a foreword that remained unpublished (perhaps because the proud Krauss sensed that it could appear to be a plea for indulgence and gentle criticism)—Krauss had hoped for scholarly dialogue instead of political denunciation. In this foreword, Krauss explains that he had received a decisive impulse from the research on Gracián insofar as he had preferred to highlight in the *Criticón* a revision of the radical opinions of the younger Gracián, a kind of rapture in his work, instead of a development, even though this development is highly contradictory. Commenting on his own book, Krauss continues:

> The present study presupposes a coherent system, which—though it determines all works of Gracián—could not be fully developed before the frame of a broader conception of life had been conceived in order to allow all contradictory ramifications. The present study has the ambition to open up this concealed kernel of Gracián's life doctrine, i.e., the practical implications of Gracián's thought for life. To that end a precise description of that which Gracián understood as "life," as well as how he responded to it, had to be dared. The figure of Gracián is then naturally removed from an intellectual and literary historical relational field in which only a small circle of experts were truly at home anyway. In order to address a wider audience, all Spanish quotes in the text are translated into German. The particular circumstances out of which his study arose explain its character. The use of previous scholarly work and any kind of secondary materials was denied the author. Thus, earlier opinions and research results could not be taken into account. The original intention to span the horizon of Gracián's development and education in an exhaustive study had to be given up. Gracián's ancient and medieval Arabic sources and assumptions remain undiscussed, as are the significant relation of the author to the Spanish anthropology and moralism of the sixteenth and seventeenth centuries, and, in particular, to Quevedo. Also Gracián's posthumous fame in France and Germany, discussed in several interesting studies, could only be touched upon. Newer works, such as that by Fritz Schalk, were unavailable to me. And I was not even able to use Borinski. I had to use the available editions of Gracián as chance allowed it. In view of such gaps and scarcities one could call it making a virtue out of necessity to claim a radical innovation in the reading of an author still in life but asphyxiated by the burden of the exegesis. But if an understanding of Gracián based on his own assumption is to be advanced here, then the author had to praise the circumstances that were forced upon him, which held him to a greater penetration of the process itself. (*Lendemains* 208–209)

Particular Circumstances

This foreword did not appear; rather, it was replaced by another one that was considerably more laconic: "This work was written in 1943 under particular circumstances. The author was limited to an edition of Gracián that was made available to him through well-intentioned generosity. Secondary literature was not at his disposal. If, after liberation, a fundamental change of the study was not undertaken, it was because I believe that a portrayal of the worldly wisdom of Gracián based on their own assumptions could also attract general interest" (Krauss, *Lebenslehre* 7). *Captatio benevolentiae?* Frankly, the thought would be frivolous if not absolutely shameless. However, as I dare state, at least, after the review I have done here of German Gracián scholarship since Borinski, one hardly notices that Krauss's book has been written solely from memory, and that previous scholarship had not been taken into account. To say that history and literary history were absent or had been violated in this study has the charm of a bad joke—also and especially in comparison to other works such as Fritz Schalk's text, for example. More interesting and important is what had been lost in the abandonment of the longer foreword, namely, the loss of the wish for a larger audience. This wish was in no way to be bought by popularizing, especially because the (brilliant) translations into German are even completed by the Spanish quotes in an appendix. For *Graciáns Lebenslehre,* well within Gracián's own mind-set, was aimed at social effectiveness through historico-philosophical reflection.

In this regard, Ludwig Flachskampf was right: *Graciáns Lebenslehre* was and is indeed a political book, even if it does not present the Spanish Jesuit as a pioneer of Bolshevism. The impulse was in another direction, which Flachskampf deliberately overlooks, or at least does not reveal to the reader of *Romanische Forschungen.* "'A portrayal of Gracián's worldly wisdom from the point of view of their own assumptions' is what the author, in his preface, calls his work," writes Flachskampf. He continues, "A broadly laid out book, which impresses by the erudition and broad perspective of the author (among others a grasp of Jean Paul, Schopenhauer, and Dostoyevsky), and which enriches the picture of the history of Spanish (and European) literature. It is not always easy to read; a certain formlessness can be detected in certain places. But, 'this work was written in 1943 under particular circumstances'" (*Flachskampf* 260).

That was it. That was all. Did Flachskampf not know anything else? Had he not heard? Or was it—from somewhere—so generally known that one did not need explain it? Whatever it was, the silence may account for the fact that a younger generation, not all too much later, no longer knew even how to spell the name of the author of this book, whose political, philosophical, ideology-critical, and moral breadth they obviously did not seize. Nevertheless, the second of the total of three reviews of *Graciáns Lebenslehre* written by Arnold G. Reichenberger, appearing a year earlier in *Hispanic Review,* did not silently pass over the "particular circumstances":[1]

> According to the prefatory note this book was written in 1943 *under particular conditions,* which made it impossible for Professor Krauss to use any critical literature on his author. . . . To call the conditions under which this remarkable book was written "particular circumstances" is an understatement for detention under a Nazi death sentence in Moabit prison. It is, then, from the author's point of view, a scholar's *consolatio.* The association between the subject matter and the man who chose it under those *particular circumstances* stirs the imagination. (Reichenberger 169)

At the risk of being accused of dealing with a "personality cult," as Frank-Rutger Hausmann recently called the evocation of Krauss's destiny (Hausmann 20), I consider it to be a moral duty to recall to memory the "particular circumstances," which impressed Reichenberger as much as they met with Flachskampf's indifference (as made obvious by his political denunciation at the end of the review). This alleged "personality cult" has obviously been "corrected" by West German Hispanists through silence and denunciation. For it appears to me that no West German Gracián scholar paid respectable tribute to the "particular circumstances" before Sebastian Neumeister did so in 1993. The fact that this actually was done in Spain and in Spanish is an irony of fate that was certainly not expected or intended by Neumeister. But it expresses adequately the process of repression of Krauss's resistance activity in Germany. Whatever the case, here is Neumeister's text in full, which we only briefly cited above:

> The merit of such success [of German Gracián criticism as being "one of the most attractive"] is due above all to two people: Werner Krauss and Hugo Friedrich. Werner Krauss, a militant antifascist, escaped imminent execution thanks only to the help of a doctor friend who declared him mentally ill. In 1943, during a period of extreme menace and perils, Krauss wrote with shackled hands the first monograph on Gracián after Borinski, without the help of a library and referring in part only to some old editions that were available to him. He understands Gracián as a court psychologist, with a humanist culture—a refined person of the so-called "internal emigration" during Nazism—[his book] belongs among the best studies on Gracián's work.[2]

As sympathetic as Neumeister's text is, it does contain some errors. First, Krauss owed his survival not only to a physician friend, but also to the engagement of many brave men and women (among them the philosopher Hans-Georg Gadamer). Also, Krauss did not belong, precisely, to the realm that we used to call the "internal emigration." Rather, he was part of an active resistance against the Nazi regime (see *Lendemains*). It should therefore be remembered here that Werner Krauss was arrested on November 24, 1942, as a member of the Schulze-Boysen resistance group and, after a farcical trial in the Reich's war tribunal, was sentenced to death on January 18, 1943. Until September 14, 1944, the day on which the death sentence was commuted to five years imprisonment, Krauss vegetated in the death cell. He wrote a report on these experiences, and selections from the report were subsequently published. "In the death house," Krauss wrote,

> I immediately requested of the director permission to continue work on my Gracián manuscript. The director, a not unfair man who allowed much, including the strictly forbidden delivery of small packages of edibles, let it be known that he could not create any illusions for me. He knew little of my case but wondered what should be done with such a manuscript. Whenever I then set myself to work on the manuscript with bound hands, I understood the justification of his warning and the paradoxes of my

> work. Someday, in the middle of the day, I would inevitably have to interrupt my work, because you cannot keep the hangman waiting." (*Lendemains* 157–158)

We are unsatisfactorily informed about the concrete conditions of Krauss's work. But we do know that parallel to *Graciáns Lebenslehre* he must also have been working on his novel, *PLN—The Passions of the Peaceful Soul*. In his foreword to the eastern zone edition of the novel in 1948 he writes, "*PLN* was written in shackles and is a shackled book. The writing began in 1943 in Plötzensee penitentiary (Dept. VIII) and was brought to a close in the Wehrmacht prison in Lehrter Street 61, from where Alfred Kothe, not without risking his own safety, smuggled it into freedom." Krauss had other helpers and coconspirators both inside and outside the prison, one of whom was Gadamer. Gadamer sent him the news for the *persona* chapter of the Gracián book that the "i[n]d[o]g[erman] *pesah*," in Hans Rheinfelder's famous investigation of the concept of *persona*, was not connected to the *persona*. At this time, then, Krauss must have been working on *Graciáns Lebenslehre*. Again, through Gadamer, we know that he must have finished it by July 1944 at the latest. For, on July 9, Gadamer wrote to Krauss, "That was finally a bit of good news that *Gracián* is finished and I am compelled from the heart to wish you congratulations. That makes up for much of the exhaustion or failure for which one often reproaches oneself, when someone realized such a work under such conditions. May we soon be allowed to communicate again."

That this book was unusual, that it perhaps was and even is comforting that "such a book under such conditions" was able to succeed was something that others, too, knew at that time. On July 7, 1947, Karl Vossler wrote to Krauss, who had a copy of *Graciáns Lebenslehre* delivered to him, that he had just finished the "in no way easy but informative and enjoyable reading." He wanted to "immediately express his joy and admiration" that Krauss, "despite the great misfortunes of the time, could accomplish this work and bring it to beautiful perfection. . . . Gracián, who possessed an unmistakable feeling for success and failure, would have enjoyed it" (*Nachlass*, Werner Krauss). A bit later Erich Auerbach wrote from the United States:

> Dear Krauss, in the last days I received a bundle of your works, which made a roundabout way: a second copy of *PLN . . . , The World in Spanish Proverbs* (enchanting), Lope, Cervantes and the Jesuits, again [an issue of the magazine] *Die Wandlung* with the essay on the "dictionary" as well as your *Gracián,* sent directly from the publisher. Because I am living in such a bustle I only fleetingly peeked at everything. The conclusion to *Gracián* is impressive and very characteristic of you. I think I will have a chance to read it in peace at sea, crossing back.

Auerbach wrote again on October 13:

> Dear Krauss, a piece of paper with notes, which I had written on the ship while reading your writings at the very beginning of my trip just fell into my hand. If I am not mistaken, I have not written to you about them. In my recollection—my capacity of memory is extremely exhausted at this moment—everything pales in light of the *Gracián* book, whose density and richness are still present to me. Not only the figure of Gracián himself, but also the connections and conditions that you discover and tie together, such as the courtly sphere and the concept of measure, are of most interest to me and are most fruitful for my own work. And, in addition to that, the connections that are opened up to Montaigne, to the French of the seventeenth century, or also to our contemporary status. You are, I believe, the only fellow scholar whom I read with true interest, that is with the intention of learning more than material information. Likewise, you are the only one who works with intentions similar to my own; and in the end you observe things that I would never see. You are more original and at the same time more eccentric. The first chance I get, I want to give the book to [Américo] Castro, or does he already have it? I would at least like to get him moving on it.

On May 22, 1949, Auerbach wrote again regarding *Gracián*:

> A few days ago I discovered a good and sympathetic review of your *Gracián* in the *Hispanic Review,* published in Philadelphia, a photocopy of which I have sent by regular mail. I have, by the way, received two copies of the book, probably by mistake. To whom should I give the second copy? Castro? Alonso? Clavería? Spitzer? A library? Or to

> Mr. Reichenberger, who wrote the *Gracián* critique. He is an "Instructor" at the University of Pennsylvania, in the same department as Clavería in Philadelphia, obviously still a young man.

. . . and an Omitted Reading

Regardless of where the second copy ended up, Vossler died on May 18, 1949. Erich Auerbach, who appears not to have pursued Gracián further, died on October 13, 1957. With those two the consciousness of the meaning of the Gracián book appears to have been lost. Furthermore, the explicit polemical and political exclusion in the *Romanische Forschungen* was complemented by a silent exclusion in Ernst Robert Curtius's *Europäische Literatur und lateinisches Mittelalter* (European literature and the Latin Middle Ages), the Gracián chapter of which fails to mention *Graciáns Lebenslehre.* Naturally, one could counter that it was hardly possible to mention Krauss's book, since *Europäische Literatur* first appeared in 1948. Nevertheless Curtius supplemented his bibliography in later editions, such as this, which one finds in the Gracián chapter itself: "After the publication of this book I learned of the interpretation of *Agudeza* by T. E. May in *Hispanic Review* in 1948 . . . which clearly ignores the Latin background of this work." There would have been nothing stopping him from extending his polemics, written in his habitual *pluralis majestatis,* against the "schoolmaster-like" judgments of others, who understood little or nothing about Gracián, to *Graciáns Lebenslehre.* "If one looks at things from the French perspective," writes Curtius,

> one sees in cultism and conceptism two "dangerous" pathologies of the Spanish intellect that one can explain by noting that Spain to its own disadvantage never "had schoolmasters as Malherbe, Vaugelas, and the Academy." It goes without saying that such schoolmaster-like censorship will fail in the face of the task of historical knowledge and aesthetic estimation. We observe here again that the force of the system of the French normal classicism three hundred years after Vaugelas is still doing scholarly damage. The value of Gracián suffers from this even today. Is there no guide through Spanish literature whose knowledge is every bit as impeccable as is his love

> of Spain, one who is unhindered by French blinders? Indeed!! There is Ludwig Pfandl. He displays a sympathetic understanding for Spanish "Baroque sensibilities." But even he does not help further historical understanding, for he explains the "Spanish Baroque" . . . from the very essence of the Spanish Baroque. (Curtius 304)

Was there not also in the meantime a book by Krauss? Was it not engaged in a totally new "evaluation of Gracián," in which, among other things, the relationship, also addressed by Curtius, between "ingenium" and "judicium" plays a role? However, just as Curtius, who also fails to mention Fritz Schalk's wholly relevant study, conjures Krauss away through not mentioning him, he devastates Pfandl's *Geschichte der spanischen Nationalliteratur in ihrer Blütezeit* through teeming irony. To this end Curtius, who obviously misunderstood the ingenious Catholicism of Pfandl as an intellectual challenge, is not even afraid to manipulate quotes.[3] Nevertheless, Curtius's critique would certainly have been insignificant for ingenious Gracián scholarship if his Gracián chapter had not paved the (rhetorical and Latinist) orientation in (West) Germany for the majority of the inquiries into Gracián's work. These inquiries saw themselves as being exempt from having to think about (or even to read) *Graciáns Lebenslehre.* Likewise nobody called into question the judgment expressed in the *Romanische Forschungen* about the communist co-optation and castration of Gracián, as well as the violation of literary history and the liquidation of the cultural European memory by Werner Krauss, to say nothing of actually revising this judgment. I do not, by the way, believe in a general conspiracy; rather—from my own experience—I am convinced that the young Hispanists of the postwar era acted *bona fide.* To be sure, Krauss was a communist. One had heard this and knew this. And communists, one heard and also knew, had knives between their teeth. In short: *Graciáns Lebenslehre* was lost in (West) German Hispanic studies. And this was a tragedy for all of us in Germany, for Krauss and for Hispanic studies, indeed—above all because Krauss was only one among many.

Almost a half century after the slandering in *Romanische Forschungen* we should declare that Werner Krauss in no way claims

Gracián as a "party comrade," especially since, at the time he wrote the book in the death cell, he himself had not yet joined the party. What Erich Auerbach praised about *Graciáns Lebenslehre,* "the connections that are opened up to Montaigne, to the French of the seventeenth century, or also to our contemporary status," Flachskampf fundamentally misunderstood, although after the collapse of the "Thousand Year Reich" it should have been obvious to every reader what Krauss meant when he reported how Critilo and Andrenio, after their ascension to the *seso,* subsequently lose it—because nothing is lost as easily, even when one has experienced how a "betrayer of the people" spits out

> puffs of smoke screen from his mouth, a mouth that is accustomed to lying. . . . They [those who have lost the seso and thereby also their orientation] will be bestowed a final leader and Cicerone of ultimate wisdom for their march on Rome: the converted courtier. The sagacity of Argos is exceeded by him, as are the hermeneutics of the decipherers and the empathy of the wizard. For Rome is "the workshop of all great individuals." Both the nations that, in Gracián's view of the world, are called to the leadership of humanity encompass themselves in this "Courtier." He is "a Spaniard, set into an Italian soul." (Krauss, *Lebenslehre* 33)

Is one to seriously believe that Werner Krauss, sitting in the fascists' death cell, used the "March on Rome" formulation *in complete innocence*? This was in fact a socialist-turned-fascist "converted" leader, who brought about the "March on Rome." It was a *duce* with the soul of a *caudillo* or vice versa (for Spain in 1936–39, they collapsed into one). And "the March on Rome," organized by this *duce,* led to death, as does the "March on Rome" under the guidance of the last leadership in *El criticón.*

We may rest assured, that as little as Krauss sees in Gracián a communist comrade, he sees him even less as a fascist. The truth of this text, which because of its historical, dialectical, and philosophical complexity obviously had overchallenged the commentators, is a much different one. Just as Krauss sees in Gracián the Renaissance humanist who actually belongs to a new time and—optimistically turned to the future—mourns the loss of the past, he also sees in Gracián's work emancipatory potential. This emancipatory potential belongs in the onset of philosophical renewal of anthropological thinking through linguistic means, which Spain will no longer know; in the emancipation of aesthetic reflection; in the inclusion into the sciences of the conception of the soul and world; and in the judgment of human action from the perspective of a pragmatics (which already completely foreshadows American pragmatism)—in the realm of the early Enlightenment affirmed by Krauss. But he also sees the dangers that result from Gracián's deficits, on account of which he juxtaposes Gracián with his French counterparts, to simultaneously mediate between the author of *El criticón* and the tendencies of the French early Enlightenment as a task of reception:

> Gracián's worldly wisdom marks both a high point and an end. Already in one's first pass at his intellectual world one becomes easily aware of the limits of worldly experience. The polarity of the sexes, the occurrence of the passions of love in no way partake in the construction of the masculine world of striving, of business, of fame, and accomplishment. This lesson of life creates a most striking contrast to the portrait of the human of the French moralists, which forms itself with the appropriate consideration of the female role as partner. The psychology of the sexes is not a topic with which Gracián busies himself. The existence of irrational powers through the conversational situations of man and woman was already integrated into thinking in seventeenth-century France, and the hopelessness of reasonable behavior was again—under the sign of Jansenism—understood as a fundamental Christian experience of the world. (Krauss, *Lebenslehre* 156–157)

That would—as an overture to the enunciation of Gracián's rootedness in belief, which I quoted earlier—indicate that a worldly behavior such as Gracián's aimed at a total, indeed totalitarian, rationalization of action and could only be prevented from falling into inhumanity through a *salto mortale* in the unquestioned faith, unmediated by human action. It is better, more reasonable, and more enlightened to allow the sensual observation and the world of sensations to flow with equal right into the concept of world-changing action: "The great courage of human strife elevates itself [in Gracián] above the defeatedness of coming up short and may boldly snatch the saint's crown—a strife without internal rupture and therefore without return and without the deepened consciousness that led in France always again to the discovery of repressed ontological energies: to the double valuation of a masculine and a feminine truth, to recognition of the irrational facts of life that, at first sight, dares to face the so long misrecognized existence of the people" (Krauss, *Lebenslehre* 157–158). Gracián's disdain for women and for the people frightens Krauss, just as does the possibility of his reception by those who would want to or could misuse or misunderstand his call for a perfect human in the form of "héroes," as a propagation of "Herrenmoral" in the manner of Schopenhauer or Nietzsche, or by the theoreticians of "Vitalism" and the "psychologists of the unconscious" with C. G. Jung as their leader, who loved to dive into the supposed ground of the soul of the people:

> Gracián could be taken as the precursor to modern psychology. But his vision of the world runs naturally in an entirely different, indeed contrary, direction from that of psychology. While the modern depth psychology delves into the streams of irrationalism, Gracián's attempt expands and fortifies new territory for the soul in the realm of human self-governance, in line with intellectual aristocratic, early Enlightenment attitudes. The irrationalism of modern psychology should be understood as a counterattack to the borderless expansion of the natural sciences' claim of an explanation through the principle of causality. Hence the love of all things abysmal, the discovery of a death and destruction drive in the dark strata of the human soul, the setting free of its primitive and archaic originary affinities. Irrationalism necessarily leads to a complete renunciation of reason and human essence in front of the destructive activities of the forces of a technological age, abandoned to themselves and without the control of a higher order. Indeed, these destructive tendencies were frenetically welcomed in light of vitalism and of a newfangled beauty and a new moralism. (Krauss, *Lebenslehre* 160–161)

Let us not forget that this man is writing in his death cell, having been judged by the judicial center of the terroristic Nazi injustice, and those who "frenetically welcomed" with cries of "Heil" the representative of "newfangled beauty and of a new moralism," namely the "Führer," had in fact, with their reason, with their *seso*, rejected reason for the "destructive activities of a technological age abandoned to themselves and without the control of a higher order." And here Ludwig Flachskampf did perhaps understand something, even if he got the *dramatis personas* of the historical tragedy confused. The "order" to which Krauss refers is not the systematizing reason of a communist comrade, Gracián, but rather the Christian *telos* and ethics, or for that matter, that which in a godless world must take its place in order to hinder the use of technology for the destruction of humanity (for example, the concentration camps and weapons of mass destruction). Faced with irrationalism and its destructive tendencies, Krauss continues, "the unbreachable codification of Gracián's human being who is bound to himself can serve as an indication that, even in the realm of the soul, truly fruitful discovery cannot come out of the thoughtless repudiation of all traditional knowledge, rather out of the boldly gathered power of a renewed establishment of goals" (Krauss, *Lebenslehre* 161).

In fact, Krauss, under the death sentence, allows himself the liberty to view the "renewed establishment of goals" not as an unconditional ruling ideology, but as a balancing act between the intellectual elites and the people, between science and the spontaneous life of creatures, just as he thought he recognized it in the past as the promise of the future and as a humanist program in the soulful moment of fortunate balance of powers in Cervantes and also—this, too, was the harshest critique of German fascism—in Goethe, Herder, and the Romantics. The outstanding human being (or the one who understands himself as such) does not have the right to impose his standards upon others if he does not want to become an enemy of the people and thus the enemy of the individual, as happened in the Nazi empire, where one could hear and read this even in the daily usage of the language: "There are some 'measure-giving circles' at work, that, hidden from us on the margins of our existence, make history 'for us,'" Krauss states bitterly, continuing, "Humans have ceased to be the *measure* of all things" (*Lebenslehre* 152).

No, the outstanding man, the "hero," as Goethe says, must—according to Krauss—function as a member of the people for the people. And here, only in this place (remember that the Nazi army is on the run from the Soviet Union), Krauss dares to waste his thought on the hope that the balance between the particular individual, the intellectual, the scholar, and the people could perhaps be realized in communism:

> It is certain that such ideas [as Goethe's] are only able to unfold the entire expanse of consciousness in a new age, through Herder's designs, through the early Romantics' attempts, and then through the philosophy of the late Romantics and the historical school, and the fame of its last fulfillment is not to be found in the West, rather in the great Russian literature, which, beginning with Pushkin, achieves perhaps the only unmetaphorical conceptualization of the "people." Here the heroic nature not only sinks its roots into an archaic protoreality called "people," rather it is at one with its essence and represents nothing but an oscillation, a pacifying energy of the people that comes about through the impulse of its movement. But even this interpretation of the heroic touches upon a very old tradition, on the heroic epic of Igor, on the Bylines, etc. . . . , just as Cervantes and Lope de Vega took up the epic tradition of the ballads. (Krauss, *Lebenslehre* 158–159)

Certainly, Werner Krauss's historical optimism may have been too great. He may have been mistaken. But others have grossly erred for worse reasons and in much more comfortable circumstances. He, however, dared what very few others have dared: to combat (even according to Gracián's rules) the enemy, concretely the Nazi murderers, in supposed total defeat, in the face of death. With the masking style he learned from Gracián, which he unleashes even more radically in *PLN,* and with the dialectical art of *pointe,* he holds court over the grand tyrant and dismantles—though the critique of Gracián and especially through the analysis of misinterpretations of Gracián—the central mythical motive of Nazism: the image of the leader framed by *fasces*:

> The essence of these ruling men [*dieser herrschaftlichen Menschen*] cannot be analyzed through portrait art, rather it is brought to intuition through the rays of a panegyrical glorification, just as, on the other hand, the essence of the age in which we live sinks into the turbulent impression of a hostile mass and appears to encourage the silhouetted style of the satire. The wonder [*prodigio*] of heroically glossed-

> over essence and the monstrous un-nature of the all-too-many produce two aspects that fall onto humanity from infinity. The manifold of defective characters is legendary; its lost-ness and its immense over-weightedness make up the hellish character of the world, which lifts itself up to godliness with every hero. (Krauss, *Lebenslehre* 153–154)

Blond to Their Very Tongues; or, Laughter in the Death Cell

Naturally there will be many of those who will now claim to have always known that *Graciáns Lebenslehre* is not a scholarly work, but political literature. Or, one could, since this condemnation of Nazism and of all inhuman-irrational ideologies in *Graciáns Lebenslehre* has up to now remained untreated, draw the conclusion that such forms of resistance are (and have been) ineffectual. To the latter, one can perhaps respond that there are obviously people for whom it would be unbearable to fail morally even for themselves, and who, therefore, like Krauss, dare the impossible. The former can be refuted immediately, even if what the respectable Gracián specialist Sebastian Neumeister wrote just yesterday no longer holds true: "Krauss's book is among the best studies of Gracián's work." That which—because of the indifference among the scholars—may be unimaginable is namely that Krauss—as in his *Corneille als politischer Dichter* (1936), where he condemns the "Führer" (state)—does not project anachronism in his historical, analytical work with the text. And he does not produce cheap analogies between the past and present. Rather, by opening up the historical mechanisms, he allows these analogies to make their own judgment on our times from the facts of the texts, whereby that which we would like to call "scholarliness" remains untouched. The fact that this requires much "ingenio" and "agudeza" of "entendimiento," that is, much wit, may be acknowledged. And although Krauss never betrayed his witness, he believed that he had to excuse himself to Gracián: "It is a historical injustice; . . . one must therefore always encourage oneself to measure the past ideology on its effects on later times" (Krauss, *Lebenslehre* 160).

Krauss's artifice of a just and at the same time scholarly correct use of the witnesses of the past, that is to say, of Gracián, is completely evident when Krauss, in his critique of "the study of national character" and the "typologies of nations," as well as their topics in *El criticón*, ridicules the nationalist "psychology of peoples," hobbyhorse of German "Romance philology" until 1945. In uncovering the factual comedy of the supposed "inherent enmity" between France and Spain, he pillories the foolishness of the "inherent enmity" between Germany and France. He also reveals, through the apology of Charles V, the absurdity to which the belief in blood purity leads: "Through blood-mixture, through education, and through the continually and carefully developed intimacy with his peoples Charles V unites the essence of character of the various Occidental cultural nations" (49). The worst thing that Krauss, in his precarious situation, could do to the Nazis, however, was to quote at great length the biologically grounded negative judgment of Critilo about the Germans, which no "good German" could accept, a judgment that exposes to laughter the Nazis' own biologically racist self-evaluation as blond-haired and blue-eyed. Andrenio, the overall opportunist, explains that he would dare claim that the Germans are "the greatest people of Europe." Whereupon Critilo replies:

> Yes, the greatest in size, but not in other regards. Every German has twice the body of a Spaniard. Indeed, but only half the heart. How stately in size, but without a soul. How daring, yet cold. How brave yet, furthermore, how brutal! How beautiful, but without elegance. Great in height, yet small in sensibility. Blond to their very tongues. What great strength they have, but no elán (*brío*). They are giants of body and midgets of soul. They save money on clothing, but not on food. They are cheap in appointing their beds and in furnishing their homes, yet spend beyond control in their drink. . . . They speak the oldest language of all and at the same time the most barbaric. There are great technicians, but no great scholars. To the very tips of their fingers they have a fine touch—better they would have it in their brains. (Krauss, *Lebenslehre* 62–63)

Loss and Mourning: On Hubert Sommer and Edgar Zilsel

There is no doubt that, having been condemned as a resistance fighter against the Nazi state, Werner Krauss, the German Romance scholar, our colleague, not only wrote in his death cell with bound hands one of the best German books on Spanish literature—which alone should grant him a place of honor in the intellectual history of our nation—but in his cell he also set forth with this book his battle for a better Germany, unmasking and condemning the inhuman Nazi ideology. What devil enjoined us to disparage, repress, or forget this book? Would not German Romance studies, which, apart from the exiled and the persecuted, in the majority fell into line with the Nazis or at least merrily went along with them (see Hausmann), have had cause to enshrine Krauss for having saved their honor, most impressively with *Graciáns Lebenslehre*? His original sin of being a communist and going to the other Germany, from which he had hoped for something better, made him and especially his book on Gracián disappear from our view. But we lost even more in this process, which becomes apparent when we ask ourselves how Krauss came to Gracián when condemned to death, although up to that point he had taken only a cursory position on him. Actually, around 1940 he wanted to finish writing his book on Cervantes, as we know from his correspondence with Martin Hellweg (Nerlich, *Verhältnis* 91–136). Even if we accept that he had already been working on Gracián when the Gestapo arrested him, it remains to be explained what at that very moment led him to Gracián. An indication of this is to be found in *Graciáns Lebenslehre* itself. It is in a footnote on the relationship between "genio" and "génie": "cf. the Marburg dissertation by Hubert Sommer" (Krauss, *Lebenslehre* 200; cf. Nerlich, *Verhältnis* 69–70, 91–136, 170–173).

Hubert Sommer was born on March 9, 1917, and among other academic pursuits engaged in Romance studies with Elena Eberwein, Glaser, Hellweg, Kuhn, Franz Walter Müller, Schürr, and Krauss, under whose direction he wrote a dissertation on "génie": "A Contribution to the Meaning of the Word." As he was drafted into the German army on November 21, 1941, he was allowed to take his oral examination on November 18, before the dissertation itself had been accepted. The dissertation was accepted on March 26, 1942, by Werner Krauss, who was at the time ex officio his doctoral adviser. Thus Krauss at this time would have had to grapple with Gracián himself. For Sommer separates the definition of the word "génie" into three sections: (1) "Genius" and "génie" from the *Roman de la rose* to Scaliger; (2) "génie" in the seventeenth century; and (3) "génie" in the eighteenth century. In the second section he delves specifically into the concept of "genio"-"ingenio" in Juan Huarte de San Juan's *Examen de ingenios para las ciencias* (1575) and in Gracián and his French reception. It is a brilliant piece of research, which, apart from a couple of chapters that Paul Zumthor published postmortem because he and Walther von Wartburg held them—rightfully—as exceptional, has remained unnoticed by those who have worked on "genio"-"génie" since the war.[4] That is all the more tragic since Hubert Sommer is among those to whom we owe gratitude. After he was granted his doctoral degree on January 4, 1943, fourteen days before Krauss was condemned to death, he himself was arrested on September 27, 1943, for having warned members of the French resistance of a pending SS raid. Immediately thereafter he was degraded and, like Werner Krauss, sentenced to death. Like Krauss he survived, in that his sentence was commuted to five years' imprisonment, of which he spent part in a military prison in Freiburg im Breisgau, before he was released to the "defense of the front" and put into a "delinquent battalion" in August 1944. He fell in France on September 29, 1944.

Upon his return from Nazi imprisonment to Marburg in 1945, Werner Krauss heard of the tragic fate of his student from Sommer's wife. It must have affected him deeply in that he owed to Sommer (apart from all of the other ties and memories) not only a deepened understanding of Gracián and of the theme of the "genio"-"ingenio" but also the acquaintance with the work of Edgar Zilsel, who, like Sommer, has been forgotten in German intellectual history, at least in German Romance studies. Sommer, who also draws upon Zilsel's *Die Geniereligion: Ein kritischer Versuch über das moderne Persönlichkeitsideal* (1918), understood his dissertation as a sequel to Zilsel's book *Die Entstehung des Geniebegriffs* (1926), which traces the development of the concept (of genius) to the Renaissance. He writes in the foreword to his dissertation:

> In recent times multiple works on the concept of genius have been written.... Edgar Zilsel goes beyond everything else that has been done with his work on the emergence of the concept of genius. A work that one would like to read often, that analyzes the cult of great men from ancient

> times up to the Italian Renaissance with its history, meaning, its mythical and sociological basis. The French concept of genius has not yet been taken up in a general study. Also the occasional studies on the French concept of the genial human being, undertaken by the Germanistic side, reveal to us very little. They often suffer from the . . . image of French classicism, of the "raison" and of Boileau. The few allusive sentences of Edgar Zilsel concerning the planning of a second, and unfortunately unpublished, part of his work, tell us more, with their caution, about the French concept of genius as many of the pages of [Kurt] Bauernhorst [*Der Geniebegriff, seine Entwicklung und seine Formen, unter besonderer Berücksichtigung des Goetheschen Standpunktes*, Breslau 1930].

The courage with which Hubert Sommer storms into the house of his Marburg doctoral commission is admirable, given that Zilsel, a mathematician by formation, was persona non grata in Nazi Germany. Born in 1891, the Jewish-born Austrian, Edgar Zilsel, published his *Die Geniereligion* in 1918 as a result of a confrontation with the same "Herrenmoral," or "master's moralism," that Krauss abhors (above all, that of Houston Stewart Chamberlain). He attempts to "habilitate" in the Vienna philosophical faculty in 1923 with his *Beiträge zur Geschichte des Geniebegriffs*. However, despite a positive evaluation from Ernst Cassirer, the Vienna faculty rejected his work as sociologically oriented and therefore an unphilosophical contribution (as a work that "obviously moves in the margins of intellectual history"). Zilsel, an active Social Democrat, worked as a secondary school teacher and in the Viennese continuing education program. In 1934 he was dismissed by the Austro-fascist regime and was forced in 1938 after the "annexation" to flee with his wife and child. Stopping for a while in England, he finally made it to the United States, where he committed suicide on March 11, 1944. *Die Entstehung des Geniebegriffs* (1926) was reprinted in 1962; however, almost no one seems to have taken notice. Not until 1977 did a selection of his essays written in the United States appear (*Die sozialen Ursprünge der neuzeitlichen Wissenschaft*, Suhrkamp). In 1990 a new edition of his *Geniereligion* appeared (again with Suhrkamp). And in 1993, simultaneous with the appearance of the first reference to the fate of Hubert Sommer in *Lendemains*, a French edition of the *Entste-*

hung des Geniebegriffs appeared, under the title *Le génie: Histoire d'une notion de l'Antiquité à la Renaissance,* edited by Nathalie Heinich in Editions de Minuit. It is probable that Sommer had his first encounter with Gracián in this history of the concept of genius, which, with one exception, remained unnoticed by Gracián scholarship even in postwar Germany.[5] The dialogue that Sommer held with Krauss on Gracián and Zilsel ended in 1944, as Krauss, in the shadows of the gallows, finished his Gracián book. It ended with the death of Zilsel and Sommer. Perhaps herein lies the reason why Werner Krauss never again returned to Gracián.

A Look at José Antonio Maravall, at Werner Krauss, and at Ourselves

Not only did Edgar Zilsel, Hubert Sommer, and, finally, Werner Krauss get lost in (West) German intellectual history after 1945 in terms of the conceptualization of genius, but also in regard to basic methodological orientation: the social and historically grounded cultural and literary sciences—called "sociologism" under the brand of Cain (see Krauss, "Literaturgeschichte") and later "materialism" or "Marxism"—that had been made taboo by the Cold War. The consequences were more grave than one could imagine. And it is to be hoped that now, after the fall of the Berlin Wall, certain phobias will vanish, that omissions will be worked through, and that the damages will be repaired, as much as possible. While no exhaustive inventory to outline a calamity that is especially obvious in (West) German Gracián scholarship will be undertaken here, let it be said that the avoidance of a dialogue with Krauss and with his Marxist-inspired literary studies coincided with the total domination of the history of ideas and rhetoric in Gracián's work in the tradition of Ernst Robert Curtius. This Curtius-inspired research on Gracián occasionally bound itself with Hugo Friedrich's approach, both currents leading to an ever greater silencing of Werner Krauss and—*dans la foulée*—of the international sociohistorical and/or sociological-cultural and literary sciences that engaged themselves with Spain.

It shall be said that this German impoverishment of Gracián scholarship did not exclude first-rate studies (above all, after 1968, when the borders loosened up a bit [see the works of Blüher, Hidalgo-Serna, Janik, and Schulz-Buschhaus, among others]). But it is obvious that the German one-sidedness has not been to the benefit of international scholarly dialogue. This can be read spectacularly in the studies of Gerhart Schröder, who has been working on Gracián for almost forty years and links up with social-historical literary scholarship in an excellent essay on the life and work of Gracián, an essay that could and should have found in *Graciáns Lebenslehre* a genial model (Schröder, "Moralistik"). Indeed, Schröder quotes Krauss in his bibliography. But in his text—at least explicitly—no reference is made to Krauss. Even more curious or telling is the fact that the relevant works of José Antonio Maravall (*La philosophie politique espagnole au XVIIe siècle dans ses rapports avec l'esprit de la Contre-Réforme* [Paris, 1955] or *Bases antropológicas del pensamiento de Gracián* [Madrid, 1958]) are not taken into account. For obviously the Cold War taboo extended to Maravall, a Marxist cultural sociologist and historian under Franco. That is all the more curious in that Maravall has found acceptance in international Hispanic studies from France to the United States (indeed, it is not an exaggeration to say that Maravall plays the role for international Hispanic studies that Max Weber performs for sociology).

The strange situation to which this (West) German reception avoidance leads becomes even more evident when one sees that no one other than Werner Krauss holds a singular dialogue with Maravall, one that is characterized by mutual respect. This is manifested among other ways by the reception that Maravall accords to the book that in Germany had fallen into oblivion: *Graciáns Lebenslehre.* Thus he writes in, among other places, *Culture of the Baroque* (1975) in reference to Werner Krauss on the latent "commodity aesthetics" in Gracián: "W. Krauss has indicated the presence of an 'economy based on laws,' literally, of an *ökonomische Gesetzlichkeit*" (Maravall, 167).

What makes Maravall interesting in our context is the paradoxical fact that he who received Werner Krauss's Gracián book has not even been acknowledged by literary and sociologically oriented German Gracián scholarship since 1968. This can only be read as perplexing when one notes that Gerhart Schröder does not even mention Maravall in his notable and thought-provoking habilitation thesis *Logos and Artifice: On the Development of*

Aesthetics in Early Modernity, in which he, in a further attempt to show Gracián as the founder of modern aesthetics and precursor of Kant, returns to the positions of Borinski (whom, curiously, he does not mention) and Krauss in *Graciáns Lebenslehre* (which is at least mentioned in a footnote as a study among others). Nevertheless, it is obvious that any sociohistorical investigation of the Spanish Baroque has no full international legitimacy without taking heed of Maravall's work. In contrast to recent German Gracián scholarship it is advisable to study Mercedes Blanco's monumental summation of the same in her 1992 study, in which Maravall, Krauss, and Borinski are not forgotten. The fact that in her bibliography Curtius figures with the first name *Edmond* R. could be interpreted as a harbinger of better times. The omitted confrontation with Maravall (and also with Krauss) is in Gerhart Schröder's case especially unfortunate, since *Logos and Artifice,* despite all such caprices, represents an important contribution to a new designation of European aesthetic history. Perhaps now, when the fall of the Wall makes it possible to see the lost scholarship, would be an opportune time to offer a colloquium on *Graciáns Lebenslehre* and the state of Gracián scholarship both within and outside of Germany. This would provide the opportunity to balance out the historical, political, moral, and intellectual deficits and omissions that have hindered us from honoring the memory of Werner Krauss, from coming clean with ourselves, and from entering timely discussions in the arena of international scholarship.

Notes

1. The third review, written by an H. Kunz, does not surpass the length of a publishing house's advertisement, and more than half of it consists of quotations. It appeared in Basel in *Studia Philologica. Jahrbuch der Schweizerischen Philosophischen Gesellschaft* 9 (1949): 189–190. H. Kunz calls Gracián "an unknown author" and Krauss's book "an excellent presentation." Aside from this he mentions that Krauss "could not take into account secondary literature," without explaining why.

2. "Debemos imputar el mérito de tal éxito [de ser la crítica graciana alemana 'una de las más atractivas'] sobre todo a dos nombres: a Werner Krauss y a Hugo Friedrich. Werner Krauss, antifascista militante, escapó a la ejecución iminente sólo gracias a la ayuda de un amigo médico, que le declaró enfermo mental. En el año 1943, durante un período de amenazas y peligros extremos, Krauss escribió y con las manos encadenadas, la primera monografía sobre Gracián después de Borinski, sin ayuda de una biblioteca y en parte refiriéndose sólo a antiguas ediciones que le eran accesibles. Comprende a Gracián como psicólogo de

la Corte, con cultura humanista, refinado de la llamada 'emigración interior' durante el nazismo, pertenece a los mejores estudios sobre la obra de Gracián."

3. Curtius, *Europäische Literatur* 299, n. 1: "Pfandl tadelt Gracián, weil bei ihm die 'eklektische Kombinierung' von *cultismo* und *conceptismo* 'an Stelle reinlicher Unterscheidung im Sinne der modernen literarhistorischen Forschung' trete. Leider—fügen wir hinzu—konnten deren 'reinliche' Ergebnisse Góngora nicht bekannt sein" ("Pfandl, to be sure, censures Gracián because he exhibits an 'eclectic combination' of *cultismo* and *conceptismo* 'instead of a clear-cut distinction as understood by modern literary-historical research.' Unfortunately—we add—its 'clear-cut' results could not be known to Góngora" [Curtius, *European Literature* 295 n. 60]). The truth is that Pfandl blames the modern literary critics, because they want to establish the abstract distinction between *cultismo* and *culteranismo,* a distinction that is denied by the work of Gracián. Still worse is the statement on p. 301, n. 3: "Es ist... unbegreiflich, wenn gesagt wird, die *agudeza* sei 'nichts anderes als eine bis in die feinsten Verästelungen ausgesponnene Tropen—und Figurenlehre' (Pfandl 551)." In reality Pfandl says precisely the contrary (551–552): "Agudeza ist also im Sinne von Gracián zweierlei: zuerst ein in seiner Knappheit vielsagendes Ordnungswort für die Fähigkeit oder Begabung, den Edelstil zu handhaben, und dann ein Sammelbegriff für die komplizierten Einzelheiten der Technik dieses Stils. Diese letztere aber stellt nichts anderes dar als eine bis in die feinsten Verästelungen ausgesponnene und fortgeführte Tropen—und Figurenlehre, den Versuch der Synthese einer gracianischen, aus *conceptismo* und *cultismo* gemischten Poetik."

4. Hubert Sommer's pioneering work remained unaccounted even in a research report written in Marburg on Gracián reception in France, although Sommer's dissertation must be available in the Marburg University library and although the author quotes Krauss's *Graciáns Lebenslehre,* in which Sommer is cited (see Oskar Roth, "Gracián, La Rochefoucald und Corbeville," 41–95).

5. In the studies that I am aware of regarding "genio"-"génie" written after 1945 by German Romance scholars as specific studies of the history of the concept or other studies that, while working through other topics, touch upon the "genio-génie" complex, Edgar Zilsel goes unmentioned. One exception, not unsurprisingly, is Gerhart Schröder, who, in his *Baltasar Graciáns "Criticón": Eine Untersuchung zur Beziehung zwischen Manierismus und Moralistik,* mentions Zilsel's *Die Entstehung des Geniebegriffs.*

Works Cited

Auerbach, Erich, and Werner Krauss. "Eine unveröffentlichte Korrespondenz." Ed. Karlheinz Barck. *Beiträge zur Romanischen Philologie* 26 (1987): Heft 2, 301–326; Heft 1, 161–186.

Azorín [José Martínez Ruiz]. *El político (con un epílogo futurista).* Madrid: Caro Raggio, 1919.

Blanco, Mercedes. *Les Rhétoriques de la Pointe: Baltasar Gracián et le Conceptisme en Europe.* Geneva: Slatkine, 1992.

Blüher, Karl A. "Gracian's Aphorismen in *Oráculo Manual* und die Tradition der politischen Aphorismensammlung." *Spanien, Ibero-Romania* 1(1969): 319–327.

Borinski, Karl. *Baltasar Gracián und die Hofliteratur in Deutschland.* Halle: Niemeyer, 1984.

Castro, Américo. "Gracián y España." *Santa Teresa y otros ensayos.* Madrid: Historia Nueva, 1929.

Coster, Adolphe. *Baltasar Gracián.* Traducción, prólogo y notas de Ricardo del Arco y Garay. Zaragoza: Institución Fernando el Católico, 1947.

Croce, Benedetto. *Estetica come scienza dell'espressione e linguistica generale.* Bari: Laterza, 1922.

Curtius, Ernst Robert. *Europäische Literatur und lateinisches Mittelalter.* 3rd ed. Bern: München, 1961.

Curtius, Ernst Robert. *European Literature and the Latin Middle Ages.* Trans. Willard R. Trask. New York: Harper and Row, 1963.

Dvorak, Johann. "Zu Leben und Werk Edgar Zilsels und zur Soziologie des Geniekults." In Edgar Zilsel, *Die Geniereligion: Ein kritischer Versuch über das moderne Persönlichkeitsideal.* Stw 791. Frankfurt am Main: Suhrkamp, 1990. 7–40.

Flachskampf, Ludwig. Review of Werner Krauss, *Graciáns Lebenslehre. Romanische Forschungen* 62 (1950): 260–265.

Hausmann, Frank-Rutger. "Aus dem Reich der seelischen Hungersnot." *Dokumente zur Fachgeschichte der Romanistik um Dritten Reich.* Briefe and Würzburg: Königshausen & Neumann, 1993.

Hidalgo-Serna, Emilio. *Das ingeniöse Denken bei Baltasar Gracián. Der "Concepto" und seine logische Funktion.* Munich: Fink, 1985.

Janik, Dieter. "Das 'Auge der Seele': Erkenntnistheoretische, moralische und ästhetische Funktionen einer Metaphor, ausgehend von Baltasar Gracián." *Texte, Kontexte, Strukturen. Beitrage zur französischen, spanischen und hispanoamerikanischen Literatur. Festschrift zum 60. Geburtstag von Karl Alfred Blüher.* Tübingen: Gunter Narr, 1987. 371–385.

Jauß, Hans-Robert. "Werner Krauss—wiedergelesen." *Lendemains* 69/70 (1993): 192–210.

Krauss, Werner. *Corneille als politischer Dichter.* Marburg/Lahn: Ebel, 1936.

———. *Graciáns Lebenslehre.* Frankfurt am Main: Klostermann, 1947.

———. "Wege der spanischen Frührenaissancelyrik." Reprinted in *Gesammelte Aufsätze zur Literatur- und Sprachwissenschaft.* Frankfurt am Main: Klostermann, 1949. 113–151.

———. "Literaturgeschichte als geschichtlicher Auftrag." *Sinn und Form,* 1950. Reprinted in *Literaturtheorie, Philosophie und Politik.* Ed. M. Naumann. Berlin and Weimar: Aufbau-Verlag, 1984. 7–61.

———. "Bericht aus der Todeszelle." *Lendemains* 69/70 (1993): 157–163.

———. Nachlass. Werner Krauss Archives, Potsdam.

Kunz, H. *Studia Philologica: Jahrbuch der Schweizerischen Philosophischen Gesellschaft* 9 (1949): 189–190.

Lethen, Helmut. *Verhaltenslehren der Kälte: Lebensversuche zwischen den Kriegen.* Frankfurt am Main: Suhrkamp, 1994.

Maravall, José Antonio. *Culture of the Baroque: Analysis of a Historical Structure.* 1975. Trans. Terry Cochran. Foreword by Wlad Godzich and Nicholas Spadaccini. Minneapolis: University of Minnesota Press, 1986.

Nerlich, Michael. "Zum deutsch-französischen Verhältnis: Werner Krauss." *Lendemains* 69/70 (1993): 8–87.

———, ed. *Zum deutsch-französischen Verhältnis: Werner Krauss. Lendemains* 69/70 (1993): 7–259.

Neumeister, Sebastian. "Gracián en Alemania." *Baltasar Gracián: Selección de estudios, investigación actual y documentación.* Suplemento. Materiales de trabajo intelectual. Barcelona: Anthropos, 1993. 121–125.

Pfandl, Ludwig. *Geschichte der spanischen Nationalliteratur in ihrer Blütezeit.* Freiburg im Breisgau: Herder, 1929. Reprint, Darmstadt: Wissenschaftliche Buchigesellschaft, 1967.

Reichenberger, Arnold G. *Hispanic Review* 17 (1949): 169–171.

Schulz-Buschhaus, Ulrich. "Baltasar Gracián: *El criticón.*" *Der spanische Roman vom Mittelalter bis zur Gegenwart.* Ed. Volker Roloff and Harald Wentzlaff-Eggebert. Düsseldorf: Schwann-Bagel, 1986. 121–144.

Romera-Navarro, Miguel. Introduction to *El criticón,* by Baltasar Gracián. Philadelphia: University of Pennsylvania Press, 1938–40.

Roth, Oskar. "Gracián, La Rochefoucauld und Courbeville: Aspekte der französischen Gracián-Rezeption in spätklassizistischer Zeit." *Aufsätze zum 18. Jahrhundert in Frankreich.* Ed. H.-J. Lope. Frankfurt am Main: Lang, 1979. 41–95.

Schalk, Fritz. "Baltasar Gracián und das Ende des siglo de oro." *Romanische Forschungen* (1940): 265–283; (1941): 113–127.

Schröder, Gerhart. *Baltasar Graciáns "Criticón": Eine Untersuchung zur Beziehung zwischen Manierismus und Moralistik.* Munich: Fink, 1966.

———. "Moralistik, Handelskapitalismus und Absolutismus." *Renaissance und Barock.* Ed. August Bock. Frankfurt am Main: Athenäum, 1972. 257–269.

———. *Logos und List: Zur Entwicklung der Ästhetik in der frühen Neuzeit.* Königstein: Athenäum, 1985.

Spitzer, Leo. *Romanische stil- und literaturstudien.* Marburg/Lahn: Elwer'sche (Braun), 1931.

Vossler, Karl. "Introducción a Gracián." *Revista de Occidente* (September 1935): 330–348.

———. *Poesie der Einsamkeit in Spanien.* Munich, 1940. 2nd ed., Beck, 1950.

Zilsel, Edgar. *Die Geniereligion: Ein kritischer Versuch über das moderne Persönlichkeitsideal.* Stw 791. Frankfurt am Main: Suhrkamp, 1990.

Afterword

Constructing Gracián

Edward H. Friedman

[Secretary to boss:]
"Sir, the following paradigm
shifts occurred
while you were out."
—cartoon by Robert Mankoff,
New Yorker, November 27, 1995

Perhaps the most accurate adjective for Baltasar Gracián is *difficult.* Gracián belongs to a literary school that relishes obscurity for its own sake. Uniting concept and conceit, he challenges the analytical and rhetorical skills—the astuteness, the wit—of his readers. The rhetoric of *conceptismo* is hardly an empty rhetoric. Discursive play is linked to social, political, and theological issues. If the words of Gracián's texts are often puzzles to be solved, the solution does not lie solely in decoding but in complex recodings of messages. The author is an exemplary exponent of the *ars combinatoria.* Practical guides or manuals become exquisite verbal artifacts and symbolic tracts. The realms of the senses are juxtaposed with the highest levels of morality, nature with artifice, action with contemplation, the expedient with the noble, the nuanced overview with the aphorism. In tropological terms, Gracián is poorly served by synecdoche, for the parts remain parts, as opposed to microcosms of the whole. The whole is, fittingly, resistant, elusive, slippery, too comprehensive and possibly too compartmentalized for easy access.

Criticism provides insights into authors and texts, while at the same time defining, or constantly redefining, the parameters and the presuppositions of the critical act. There is, in our current preoccupation (and fascination) with theory, a tendency to use theoretical models to mediate the study of texts. The process expands the object under scrutiny, in that the organizing principles that inform the text proper are the product of the organizing principles of the individual critic in accordance with a set of theoretical presuppositions. Whether one chooses to label the phenomenon deferral at the critical level or to inscribe the critic into the *mise-en-abîme,* it seems problematic to view "professional" criticism as a direct confrontation between reader and text. The critical path is often no less complex than the objects under investigation; the circuitous routes within texts may be replicated by readers who attempt to traverse—that is to say, to decode—them. *Rhetoric and Politics: Gracián and the New World Order* is a testament to current theoretical modes. We gain access to Gracián through studies that propose a series of mediating categories. The question of how to read Gracián becomes a question of linkage, of selection, of a particular movement from signifier to signified, from vehicle to tenor. We may find ourselves in a baroque age of theory, in which the initial mysteries to be resolved are the demarcation of the text and the aims of criticism.

There is a certain joy—derived from the pleasure of the text, as it were—in noting how the same words can strike different readers in different ways. Consider, for example, the closing chapter of *Don Quijote.* One may see, in Alonso Quijano's death, the character's disillusionment and acceptance of reality or Cervantes's coming to terms with his own mortality. Carnival is over, and the errant knight and his creator must return to the real world. If one chooses to analyze the ending within the parameters established by the prologue to Part 2, in which the authorial figure announces that Don Quijote will be dead and buried by the novel's end in order to ward off false sequels such as Avellaneda's, the focus will not be on Don Quijote's psyche but on his marketability and on his endurance as text. Theology, spirituality, madness, techniques of characterization, and the rhetoric of *desengaño* can all be brought to bear on the demise of Alonso Quijano, but from the other end of the spectrum the very literariness of the knight and the adversarial relation between the literati Cervantes and Avellaneda may lead the reader to favor a secular and ironic reading of the conclusion. While the metafictional thrust of the novel leads me to favor the second direction, it is clear that brilliant arguments have been made for the serious reading of the ending, arguments that help to enrich and energize the other view. Consideration of the means by which elements within the text engage theoretical connections is, arguably, as much a part of the critical enterprise as the interpretation of texts per se, in large part because the two are inextricably intertwined. When we endeavor to discern the subject of criticism, we often find self-fashioning at work. This is not to eradicate the significance of the text but, in the Baroque and poststructuralist lexicons, respectively, to obscure and to defer meaning. Pluralism, in the semantic sense, represents the impetus rather than the defeat of criticism.

Baltasar Gracián lends himself to the open spaces of criticism. Manuals of literature project a Gracián who epitomizes the Baroque artist, the maker of conceits and a traveler on numerous discursive paths. Gracián offers moral and political commentary. He writes fiction, and he dissects rhetoric. He is an allegorist and an empiricist. We may admire his adherence to propriety and his delight in excess, his abstract nature and his respect for practicality, his devotion and audacity, his devout spirit and his enthusiasm for the worldly. We know that Gracián was censured in Valencia (between the publication of *El político* and *El discreto*) for announcing from the pulpit that he would read a letter sent from hell. He spent his last years paying the consequences of having published *El criticón* without the permission of his superiors. His personal circumstance brought creative vigor and a desire to communicate with his fellow man into conflict with a restrictive environment. The Gracián extracted from his biography and from his works is hardly an easily constructed or consistent figure. The revelation of the self, the sage advice, the verbal and conceptual puzzles, and the play of the mundane and the eternal inevitably will point to more than one inscription (and description) of authorial consciousness. The frame is not so much enigmatic as overdetermined. Thus, the task will involve the positing of a frame and the elaboration of a critical protocol, or mediating ground. The consciousness that motivates the operation may identify its object as the historical Gracián, the implied author, the state, the Baroque age, or the reader, among other options. The goal is to expose a structure, a rhetoric, be it encoded or inherent, through which to comprehend the text. I do not intend, in what follows, to confuse afterword with final word. Rather than pass judgment on the approaches to Gracián, I hope to show how one reader elects to frame the essays and to designate areas that could be deemed as open for further exploration.

Nicholas Spadaccini and Jenaro Talens initiate the collection of essays on Gracián with an allusion to relations of power. The very fact that one may look to Gracián for instructions on worldly power is paradoxical. A mediating agent of the introductory chapter is José Antonio Maravall, who in his effort to delineate Baroque culture relies heavily on the domination of the state. Spadaccini and Talens advance a dialectics of creation, in which the individual strives for self-preservation amid the burdens of institutionalized authority. In many of his writings, Gracián casts his gaze on the *hic et nunc* of social interaction, and the relative nature of his recommendations may surprise us. Gracián's universe seems undeniably logocentric, but meaning is variable, subject to the whims of context and of the speaker or writer. When Gracián advises us to maintain a degree of ambiguity in word and deed, he deviates from what could be categorized as a fundamentalist semiotics in order to set forth a formula for success, a formula through which the individual may succeed within the system. Moderation, control, and, perhaps most important, knowledge can promote the gaining of control in a limited, but crucial, manner. The notion of absolute values, whether linguistic or political, is replaced by a rhetoric of pragmatism. Spadaccini and Talens focus less on the declining imperial power than on the strategies by which citizens and writers may empower themselves. The state presupposes a compliant subject, while the individual takes advantage of gaps, or inadvertent flexibility, within the hierarchies of control. The Jesuit moralist concentrates on the outer being, on self-(re)presentation, on elitism, on rhetoric.

One may contemplate, as do Spadaccini and Talens, how the masters of Spanish Baroque art perceive the role of the individual writer in light of the power structure and how Hispanists have tended to "accommodate" Gracián in the scheme of things. Although the editors accentuate points of contact with current discourse on the political status of writing, I would suggest that their commentary on the topic may inspire the reader to recontextualize the *Criticón,* the centerpiece of Gracián's writings, whose allegorical, and self-consciously bipartite, structure should reflect the precarious balance of power, together with the interplay of earthly and higher orders. The connection between *El criticón* and structuralism is evident. Poststructuralism adds, perforce, attention to the mediating space, and this is where the essays of *Rhetoric and Politics,* I would submit, find a common denominator. Each of the authors elucidates a method of access to Gracián. The process yields both discovery and a necessary absence of plenitude, which the juxtaposition underscores and helps to diminish.

Gracián is a Spanish Baroque writer. Our concepts of the Baroque facilitate our attempts to situate him, just as he serves to epitomize, and to characterize, the Baroque. Alban K. Forcione discusses Gracián's confrontation with tradition as a challenge to the philosophical and theological intertext, analogous to Cervantes's challenge, most notably in *Don Quijote,* to the literary intertext. Forcione deploys terms associated with rewriting, terms such as "imaginative reconstruction" and "recreation." It is in this setting that "the traditional rational cosmos has metaphorically reconstituted itself as the Baroque court, in an image of plenitude integrated not through reason or love but rather through power and charismatic self-display." Gracián recasts the miracle narrative, which relies on the incomprehensibility of divine power, as hexameral narrative, through which God chooses to make himself comprehensible to man, while bearing in mind man's limited capacity for understanding. Literary creation and ideology unite to protect the orthodoxy, to defend the rationality of the universe. Significantly, the verbal constructs are able to incorporate contemporary political concerns and to find a place for man as microcosm, bound always to the image of God.

Forcione contends that Gracián's "most astonishing innovation" is the transformation of man as reader of the world around him. From Cicero to Milton, man stands before a "completed" text, whereas in *El criticón* man has a measure of imaginative freedom that would permit individual readings, uncharted interpretations: "At this most subversive moment of Gracián's articulation of the Book of the World, man's cosmic connection springs apart, the created world loses its essential and indelible character, a new subject stands as reader and creator before a potentially chaotic reality, the imagination (*ingenio*) makes a powerful ontological claim in the face of reason's traditional enthronement and present collapse." The theological frame of *El criticón* displaces the cosmic order with "disquieting scenarios of contemporary absolutist politics." The absolutist state and the Baroque artist operate through the imagination, which often replaces the rational with the irrational. Individualism has its internal contradictions; the mind is liberated, maintaining a distance from any predetermined metaphysical order, but the individual remains a subject of the state. In Forcione's view, the most decisive effects of this change—of this vision of man as a "*distanced* being"—lie in the area of worldly philosophy, in pragmatic self-fashioning. The consequence of the shifts in focus is, in essence, disillusionment, *desengaño*. Man is free to rediscover—to reinvent—the world, but what he finds behind dazzling surface appearances is frighteningly empty.

There obviously can be multiple readings of Forcione's reading of Gracián, some of which would be deconstructive. The freedom of man is, in the final analysis, illusory and ironic. The imagination liberates humanity from the binds of determinism and passivity, but the new engagement with the cosmos only forces individuals to realize that the substitute reality, in part of their own making, is infinitely inferior to the totality that they have rejected. How does the overriding spirit of disillusionment affect the early lessons in worldly philosophy? Are the self-help manuals and the impact of aphorisms and examples rendered inactive by the hollow core of appearances? How does self-representation fare in a context distinguished by a lack of substance? If everything leads toward *desengaño*, what, in retrospect, is the value of the quest? Stated a bit differently, does disillusionment rewrite its textual precedents? Do the encounters of Critilo and Andrenio on their journey reenact, in conclusive ways, Gracián's encounter with philosophical, ideological, and artistic traditions? Does imaginative energy, as a means of moving beyond the fixed patterns of the past into new realms of subjectivity, become a paradoxical first stage of refutation and nostalgia? Does liberation free man from the binds of security and harmony only to expose the alternatives as treacherous and insubstantial? Do the insights at the end of the road bring increased knowledge or a demystification of knowledge? What is Gracián's authentic trajectory, and how can one describe the convergence of allegory and metanarrative in *El criticón*? Does the critical act, informed by recent theory, uncover or fabricate Gracián? Together with the introductory essay by Spadaccini and Talens, Forcione's contribution lays the groundwork for a reevaluation of Gracián.

Isabel C. Livosky emphasizes the Machiavellian overtones of Gracián's political treatises. The model is not Philip IV, with whose policies the writer often disagrees, but Ferdinand the Catholic, and the goal is victory at any cost. Elitist, probabilist, and self-promoting thoughts can enable the cultured, discreet man to carve a niche for himself in society. Livosky quotes R. O. Jones, who holds that the subject of the *Oráculo manual* is *worldly* prudence, for the divine is taken for granted. This stance appears to beg the question. Livosky sees the politician, the hero, and the discreet man—and Gracián's portrayal of the three prototypes—as part of a movement toward the introspection and the disillusionment of *El criticón*. Her essay invites us to reexamine the mediating spaces between the early texts and the culmination of Gracián's artistry, for Livosky leaves open the points of connection. The political essays are not presented as self-consuming artifacts, and one may wonder if Gracián leaves a trail of evidence that would mark the transition from this life to the higher order, from the triumphant resonance of self-fashioning to a quest for the soul of man. Is it the failure of the present to live up to the past, or is it something even more decisive, more profound? Among the most respected of theological precepts is the ultimate equality of all human beings, who are to be judged by their works, not by their social status. How can one reconcile the cultural and ideological elitism of Gracián with the egalitarian principles of eternity?

For Malcolm K. Read, the answer may lie in language itself, as a guide to truth. We are victims of appearances until we rise above the delusions to recognize that true values are unadorned, directly accessible to us. Gracián is aware of the mutability of language, of its suitability to diverse associative fields. Rhetoric, moral philosophy, and history, for example, stem from, and acknowledge, different linguistic contexts. That this "ideologue of the Absolutist State" advocates semantic relativity is not necessarily a contradiction, given that absolutism itself must account for an increasingly alienated society. Interestingly, Read demonstrates that commercial metaphors bridge the gap between the verbal and ideological extremes of Gracián's writings. Here, the idea of language as commodity serves to synthesize Gracián's process with his product, his Baroque invention with the realities of life and art. I consider both intriguing and convincing Read's argument that, for Gracián, obscurity—inaccessibility—imitates the way in which God sustains the admiration of his subjects. If (obscure) language is power, however, how does the story of disillusionment in *El criticón* put forward, that is, display, its discursive analogue? When, and how, do linguistic theory and practice merge? And, finally, to what extent do we need to differentiate between the metaphorical structures of Gracián and the metaphorical frames of our own critical conventions?

Several encompassing metaphors direct Luis F. Avilés's examination of subjectivity in *El criticón*. One, not surprisingly, is the journey of Critilo and Andrenio. Others include sight, vision, and mirroring, the latter of which provides a link to Lacan's "mirror stage." *El criticón* allows the reader to see the development of Andrenio, a tabula rasa brought into contact with culture, as part of an allegorical depiction of society at large, both of which may be disproportionately molded by "the gaze of the father." Avilés's metaphors are conspicuously modern. He refers to "technologies of control, power, and domination," as well as to stages of development and gender issues in the lexicon of post-Freudian psychoanalysis. When the essayist claims that "allegory becomes the productive signifier trying to supplement those gaps and insufficiencies perceived in individuals, but at the same time demonstrating its shortcomings and slips," we may question the completeness of—to cite one case—the Lacanian system, both in general terms and as a model for evaluating the characterization of intensely allegorical figures. We cannot question, however, the advantages of breadth and distance in Avilés's treatment of *El criticón*.

Also in search of the subject in Gracián, William Egginton reads Kant through Lacan and the Baroque through the Enlightenment. He makes the important point that Descartes's *Discourse on Method* predates *El criticón*, while showing that place as well as time will affect the emergence of the "modern subject." Egginton's essay accentuates issues raised by Livosky and Avilés: the reconciliation of personal advancement and power politics with morality (with special focus on the *Oráculo manual*) and the psychology of self-fashioning. The rehistoricizing of the Baroque subject—a more modern subject than we may have conceded—allows us to observe Gracián's work within a broader philosophical tradition. The merging of intellectual history, philosophy, psychology, and literature foregrounds not only the creation of the subject but also the formulation of a code of ethics. We are inclined to analyze Gracián the sociopolitical thinker through Gracián the moralist, and, as Egginton's essay confirms, the philosopher and the critic have a certain freedom to construct ethical frames. To assert that "Gracián is the ideal of that very pathological morality that the Enlightenment had to efface in order to institute the symbolic law of modernity" is to configure what could be called the raw material furnished by the relevant texts and disciplines. The raw material is, at best, dialectical, in need of emplotment.

This latitude in the organization, or disposition, of elements is, I believe, a key message of Jorge Checa's essay on *El criticón.* Using the works of Gracián's contemporaries Diego de Saavedra Fajardo and Baltasar Alamos de Barrientos, among others, to examine the projection of history within texts, Checa argues that the author of *El criticón* is not concerned with " 'discovering,' within ethical reality, a syntax supposedly made up of a number of elements," but with the need continuously to rewrite morality, to translate the blurred and conflicting world of appearances into a language that is "dynamic, provisional, and open-ended." Recognizing that unity is as much invented as inherent, Checa recasts the topics of unity and symmetry in the narrative and in Gracián's political thought. In the world of axioms and aphorisms, and in the figurative world of *El criticón,* the propensity toward the normative vies with an "other," be it disjunction, free will, or a sense of progress. Checa's essay reminds us that the text does not lie in wait, ready-made, for interpretation, but instead, and by virtue of its polysemy, becomes the catalyst for decoding.

Influenced by Maravall's studies of Baroque culture, David Castillo deals with subjectivity as redefined by alterations in the social fabric of absolutist Spain. The Gracián that he projects is conscious of a weakening of the aristocracy, as a result of the shift from lineage (as the primary determinant of position) to a new class of nobles, who bring wealth, education, and professional offices to bear on the social roles. Gracián seems to respect the changes wrought in the composition of society without moving away from a strong resentment of vulgarity, in people and in art. This is why he cannot applaud the printing press and increased literacy. His social conservatism will permit the incorporation of a new power elite based on intellectual achievement and slightly modified criteria for nobility. Gracián replaces the self-made man with a self-making man, aware of the complexities of projecting the public persona. The broadening of the boundaries of nobility (and, therefore, of power) to embrace the artist recalls Velázquez's struggle to bring prestige to his profession. Castillo underscores the aspect of adaptability in the worldly wisdom of Gracián. A question that remains open, I would submit, is the relation of Gracián's "moralistic thought"—which Castillo associates with Descartes, Leibniz, Hobbes, Machiavelli, Bodin, Montaigne, and Locke, but which seems to fade from the picture—and his sociopolitical philosophy.

Francisco J. Sánchez locates in the word *caudal* a wealth that extends to the material, the social, the political, and the discursive. He draws parallels between varieties of economic exchange and the formation of symbolic structures, through which *caudal* becomes "symbolic capital," an intersection of political behavior (*prudencia*) and symbolic production (*agudeza*). Noting the implied strategies of performance within this system, Sánchez places in the same middle ground between prudence and wit the concept of *despejo,* which can be understood as lucidity, elegance, good taste, and, perhaps most significantly, self-assurance. In Sánchez's reading of subjectivity, theatricality dominates; the bottom line, so to speak, is self-interest, intimately connected to the conventions of self-representation. By stressing the interrelation of literature and society, the essay advances a new way of looking at the conceit, which is not only intellectual and abstract but performative, "a description of society and individual competition achieved by a textualization of social performance." For Gracián, the deciphering of verbal signs duplicates social reality, full of mysterious signs that must be grasped and mastered. The interpretive tools depend, in each case, on mental activity and histrionic force. As an introduction to Gracián's use of *caudal,* Sánchez draws upon contemporaries such as Cervantes, Alemán, López de Ubeda, and Zayas. The correspondence is fascinating, and it would be instructive to see where Sánchez would place Gracián in terms of similitude and difference on a more comprehensive plane.

Acknowledging the work of Martin Jay and others, Oscar Pereira approaches Gracián through the motif of vision. While Gracián favors sight over the other senses, Pereira notes that the model that he presents in the *Criticón* is multifaceted. Sight and insight, appearance and reality, surface views and in-depth knowledge, passive observation and the penetrating glance, artificial light and natural light represent variations on the theme of vision. Gracián gives added weight to perspicacity, which combines sharpness of vision with sharpness of wit or understanding. To see is to submerge oneself in reality, while to contemplate is to observe in a detached manner. The two methods of viewing put Critilo and Andrenio in the range of the divine gaze. Among the issues that Pereira's essay raises is interpretation itself. How do obscurity and perception interact? Why would an author want to cloud the reader's vision? If "what is obscure generally connoted negatively in Gracián's work," and if, "all things considered, the aspects that characterize the Baroque regime do not constitute an ideal for Gracián, but rather the other side of utopia represented by the 'city of truth,'" how does vision, as inscribed into literature, lead the reader toward truth?

Anthony J. Cascardi builds upon Hans-Georg Gadamer's commentary on the origins of taste in Gracián. Cascardi questions Gadamer's view that, although taste is a historical idea, Gracián presents a view of education (that is, *gusto,* educated taste) as independent of class. Cascardi aims, then, to historicize Gracián's commentary on taste with respect to class structure, while noting that the constitution of society generally precedes the establishment of criteria for evaluating taste. Cascardi is especially effective in elaborating the paradoxes of taste, not the least of which is the move from a rigid hierarchy based on bloodlines to a more flexible range of nobility and the consequent need for stronger judgments of worth and acceptability. Good taste allows the individual a modicum of independence from society at large, while it validates the primacy of the body social. Cascardi applies the notion of taste to debates surrounding Baroque style in literature and to the thorny area of authority in life as well as in art. He sees the problem as never completely resolved, but "displaced onto an anonymous voice." The displacement suggests that, like other signifiers in the Golden Age, *gusto* is not merely a marker of displaced authority but a symbol of displacement itself. Naming, measuring, ranking, appraising, segregating, and, of course, excluding are means of challenging individualism; the result may satisfy those who pass the test, but this is quite probably the antithesis of social cohesion.

Carlos Hernández-Sacristán reads the *Oráculo manual* through the filter of the sociology of everyday life, as developed by Erving Goffman. Gracián alludes to conversation in a number of aphorisms, and social dialogue is fundamental to the formation and maintenance of one's image; speech is a "power relationship." In conversational practice, an individual speaker has the opportunity to correct misstatements or strategic flaws. The majority of the aphorisms recognize the perspective of the speaker, but others relate to the listener. Conversational etiquette allows one to emulate royalty, to achieve a personal air of majesty. According to Hernández-Sacristán, "Morality and justice are the same for Gracián and Goffman: both are founded on the believability of the self or person, understood as a subject involved in the construction of social reality." This is an intriguing extension of his commentary on conversation and a topic that invites further development.

Michael Nerlich works to correct "one of the most shameful chapters in reception history," the virtual disappearance of Werner Krauss's *Graciáns Lebenslehre* (1947). The act of critical redemption is to be applauded on many counts. Following a survey of the critical tradition on Gracián in Germany, Nerlich demonstrates the strength of Krauss's reading and contextualization of Gracián. Krauss treats literary, social, and philosophical aspects of the texts, and their place in intellectual history, in a manner that is both systematic and learned. Nerlich fills in gaps while producing a critique and a history of his own, and the rigorous, penetrating judgments are rendered in a spirit of fairness.

It is edifying and awe-inspiring to note how cultured (de rigueur), theoretically informed, and subtle critics undertake the reading of Gracián. The task is potentially intimidating precisely because complexity is at the foundation of every contact between text and reader. The more one knows of Gracián—Baroque citizen and writer—the greater the mediating space between signifier and signified. Binary oppositions have preoccupied theorists in recent decades, and the space that separates the antithetical elements is the primary locus of poststructuralism. I have used the term "constructing Gracián" in order to emphasize that our access to Gracián's writings, the identifying mark of which may well be a never-ending system of dualities, derives from a process of *reading through* (e.g., reading Gracián through Lacan, reading Gracián through the sociology of everyday life). Curiously perhaps, critical approaches are defined through deferral; we rely on intervening agents, or bridges, to point us in a valid direction. When we contextualize a given document, we introduce values from without. If we speak of Gracián's works as part of Baroque culture and wish to evaluate them in that light, from what source do we attain a systematic view of Baroque culture? If Maravall, to cite an illustrious example, is our bridge, how do we bring into the equation the fact that Maravall's Baroque culture is only a construct, a selected reading, which for all its merits remains undeniably incomplete and open to debate? Or the fact that Gracián and his contemporaries contribute to the formulation of "Baroque culture," only to be judged through, or against, this formulation? Despite poststructuralism's distrust of origins and endings, criticism has to start and end somewhere. As we resist impasse, we strive to approach, to *approximate,* the objects of investigation. What make Gracián especially difficult are the internal contradictions, of which the interplay of the worldly and the spiritual may be the most evident.

Understandably, any approach will have its strengths and shortcomings. It would seem that the greater one's understanding of the philosophical and theological traditions that inform Gracián's writings, the more accessible the texts will be. Nonetheless, we need to take into account that the philosophical-theological intertext is itself a construction and, further, that a comprehension, necessarily partial, of the intertext cannot guarantee our ability to read Gracián's response as conformity or critique. There is also the matter of competing intertexts. How are philosophy and theology mediated by politics, for example, or by aesthetic considerations? Gracián *politicus* is arguably the most unfathomable of the implied personae. How does one deal with the fact that the political writings do not seem to be mediated by religious principles? Gracián appears to aim his messages at "worldly" individuals and at levels of success bereft of eternal priorities. He reveres the accomplishments of eminent figures of the past, but he wants to prepare a new type of hero to triumph in a world order in transition. Success is inflected by class distinctions and thus by an antidemocratic temper. The normative becomes exclusionary; art is a function of culture, and culture manifests itself through unyielding hierarchies. Renaissance humanism's elevation of the individual is, at the same time, the key to and the point of deviation from Baroque individualism. The literature of the two periods bespeaks a concern for the formation and advancement of the individual, within a series of protocols. *El héroe, El político, El discreto,* and *Oráculo manual* seem to be inspired by a goal of refinement, enrichment, and self-presentation, and their orientation is resolutely secular, apparently geared toward achievement in a labyrinthine and changing social structure. What is the rationale for joining the spiritual to the secular, or for maintaining a separation? Is the pseudonymous Lorenzo Gracián an autonomous entity or a supplement to Baltasar Gracián? What are their places, and ours, in the hermeneutic circle?

It may be a sign of the current moment in literary studies that *Rhetoric and Politics* decenters the *Agudeza y arte de ingenio,* an inquiry into the nature of wit and the forms of art. Gracián expounds upon the formal, ideological, and intellectual properties of art, synthesized in the conceit. Rhetoric creates beautiful objects, highly textured and rich in ideas. Only the sharpest mind can conceive—and comprehend—stylistic and conceptual intricacies. Here is a link to the metaphorical language of the political writings, the institution of a new power elite, and the cult of good taste, among the topics treated in the essays in this volume. Language is a convenient starting point, but Gracián's manual of style and wit is not about language as an end in itself but about language as a tool. Superior performance in speech and writing can take one to sublime and exclusive domains. The *Agudeza y arte de ingenio* is a handbook of sorts, filled with examples and elaborate details, but it is also a guide to the operations of the mind. Its rhetoric presupposes a sensibility based on rank, that is, a deep structure in which blood, social authority, and mental capacity reflect the same gauge of quality, the same elitist paradigm. When we look at the lessons of *Oráculo manual,* along with a group of political treatises, we have to ponder the question of the intended audience. What is the objective of this worldly wisdom? Is it to help men achieve their maximum promise, to survive at the top, or to disengage themselves from the vulgar? Do the ends always justify the means? Are we trained to detect irony and disapproval within a period of censorship? Do we pursue the positive values in a philosophy and a rhetoric of elitism, or are we willing to condemn what Gracián obviously esteems? Do we somehow assign ourselves the role of the resistant reader, forced to contemplate formulas for success from the margins of our own displacement, our allegiance to equality, our vulgarity? Does it matter, for analytical purposes, that Gracián's writings fall into different genres (some distinctly nonliterary), or do we refuse to privilege one kind of text over another?

The varied nature of Gracián's writings animates the critical search for internal consistency in a given text or consistency (or justification of inconsistency) among the texts. The biographical data are telling but rarely an aid to consistency. Baroque culture and Baroque politics are, appropriately, convoluted, dense, awaiting emplotment. Doctrinaire theology configures self-motivation in a manner radically different from that of political expediency. Similarly, a universalist reading would differ from a rigidly contextualist reading. When the mechanism for "reading through" is based on models developed a posteriori, the structuring recourses become more prominent. A case in point is the concept of subjectivity, which adapts methods from philosophy, psychoanalysis, sociology, and other fields. Like the metaphors upon metaphors of Baroque literature, readings of subjectivity become escalatingly figural. Because the processes by which we find expression for abstractions or for the disposition of amorphous data (events, facts, records) are developed from rather than intrinsic to the material, textual analysis must concede that there is, for better or worse, a degree of openness in the mediating space(s). When we use a given model, we add our own discretionary space to that of the theorists and critics whom we follow, thereby compounding the distance between datum and enunciation. The reality of multiple configurations becomes problematic only when the constructive process is overlooked. When we forget, for example, that the parameters of "Baroque society," "Baroque culture," "Baroque literature," and "the Baroque subject" are determined by individual critics or that "Jesuit theology," "Kantian philosophy," "the absolutist state," and "miracle narrative" are anything but closed categories, we may perhaps put too much faith in the power of (hi)stories to tell themselves. A beauty of structuralism is the revelation of deep structures. A beauty of post-structuralism is the message that there is no such thing as pure description, agency without an agent, or a self-revealing deep structure. Not only are we actively involved in the construction of Gracián, but we select (and, it could be argued, invent) the contexts through which to display our findings.

The history of hermeneutics and phenomenology shows a crucial shift from the author to the reader. An attitude of skepticism begins to affect the pursuit of intention and of the consciousness of the author. The reader becomes a conduit and then a player in the interpretive venture, and hermeneuticists and phenomenologists find themselves cataloged under reader-response. Each of the essays in *Rhetoric and Politics* illustrates the weight of theoretical models and the individualizing touch of the critic. Readers will note numerous meetings of the mind in the essays, but these critical crossings are bearers of difference as well as of similitude. Several commentaries are built around the motif of sight, which serves to demonstrate, consciously or unconsciously, that significance is in the eye of the beholder. The essays in general focus on a rhetoric of politics in Gracián, that is, on the manner in which the writer frames the education of man as an individual within the social system. We are left to make connections with the class structure at large, with the spiritual macrocosm, and with the literary corpus, and this is as it should be. The collection leaves me with a stronger perception of Gracián, author and historical figure, and with an awareness of the indeterminacies that stimulate critical inquiry. Issues that strike me as open for investigation include the significance of genre (for example, the role of genre in the political and literary writings of Gracián and Quevedo), the relation of Juan Huarte de San Juan's examination of wit with Gracián's, the allegorical structure of the *Criticón* and its ties to Cervantes's *Persiles,* and the place of women in the works of Gracián, and, more generally, in formulations of Baroque subjectivity. Other readers will have their own questions, their own lists, and their own engagement with the texts. *Rhetoric and Politics* does much to advance our knowledge of Gracián and to provide openings for further study.

I would like to end with a narrative of sorts, prompted by Forcione's essay and influenced by the others. Two men, who represent the dual nature of all human beings, undertake a journey, which in turn depicts the lessons of experience and the stages of the life cycle. The allegory into which the protagonists are encoded suggests that growth can foster a sense of independence. Man ceases to be a pawn of fortune or of determinism, but becomes instead a participant in his own destiny. The celebration of individual freedom unfortunately has a down side, for the price of separation is a loss of the comforting order and security of the earlier design. The ultimate lesson is one of disillusionment. Man is enlightened only to see that glitter is insubstantial, that emptiness underlies the appearance of depth. Equally disorienting is the recognition that once man has asserted his autonomy, the protective cover of the past is no longer available, no longer an option. He may react with despair, with a hunger for the past and a resentment of the present; that is, he may take *desengaño* very much to heart. He may strive to conform to, and to improve, his condition. He may develop his proficiency for self-representation, through word and deed. He may attempt to restructure his notions of the divine, now that earthly patterns have been altered. His security may have been disturbed, but the possibilities seem infinite.

If disillusionment is the most commanding of the internal mediators of *El criticón,* it also may be the impetus for a repositioning of Gracián's writings, in line with the deceptive closure of the narrative. I hope to have indicated, in the allegory of an allegory, that there are ties between Baroque disillusionment and poststructuralist doubt, both of which stem from liberating drives, disrupt the balance of an accepted order, and press the limits of self-consciousness. Insight has its advantages and disadvantages. We may not like what we see, but we must choose vision over blindness. Deferral supplies a paradoxical means of access to texts and to critical strategies. Having relinquished the master frame, we must be content with what Borges calls "partial magic." Having sharpened our wits, we must labor to feast on wisdom.

Contributors

Luis F. Avilés. Assistant Professor of Spanish at the University of Massachusetts at Amherst. He has published several essays on Gracián's *El criticón.*

Anthony J. Cascardi. Professor of Comparative Literature and Spanish at the University of California, Berkeley. He has published *The Bounds of Reason: Cervantes, Dostoevsky, Flaubert* (1986), *The Subject of Modernity* (1992), and, as editor, *Literature and the Question of Philosophy* (1987), as well as numerous essays on the relationships between philosophy and literature.

David Castillo. Lecturer in Spanish and Portuguese at the University of Minnesota. He has published several essays on Spanish Golden Age literature and culture and is interested in the multifaceted representation of subjectivity in early modern Spain.

Jorge Checa. Professor of Spanish at the University of California, Santa Barbara. His studies include *Gracián y la imaginación arquitectónica: Espacio y alegoría de la Edad Media al Barroco* (1986).

William Egginton. Doctoral candidate in Comparative Literature at Stanford University. He has published several essays on Spanish Golden Age literature and culture and is interested in the relationship between literature and Lacanian psychoanalysis.

Alban K. Forcione. Walter S. Carpenter Jr. Professor of Language, Literature, and Civilization of Spain, and Professor of Comparative Literature, Princeton University. His studies include *Cervantes and the Humanist Vision* (1982) and *Cervantes and the Mystery of Lawlessness* (1984).

Edward H. Friedman. Professor of Spanish and Comparative Literature at Indiana University. His primary field of research is Spanish Golden Age literature. His publications include *The Unifying Concept: Approaches to Cervantes's Comedias* (1981) and *The Antiheroine's Voice: Narrative Discourse and Transformations of the Picaresque* (1987).

Carlos Hernández-Sacristán. Associate Professor of Linguistics in the Department of Theory of Languages at the University of Valencia, Spain, where he teaches linguistic epistemology and intercultural studies. He has published widely on linguistic theory and translation. Among his recent books are *A Phenomenological Approach to Syntax: The Propositional Frame* (1992) and *Aspects of Linguistic Contrast and Translation: The Natural Perspective* (1994).

Isabel C. Livosky. Professor of Spanish at Knox College. She has written extensively on Gracián and on various other aspects of Spanish Golden Age literature and culture.

Michael Nerlich. Professor of Romance Literatures at the Technische Universität Berlin. He is editor-in-chief of *Lendemains* and author of *Untersuchungen zur Theorie des klassizistischen Epos in Spanien (1700–1850)* (1964); *Kritik der Abenteuer-Ideologie: Beitrag zur Erforschung der bürgerlichen Bewu§tseinsbildung 1100–1750,* 2 vols. (1977; English translation, *Ideology of Adventure: Studies in Modern Consciousness, 1100–1750,* 2 vols., University of Minnesota Press, 1988); and *Apollon et Dionysos; ou, La science incertaine des signes: Montaigne, Stendhal, Robbe-Grillet* (1989).

Oscar Pereira. Assistant Professor of Spanish at the University of Nebraska. He has written several essays dealing with the literature and culture of early modern Spain and has finished a book titled *Literatura y representación pública en la primera modernidad española.*

Malcolm K. Read. Professor of Spanish at the State University of New York at Stony Brook. His publications include *Juan Huarte de San Juan* (1981), *The Birth and Death of Language* (1983), *Visions in Exile* (1990), *Language, Text, Subject* (1992), and *Borges and His Predecessors* (1993). He is currently writing a book on Spanish Romanticism.

Francisco J. Sánchez. Assistant Professor of Spanish at the University of Iowa. He has written on various aspects of Spanish Golden Age literature and culture and has recently published *Lectura y representación: Análisis cultural de las novelas ejemplares de Cervantes* (1993).

Nicholas Spadaccini. Professor of Hispanic Studies and Comparative Literature at the University of Minnesota. He has written on the Spanish Golden Age and colonial cultures and has edited a number of Spanish classics and several volumes on literary theory and criticism. His most recent book (coauthored with Jenaro Talens) is *Through the Shattering Glass: Cervantes and the Self-Made World* (1993).

Jenaro Talens. Professor of Literary Theory and Film and Head of the Department of Theory of Languages at the University of Valencia, Spain. He has been a regular visiting professor at the University of Minnesota since 1983, and has also taught at other U.S. and European universities. He has authored seventeen books of poetry and has translated many classics of German and English poetry into Spanish. He has published widely on semiotics, poetic discourse, and literary and film history. His more recent books in English are *Through the Shattering Glass: Cervantes and the Self-Made World* (coauthored with Nicholas Spadaccini, 1993) and *The Branded Eye: Buñuel's "Un Chien andalou"* (1993).

Index

Compiled by Bradley J. Nelson